PRENTICE-HALL, INC.   ENGLEWOOD CLIFFS, NEW JERSEY

CHARLES J. BRAUNER   OHIO STATE UNIVERSITY

American
Educational
Theory

PRENTICE-HALL INTERNATIONAL, INC. London
PRENTICE-HALL OF AUSTRALIA, PTY., LTD. Sydney
PRENTICE-HALL OF CANADA, LTD. Toronto
PRENTICE-HALL FRANCE, S.A.R.L. Paris
PRENTICE-HALL OF INDIA (PRIVATE) LTD. New Delhi
PRENTICE-HALL OF JAPAN, INC. Tokyo
PRENTICE-HALL DE MEXICO, S.A. Mexico City

Library of Congress Catalog Card No.: 64—12855

Printed in the United States of America

02401

When you are criticising the philosophy of an epoch, do not chiefly direct your attention to those intellectual positions which its exponents feel it necessary explicitly to defend. There will be some fundamental assumptions which adherents of all the variant systems within the epoch unconsciously presuppose. Such assumptions appear so obvious that people do not know what they are assuming because no other way of putting the things has ever occurred to them. With these assumptions a certain limited number of types of philosophic systems are possible, and this group of systems constitutes the philosophy of the epoch.

(A. N. Whitehead, *Science and the Modern World*. New York: © 1925, The Macmillan Company; copyright renewed, 1953 by Evelyn Whitehead, pp. 49-50. Reprinted with the permission of The Macmillan Company.)

The commonly accepted dichotomy in education— theory vs. practice —takes "theory" for granted. Professionals talk so much about the importance of philosophy of education in teacher training that the assumption that education has a philosophy or philosophies is too often overlooked. Education's presence as a department in most universities strengthens the unexamined conviction that there must be a body of subject matter worthy of being called a discipline. The absence of standards for discerning discipline status goes unnoticed. And the difficulties associated with the mixing of sense with nonsense defy analysis because they escape scrutiny.

In what follows much use is made of three relatively undefined common-sense distinctions. The importance of these distinctions in connection with education as a subject of study was first made evident to me in 1956 by Professor W. H. Cowley of Stanford University in a course on higher education. He referred to three categories of professional expression and named them logodemic, practidemic, and pandemic. Though I was impressed by the distinctions and their utility in discussing the kinds of talk educators engage in, I found myself more comfortable with what I took to be their common-sense equivalents, respectively: scholarship, practical

Author's
Preface

explication, and popularization. Practical explication often involves popularization, so I have directed attention to the core of concern by calling it practice-centered talk. Much popularization of educational ideas has taken place in the mass media, and it seems that in keeping with the distortion and bias so frequently made central that this brand of reporting and editorializing, popular indeed, can be called journalism. Attempts to give clear, precise, and consistent definitions to each of these categories could lead so far down the primrose path of pedantic abstraction that it seems more is to be gained by relying on the common-sense meaning built into them by ordinary usage. Whatever is lost by way of ambiguity seems not nearly so terrible as the deformity wrought by worrying them beyond recognition.

In the search for an honest objectivity a researcher must so detach his personal outlook from his considered reflections that "scholarly" remains a synonym for dull—in the work and in the man. Few writers have even a little of the powers and the command that permit a Whitehead, a Veblen, or a de Voto to raise a piece of scholarship to the level of art. Next best would be Orwell's facility or Mencken's merciless wit. Doctoral dissertations and government research grants, needless to say, encourage no such liberties. (Bread and butter projects that they are, who can complain?) So to keep myself amused, and to keep the research relatively honest, I put my most personal opinions in the bottom margin, related to the text by an asterisk.

Acting under Public Law 531 of the Eighty-Third Congress, the U.S. Office of Education, with Stanford University as co-operating and administrating institution, supported the project from which this book developed. Professor W. H. Cowley directed the project for the two years of its duration: July 1, 1957 until June 30, 1959

As director of my dissertation Professor Cowley helped me learn to use the idea-summation and classification techniques associated with his approach to file-card indexing and "conceptual research." As director of the U.S.O.E. project he provided much needed financial help. As teacher, he awakened many ideas which have profoundly influenced my outlook.

In connection with the initial proposal to the U.S.O.E. Ralph W. Tyler and Mrs. Ruth Eckert must be thanked for their interest in the theoretical problem.

Chief among those who provided intellectual stimulus and guidance are Professors Lawrence Thomas, Arthur P. Coladarci, and Jeffery Smith of Stanford University. For his continual encouragement and his help in bringing this work to the attention of Prentice-Hall, I am most grateful to my friend, Dean Hobert W. Burns of Hofstra University.

The author wishes to make the following acknowledgments for permission to use the material included in this book:

Professor Harold Alberty, for excerpts from his book, *A Study of the Project Method in Education,* published by the Ohio State University Press.

Alfred A. Knopf, Inc., for two excerpts from H. L. Mencken in *Prejudices: A Selection,* edited by James T. Farrell, in Vintage Book, Vol. 58, published by Random House, Inc., and for an excerpt from *The Art of Teaching,* by Gilbert Highet, published by Alfred A. Knopf, Inc.

Professor R. Freeman Butts, for excerpts from his letter to Professor W. H. Cowley.

The Department of Health, Education, and Welfare, for permission to reprint the results of the author's research which was supported through Cooperative Research Project #245.

Harcourt, Brace & World, Inc., for excerpts from *Foundations of American Education,* by Harold Rugg, published by Harcourt, Brace & World, Inc.

Harper & Row, Publishers, Incorporated, for an excerpt from *NEA: The First Hundred Years,* by Edgar B. Wesley, and for an excerpt from *Education and the Common Good,* by Philip H. Phenix, both published by Harper & Row, Publishers, Incorporated.

Harvard University Press, for an excerpt from *Introduction to the Scientific Study of Education,* by Charles Hubbard Judd, published by Harvard University Press; and for an excerpt from *Augustine to Galileo,* by A. C. Crombie, published in Toronto by William Heinemann Limited.

Heinemann Educational Books Limited, for an excerpt from *Augustine to Galileo,* by A. C. Crombie, published in Toronto by William Heinemann Limited.

Houghton Mifflin Company, for an excerpt from *Introduction to Child Psychology,* by Charles W. Waddle, published by Houghton Mifflin Company.

John Wiley & Sons, Inc., Publishers, for an excerpt from *The Sociology of Teaching,* by Willard Waller, copyright 1932, by John Wiley & Sons, Publishers. Reprinted with permission.

Acknowledgments

Liveright Publishing Corporation, for excerpts from *The Sources of a Science of Education*, by John Dewey. Reprinted by Permission of Liveright, Publishers, N. Y.

The Macmillan Company, for excerpts from *Adventures of Ideas*, by Alfred North Whitehead, copyright 1959. Used by permission of The Macmillan Company.

Meredith Press, for two excerpts from *Lay Sermons, Essays and Reviews*, by Thomas Henry Huxley.

Lawrence Metcalf and Mrs. Roberta Dewey, for excerpts from John Dewey in *Progressive Education*.

Ellis Monroe and Jeannette Monroe Bassett, for excerpts from Edwin A. Kirkpatrick, John Dewey, and Edward H. Cameron in *A Cyclopedia of Education*, Paul Monroe, editor.

The Ryerson Press, for excerpts from *The Concept of Mind*, by Gilbert Ryle.

School and Society, for an excerpt from Guy M. Whipple in *School and Society*.

Teachers College, Columbia University, Bureau of Publications, for two excerpts from *The Evolution of the American Teachers College*, by Jessie M. Pangburn; two excerpts from *Philosophies of Education Current in the Preparation of Teachers in the United States*, by Francis Edwin Peterson; and several excerpts from *The Lancasterian System of Instruction in the Schools of New York City*, by John Franklin Reigart.

Teachers College Record and Dr. William Heard Kilpatrick, for four excerpts from William H. Kilpatrick in *Teachers College Record*.

The University of Chicago Press, for excerpts from V. A. C. Henmon, S. Chester Parker, and William C. Ruediger in *The School Review Monographs, No. II*, and from Paul Monroe and Edward L. Thorndike in *The School Review Monographs, No. I*; an excerpt from Ernest Nagel in *International Encyclopedia of Unified Science*, edited by O. Neurath, R. Carnap, and C. Morris; and for an excerpt from Joseph J. Schwab in *The School Review*.

The Bureau of Research and Service, the College of Education, the University of Illinois, for several excerpts from Archibald W. Anderson, *et al.*, in *The Theoretical Foundations of Education;* and several excerpts from W. S. Monroe in *The University of Illinois Bulletin*.

Table
of
Contents

The truth is that criticism, if it were thus confined to the proposing of alternative schemes would quickly cease to have any force or utility at all, for in the overwhelming majority of instances no alternative scheme of any intelligibility is imaginable, and the whole object of the critical process is to demonstrate it. . . . the thing they [alternate schemes] propose to accomplish is intrinsically, or at all events most probably, beyond accomplishment. . . . Unluckily, it is difficult for a certain type of mind to grasp the concept of insolubility. . . . It is the settled habit of such credulous folk to give ear to whatever is comforting; it is their settled faith that whatever is desirable will come to pass.

H. L. Mencken, "The Cult of Hope," Prejudices: a Selection, in *Vintage Book,* v. 58, Random House, N. Y., pp. 84-85.

Works of scholarship, like works of art, can be designated upon inspection, but general standards for either cannot be expected. New scholarship, like new art, must be free to set new standards of expectation. When such expectations become requirements, future works cannot break from the mold set by past works. This crystallization of forms sometimes happens in folk art, in academies that prescribe how language must be used, among critics, and among scholars, but it is a human weakness paraded as if it were an intellectual virtue. If the vast sets of opportunities for innovation are to be left open for both scholars and artists, neither scholarship nor art can be circumscribed by rules, and as a consequence, the term *scholarship* and the term *art* remain undefined except in connection with past performances. Standards of scholarship in education as a subject of study must be developed from an examination of past works.

"Art," however, remains a useful concept, as does "scholarship." Further, within art it makes sense to distinguish between prose and poetry even though the border between the two remains a no man's land of dispute. It is not necessary to know the boundaries in order to be able to point to the central tendency that a concept specifies. It is in this sense that scholarship, in talk about education, is to be distinguished from that which is practice-centered on the one hand or journalistic on the other. "Scholarship" refers to the disinterested pursuit of knowledge for its own sake and is opposed to journalism which slights thorough qualification in favor of simplicity, to extremes and devices

Introduction

which popularize and persuade at the expense of enlightenment. Practice-centered talk, with its primary concern for application, is different again from both journalism and scholarship, although it sometimes incorporates both.

Dividing comment or talk about education into that which is scholarly, practice-centered, and journalistic requires the same kind of careful judgment that art critics must give to evaluating paintings. In the case of talk about education, all three kinds may appear in a single work. Further, this tripartite division does not cover the whole range of comment about education. For instance, George Orwell's "Such Such Were the Joys" is a fine, entertaining, even informative autobiographic essay. It may best be set aside as a work of art, yet it could not be called scholarly, practice-centered, or journalistic.

In this examination of the development of general methods and general disciplines as major components of American educational theory, such qualifications play quite a significant role. Until talk about education is crudely divided as to its scholarly, practice-centered, and journalistic components, finer distinction—and, hence, better theories and a better discipline of education—will be more difficult to arrive at than need be.

The terms *theory* and *discipline* (academic, not corporal) also defy definition, because both entail qualitative considerations of the same kind as are implicit in judging works worthy of being called scholarship.

Discipline is a collective term, encompassing both "theory" and "scholarship." In the case of education as a subject of study, "scholarship," "theory," and "discipline" have all been called into question. Until scholarship in education is accurately judged and found worthy by a respected jury of critics, "theory" will remain even more difficult to evaluate. Throughout this work I have had to try to distinguish scholarly, practice-centered, and journalistic statements so as to identify some of the ingredients in what ordinarily passes under the broad heading of "educational theory." With scholarship tangled up in practice-centered and journalistic ways of talking about education, there can be little basis for exhibiting any part or all of education as a subject of study to an academic jury for acceptance as a discipline. Yet these have been judgments resulting from intuition on my part. I have no pat definition of scholarship that will enable the reader to identify scholarly statements as distinct from practice-centered or journalistic ones. Further, although my research carries the documentation that qualifies this as a work of scholarship, there seems no way of defending some of the arguments against the accusation that they contain journalistic elements. No matter how careful one strives to be, since these arguments defy technical demonstration in formal logic, questions of adequacy are always pertinent.* These problems

---

* Some of the least defensible statements that I could not resist making have been set forth in footnotes such as this.

of proof and scope come to a focus in a peculiar way in what has been called "conceptual research."

Conceptual Research

In 1911, Paul Monroe, then just completing the editing of *A Cyclopedia of Education,* worried in these words over the decline of what had previously been the backbone of scholarship: "The traditional methods of logical investigation which appertained to such scientific study as existed in centuries preceding the nineteenth have ceased to receive any great consideration." [1] The worth of careful observation and detailed description of practical problems small enough to be thoroughly examined had just been fully appreciated in connection with building a discipline of education. The direction of development since then can be seen by comparing Monroe's statement with the one which follows, from the educational psychology section of the 1957 *Annual Review of Psychology:*

> The tendency to neglect theoretical research and to concentrate on immediate and perhaps more practical problems, which may contribute little to the development of a systematic science, has been a frequent criticism of educational psychology. No marked change in this pattern of emphasis could be noted in the review period. . . . Concern about the responsibilities which educational psychologists have for theoretical development is not, of course, inconsistent with their responsibilities as applied psychologists. . . .[2]

The key question becomes, "What is theoretical research in education?" Does it require a return to the traditional methods of logical investigation ubiquitous to all but the most highly quantified subjects before the twentieth century? In a modified "yes" to this last question, W. H. Cowley of Stanford University suggested that conceptual research should supplement and give meaning to factual investigation. Clarifying his terms in a 1956 article, Professor Cowley offered the following distinction:

> By factual research I mean adding new facts to the store of knowledge, facts which enlarge on present knowledge or which open up new, unmined veins. . . . Conceptual investigation differs from such studies in that it either organizes facts already on hand or critically appraises existing concepts.[3]

Two years earlier Cowley had explained the limited extent to which conceptual research would return to the more traditional mode of logical

---

[1] Monroe, 1911: 71.1 (in Bibliography at back of book).
[2] Keller, 1957: 52.
[3] Cowley, 1956: 15.

investigations so current before this century. Conceptual research would guide factual investigation by providing a historical framework in this way:

> This means the tracing of the history of the ideas involved in them [existing concepts] and appraising their present status and their future prospects in the light of the historical continuum thus plotted. Only when this has been done is it possible to decide what factual investigations have relevance.[4]

Conceptual research is the missing link between a logical-speculative tradition prematurely abandoned and a body of immediately useful facts without theoretical portent.

Yet the term *conceptual research* is both ambiguous and vague. All philosophic and historical inquiry, for example, involves the examination and development of concepts, ideas. On the one hand, however, modern philosophic analysis pays such minute attention to the logical adequacy of individual statements as to make it quite difficult to see the relationship among a vast number of concepts. Then, on the other hand, concern for the authenticity of each fact in historical research is often so all-demanding that broad perspective is prohibited. Hopefully, without forsaking logical soundness or factual authenticity, conceptual research seeks to rise to a panoramic view of the relationships among major concepts. Some attention to detail must be sacrificed for the sake of scope. By looking at the forest instead of microscopically inspecting each tree, it strives to discover patterns in planting that may have gone undetected. In literature, Lovejoy has done this kind of research in *The Great Chain of Being;* Whitehead has done it in the first half of *Adventures in Ideas.* Conceptual research of this sort seeks a new synthesis. Thus, by being speculative, it attempts to retrieve the notion of scholarship from its narrowest confines, described this way by Whitehead:

> The difference between the two, namely the Hellenic and the Hellenistic types of mentality, may be roughly described as that between speculation and scholarship. For progress both are necessary. But, in fact, on the stage of history they are apt to appear as antagonists. Speculation, by entertaining alternative theories, is superficially sceptical, disturbing to established modes of prejudice. But it obtains its urge from a deep ultimate faith, that through and through the nature of things is penetrable by reason. Scholarship, by its strict attention to accepted methodologies, is superficially conservative of belief. But its tone of mind leans toward a fundamental negation. For scholars the reasonable topics in the world are penned in isolated regions, *this* subject-matter or *that* subject-matter. Your thorough-going scholar resents the airy speculation which connects his own patch of knowledge with that of his neighbours. He finds his

---

[4] Cowley, 1954: 16.

fundamental concepts interpreted, twisted, modified. He has ceased to be king of his own castle, by reason of speculations of uncomfortable generality, violating the very grammar of his thoughts.[5]

Conceptual research injects a speculative cast of mind into many areas of narrow scholarship in the hope that the expansion thus forced will cause separate areas to merge without bursting the extreme limits of the definition of scholarship, in which case there would be merely a release of hot air. It sets up a controlled intellectual reactor for the production of new, but not undisciplined, thought. In that larger sense, this study seeks to be scholarly by being both factual and speculative.

To neglect conceptual research is to overlook a valuable approach to the improvement of education as a subject of study. Continuance of such neglect will insure that scholarship in education will remain undistinguished from practical and popular talk, thus making it impossible to defend education as an academic subject of study. This whole book is a probe in the direction of standards of scholarship for education as a discipline.

---

[5] Whitehead, 1959: 111.

American education changes according to major historical, economic, political, and philosophic developments within the society itself. These forces lash the seas of debate by which instructional practice must justify itself. Knowledge, however, does not necessarily lead to sound action. Awareness of the population expansion, for example, has not always resulted in the provision of adequate classroom space. Ignorance of the problem could be catastrophic. Matching pupils to seats requires as detailed a knowledge of classroom space and cost as it does of population size, composition, and expansion. Yet this problem is relatively simple, since it contains so many elements of factual information and reasonably reliable prediction.

The obviousness of the trend toward automation and the probability of increased leisure in the future have resulted in an emphasis on occupational skills, on the one hand, and recreation skills, on the other. The equally obvious threat of Russian political and scientific ascendancy has exerted a contrary emphasis, and has put academic subjects, especially mathematics, physical science, and foreign languages, at peak priority. Shallow expedients quickly put forth as a society's most pressing need are bound, however, to be superficial and incomplete when they derive from a panic-stricken shortsightedness which mistakes exposure of the most obvious part of the problem for a complete examination. Such inquiries into the problems facing American education fail to examine the many and complex forces at work in the long run of social development and can too easily conclude that the Communist threat demands

1

Perspective: Practice As the Context for Scholarship

that certain books be removed from school libraries. Such shortsightedness sees no threat to freedom of speech, inquiry, and opinion in that kind of censorship. Quite the contrary, it claims to protect each.

John Dewey has had a lasting influence on American education because he welded his detailed inquiry into the many facets of social and philosophic issues to key elements of classroom practice. His understanding of practice had to be as many-sided and as thorough as was his understanding of philosophy. Looking below the obvious, he saw clearly that mere occupational training, simple recreation, and the technological problems of an industrial society meant relatively little when set against the difficulties of communication in a society that found itself sustained by machines and in danger of becoming dominated by them. In the face of such a moral problem, he attempted to show how the classroom could be used to initiate inquiry of a new sort. Collective and cooperative decision-making were offered as general models of instruction; these were patterned after what seemed to be a method common to all science. Educators saw in that idea a workable general method of instruction.

Unlike some of his followers, Dewey realized that the techniques for implementing such instruction would have to be thrashed out by trial and error in the classroom. His experimentalist pedagogy simply attempted to set forth some of the ground rules by which the trials could be made somewhat systematic and the quantity of error minimized. That search for ground rules led him to explain the parallel between freedom of inquiry and expression in the classroom, in empirical science, and in the open democracy. Although "democracy in the classroom" soon became a slogan and eventually became the subject of ridicule, the original conception had considerable meaning because it developed in connection with a detailed analysis of the conditions of practice. It was his inquiry into the elements of instruction which preserved Dewey from the error of building a grand intellectual structure with no foundation in practical social action—in this instance, the institution of public instruction.

It is no reflection on the quality of work done by men such as Plato or Hobbes to say that, apart from reflections on human nature and society, their comments on teaching did not result from analysis of instructional practice. As with afterthoughts or with a priori convictions, statements without detailed grounding in an analysis of practice cannot occupy a central position in a practical discipline.* Classic as their comments may be, Plato and Hobbes, for example, cannot be looked to as the source of an educational discipline, although they need not be ignored.

Talk about democracy or morality, no matter how fine as philosophy,

---

* Ideas grounded in an examination of practice need not be practice-centered, however, just as research into methods of auto manufacture need not focus on immediate utility.

as law, or as political science, must remain "general" so far as education as a discipline is concerned, unless it occurs in conjunction with, and as an integral part of, some analysis of practice. Such general talk belongs no more to a discipline of education than Joyce Kilmer's "Trees" belongs to the science of botany. Poetry, bad or good, cannot be pressed into service as science, and general statements cannot serve where specialized ones are called for. A proper analysis of practice may provide the basis for converting a general statement into a specialized one, just as the proper training may turn a civilian into a tail gunner. But conversion is required, and only inquiry into practice can extend the hope of utility.

To build a parallel, legitimate art criticism must be clearly traceable to the direct examination of actual works, and to be complete, it must result in implications for the examination of subsequent works. Many excellent biographies, with provocative psychological theories about the kind of complex that led this painter to portray harlots instead of ballerinas, drop through the net that sifts art criticism from the broad body of biographical talk about painters. Similarly, many provocative philosophic, psychological, sociological, and political considerations must remain peripheral to education as a discipline until an examination of practice makes them relevant. Without a clear link to practice, they remain general and, hence, belong properly to their own special discipline. The insistence on talking about Idealism, Realism, Scholasticism, and so forth, has kept philosophy of education general in this same sense, and this has raised the question of how it differs from philosophy itself, except for deficiencies in scholarship. It is the absence of just such a connection to practice and the disinclination of specialists in psychology and sociology to examine classroom practice itself that make it impossible for departments of education to get more than casual help from findings established in specialized disciplines.*

PRACTICE IN THE BROAD—THE SCHOOL REVOLUTION

Imagine an inquiry into American society which overlooked the Industrial Revolution. How could a discussion of the population crisis proceed without reference to changes that have taken place in medicine and contraception? Yet criticism of the American school system often ignores changes that have had as profound an influence on instruction as

---

* Hence a middleman theorist called an educational psychologist or an educational philosopher must be trained to speculate about possible applications. Such speculation, whether scholarly, practical, or popular, becomes the content of such a field as educational philosophy.

atomic weapons have had on warfare. Five such changes which add up to a school revolution are:

1. The change in available information
2. The change in tolerated behavior
3. The change in school clientele
4. The change in teaching personnel
5. The change in purpose

THE CHANGE IN AVAILABLE INFORMATION

Available factual information about everything from zeppelins to astronautics has increased by the square, and recently by the cube, over what it was when American public schooling began. Present library techniques for cataloguing information seem to be approaching the limits of utility. The greater amount of information means that more must be mastered if command of an activity or area of inquiry is to be thorough. As each specialty grows, the longer it takes to master it. Students feel the pressure to specialize earlier and earlier. Having specialized, they find it ever more difficult either to change from one area to another or to gain an overview of several fields.

To be efficient in passing on the information needed for mastery of a special area of investigation, instruction must be packed tightly with factual information.* Books must be written along new lines in order to minimize outworn, incomplete, erroneous, and insignificant concepts while at the same time maximizing key information and ideas. Each generation has more to learn than its parents had. Yet it is inevitable that course content and books will lag behind the best available information, because it takes time to prepare them and more time to get new approaches accepted.

As the amount and complexity of information grow, the gap between what is known by specialists and what is learned in school increases; and, as the gap grows, so does the alarm of specialists, teachers, and parents. Teaching seems to decline in quality as the problem of communicating complex concepts grows more difficult. At the moment, the solution seems to involve getting experts to explain the subject simply and clearly by means of texts, tapes, movies, television, or teaching machines. Then if the student does not get it, it's his fault; at least, the correct information

---

* Programming for teaching machines often shows the teacher how inefficient and confusing his lectures have been (raising the embarrassing question as to whether previous failures were primarily his or the student's fault).

has been broadcast. Forced feeding of compact information packages by intense bombardment becomes the operating policy. Yet the changes in tolerated classroom behavior have made this difficult.

THE CHANGE IN TOLERATED BEHAVIOR

While the technology for forced feeding of information has grown, the techniques for making youngsters endure such feeding have been restricted. Variously, in the names of Christianity, Democracy, Liberalism, and Humanitarianism, child labor has been outlawed, spanking frowned upon, ear-boxing eliminated, mouth-washing with soap abandoned, and left-hand writing permitted. Forcing a child to do what he's told isn't the straightforward matter that it used to be.

To further upset the program of forced feeding of information, youngsters were encouraged to ask questions, to dispute opinions, to contest fact, and even to complain. Instead of remaining a place in which to absorb and recite, the classroom became the place where neatly packaged bundles of content were unwrapped and where children rummaged around in the parts.

Even so, the change in behavior tolerated by teachers failed to keep up with the changes recommended by specialists in the study of human behavior. By the time teachers learned to tolerate a silent youngster in the back of the classroom, psychologists were urging that he be regarded with suspicion and brought into the circle of social activity. Just as factual information outstripped instructional content, so the outlook of clinical psychologists outdistanced efforts of teachers to modify their attitudes toward student conduct. Teachers had barely identified slow, average, and fast readers when they were urged to let each child proceed at his own rate. As the understanding of human behavior advanced, the specialists could see that practices in the schools were falling behind the practices recommended by psychologists and sociologists.

Each invitation to question a matter of fact and each division of the class into slow, average, and advanced learners slowed up the forced feeding of information-packed, prefabricated lessons. Both the change in content and the division of classes into groups became increasingly necessary because of the change in clientele served by the schools.

THE CHANGE IN SCHOOL CLIENTELE

Just as the Supreme Court decision to end segregation in public schools was the tardy legal backbone which would give strength to Lincoln's Emancipation Proclamation, so was the inclusion of all youngsters in the public school the tardy institutional realization of the sentiment expressed by Jefferson.

Political expedience aside, acts like the Emancipation Proclamation have a certain mechanical property which contributes to their significance. Slaves were declared free in the middle of a war with little consideration of their capacity to enjoy their new status and with no provision for their survival. In the same way, new African nations have been granted autonomy even though they lack the economic facilities, the political institutions, the leadership, the military organization, the agencies of welfare, and the experience to be assured that they will survive at all, much less survive as nations in a climate of political cannibalism. In the same mechanical way American education set out to serve a new clientele.

As the twentieth century got under way, more and more youngsters were herded together into classrooms and held there for longer and longer periods. Youngsters had to occupy seats in school regardless of their capacity to profit from the instruction offered them. No one could insure that youngsters would master the lessons presented or even would benefit from being present in school. But as the youngsters filled the schools to overcrowding, the percentage of pupils in any class who could be expected to benefit from the old methods of forced feeding declined considerably. Just as emancipation made freedom a legal fact long before it became a living actuality, so did the clientele revolution make schooling for the new clientele a regulatory fact before it could assure them an education. Success has not yet been assured.

Since the situation was novel, students and teachers had to work things out for themselves without the benefit of any precedent that was known to be useful. The unalterable factor was that teachers had to keep all the youngsters sent to them. This ground rule meant that something had to be found for each youngster to do, and that something could not be the continual absorption of factual information.

It seemed unreasonable to assume that all youngsters in secondary school could master the informational lessons prefabricated for those in the top ten per cent as rated by academic ability. As the supply of information to be mastered grew even greater and more complex, the school presented less. Further, it simplified what it did present so that the average student could grasp and hold it. Even so, the new generation of students would not sit still and listen the way more able youngsters had submitted to their teachers in earlier years. Some of the more effective methods for holding pupils still were banned as brutal, and many other methods could not be used because psychiatrists and parents frowned upon their use. The new schools invited the expression of parental opinion; hence, what the parents wanted and would allow became increasingly influential.

As control became more difficult, the instruments available for exercising it grew weaker and fewer.* The way out seemed through some-

---

* Critics of United States education often speak as if teachers should have risen as a man and done something about this.

thing everyone could do and that most would do voluntarily.* On this cue, in walked the self-proclaimed Messiah: audio-visual aids. Advance advertising boasted that the "aids" could present information simply, clearly, and precisely while holding interest through clever programming. In many cases, however, the information that all could master was trivial, and the program that all would sit still for was informationless. Thus, teaching by projector became entertainment, and one that provided only a modicum of interest in an oversimplified idea made trivial by its isolation.

Teachers with less concern for information that all could master and with more concern for activities that all could perform explored projects, field trips, camping, and such socializing activities as dancing. The diversity of activities necessary on a camping trip or in putting on a play assured a wide range of things to do. And in that broadened range it was hoped that there would be something everyone could, and would want, to do. In the intellectual climate of the 1930's, it seemed reasonable that by cooking a meal or by painting some scenery each child could benefit socially by contributing to the group effort. But, further, there was the hope that the fun of camping or the excitement of play production would turn a hitherto lethargic child into a curious and interested student. Briefly, there seemed to be a naïve faith that academic interest in a subject such as history, mathematics, or literature would rise as spontaneously and as unanimously on contact with the proper project or activity as interest in swimming, dolls, or football usually did. That this did not happen proved a great disappointment. Part of the reason why projects and activities failed for some was that teachers did not have the academic background necessary to make the subjects to which these pertained exciting. There had been a change in personnel that paralleled the change in clientele. With more facts and more complex theories to be passed on to more and more students, the logical thing to expect would be that fewer and fewer people would have the ability to do all that was required of teachers.

THE CHANGE IN TEACHING PERSONNEL

The increase in the numbers of students in school called for a proportionate increase in the number of teachers. With the bulk of college-trained talent being absorbed by business, medicine, law, engineering, and government service, the supply of new teachers around 1900 could be found only by digging deeper into the barrel of talent. Like an apple barrel, the talent barrel gets soggy near the bottom.

---

* This is often treated as some dark conspiracy a good deal more sinister than the desire to keep everyone in a school.

As information grew in volume and complexity, and as the problem of maintaining control over youngsters became more difficult, teacher preparation had to take in candidates for teaching who had less capacity to master complex concepts and less talent for maintaining discipline.*
Normal schools, teachers' colleges, and departments of education had to initiate their own courses in mathematics, physics, history, and literature in order to protect teacher trainees from the stiff requirements of such courses in the liberal arts sections of the colleges and universities. Thus, the prospective teacher was exposed to less of the available supply of information and was expected to master less than was his counterpart in the liberal arts program. As attention to projects and social activities replaced some of the academic content in teacher training, the gap between the man who was training to teach history or literature and the liberal arts major in either of those subjects grew to embarrassing proportions.†
Teachers' college and department of education graduates earned a reputation for being inferior students; and, on top of that, they were given such oversimplified explanations of key concepts in such fields as physics and literature that, when they did master what they were taught, they often embarrassed themselves by exhibiting what they had learned.‡

Accurate simplification and significant selection of the most important parts of a subject demand a thorough mastery of content rather than a diminished command. Bargain-basement trainees in a cut-rate program thought that they were studying history, economics, and physics. They mistook the oversimplified generalizations drawn from summaries of the subjects for the real merchandise. Thus, they passed on the same generalizations (or even more simplified versions of them) to their students in the public school, without being aware that a whole order of understanding and information not available to them as teachers constituted the basic content of the academic disciplines. Though it be mere conjecture, this or some similar avenue seems to be the way in which scholarship deteriorated in both teacher training and public instruction.

Scholarly information and concepts continued to grow more complex and harder to teach. More and more students of reduced academic ability had to be taught. Teachers with less command of the content and with less talent for presenting what they had learned in simplified form kept

---

* It is hard to say where the blame for this should be put—maybe the ratio of teachers to students should have been held to 1 to 775, as is the case in medicine. Of course, there is the resulting problem of overcrowded classes.
† Notwithstanding the fact that liberal arts departments have always graduated enough incompetents to give teacher trainers encouragement.
‡ Nor does this mean that one could not get a good education in a teachers' college. It may have been a little more difficult, however, since doing so required the willingness to work harder than would be necessary for passing.

increasing in number. Ever more oversimplified generalizations replaced command; arrogance too often exhibited itself as the other face of ignorance. Under such conditions, though one may disagree with the specific conditions of teacher certification, can the need for some control be denied?

THE CHANGE IN PURPOSE

So long as schools taught only those students in the top ten per cent as rated by academic ability—the majority of whom came from families with comfortable economic and social positions—scholarship, like art and virtue, could be its own reward. With social position assured and economic matters well in hand, taste and understanding became the playing field on which the able sought to demonstrate their superiority. When material differences can be ignored, intellectual distinctions can be pursued intensely.

The middle and lower economic classes had many material, financial, and social "wants" to satisfy; and they usually insisted on knowing how what they were expected to do would lead to the satisfaction of these wants. As the new clientele from the lower- and middle-income classes filled the schools, education for its own sake could no longer satisfy parents or students. Least of all could such a justification extract the financial support which public schooling required. Education for economic and social success made more sense to the new clientele. Education for the success of democratic government made some sense, but it remained to be shown in tangible terms what such a program would yield and how it would work. In the narrow sense, increased earning power provided the best justification for public schools. In the broader view, increased security and welfare held a strong appeal. The depression welded the narrow and broader views together.

When academic work as apprenticeship for material gain replaced scholarship for its own sake or for reasons of social prestige, mere information could not survive in the schools. Information had to be useful beyond pedantic demonstration and below the level of advanced scholarship. It had to fit into the larger framework of job training and work performance. Scholarship for curiosity's sake had held Latin at least equal to mathematics, and taste was not to be disputed. The utility of mathematics in engineering and the importance of chemistry in agriculture, as against the declining utility of Latin in medicine and botany, now set the order of priority.

The vocational guidance and occupational training programs, so important in the 1930's, dramatically illustrate how this emphasis on the utility of schooling could be turned into a shortsighted expedient under the intense pressures of the depression. The importance of getting a job after leaving school became so urgent that academic subjects seemed almost a luxury which could not be afforded.*

The change in purpose from academic to vocational cannot be dissociated from the changes in personnel, clientele, tolerated behavior, and available information. It seems unfair to accuse vocational training of driving scholarship from the schools. Once teachers no longer imported it in relatively pure form, the decline set in. When students could no longer cope with the academic subject matter that teachers did bring into the program, vocational training was one of the few things available to fill the vacuum. Yet able teachers and able students have always kept islands of academic learning afloat in the rising tide of nonintellectual school activities. It may be difficult, indeed, to find a healthy academic program that has been smothered by commercial interests. More often, Latin, ancient history, and trigonometry have decayed, become archaic, or grown spitefully difficult, thus losing out to home economics, driver training, music, art, and shop by default. Many factors went into the change in purpose, and the problem of determining which ones were most responsible is at least as difficult as figuring out what made Hemingway commit suicide.

HISTORICAL NECESSITY

The contexts within which practices in American public schools have changed resemble the old spiritual about the "wheel in a wheel way in the middle of the air." Changes in information, tolerated behavior, clientele, personnel, and purpose have added up to a revolution in practice. The search for something that everyone could do and benefit from could not take place isolated from the forces acting upon society and, hence, upon the attention of the public. The depression of the 1930's set the basic economic and social context in which the revolution in practice matured. All students needed as much preparation for work as they could get, and everyone had to learn to adjust to new circumstances and to one another. To have ignored job training during the depression would have been impossible. Public schools were the only available institution for reaching all youngsters over an extended period of time. To have ignored social adjustment would have been almost as difficult. The practical revolution had its own internal forces which brought it to boil, but the forces which surrounded it in society at large gave direction to the whole movement and determined how the internal forces would develop.

---

* One might speculate whether or not the liberal arts graduates, so contemptuous of teaching, could have convinced students, teachers, parents, administrators, and board members of the folly of such shortsighted vocationalism had they stooped to teaching.

It is one thing to protest against sin, cancer, alcoholism, and appease-
ment. It is another thing to try to understand any one of them sufficiently
to guess at the causes and change the conditions in such a way that changed
behavior ensues. Evangelists who would have us repent the sins of American educational practice have neither the patience nor the talent to
analyze the situation so as to distinguish between the arbitrary and the
inevitable. The passion that leads to wholesale condemnation does not
nourish careful examination. It remains true, however, that the worth of
a recommendation is directly related to the depth and care of the analysis
that leads to it.

It may be true that by 1945 vocational training, physical training,
competitive athletics, social adjustment courses, and watered-down subjects had formed a nonintellectual (even anti-intellectual) impaction in
the system of public schooling. But the cure recommended will depend
upon whether the ailment is viewed as a conspiracy, an accident, the result of improper diet, the consequence of emotional upset, or the inevitable malfunction of an organism at a certain stage of life.

Was it wrong to bring virtually everyone into the public schools?
With most youngsters in the appropriate age groups in school, was the
mistake that of attempting to keep them there? Should they have been
kept there and somehow forced to work, even if they could not expect to
master the lessons? Was the search for something that everyone could
and would do ill-advised? Given the new clientele, should the schools have
continued to operate with the old personnel? Given the depression, should
the new personnel have insisted that Latin and ancient history remain
cornerstones of the curriculum?

The failure to analyze forces acting upon the school revolution and
within it led, first, to exaggerated hopes of what it would achieve and,
second, to excesses of recent discouragement. Just as ignorance of the
forces behind the Castro revolution in Cuba led to early optimism and later
pessimism, so did Americans overestimate and then underestimate what
their school revolution could do. Failure to take into account such fundamental conditions as the extensive and influential local control has often
led to recommendations for the improvement of practice that have no more
effectiveness than New Year resolutions.

Even in this brief overview, the questions that arise concerning what
the schools should be doing and how they might best go about it extend
in almost any direction we might wish to pursue. The practical question
of how much discussion to allow in a history lesson can lead to the prior
question of what the lesson is supposed to accomplish and whether the
aim offered is more or less worthy than some alternative purpose available.
The question of how much freedom of expression is appropriate in this
class or that might be carried back through Dewey, G. Stanley Hall, and
Pestalozzi to Rousseau and the basic view of human nature that sees the

child unfolding best in as near a state of nature as permits survival. In such a way, all educational problems soon become philosophic questions, and educational philosophy comes forth as the fundamental core of education as an intellectual discipline.

ORGANIZATION

This book seeks to set forth a narrower view of the subject matter that is most centrally relevant to education as a subject of study. Cast in the chronological framework of major changes in American educational thought, primary attention falls on analysis in the following areas:

1. Nineteenth-century explanations of instruction and teacher training.
2. Early twentieth-century conflicting views of a science of education.
3. Post-World War I suggestions for unifying professional course work.

Monitorial method, object-teaching, Herbartianism, and child study have been appraised as key nineteenth-century antecedents to the idea that education might eventually become a science.

Monitorial Method. Before the Civil War, monitorial training explained particular technical skills of instruction and control in practical, descriptive terms which led toward non-theoretical talk about method.

Object-Teaching. Carrying monitorial practicality on into the post-Civil War period, object-teaching broadened discussions of method. Yet interest in Pestalozzi's appeal for sympathy in child handling focused attention on introspection. Meanwhile, Froebel's stress upon the symbolic and spiritual significance of objects had introduced speculation about educational concepts.

Herbartianism. Under Herbartian influence, the object-teaching trend toward psychological introspection and philosophic speculation took precedence over matters of technical skill and instructional method. The logical relation of talk about human nature to instructional practice initiated the first attempt at building a comprehensive educational discipline.

Child Study. Opposed to the Herbartian emphasis on logical theories about human nature, child study concentrated upon the observation of children. This process yielded a body of reports which would become the initial content of education as a descriptive science.

Reflecting increased complexity in discussions of education, these nineteenth-century viewpoints set the pattern of controversy within which conflicting views of a science of education found expression early in the twentieth century.

Ideas about science that were made popular by Thomas Henry Huxley, Charles Peirce, Josiah Royce, William James, and John Dewey give general meaning to the differences between Herbartian and child-study concepts of educational science. Coupled with statements by such investigators as Hugo Münsterberg, Paul Monroe, and Edward L. Thorndike, these conceptions of science promoted the idea that an educational discipline must be distinguished from the task of training teachers by emphasis upon scholarly descriptive research.

Although a clear notion of observation-centered science was being ably fashioned around 1912, a considerable gap developed between it and the kind of content achieved by the measurement and survey movements which emerged about the same time. Reasons for the gap have been sought by comparing Paul Monroe's *Cyclopedia of Education* of 1911 and Walter S. Monroe's *Encyclopedia of Educational Research* of 1941.

The discrepancy between the advocacy of educational science and the limited findings of measurement research bred dissatisfaction in those who needed theories to give substance to teacher training. To keep scientific findings basic to teacher training, John Dewey wrote *The Sources of a Science of Education* in 1929. Comparison of this book with writings of Harold O. Rugg and others reveals it to be the source of the "foundations of education" concept propounded at Teachers College, Columbia University, in the early 1930's. Going beyond Dewey, however, Rugg and his associates promulgated a program which synthesized information from all sources, not merely from science.

As Herbartianism had done earlier, the "foundations" concept made the study of education theoretical at the expense of careful scientific description. It thus obscured the distinction between a discipline of scholarly research and content useful in the practical task of training teachers.

GENERALIZATIONS REACHED

In sum, two guiding ideas emerge from this attempt to reconsider the nature of education as a subject of study. First, under monitorial method, object-teaching, Herbartianism, and experimentalism, specific practical recommendations were set forth as general methods which could guide instruction. And second, under Herbartianism, child study, experimentalism, and the foundations of education concept, great confidence in a general discipline of education was encouraged. The general methods were credited with being a working description of how to teach in the same sense that T. H. Huxley's general method of science was credited with being a working description of how to do science. The general disciplines of education were credited with being systematic, comprehensive, usable theories much akin to the grand systems in philosophy. Like powerful magnets attracting iron filings, the general methods drew the rationalisms for a general discipline in such number that they sometimes obscured the core. The stronger the general method, as in the case of Dewey's application of scientific method to moral problem-solving, the more power it had to attract distant rationalisms deeply embedded in philosophy. But when the bits of philosophic ideas originally packed around a core of general method take on adhesive properties that hold them together as parts of a general discipline, the hard core of general method can go completely dead and no one will notice. This is why there is so much useless educational theory.

Part 1

Four Nineteenth-Century Traditions that Bred Confidence in General Method

If a nation expects to be ignorant and free, in a state of civilization, it expects what never was and never will be.[1]

The withdrawal of British troops and rule confronted the Americans of 1783 with the task of sustaining the spirit which had conceived the Declaration of Independence and would soon produce the Constitution of the United States. One of the citizens most responsible for capturing that spirit in prose, Thomas Jefferson, hoped to insure its continuance through widespread national education. As part of his argument he offered the following contrast:

In Turkey, where the sole nod of the despot is death, insurrections are the events of every day. Compare again the ferocious depredations of their insurgents, with order, the moderation and the almost self-extinguishment of ours. And say, finally, whether peace is best preserved by giving energy to the government, or information to the people. This last is the most certain, and the most legitimate engine of government. Educate and inform the whole mass of the people. Enable them to see that it is their interest to preserve peace and order, and they will preserve them. And it requires no very high degree of education to convince them of this. They are the only sure reliance for the preservation of our liberty.[2]

Other leaders of the period shared Jefferson's views. Benjamin Franklin and Benjamin Rush outlined conditions that a national system of education should

---

[1] Jefferson, 1816: 49.
[2] Jefferson, 1787: 48.

2

Practice As a Basis for Theory: Monitorial Method

take into account. In 1791 Robert Corman and James Sullivan both added their support to the view that (1) higher education in the United States should be viewed as comparable, if not superior, to European training, and (2) utilitarian training should be considered at least as valuable as classical learning.

The ideas so vital in precipitating the Revolution proved no less revolutionary once the new nation had been achieved. In place of military plans, leading citizens proposed formulas for a system of national education. Drawing out the summary view of this interplay of philosophic thought and practical planning, A. O. Hansen wrote in 1926:

> The principles advocated by Tom Paine and others led many at the close of the Revolution to think that some social instrument must be invented whereby this liberal philosophy could become a permanent part in determining the thought in the new republic and in fashioning institutions in harmony with these principles.
> Chief among the means sought was a system of national education that would promote such a national culture as would be an expression of these principles. Many plans were suggested.[3]

Despite the proposals published for the widespread education of youth, a practical formula won out. It went under the name of Monitorial Method.

The Bell-Lancaster Monitorial Program

Duplicating the pattern of immigrant arrivals during the early 1800's, the monitorial method crossed half the world only to settle in the major cities of the United States for at least a generation.

A Scot, Andrew Bell, developed the modern form of Monitorial Method.* In 1791 he accepted the post of chaplain and superintendent of the Military Male Orphan Asylum at Madras, India. After dismissing one of his teachers for refusing to use the native-school method of writing on sand tables, Bell hit upon the expedient of filling the vacancy with one of the more able students. The boy succeeded so well that Bell felt encouraged to experiment further. Eventually, boy monitors took over the conduct of instruction, and the adult teachers were dismissed.[4]

Five years later the program appeared in England, where St. Botolph's, Aldgate, the oldest parochial charity school in London, first

---

[3] Hansen, 1926: 40.
* The concept was not new. Many of its elements date back to Greek and Roman instruction.
[4] Gill, 1887: 35.1.

put it into practice.[5] The next year, Joseph Lancaster, former naval seaman and not yet twenty, began instructing the "destitute poor." Almost entirely without funds, he taught along the lines of the Madras system and quickly expanded his school to include a thousand students. Considering the problems of cost and control in an enterprise of that size, Lancaster's success speaks well for the efficiency and order made possible by the monitorial approach.*

Lancaster toured both Europe and America, speaking about the marvels of the monitorial method. Such men as John Adams and De Witt Clinton became convinced that the method offered just what this country needed. Laymen and educators began referring to it as "the Lancasterian method." Bell and the Madras system gradually faded into the background.

From the perspective of 1891, J. P. Gordy, Professor of Education at Ohio University, traced the growth of the program in the settled regions of colonial America. He explained that the monitorial method was almost universally adopted in large cities such as New York, Albany, Hartford, New Haven, Philadelphia, Baltimore, and Washington. By 1820, some twenty Lancasterian schools flourished in the State of New York alone.[6]

A quarter of a century after Gordy, John F. Reigart, Principal of Public School 166 in New York City, described the suffocating hold which the monitorial program had in that city. Mentioning its grip on general instruction, Reigart wrote:

> The Lancasterian system of instruction was the official system of the New York Public Schools from their foundation in 1806 until 1853, when the schools of the Public School Society were taken over by the Board of Education. Until the establishment of ward schools in 1843, the system constituted a practical monopoly in the field of public education; it was supported mainly by taxes, administered by a self-perpetuating body of trustees. Teachers were forbidden to make any departure from the plans laid down in the by-laws and manuals.[7] †

Lancasterian method had broken instruction up into separate classroom packages. Each teaching unit had to be completed before the next

---

[5] Gill, 1887: 35.1.
* This fit the specifications for minimum literacy which Jefferson seems to have had in mind when he said that "it requires no very high degree of education to convince" the whole mass of people that peace and order are in their own interest.
[6] Gordy, 1891: 36.1.
[7] Reigart, 1916: 86.3.
† Here, at the beginning, is the heavy emphasis on the fixed curriculum so thoroughly enforced by the New York State regents' exams. Standardization was initially necessitated by the fact that teachers could not be expected to know the subject thoroughly enough to insure coverage.

could be begun.* Lacking teachers with professional training and adult competence in judging what a student needed, school boards legislated lock-step instruction. Such legislation brought attention to the need for teachers, but, as Reigart stated in the following sentence, the remedy was a long way off: "Until the foundation of the Normal College in 1870, the only training for the teachers of the New York Public Schools was secured through the monitorial system." [8]

Part of the staying power of the monitorial approach came from its capacity to supply a kind of teacher or monitor in quantity. This capacity, in turn, came from administrative simplicity—by separating classroom instruction from discipline and the supplying of teaching materials, each could be reduced to routine.† Maximum specificity of content goals, such as memorizing a poem or drilling in spelling, did not interfere with explicitly stated discipline, such as not whispering and standing to recite. On the contrary, they supplemented one another: rote memorization of passages from the Bible dovetailed with obedience to orders, and both served as moral training.

Responsibility carried appropriate authority within an almost military hierarchy of obedience (fitting to the tradition of the Military Male Orphan Asylum at Madras, India). Or, viewed from another direction, the same program which provided economy and efficient control in turning out clerks for colonial India offered the key to large-scale education on a minimal budget in the newly decolonized United States. The heart of the program rested on a unified method: the same program provided teaching and teachers. In the war against illiteracy, this amounted to making each enemy a comrade-in-arms simply by defeating him. Not only did each student gain a victory over illiteracy: at the same time, he became a potential teacher.

The Method of Monitorial Instruction

Monitorial Method separated administration and instruction within a hierarchical chain of command that matched authority with responsibility. In this way, the number of children under instruction could be expanded considerably without loss of control or quality of learning. John

---

* The rigid divisions between fields of knowledge and branches within a field were necessitated by the low level of teacher competence.

[8] Reigart, 1916: 86.1.

† The much-emphasized journalistic dispute between freedom and democracy in education, on the one hand, and authoritarian-fascistic control, on the other, seems, in retrospect, to have been the struggle between a system's need for bureaucratic routine and its need to keep routine from becoming mechanical by introducing novelty.

Gill, professor of education at the Normal College, Cheltenham, England, listed the steps in that hierarchy as follows:

> The *tutor* had one child to assist in the preparation of his lessons, all the children of one class becoming the tutors of the next class below. The *assistants* had charge of a class. They were overlookers and examiners. . . . The *teachers* had charge of two or three classes. It was their business to take each class in turn, examining and stimulating both assistants and tutors. The sub-ushers were chargeable with the order and general arrangements, and with the supply of books and slates; and they were expected to report to the ushers the names of such children as they could not control. The duties of the usher were to conduct all the changes of the school, to act as a sort of general superintendent, and take the names of all such as continued disorderly after they had been reported by the sub-ushers. These officers were to prevent the too frequent appearance of the master in matters of discipline and general management. . . .

> The second feature of the Madras organization was its classification. It consisted of large classes formed into hollow squares, and was based upon reading only.

> The third feature . . . was the arrangements of the schoolroom. The objects to be secured in this part of organization are effective superintendence, combined with such isolation of the classes as will prevent one class interfering in any way with the efficiency of any other. Dr. Bell doubtless took his whole organization from the parade-ground.[9]

Lancaster inherited the method and passed it on to the organization of schools in England, Europe, and the United States. To it he added the idea of competition[10]—not the matching of man against man, but, in the emerging military and social tradition of his day, group against group, class against class.

Monitorial method was a great practical success. Economy of instruction and the speed with which new monitors could be produced promised the minimal education on the national scope that Jefferson had envisioned. The strict obedience and mechanical learning of the monitorial schools, however, contradicted the spirit of Jefferson's appeal for improved social action and increased understanding. Moralists who would have most social problems solved by the "strengthening of will" and the memorization of commandments must have found this program quite suitable. Those who found the old dictum, "Spare the rod and spoil the child," a reliable rule of thumb* for child rearing had all the opportunity to apply it. By issuing the proper commands for rote learning so successful in training a clerical

---

[9] Gill, 1887: 35.3.
[10] Gill, 1887: 35.4.
* Much so-called educational theory amounts to little more than elaboration on rules of thumb that represent the distilled experience of the profession.

force at Madras, the advocates of monitorial method sought to march
mental forces to the front lines of social action in America. The system
so adapted to the purpose of empire in India had invaded the public
schools in a country dedicated to freedom and searching for self-direction.
And here began the practical phase of the educational debate over what
kind of child rearing and teaching would be most in keeping with producing citizens in and for a democratic society.

Monitorial method constituted a practical but minimal approach to
making information and skills of proven value available to many pupils
by mechanical means. Behind the need for a practical program, however,
lay the hope for something more which mechanically gained skills and
memorized information could not provide. Jefferson had looked forward
to a changed people well adapted to using, as well as to preserving, the
liberty which their new government assured. Monitorial method organized
instruction but resisted the hopes of those who desired to make the
schools both the expression and the instrument of a democratic social
philosophy. To fill the gap between attainable practical instruction and
a hoped-for future, only partly defined but deeply felt, much talk about
education developed. Practical as low-cost instruction, monitorial method
proved ill suited to the broad social visions which Americans expected to
realize through the institution of the public schools. These visions permeated the talk about what the schools should do. Scholarly, practical,
and journalistic speakers speculated about aims, methods, policy, and
programs.

The gap between the vision of the desired society and the practical
techniques of classroom instruction set the stage for the separation of two
ways of talking about American education. The practice-centered viewpoint initiated by monitorial method called for the careful explication of
rules and activities found useful through personal experience. Speculation
as to the desired society and the place of the school in realizing it generated essays in social philosophy which passed as educational theory.
Interest in improving the quality of teaching became welded to speculation about the good society. This mixture of practical explication and
philosophic speculation gradually filled programs of professional preparation. The sorting of those different mixtures and the cataloguing of the
various kinds of ideas which threaded through talk about education could
expose the evolution of education as a discipline. Just distinguishing the
scholarly concepts from those having a primarily practical focus would be
a major undertaking. From each the journalistic elements would have to
be isolated. Without the cutting edge which a thoroughly acceptable definition of journalism would provide, it remains the task for a jury of acknowledged experts.*

---

* The best such jury seems to have been the editors whom Paul Monroe
brought to the task of helping build the *Cyclopedia of Education,* published
in 1911-1913.

Monitorial Teacher Preparation

On Quintilian's cue that he who has just learned is best fit to teach, the followers of Bell and Lancaster combined the method of classroom instruction with the teacher-training process. As each student learned, he absorbed the ability to teach. Academic departments in colleges and universities adopt the same practice when they assume that mastery of a body of content brings with it the capacity to teach it. Instead of meeting the problem of how people can be trained to teach, such an approach either denies that there is a problem or else assumes that nothing can be done by direct attention. In either event, no significant body of pedagogical thought can be expected to emerge from such an anti-theoretical point of view.

The explanations and reasoning underlying monitorial method remained quite practical and seemed to show common sense, since the process of instruction had to be made intelligible to partly trained boys and to only slightly better-trained adults. Although educational thought had a long history before Bell began his program at Madras, scholarly reflection had to be minimized in favor of a practical plan which could be used in the city, where many children could be gathered into classes with ease. Consisting mainly of explanations about how to conduct practice, talk about monitorial method did offer a workable method of combining teacher training and classroom instruction in a field too young and too poor to cope with duplication or complexity.

The Cost of Operation Give and Take

Praising monitorial method for its ability to provide public instruction cheaply, Reigart offered this comparison:

No city in the early part of the century could have undertaken a system of public school as maintained at present (1916). It was largely through the cheapness of monitorial plan that the community was gradually led to assume the expense of public education. In 1823, 4090 pupils were taught at an expense per pupil of $1.80. Under the Board of Education, expenses based on the average attendance rose to $12 in 1851 and $30.54 in 1867.[11]

In addition to financial benefits, monitorial training offered three attendant advantages:

1. Rote learning of information and skills required a minimum of materials.

---

[11] Reigart, 1916: 86.5.

2. Widespread control and instruction could be achieved with a minimum of adult personnel.
3. Teacher production developed in a geometric progression, since one monitor prepared several students as instructors.

In return for such gifts, the monitorial method made only two demands:

1. Teaching and learning had to be defined in terms of rote-learning outcomes.
2. Administration had to be separated from instruction, so that a child could be handed that portion of the monitorial task best fitted to his talent and training.

Comprehensive public schooling could not have gone beyond the talking stage if a method for rapidly achieving minimal literacy and for supplying a vast supply of barely competent teachers had not been found.* Bell and Lancaster supplied both in the same monitorial package, consisting of the following six ingredients:

1. A method of instruction and a body of content: *memoriter* learning and drill in skill.
2. A method of monitor training: mastery of content and skills.
3. A method of control: unquestioned obedience.
4. A method of grouping classes: the hollow square based on reading ability.
5. A method of testing for mastery: faultless repetition from memory.
6. A method of administration: a chain of command which matched authority with responsibility and proven competence.

Each of the six methods was completely practical in that it outlined specifically how the conduct of some phase of the school was to be handled. Each was as nearly mechanical as possible in order to insure that practice would be routinized to such an extent that "even a child could do it." Concerning this facet of Bell's program at Madras, Gill made the following comment:

> As he attached little weight to what is done *for* a child, and highly valued the teaching of children by children, the result was that the instruction was mere rote, and consisted chiefly of what was mechanical and verbal. It consisted chiefly in mechanical reading, writing, and arithmetic.[12] †

---

* It is interesting to contemplate where public education would be if it had had to wait either until an adequate supply of well-trained teachers became available or for liberal arts colleges to undertake the task of teacher training on the scale which normal schools and teacher colleges have done.
[12] Gill, 1887: 35.2.
† At the beginning of public instruction, excesses of mechanical rote instruction and uncomprehended verbalisms were present. Subsequent programs have tried, often unsuccessfully, to eliminate these elements.

The journey halfway around the world from Madras to the eastern seaboard of the United States did not alter the mechanical drill in basic skills or the rote memorization of verbal content. It was just such practical simplicity in what was to be learned as well as in the techniques of instruction and in the extraction of obedience that made it possible for the monitorial schools of the United States to produce the number of teachers needed in the new schools being built early in the nineteenth century. Here, for once, the analogy of a school system lifting itself by its boot straps seems appropriate. With few scholars willing to go into the field, the school system had to produce its own teachers and it had to employ all it could produce.*

Beginning Normal Instruction

In 1818 the Public School Society of the City of New York undertook the task of training adults to run the public monitorial schools then being built. To insure an accurate explanation of the monitorial method, they invited Charles Picton from England to lead their teacher-training program. When he was ready to begin instruction in the monitorial method, the Society issued the following summons:

> With deep solicitude for diffusing the means of education among the poor, and for the general extension of the Lancasterian system throughout the country, the trustees invite all those persons who are desirous of obtaining a knowledge of this method of instruction to repair to the schools under their charge, where in the space of six or eight weeks, a competent knowledge of the Lancasterian Methods of instruction can be obtained without fee or reward.[13]

Six weeks would be just long enough for a very practical explanation of methods of (1) instruction, (2) control, (3) monitor training, (4) grouping classes, (5) testing for mastery, and (6) administration through a chain of command. Such practical talk about methods of teaching to be understood by the average citizen probably contained little scholarship. This was the domain of practice-centered concern.†

Despite its organizational and instructional practicality, the monitorial method ran into financial difficulty because the increasing demand

---

* Critics who find teachers badly prepared seldom bother to find out how far they have come.

[13] Gill, 1887: 35.4.

† It was such practice-centered concern that prepared the way for the accusation that teacher training was nothing but recipes called "methods." And the failure of methods when tried led to the counter accusation that normal schools were too "theoretical."

for clerical and other kinds of literate workers in the cities was so high.
Describing this snag in the New York City program, Reigart had this to
say in retrospect:

> It was difficult to secure a supply of monitors, and very few children
> remained in school after the age of eleven. Of those who were mature
> enough to become monitors, few could be induced to remain after their
> parents discovered that more money could be earned in other occupa-
> tions.[14]

As monitors left teaching to go into other occupations, public school
instruction had to depend more and more on adults who were willing to
teach. A major step in replacing monitors with adult teachers was taken
when the four lower classes were dropped from the monitorial schools
and made into a primary department. On this pre-monitorial level, women
teachers replaced boy monitors shortly after the establishment of the Infant
School Society in 1827.[15] At a salary of twenty-five dollars for the first
year, however, the adult women who took over primary department instructions could not be relied upon to provide even the low-level standardized instruction which trained boy monitors had assured. To normalize,
or standardize, instructional methods and materials, the Public School
Society of New York City provided Saturday classes for the new women
teachers.

At first, these normal classes amounted to very little. Thus, Commissioner Isaac Bell observed, in a speech quoted by Reigart:

> The committee formed supplementary classes in nearly all the female
> departments of the public schools—many of them small and expensive;
> and although teachers were mainly appointed from them, there was no
> pretense even of imparting instruction in methods and principles of
> teaching. There was no training in government and discipline, and,
> therefore, thousands of children were compelled to suffer loss and in-
> jury before these teachers acquired the necessary tact and power to
> manage their classes.[16]

For a long while normal instruction reflected monitorial practice. Gradually, however, as the idea of a teacher—as distinct from a boy monitor—
became more clearly defined, the Saturday classes promised to become
agencies for improving practical competence. Always behind the fumbling
efforts at normal instruction stood the basic skeleton of a belief that with
a little training people of average ability could become competent professionals. And solidly behind that idea stood such energetic educators as

---

[14] Reigart, 1916: 86.4.
[15] Reigart, 1916: 86.4.
[16] Reigart, 1916: 86.2.

Horace Mann, always ready to draw sharp and useful, even if journalistic, dichotomies, such as the following quoted by Gordy:

> One must see the difference between the hampering, blinding, misleading instruction given by an inexperienced child and the developing, transforming, and almost creative power of an accomplished teacher—one must rise to some comprehension of the vast import and significance of the phrase "to educate"—before he can regard with sufficient contempt that boast of Dr. Bell, "Give me 24 pupils to-day and I will give you back 24 teachers to-morrow."[17]

Like such intellectual leaders as Thomas Jefferson, who thought about social philosophy while talking about the public schools, Horace Mann and other advocates of the full-time normal school thought in ideal terms about the "creative power of an accomplished teacher" even though their understanding came more from a depth of feeling nourished through years of practical experience than from detailed observation and precise definition. Talk about the ideal teacher fitted well with speculation about the social philosophy of the "good" practitioner. Thus, on quite common-sense grounds, the ingredients for developing a speculative theory of education to be used in the normal schools had begun to accumulate along with the practice-centered explanation of monitorial method. But speculation about social philosophy that develops from common-sense grounds can quickly degenerate into journalism, especially in the climate of polar extremes of good and bad.

The normal schools, which developed after 1840, became the major training ground for the teachers who supplanted monitors in the public schools. Yet those training schools had been so severely influenced by the Lancasterian approach to teaching that the adults taking the places of boys often had substantially their same outlook. The simple process of insisting on obedience within a hierarchical chain of command had allowed classes to grow to such size that military control and rote learning remained the only practicable kind of teaching. Public schooling had to become bureaucratic, and bureaucracy cannot exist without routine. The same rigid standards of classification that enabled a bright boy to take charge of instruction had been translated into methods and rules of teaching which came into vogue with the people from whom reform had been expected. Summing up the retardation effect of the monitorial method, Reigart wrote:

> The spell of Lancaster has hindered all reform movements. Pestalozzian methods which were supposed to be used in the infant schools were cast in the Lancasterian mold. The imparting of information rather than

---

[17] Gordy, 1891: 36.3.

training in observation and eliciting of thought became the aim. There was developed a catechetical method of teaching which could readily be acquired by the monitor or the unskilled teacher. With the introduction of the higher studies into the grammar grades, a similar adjustment was made to the capacity of the monitorial type of teacher. The chopping up of all subject matter into easy mechanical stages, and the estimation of the pupil's attainments on the basis of memory became the almost universal practice.[18]

Monitorial method had attacked illiteracy by the steady, if slow, approach of implementing mechanical drill and verbal memorization. That same steady pace resisted being hurried, however.* The characteristics which made it practical as a preparation for Pestalozzian ideas and techniques stood in the way of the rapid and thorough adoption of those ideas and techniques. Efforts at realizing the better-trained teacher and the more humane pupil-teacher relationship central to Pestalozzi's plan had to take into account the permanent heritage the monitorial method had left behind, and sometimes that heritage was a hindrance.

As a practical program of control and instruction, the monitorial method did not encourage scholarly talk about educational matters. Organized around the single explanation and description of mechanical methods of instruction and military techniques of control, monitorial talk set a narrowly practical precedent. Using the common-sense approach that a mechanic might employ to explain how to fix a car, talk about practical methods tended to remain linked to things, content, and activities that might be seen, read, and touched rather than to more subjective humane feelings about children and speculation about the needs of individuals and of society. Ordered according to practical activities, such talk about education did not encourage theorizing. Such practice-centered thinking encouraged talk about education only insofar as it promised to increase the immediate efficiency of the conduct of instruction, thus setting a basic pattern for normal school instruction.

Monitorial method encouraged the development of narrowly practical rules of thumb to be used as methodology for teacher training in the newly established normal schools. Designed expressly to supply routines which could be carried on in school systems having an increased turnover of boy tutors, monitorial method sought after interchangeable parts. Method became a set of standardized instructional units and control techniques which could be routinized for handling large numbers of

---

[18] Reigart, 1916: 86.6.
* Each attempt at instructional reform had to combat the inertia of an ever-increasing weight of practice. Hence, what began as the weight of monitorial tradition grew to be a hated *traditionalism*. The objection has often been against overly mechanized routine and has been made in the defense of novelty in instruction.

children. Divided into separate, standardized rules of thumb, talk about education was impersonal, non-theoretical, and utterly practical. Such practice-centered talk could claim neither the scholarly unity of a philosophic framework nor the subjective unity of a practitioner committed to a belief he had intuitively grasped. There was no comprehensive view of the teaching task which could be explicitly stated as a theory of education.

In their effort to supplant monitorial teacher training and instruction, advocates of object-teaching fostered the belief that an intuitively felt philosophy of life would produce the ideal practitioner. The intuitive feeling would be developed through speculative, if somewhat poetic, talk about "reality"—metaphysics.

The philosopher Johann Gottlieb Fichte referred to the Swiss educator [Pestalozzi] in his famous *Reden an die Deutsche Nation* [*Addresses to the German Nation, 1807-1808*], in which he emphasized the idea that the regeneration of Prussia, just defeated by Napoleon, could not be attained without a thorough-going moral and spiritual recovery. As a means for this recovery he recommended a new education according to the principles of Pestalozzi.[1]

Placing spiritual and moral concerns first, Fichte recommended the widespread adoption of Pestalozzi's educational practices and theory throughout Germany. By following Fichte's proposal, Germany achieved a position of influence and leadership which made her the capital of the American pedagogical world from the close of the Civil War to the beginning of World War I.

Fichte's educational lodestar, Johann H. Pestalozzi, conducted his school at Yverdon during the same score of years (1804-1824) that the Lancasterian Monitorial programs were being established in the major cities of the United States. Pestalozzi and his followers emphasized the importance of affection and individual attention within the framework of the method of object-teaching. This view of teaching differed fundamentally from the verbal drill and military routinization developed under the monitorial method. As Pestalozzi's ideas became known in the United States,

---

[1] Ulich, 1935: 103.

3

Feeling As a Basis for Thought: Object-Teaching

American educators came to envision the teacher as a well-trained, well-informed, sympathetic adult who taught in accord with the principles of the object method, and on this concept they built an idealized model of the future teacher.* In contrast with these hopes, the boy monitors of Lancasterian origins seemed as unfit for teaching as the youth of the Children's Crusade had been for fighting the Saracens.

Joseph Neef introduced Pestalozzian practices in the United States. Beginning an object-teaching school in 1809 in Philadelphia, he employed and wrote about many of the ideas he had learned while working with Pestalozzi in Europe. Other Americans carried forward this new approach to teaching. The unsuccessful experiment in communal living initiated by Robert Owen at New Harmony, Indiana, in 1825 set the sympathetic understanding of the child as a primary goal for the teacher. Similar in purpose, but with greater success, the kindergarten took hold in this country just before the beginning of the Civil War. With it came Froebel's expansion of the rationale behind object-teaching. All this established an ideational and a practical basis for the rapid development of this anti-monitorial view of teaching once peace came again.

Along with the ideational and practical foundations of object-teaching, the economic basis for abandoning monitorial instruction gained momentum during the first half of the nineteenth century. When the monitorial program had first gotten under way, the United States had just acquired the wild and unexplored Louisiana Territory. Monitorial method succeeded in providing a program for establishing minimal literacy during a thirty-year period when the West borrowed wealth, manpower, and trained talent in great quantities from the eastern part of the country. However, when the repayments from western territories mounted, in the form of cattle, lumber, wheat, and gold, the nation could afford to entertain more ambitious, more complex, and more expensive programs of public instruction. Increased prosperity accompanied talk of a more speculative cast than the narrowly practical explanations that monitorial method supplied. The object method, so successful in Germany, had a speculative flavor as well as sufficient novelty and complexity to seem attractive without appearing impractical.

As the Civil War threatened, Edward Sheldon organized a program to train practicing teachers in the use and the rationale of object-teaching. Hoping to remedy the faults of rigid monitorial instruction, he encouraged demonstration and practice teaching. In demonstration teaching, an expert would show the student teacher how the method worked. In practice teaching, the student would show how well he had mastered the new method. Hoping to provide the teacher with a broader understanding

---

* Hence the gap between what a teacher should be and, under the circumstances, what kind of person could be found to teach.

of the method than practical explanation and "showing" would supply, Sheldon encouraged the speculative discussion which Pestalozzi, and later Froebel, had developed as a rationale of the object method. As the local impresario of the object method, Sheldon drew together a three-act program of teacher training: practical explanation, show (demonstration and practice teaching), and speculative talk. In those elements he had the ingredients of a discipline of education, although the primitive state of the speculative discussion did not provide the kind of unity which the Herbartians developed later. At such an early stage of development, it would be demanding a great deal, indeed, of the people at Oswego to expect that they would distinguish among scholarly, practice-centered, and journalistic ways of talking about education.

Speculative Talk about Object-Teaching

In works like those of Kant, Fichte, Schelling, and Hegel, eighteenth- and nineteenth-century Germany exhibited such an outburst of speculation on the nature of man, nature, and God that it would seem odd, indeed, if the pedagogy imported from that nation lacked such elements. In fact, it did not. The educational theories which Froebel and Pestalozzi developed for the support of the object method fixed long-standing rules of thumb about teaching to that same tradition of philosophic speculation.

METAPHYSICAL SPECULATION

In 1856, Froebel's kindergarten program came into the United States in its German-speaking form through the labor of Mrs. Carl Schurz, at Watertown, Wisconsin. Spreading to Columbus, Newark, Louisville, and Detroit, it took English-speaking form at Boston in 1860.

Emphasizing self-expression and contact with the objects which Froebel called "gifts," kindergarten teachers brought physical activity into the classroom in a manner quite foreign to the routinized and verbal concept of learning that the monitorial method had enforced. Froebel had a rationale with which to support this change in technique. Under Froebel's educational theory, each cube, block, pyramid, and sphere— each gift—had a special symbolic significance. For example, the oneness of humanity emerged from the unity of the sphere. In another instance, a ring-around circle of children holding hands led to the unity of Christian brotherhood under God—physical objects stood as symbols in this analogic reasoning, much as the appearance of order in nature suggests Divine purpose to the devout.

With this concern about the mystical nature of things leading him toward philosophy—in particular, to metaphysics—Froebel might be called "the metaphysician of the object method." He filled his talk about the object method, or reality teaching, with speculation. Summing up the philosophic nature of Froebel's educational theory, Jessie White, formerly vice-principal of the Home and Colonial Society's Kindergarten College, supplied the following list of claims made for the object-method concept:

(1) The training of the spiritual energy of man as one sprung from God, the child of God.
(2) The training of the body as the tool of this spirit.
(3) The correct apprehension of all the objects of the external world.
(4) The correct designation of them and their relationships.[2]

By attaching symbolic significance to objects of instruction and classroom activities, Froebel made theologic and philosophic speculation a matter of direct educational concern. As a strong man might make opposite ends of an iron bar touch one another, Froebel brought metaphysical matters into contact with classroom practice. Having a clear view of God and a "correct" apprehension of the world as it "really is," Froebel anticipated a kind of osmotic absorption of these insights through contact with the pure form of the gift or the symbolic classroom activity.* Once introduced into talk about instructional matters in the United States, such speculation about the symbolic significance of acts and objects developed a life and history of its own as educational philosophy.

By 1900, philosophic questions had become issues of dispute to be defended, justified, and affirmed before talk about instructional method could proceed. Speculation attempted to set forth a world view of what lay beyond sense perception. To reach beyond sense perception, it became necessary to speculate in terms of poetic devices, since reality could not be directly perceived. Emphasizing the social rather than the metaphysical side of Froebel's speculation, MacVannel of Columbia University provided the following example of how his analogic reasoning was being employed in 1906:

> . . . in the *Mother Play*, his "most triumphant achievement," it may be
> noted how Froebel works out the idea of education as a process of in-
> teraction between the two factors of the experience-process, society and
> the individual, represented by the mother and child. On the one side you
> have the child with its impulse, the need, the unformed activity; the

---

[2] White, 1905: 113.
* Belief that all educational (and all moral) matters are at bottom dependent on a metaphysical commitment (often called a philosophy) is still quite strong, though the views suggested are seldom so concrete, direct, and naïve as Froebel's. Even so, Froebel cannot be adequately characterized as merely a realist or idealist.

mother (who represents the social or normative side of the process) contributes the direction, the habitual form, the value or interpretation. As Miss Blow expresses it, Froebel *sought for the point of contact between the manifest needs of the one and the instinctive effort of the other to meet such needs.* The child and the mother (or what the mother through *thinking love* does for the child), for Froebel and his *Mother Play,* therefore, are the terminal aspects of a unitary educational process. What Froebel would have the mother do, therefore, is so to correct, organize, and enrich the child's crude but very real experiences, that its experience at any moment may be full and rich and therefore preparatory to a still fuller and richer experience in the future. [3] *

Yet Froebel's social and metaphysical speculation and the uses to which they were put represented only the top layer of talk about object-teaching. Beneath that lay the rational psychology that Pestalozzi had begun in his effort to make instruction accord with a philosophy of mind.

SPECULATION ABOUT MIND

Under Pestalozzi's direction, a full-scale program for maximizing the instructional and child-development benefits of object-teaching developed at Burgdorf and spread its influence across Europe. At Pestalozzi's school, the demands of management, attention to the perfection of method, and controversy with staff members kept much of his attention focused on practical, everyday affairs. In reflecting about education, however, he approached the practical problem of classroom instruction with a philosophic question in mind, as his statement revealed:

> I am trying to psychologize the instruction of mankind; I am trying to bring it in harmony with the nature of my mind, with that of my circumstances and my relations to others. I start from no positive form of teaching, as such, but simply ask myself: "What would you do, if you wished to give a single child all the knowledge and practical skill he needs, so that by wise care of his best opportunities he might reach inner content?"[4] †

By reflecting on his own mental processes and by reasoning about the nature of the mind of the child, Pestalozzi sought to understand what he

---

[3] MacVannel, 1906: 61.2.

* Important words so necessary to the journalistic debate between Progressive and Traditional education are here: *interaction, experience-process, impulse, need, rich, real experience.*

[4] Pestalozzi, 1898: 83.

† By looking at the inner workings of his mind for guides to understanding behavior, Pestalozzi did for normal children much of what Freud did for upset adults—each caught some insights into causes of activity.

should do and to use the insights of such thinking to improve his practice. Instead of limiting talk to rules of thumb about pupil conduct and methods of instruction, as monitorial method had done, Pestalozzi encouraged speculation as to what man's mind might be like and how he might best attain "inner contentment." *

This mixture of rational psychology and personal philosophy became inseparable from the practical explanation which surrounded object-teaching as is came down from Pestalozzi and from Froebel. Although monitorial method in the United States had set up obstacles to the practice of object-teaching and had influenced the practical explanation of method, the fact that the followers of Bell and Lancaster had not developed any extensive speculation left the ground floor of educational theory easily accessible to the ideas attached to the object method.

Beginning a Discipline at Oswego

Lancasterian instruction held fast in many of the major cities of the United States through the first half of the nineteenth century. In a few spots, however, a different kind of program emerged like spring flowers through the snow to announce an imminent change of climate. The first such program for the development of object-teaching Joseph Neef introduced at about the same time that the Lancasterian programs took hold in the cities. Neef's program, Will S. Monroe, professor of psychology at the State Normal School, Westfield, Massachusetts, later declared, chronicled the early appearance of object-method-oriented schools. Writing in 1907, Monroe made the following statement:

> In America object-teaching was employed in various Pestalozzian schools of Joseph Neef in Philadelphia in 1809, in Village Green, Pa., in 1813, in Louisville, in 1816, in New Harmony, Indiana, in 1825. Neef, formerly associated with Pestalozzi at Burgdorf, published this country's first book on method and probably the earliest book on pedagogy in English: *Sketch of a Plan and Method of Education* (1806).[5]

Several good examples of Pestalozzian object-teaching had broken ground for a new approach to education in the United States, and the success of kindergarten programs after 1856 introduced a new batch of seeds. Coming at a time when the Lancasterian system had run full-course, to end in the senile knotting of military-type control and routinized drill, the object-teaching of the kindergartens brought the youthfulness of unfettered

---

* The whole vocabulary of inferred processes, such as judging, conceiving, and creating, is what Ryle finds so objectionable in *The Concept of Mind.*
[5] W. S. Monroe, 1907: 72.

movement to the attention of teachers and parents. Children began to get a little elbow room. There was room for novelty in the content taught in the classroom.

DIVERSIFYING TALK

In 1861 Edward Sheldon began systematically training teachers in the use and the understanding of the object method at Oswego, New York. Faced with objection about the difficulty and impracticality of object-teaching, Superintendent of Schools Sheldon set out to demonstrate that the old job of teaching spelling, arithmetic, geography, and grammar could be done "in a much more rational and efficient way."[6] Beginning with an in-service Saturday training program for the teachers of Oswego, New York, he built his program to full-time normal school proportions. To insure that the distortion of European ideas would be minimized, Sheldon brought Miss Margaret E. M. Jones, of England's Home and Colonial Training Institution, to Oswego as a lecturer on the theory of object-teaching. By way of maximizing the effectiveness of her one-year stay, Dr. Sheldon attended her lectures regularly and took notes, such as those listed by Dearborn after the following introductory statement in his 1925 book:

> The theory courses, such as mental and moral philosophy or philosophy of education, were a mixture of the history of education, physiological psychology, and general principles of education. As in the Home and Colonial Training Institution the psychology was limited, and comprised discussions concerning the nature and order of development of the various "faculties" of the child—mental, moral, and physical. . . . No better authority can be presented in setting forth the principles which formed the framework of these theoretical or philosophical courses than the notes of Mr. Sheldon taken while attending, as a regular student, the classes at Oswego given in 1861-62 by Miss Jones. The following statement of Pestalozzian principles is transcribed from the original manuscript:
>
> 1. Begin with the senses.
> 2. Never tell a child what he can discover for himself.
> 3. Activity is a law of childhood. Train the child not merely to listen, but to do. Educate the hands.
> 4. Love of variety is a law of childhood—change is rest.
> 5. Cultivate the faculties in their natural order. First, form the mind, then furnish it.
> 6. Reduce every subject to its elements, and present one difficulty at a time.
> 7. Proceed step by step. Be thorough. The measure of information is not what you can give, but what the child can receive.

---

[6] Gordy, 1891: 36.5.

8. Let every lesson have a definite point.
9. First develop the idea and then give the term. Cultivate language.
10. Proceed from the simple to the difficult, i.e., from the known to the unknown, from the particular to the general, from the concrete to the abstract.
11. Synthesis before analysis—not the order of the subject, but the order of nature.

In elaborating on the development of the intellectual powers of the child, he (Pestalozzi) held that there is a certain order in which they unfold and increase in strength. It follows that there should be an orderly or a systematic procedure employed in stimulating and directing the growth of childhood. Two questions, then, emerge for serious consideration. First, in what order do the intellectual faculties of a child develop? Secondly, how shall teachers act in paralleling this order by the educational procedure employed?[7]

Dearborn's introduction, just quoted, identified the philosophic nature of the educational talk dispensed by Miss Jones at Oswego. Mental and moral philosophy, which mixed historical information with rational psychology and general principles drawn from both successful experience and self-evident assumptions, is an apt description of what usually passed as educational theory. Sheldon's notes show that the philosophy of education taught at Oswego had a thin veneer of pedagogical thought drawn from "laws" of childhood used as practical rules of thumb. These guides appeared theoretical on six levels: (1) observation, (2) common-sense reasoning, (3) the more technical sense of specialists, (4) definition, (5) deduction from premises, and (6) insight into both paradox and contradiction.

On the observational level, everyone who had ever watched children had to agree that they were active in a variety of ways. In an excessively broad sense, such "laws of childhood" could claim to be the product of scientific observation. On the common-sense level of ordinary thought, it certainly seemed obvious that every lesson should have a point, and that the basic elements of the subject should be presented step by step, one difficulty at a time, until thorough mastery had been achieved. In a slightly more technical way, it was just as obvious to many teachers that the child should discover things for himself—although just when one should stop trying to have him discover something he keeps missing isn't discussed. By definition, learning had to be based on achievement, not on the amount of material presented, even though many lectures remain mere broadcasts. From the particular to the general, from the concrete to the abstract, was implied in the basic assumption of object-teaching: that learning must begin with the senses; thus, such derived principles had a simple logical

---

[7] Dearborn, 1925: 19.1.

truth. And finally, in the context of the rest of the rationale, paradox and contradiction melted into profound insight under the realization that, when conducted in harmony with the real operation of mental processes, educational practice could contain no discrepancies no matter how words might be arranged.

Philosophic speculation about the nature of nature, of the child, of the mind, and of learning was transposed into terms which supported rule-of-thumb methods for conducting classroom instruction. The wide-ranging metaphysical speculation of Froebel and the narrowly practical talk about how an object must be handled had been verbally joined. The linking of such "talk" about education with the "show" of the practice-teaching program at Oswego marked the beginning of a comprehensive attempt to fashion a discipline for the professional training of practitioners. Theory was being joined to practice.*

LINKING TALK WITH SHOW

Although introduced into American teacher training by Dr. J. W. Dickenson, principal of the normal school at Westfield, Massachusetts,[8] practice teaching reached full-scale proportions under Sheldon at Oswego. There the use of practice teaching in all grades of the public primary and high schools first found expression. By carefully etching out each corner of its practice-teaching program, the normal school at Oswego traced out the first figure of the new fresco depicting education as a profession enlightened by theory. In order to illustrate practice teaching on such a scale, however, the Oswego people had to routinize their program thoroughly. In 1865, Professor S. S. Greene, president of the National Teacher's Association, made the following report, in which he described the practice-teaching routine at Oswego and explained how it functioned in connection with the training of teachers in the use of the object method. He reported his observations and impressions this way:

> Let us now pass to the Training School. Here, it should be borne in mind, are regular Primary and Junior schools under permanent teachers, who act the part both of model teachers and critics before the members of the Normal School—or Training class. . . . The regular teacher gives a lesson to the class. The assistants observe and mark the methods as models for imitation both as respects the steps in the lesson, and the management of the class under instruction. One of the assistants—a pupil teacher —next gives a lesson. She is now under a double criticism; first, from

---

* Little attention was paid to whether reasoning was strictly logical or ana-logical, or whether a well-turned phrase was true by definition rather than by what it revealed.
[8] Gordy, 1891: 36.11.

her equals, the other pupil teachers present; and second, from the regular teacher. She is not doing *fictitious* but *real* teaching. . . . But now the scene changes. . . . In this room the theory of teaching is discussed and exemplified by practical lessons given by the Normal teachers to small classes of children brought in from the Primary and Junior grades. These lessons are to be drawn off by the class and examined as illustrations of the theory. Then, again, a pupil is called upon to give a lesson to a similar class, while both the Training class and teacher act as critics. The points of excellence and of defect are freely discussed, and practical hints as to the method of the lesson, its effects upon the class, etc., etc., are freely given.[9]

Professor Greene's report described the double demonstration program at Oswego. First, the process of show presented a model teacher in a model demonstration. The novices, in turn, each showed their ability to emulate the models. In the climate of such demonstration and exercising of skill, the normal school teacher and the students talked about practical educational problems which the process of showing had uncovered. Such practice-centered talk was often regarded as theory. Second, this educational program suggested activities to be demonstrated by the model teacher, practiced by the novice, and discussed by all. Speculation and practical talk were given unity of meaning through demonstration and discussion under the guidance of a specialist in both the theory and the practice of instruction.

Regular observation, guided analysis, and generalizations were reinforced by imitation, exploration, and evaluation. In a sense, the critic teacher used himself and his students as objects. This method of teacher training focused attention on activities that the student could see and do. In addition, the critic teacher defined the role of teacher by means of examples which the student tried to imitate as well as by means of explanation. The student had a concrete professional image of the teacher before him in much the same way that the child had objects to handle. In the novice's training, that image grew in meaning as he more fully realized his prowess as a teacher.*

As the model became more clearly understood, first at Oswego and then out in the field, it became a criterion for evaluating normal-school

---

[9] Greene, 1865: 37.

* This is still generally regarded as the best way to train teachers. Professional educators, as well as their critics, endorse it heavily because it is practice-centered. Implicit is the belief that there is no educational theory worth half so much as an error-trial-error exposure to teaching. Much of the high failure rate of college freshmen exposed to lecturers making their first fumbling attempts at teaching is part of the price imposed by a research-oriented Ph.D program that looks on instruction as a chore and on the ability to teach as a gift likely to impede promotion.

programs and the attainment of professional status. Sheldon himself formulated four of the essential qualifications of the model. They were quoted as follows by Dearborn in 1925:

> For this all-important work the teacher needs to be well-equipped. Among the many qualifications required the most essential are: (1) a thorough knowledge of subject matter, (2) a ready hand at drawing so that accurate representation may supplement the use of real objects, (3) easy communication with children, and (4) the power to arrest and sustain the interest and attention of children. Our normal schools must no longer be preparatory schools in the various branches of study but in the *art of teaching* alone. This reformation is not the work of a day but years. That it is destined ultimately to triumph as education becomes better known *as a science*, with its well-defined laws and principles, and teaching more thoroughly studied and practiced *as an art,* we have not the slightest doubt.[10]

More important than the items in his specifications of teacher qualifications is the fact that Sheldon had grasped the idea of making the art of teaching as full and as explicit as possible. If it could not be written out as a discipline, it might at least be embodied in a comprehensive program of talk and show. If the program as a whole could not exhibit an ideal blend of speculative and practical talk made intelligible through demonstrative and imitative show, at least one critic teacher might emerge as a standard model of the good practitioner. In fact, the critic teacher's role called for the exhibition of an expert practitioner's skill and the exhilaration of an amateur philosopher's intoxication with speculative thought. Given just this encouragement, many expert practitioners were only too willing to become amateur philosophers and, hence, theoreticians.

Practical talk, demonstration, and speculation, therefore, had to be balanced through translation of thought into action and of action back into words. All this was done by teacher trainers who were not primarily scholars. In all probability, Pestalozzi and Froebel underwent free translation, and object-teaching suffered as much distortion as poetic license could introduce. But the Oswego program did turn out a kind of standard measure of the professional practitioner, even though the degrees of tolerance varied from person to person and from time to time. And these standardized practitioners from Oswego went out to newer normal schools and passed along the approximate dimensions.

The Oswego Influence

Having begun at the same time as the Civil War, the Oswego program had four years to get under way before national conditions

---

[10] Dearborn, 1925: 19.2.

favored peaceful advance. The strength, experience, and routine developed during the war years enabled the Oswego program to accept the challenge of providing trained teachers for the normal schools being built all over the country. As evidence of the way the Oswego Normal School met the challenge, Gordy mentioned the influential role which its graduates played in staffing the normal schools of 16 states—Minnesota, Indiana, Pennsylvania, Connecticut, Rhode Island, Vermont, New Hampshire, Maine, Wisconsin, New Jersey, Nebraska, Missouri, Mississippi, California, Kansas, and Iowa. Of the seventeenth, he said:

> All the State normal schools in New York, excepting the one at Albany, have been organized on the Oswego plan, with Oswego graduates to do the work in methods and criticism.[11]

In those post-Civil War years, the spread of Oswego graduates throughout normal schools all over the United States placed a unified point of view at the base of much of this country's teacher training. It was not so much a unity of explicit statement as of common feelings and point of view toward such speculative matters as the nature of childhood, such practical talk as rule-of-thumb methods, and toward the belief that demonstration had prepared them to recognize good teaching when they saw it. The combination of show and talk had turned out models of the good practitioners who were employed to duplicate the demonstration techniques they had learned and who were dedicated to expand the speculation to which they had been exposed. It was in this spirit that they contributed to the mid-nineteenth century tendency noted by Edgar B. Wesley of Stanford University in the following paragraph:

> Discussions concerning philosophies and theories of education overshadowed the problems of classroom instruction. In fact, classroom procedure was regarded as a kind of mechanical or personal matter, quite beneath the dignity of major attention from leading educators. The teacher was thus left to work out the application of theories and philosophies, and when he failed to understand philosophic principles and resorted to devices and mnemonics, he was scolded and ridiculed for being superficial and unperceiving. In spite of the supposed emphasis which normal schools placed upon methods, the fact was that specific procedures for use in the classroom were neglected. This neglect of methods helps to explain the great popularity of Herbart in America, for he had a formula, a procedure, a set sequence of steps that promised tangible outcomes and provided guidance and assurance for the teacher.[12]

After all, a good show was worth repeating, and a good idea was worth pursuing. In the minds of amateur philosophers, wild speculation seemed identified with open-minded free inquiry while insistence on more careful

---

[11] Gordy, 1891: 36.6
[12] Wesley, 1957: 108.1.

demonstration seemed the first sign of a perverseness that would stifle investigation by taking the fun out of it and making it drudgery.

The Spirit of a Discipline

Monitorial method made principles of education out of such practical material as the organization of a hierarchical chain of command or the rules of thumb for classroom instruction. As practical principles, such talk invited little intellectual pursuit, since it was straightforward and simply explanatory. Although monitorial method had its practice-centered talk, such explanations were basically non-theoretical. Like the circumference of a circle, each part of monitorial method tended to curve around a common practical center. Pestalozzi and Froebel put doors and windows in the circular wall of practical explanation. Although the explanations of object method circled around the same kind of practical center, from time to time intellectual windows invited thinkers to look out toward the nature of mind or the spiritual and symbolic meaning of objects and activities found in the classroom. Wonder about spiritual and symbolic meanings in the minds of amateur speculators brought conversational and cracker-barrel philosophy into normal school training.

Under the Oswego program, which invited experts in the demonstration of practice to indulge in amateur philosophic talk, the normal school teacher synthesized theory and practice in both action and word. Such a speculating demonstrator seemed to personify the ideal practitioner-theoretician. Commissioned to turn out practitioners in his own image by synthesizing talk and show, he became a skilled technician in the communication of a personal philosophy of education. This often involved more journalistic popularization than careful scholarship. These philosophers in the normal schools had begun what was to pass as the intellectual discipline of education. Although their formulations centered more on an expression of feelings than on the logical relationship among ideas, they had taken the first step toward becoming conceptualists. That step was implicit in the transfer of interest which led them away from techniques for practical application and toward speculation for the sake of the idea involved. The next step in the evolution of education as a discipline was to shift the emphasis from feeling-centered thinking to logic-centered speculation. But logical and analogical thinking became even more thoroughly tangled at this next stage, called Herbartianism.

The great victories of Prussia proved conclusively that broad system of education. The well-known saying, that the victory of Sadowa was won by the Prussian schoolmaster, though somewhat one-sided, is partially true. It is an undeniable fact that the superiority of the German army was due principally to the general culture of all its members; for even the subaltern officers were graduates from the common schools.[1]

On the plains of Konigratz (Sadowa) in Northern Bohemia, the legend of German invincibility had a modern rebirth in 1866. The pronounced victory of Prussian forces over the troops of the Austrian Empire dimmed the shame of Napoleon's earlier conquest. Fichte's appeal for spiritual rejuvenation could hardly have had a more satisfying answer. Teachers became heroes; the educational system became legend.

A year later, in 1867, the German intellectual lion roared across all of Europe as Karl Marx's remarkable feat of scholarship burst forth in the publication of the first part of *Das Kapital*. Applying the tradition of Fichte, Kant, Schelling, and Hegel to social and historical philosophy, Marx gained new attention for Germanic scholarship with the scope of his synthesis. In art, science, and philosophy, the German intellectual climate had generated much of the culture most cherished

4

---

[1] Paulsen, 1897: 78.

A Rational Science: Herbartianism

throughout the world. Yet, like the Greeks before them, they had proven that a nation of great philosophic wisdom and artistic sensitivity need not forgo its ability to act in battle. How could American educators ignore such a compelling recommendation? Indeed, they could not; and they did not.

Even before Herbart's death in 1841, such immigrant educators as Joseph Neef had established a beachhead for the later invasion of German pedagogy. Froebel's quick-spreading kindergarten linked talk in education with religious symbolism. By 1861 Edward Sheldon had taken up Pestalozzi's ideas directly, and German speculative thought followed naturally. Shortly after 1866, graduates from Sheldon's normal school at Oswego began their ambassadorial work of spreading the theory and the practice of object-teaching throughout newly established training programs. As models of a way of teaching and a way of believing, these graduates were dedicated both to the rational psychology and to the humane treatment of children which Pestalozzi's pedagogy had emphasized.

Gradually, the United States of the Reconstruction era was employing teachers committed to a personal philosophy of education which they understood only in part but which they believed in completely. On all levels, the conscious understanding was German in spirit. Froebel's spiritual symbolism related practical kindergarten activities to a metaphysics of God and Man. Pestalozzi's elementary-school object method was linked to laws of childhood and learning. And in the newly developing secondary schools, Herbartian theory offered the greatest promise. Together, the ideas of Froebel, Pestalozzi, and Herbart resembled an intellectual tripod capable of supporting comprehensive public education in the United States from kindergarten through high school. To strengthen the tripod, the Herbartians sought to achieve an explicit philosophy of education based on the systematic arrangement of thought set forth as a rational science.

The Herbartians

During the second half of the nineteenth century, travel to Germany for purposes of observing the Prussian national system or contacting Herbart's disciple, Professor Wilhelm Rein, became a kind of professional avocation for American educators. The brothers Charles and Frank McMurry studied Herbart's writings with scholarly diligence. Charles De Garmo found extraordinarily attractive the amalgam of literary and philosophic thought with which Herbart had cemented together the educational side of his thinking. C. C. Van Liew paid particular attention to problems of translation so that Herbart's thought could be made available to American educators at home. These Americans and their associates quickly became expert authorities on matters of Herbartian doctrine and practice. Being quite vocal experts, they soon offered their own writings and interpretations as the basis for a new movement in American education, Herbartianism.

The Herbartians made their way into four related parts of the over-all structure of comprehensive public education: The National Herbart Society, the National Education Association, the secondary school, and university departments of education. With the foundation of the National Herbart Society, grandfather * of the National Society for the Study of Education, the Herbartians began a campaign of scholarship and publication in professional journals. In their own society and in those closely related to it through overlapping membership (such as the National Education Association), the Herbartians continued to expand their rationale and their influence. Being the first group in American educational history with a well-developed theoretical structure, their articles and books had a wide and cumulative influence. Capturing key positions in the newly established university departments of education on the basis of publications and activity in professional organizations, Herbartians quickly acquired strategic platforms for the further dissemination of their concepts and the extension of their influence.

The secondary schools of the United States remained quite undeveloped during the first three-quarters of the nineteenth century. Kindergarten and primary-school teacher training had demanded the full attention of the normal schools. With the opening of the university departments of pedagogy after 1875, a new potential for professional preparation appeared in education. These university stations the Herbartians largely commandeered, further isolating the normal schools, with their Pestalozzian ideas and elementary-school training, from the university departments of education.

Having a reputation for scholarship, the university departments also suggested the possibility of new research in education as a field of independent study. For twenty-five years, this new potential, however, lay dormant while the departments gradually grew in strength and number. By 1900, in conjunction with some of the newly organized teachers' colleges, the university departments found themselves faced with the task of training the nation's secondary-school teachers. Herbartianism seemed to meet the needs of such departments. Of the pedagogical doctrines, thanks to Herbart, it had the most scholarly content, and thus it succeeded best in overcoming the stigma picked up from association with teacher training. The Herbartians had succeeded in making themselves known for the systemization of educational thought through a vigorous program of addresses and publications. Further, their plan emphasized the same subject-matter content that the university cherished—literature, history, and philosophy. Instead of growing as upward curricular extensions of the elementary schools, the secondary schools could become downward extensions of college programs.

By 1892 the Herbartians had sufficient strength and numbers to form a club at the Saratoga Springs meeting of the National Education Association.

---

* Father of the National Society for the Scientific Study of Education.

Three years later, the National Herbartian Society for the Scientific Study of Education came into existence at the Denver meeting of the N.E.A. Although the organization disclaimed allegiance to any one educational idea, of the nine original members of the executive council, the majority were confirmed Herbartians: Charles De Garmo, Nicholas Murray Butler, John Dewey, Wilbur S. Jackman, Elmer E. Brown, Frank McMurry, Charles McMurry, Levi Seeley, and C. C. Van Liew.[2] Dewey stood out as the only active opponent of the Herbartian position.

The early issues of the society's publications carried extensive explanations of the Herbartian viewpoint, largely unopposed except by Dewey's criticism of basic principles. Following the reformation of the group into the National Society for the Scientific Study of Education in 1901, Dewey did not appear on the new executive committee.[3] He did continue his membership in the society, however. As a group, and as individuals, Herbartians became a powerful influence, as this capsule summary by Wesley stated:

> For the next twenty years [after 1895] the Herbartians wrote most of the educational books, took complete possession of several educational journals, proclaimed the issues for debate, and dominated professional discussions. Almost every prominent educator of the period endorsed all or some of the Herbartian doctrines, but the most active disciples were those who had been students of Dr. Wilhelm Rein at Jena and who were located at one time or another at Illinois Normal University—the brothers Charles A. McMurry, and Frank M. McMurry, Charles De Garmo, and C. C. Van Liew.[4]

The Herbartian Framework

Bell, Lancaster, Pestalozzi, and Froebel were not, primarily, scholars. Each thought as deeply as he could about educational matters; but whether concerned with symbolism or psychology, the theoretical side always wore the common dress of the vernacular in grammar, logic, scope of thought, and depth of background.

As successor to Immanuel Kant in the chair of philosophy at the University of Königsberg, Herbart brought the language, methodology, and complexity of careful scholarship into his theory of education. In a sense, it might better be said that he brought education into his philosophy. He made heavy use of the body of historical educational theory so long dormant. Those who followed the Herbartian approach in this country continued to incorporate scholarly content into their educational theory. Compared with

---

[2] C. McMurry, 1896: 62.
[3] National Herbart Society, 1902: 75.
[4] Wesley, 1957: 108.2.

the pedagogical thought in the monitorial method, or behind the object method, the Herbartians had an elegant geometric proof. They spared no expense of reason in trying to build a comprehensive educational theory in which rational psychology and purpose figured heavily. In turn, method played an important part in the practical side of their thought. But, most of all, each part of the theory was tied to each other part with an over-all moral concern. From their own point of view, the Herbartians claimed success in constructing the first comprehensive, logical theory of education— a rational science of systematic reasoning. The science promised a harmony of philosophic, literary, historical, and methodological concerns.

RATIONAL THEORY

At the first two meetings of the Herbartian Society, Frank M. Mc-Murry, newly appointed professor of pedagogy at the University of Illinois, expounded the American version of Herbart's pedagogy. McMurry's exposition at the Saratoga meeting of 1892 covered most of the doctrine. For convenience, his formulation can be divided into eight parts: (1) the aim, (2) the instruments, (3) the psychological means, (4) the curricular means, (5) the psychological theory, (6) the philosophical theory, (7) the pedagogical theory, and (8) the pedagogical method. Together, these parts contain vastly more complete and scholarly talk about education than had been directly linked to public instruction under Lancasterian monitorial method or Oswego object-teaching. For secondary-school teachers, it seemed the Newtonian science of pedagogy.

1. *The Aim—Moral Character.* The most comprehensive concept in the Herbartian system is both its unifying theme and its most ambiguous idea. Relying on scholarly and common-sense agreement that man's ultimate goal is a moral life, McMurry set forth the first part of Herbartian theory in the following manner:

> According to the Herbartians, the teacher cannot reach the best results by trusting merely to good fortune in the training of children. He must follow a systematic plan, the first essential of which is a definite aim. . . . With the Herbartians this supreme and ultimate object is of an ethical nature: it is the development of good character. The welfare of the child himself, as well as that of the State, gives to character-building the highest rank. All of the other objects of the school, such as useful knowledge, mental discipline, etc., are subordinate to it, and mere means for the accomplishment of the final end.[5]

Assuming that everyone knew what good character consisted of, the Herbartians fastened on this as their ultimate objective. In a climate of

---

[5] F. McMurry, 1893: 64.2.

thinking which endorsed absolute values cast in the form of Christian ethics or their counterpart as translated from other cultures, McMurry's ultimate aim of education seemed to make good sense to an increasingly social-conscious America. The well-being of both the state and the child seemed laudable, and the development of either one seemed to insure the other. By building in maximum ambiguity of meaning at the highest level of theoretical abstraction, the Herbartians could claim widespread consensus, since anyone could supply his own interpretation of "good character" and "ethical nature." With such consensus, any disagreement must be on some lower level of thinking. Here was a "philosophy" of education which, the Herbartians believed, all mankind could accept.*

2. *The Instrument—Teachers and Subject Matter.* As with a trip from New York to San Francisco, the selection of routes plays a crucial part in whether the instrument of travel is to be a plane or a boat; in a similar manner, Herbartian psychology determined the teacher's role. Earlier in American pedagogy, the monitorial method and especially the training program at Oswego had enforced the idea of the teacher as the major instrument for developing the child's character. The broader Herbartian conception F. McMurry described as follows:

> The ultimate object being determined, it remains to consider the means by which it may be realized. The Herbartians recognize two such means: the example and personal influence of the teacher as one, and instruction as the other. While they agree with Americans in considering the personal influence of the teacher a very potent factor in securing the final result, they distinguish themselves from us decidedly in the degree of importance they attribute to instruction in helping to accomplish the same end. They believe that the course of study itself, owing to the thoughts it may contain, can affect character, and they therefore place it in direct relation to the final object in view. They reason as follows: The chief element in good character is a good will. But the will is not something wholly independent of everything else; it can be influenced, it can be affected, and the instrument by which it can be affected is thought. The things which we decide to do are not simply willed outright, but are determined largely by the ruling thoughts that occupy our minds. Then, if our ruling thoughts are of the right character, so will our actions be; but if they are not, our conduct will be faulty. Certain thoughts, whether

---

* In America of 1890, before more than a handful of men took Darwin seriously, in the nation in which De Tocqueville found Christianity most deeply felt, before the popularization of "relativity," "good character" seemed to have the same Ten-Commandment concreteness as premarital chastity. Men spoke seriously of living good Christian lives. Most of what has been said about the aims of education by such well-intentioned groups as those that met at the White House Conference in 1955 has been no more than finding other ways to emphasize the importance of "good character" in schooling, that is, moral and spiritual values.

good or bad, are maxims or principles controlling our conduct. But maxims are the product of education: they have not always had control of us, nor did they secure their control instantaneously; they were slowly taught to us.[6] *

With "will" as a chief determinant of good character, the instruments which developed and directed the will became basic to Herbartian pedagogy. Along with the advocates of the object method, the Herbartians felt that the teacher served as a model to be observed and emulated as a standard of good moral behavior.† But, beyond this, the Herbartians believed in the power of ideas to influence behavior.‡ Verbal learning played as big a role in Herbartianism as it did in monitorial method, although the concepts offered were neither so limited nor so carefully memorized. The human model who provided an example did not have quite the same importance as "the word"—that is, ideas and literature—which could illustrate moral problems on a scale which no human life could approximate. The word served as the catalyst which gave work both meaning and the power to improve the will.

Work, works, and workers trained the will. The child had to work hard on those subjects which the curriculum offered him. The books contained those works with the best ideas, and the teacher was the worker who exemplified good action. Work, works, and workers instilled the habit of wanting to do what was right at the same time that they informed the will as to what it should want to do. With a reasoned psychology of a trainable will directly influenced by ideas, the Herbartians made teaching ultimately moral and morality immediately intellectual. No one who "really" understood poetry, good poetry, could be a bad man—wholly bad, that is. Yet even the Germans had to admit that Napoleon was not entirely illiterate.

This attempt to reason in literary and philosophic terms about how the will, the mind, and mankind must be and operate constituted a large share of Herbartian explanation. It has been called *rational psychology* as well as *rational philosophy*. Through such rationalism, the Herbartians tried to prove that good character and moral citizens could be produced at the low cost of introducing good thoughts into the curriculum in the right way.

---

[6] F. McMurry, 1893: 64.3.

* Here is a straightforward statement of the "mind over matter" (or, at least, over personality and behavior) doctrine. Not "wishing" but "willing" makes it so.

† Hence, the teacher had to lead an exemplary and public life, although parents did not.

‡ Not in some abstract metaphysical doctrine, but in the psychological belief that ideas quite directly influence action lies the basis for the emphasis on liberal arts as the best preparation for life and for the preference for poetry over logic as preparation for humanistic sensitivity. Advocates of liberal arts as the best general training for all later living seldom admit to such belief.

The right way, it turned out, produced the desired results because it employed the correct psychological means.

3. *The Psychological Means—Interest.*   Rational psychology, or rational philosophy—depending on whether the nature of mind or the nature of man seemed to be the subject—often appealed to commonly accepted everyday experiences, as this section by McMurry demonstrates:

> Our daily experience tells us that it is the interesting thoughts that keep our minds active; therefore, it is through interest in thoughts that that very important object of the public school, lively mental activity, is attained. . . . To the Herbartian a lively, permanent interest is the highest immediate purpose of instruction. Mere knowledge is entirely subordinate to it. Interest is not excited simply in order that one may learn better, i.e., more knowledge may be acquired. This is the usual view, but it is not the Herbartian. According to the Herbartian view, facts are learned about a subject in order that, through them, a deep, permanent interest in that subject may be awakened. The more thoroughly and accurately the facts are taught, the stronger the interest, of course. This is a fundamental principle of that school of pedagogy.[7] *

By referring to daily experience, McMurry sought to tap a commonly invoked principle of learning—the need for interest. Having learned from the advocates of object-teaching, the Herbartians saw the need to elicit interest rather than compel it or go on without it, as monitorial method had done.

In a world where good actions result from a trained will properly guided by exposure to good thoughts, interest in ideas would be a goose laying golden eggs of moral character and social welfare. By contrast, the facts and skills compelled by the monitorial method were a kind of forced feeding used in cases of "lockjaw of the mind" (if you will pardon the gruesome and garbled metaphor).

For all their concern with interest, however, the Herbartians could neither cater to it nor contact it at the expense of customary factual learning. The accumulated body of academic facts remained cobblestones in the avenue of moral character. To insure their survival intact against the whims of changing interests, a convenient common-sense maxim sufficed: the more thoroughly and accurately the facts are taught, the stronger the interest they would command.†

4. *Curricular Means—Literature and History.*   After such a simple

---

[7] F. McMurry, 1893: 64.4.

* As the amount of facts to be learned grew ever larger, the interest in problems connected with the subject had to be held off longer and longer. This frustrating of student interests upset Dewey.

† The switch from commanding interest to tapping interest marked the change experimentalists sought and shifted the emphasis from interest thought to be inherent in content to interests found to be operating in children.

maxim chaining interest to established learning, McMurry had only to ask the following questions:

> Where are thoroughly interesting thoughts of the right quality to be obtained? or, What principles should guide one in their selection?[8]

in order to give the specific means:

> Since literature and history are especially the studies that deal with the motives and actions of men, they are the ones from which the thoughts must be selected that can influence character. Hence, one or both of these branches should be taught throughout the course in the public school.[9]

Certainly, if good ideas were the bedrock of moral character, no one could ask for a better curriculum than one which arranged the best thoughts of the best minds of the best ages in their most meaningful sequence. Literature and history contained exactly those raw materials, the Herbartians reasoned. The problem was how to arrange these subjects in the most meaningful order for children. McMurry's solution introduced the theory of apperception in this way:

> The chief problem really is, to decide what truths of the desired kind will prove most interesting to children at different ages. This is plainly a question of apperception; we are called upon to decide what is most closely related to the experiences and interests of the child during each year of school.[10] *

5. *Psychological Theory—Apperception.* With the principle of apperception, the Herbartians plunged into rational psychology, to emerge with the culture-epoch theory of the nature of human nature. In rational psychology, through questions on the nature of mind, will, intellect, and thought, the Herbartians introduced the standard issues of philosophy as they pertained to a view of human nature. From this interpretation of Locke's concept that all knowledge must come through the senses, the Herbartians could either speculate toward higher abstraction about how mankind developed (the culture-epoch theory) or head in a more practical direction to deduce the best curriculum (concentrated core of history and literature) and method of instruction (the five steps). McMurry took the latter course in his 1894 account of the principle of apperception. Writing for *The First Yearbook of the Herbart Society for the Scientific Study of Teaching*, he said:

---

[8] F. McMurry, 1893: 64.5.
[9] F. McMurry, 1893: 64.5.
[10] F. McMurry, 1893: 64.5.
* Interest as used here had the same necessary characteristics of a natural law such as governs gravitation. Meaning different things, the Herbartians and their opponents could agree on the importance of good moral character and genuine interest.

The principle of apperception declares that what one can know and feel and will depends upon what he has already known and felt and willed, or that past experiences are the sole basis for intellectual, emotional, and ethical growth. Accordingly, excellence in teaching consists, first of all, in fitting newly offered ideas closely to these past experiences as their base or foundation. The first requisite to this end is that the subject matter of instruction be intimately related both to the kind of thinking and to the topics of thought which most naturally occupy the child's mind. Suitable matter will vary according to age and stage of development. There is probably a period in each person's life when any book, or indeed any thought, can be most highly appreciated. If we could only discover and take advantage of this more opportune moment for offering every bit of knowledge, what a wonderful economy of effort would result! Children's brains would then continually be stirred by what they received at school.[11]

In search of the topics and subject matter which most naturally occupied the child's mind, the Herbartians found it necessary to speculate on the nature of mind and man. The rational psychology of apperception, with its principles of how man comes to know, led to efforts to diagram the child's mind in order that the method and content of instruction could accord with the mental process. In pursuit of such an architectural plan of the mind at all ages and stages, rational psychology reached out beyond a concept of the individual to speculate about the development of the human race. A kind of rational anthropology, the culture-epoch theory brought the full range of philosophic speculation into talk about education.

6. *Philosophical Theory—Culture Epoch.* Developing a kind of rational anthropology, the Herbartians enjoyed a remarkable fluidity of thought. Thus, from the furthest speculative generalization on the nature of the race, McMurry quickly traced a line of practical deduction to Robinson Crusoe and its place in the second grade. In his 1893 article, he stated his deductions this way:

> The Herbartians, as well as Herbert Spencer, have reached this conviction; and this principle—called by them the *culturstufenidee*—is their guide in determining a course of literature and history. They see clearly a parallelism between the development of the race and that of the child. Just as one entertains itself largely at first with pictures of the imagination, then loves especially physical feats of bravery, and finally becomes reflective, so does the other. Since the two are so much alike, what interests one most at a certain age is of like interest to the other at a corresponding age. But we know what has interested races during their different periods of growth; we have their thoughts and deeds preserved to us in the form of myths and fairy-tales, legends, epics, poems, and actual history. These

---

[11] F. McMurry, 1894: 65.1.

experiences, then, are what will interest the child most if given at the proper time. In imagination he can and does live through them, just as the races have lived through them in reality. The Herbartians have, therefore, chosen fairy-tales as a regular study of the first school year; "Robinson Crusoe" as one for the second; German legends, "The Song of the Nibelungen," and other literature and history, for the grades following. Thus, classical literature or history, or both, are taught to the children during each year of school; through them good motives are implanted in the minds of the children, and thus their wills are affected.[12]

As if all the preceding pedagogic and philosophic theory had provided momentum for soaring, McMurry drew them together as a catapult for speculating about the race. Then, like a hammer poised to strike, he picked the particular phase of practice he wanted to hit, and with hawklike precision he could see "Robinson Crusoe" in the second grade.

Herbartian rational psychology (speculative philosophy) provided a deduction for practice that made it seem as if they might not need the theory to discover what should be done in the classroom but only to justify what they wanted to do. Yet, the appearance it gave was one of marvelous continuity between theory and practice and, above all, specific direction for practitioners.

What started as a speculative analogy between the development of the race and that of the child finished as something quite different. Lacking modern anthropological data, the Herbartians did not doubt that the race passed through those stages claimed for it. Without experimental psychology, they believed that the child approximated those stages. Without modern philosophy, they assumed that such analogies as they accepted had the same scientific standing as observed facts and that this justified imposition of those stages onto the curriculum. They had little doubt that the processes inferred might not exist—judging and deducing seemed real enough, if only confirmed by introspection. Finally, after the manner of literary criticism, they found that the particular works selected, and not others, exemplified certain of those stages. The analogy had been taken as a literal description yielding predictive powers. In a less naïve manner, the Herbartians reasoned much as Froebel did. From race to child to curriculum to Robinson Crusoe marked the course of this big-as-all-life idea which had so much scholarly material behind it and which offered so much guidance for practice.

This acceptance of analogy as better than fact appeared in C. C. Van Liew's defense of the cultural-epoch theory. Writing in *The First Yearbook* of 1894, Van Liew, translator of much Herbartian doctrine from German to English, tried to save the theory from criticism by asserting that the

---

[12] F. McMurry, 1893: 64.6.

child passed through epoch stages even if they could not be identified. After stating that the parallel between child and race occurs in general psychical functions and traits, he wrote:

> The "exaggerated individualism" of the cowboy, as it appears to the eye of social order, is after all, the product of one epoch of psychical development through which every healthy boy passes, though generally without becoming a cowboy; it may be that the passage is made in his literature, in his play, or in his work; it may express itself in a variety of products totally unlike that of the cowboy, and the "exaggerated individualism" may be made the source of a healthy development in the boy just as has been the case in the history of the race. For "exaggerated individualism," which was so characteristic of the early Teutonic race, was the source of modern ideals of freedom and of American institutions. So, too, may it be converted into power in the individual, if seized upon and utilized.
>
> We must insist, then, that we are dealing in this comparison not with the products of development but with the development of mental functions that have brought about the products.[13]

With self-protecting reasons Van Liew sought to answer criticisms of the culture-epoch theory by asserting that things really could not be any other way. The Herbartians believed that they were offering the most reasonable explanation of what everyone knew to be true. Every child, for example, had to have some moments of exaggerated individualism even if they came out in forms usually associated with opposite kinds of behavior. Going further, Herbartians reasoned that exaggerated individualism could be identified in any race and any child at some moment in their respective histories. No wonder that it could take any form at any time and might be overlooked altogether.

The culture-epoch theory could claim common sense and even a kind of observational validation. Similarly, connections between the early Teutonic races and colonial America could be drawn from history and writings, and could be offered as part of an educational theory. Such stages as exaggerated individualism became necessary characteristics of children at certain ages. If the curriculum were to capitalize on the features inherent in child development, it had to devote a certain part of the curriculum to work about cowboys. The efficient curriculum organized its sequence to correspond with the unfolding of stages in the child.

7. *Pedagogical Theory—Concentration.* The culture-epoch theory facilitated deduction from the nature of the race down to Robinson Crusoe and cowboys. The theory of concentration as presented by McMurry permitted reasoning to go back the other way. In his Saratoga address, Frank

---

[13] Van Liew, 1894: 104.

McMurry took the problem of curriculum and, with common-sense reasoning, reached up to encircle the over-all aim of education: moral character. To do this, he built the following case:

> Unless the teacher takes special precautions to avoid it, there is the greatest danger that their [the pupils'] knowledge will be a chaotic mass of information. The danger is quite apparent when we remember that within a single day the child studies one-half dozen different branches. . . . The Herbartians make one study a center about which all others as far as possible are grouped. . . . The Herbartians distinguish themselves by acknowledging this fact and making special arrangements to relate closely the ideas they teach. To their minds, just as the steps in a single recitation should form a closely connected series, and the parts of a single study an organized whole, so the different studies taught at any one time should make up a unit, an organized body of knowledge. It is only in this manner that the mass of facts acquired can be well mastered by the pupil, and stand at his disposal for use at any time; it is only by having all his knowledge closely related that he can have command of himself, maintain his self-reliance, and present a strong character. With these thoughts in mind, the Herbartians make one study a center about which all others as far as possible are grouped.[14] *

Once begun, this process of reasoning about the nature of man could be carried on indefinitely. As the core of subjects provided organization and order in the child's life, so the order of experience throughout many lives took on meaning in social terms. In his 1894 article on "Concentration," McMurry spun out this larger web of a priori speculation. With a final appeal to authority, he reasoned:

> The continual change of environment tends to prevent the establishment of a few central spheres of thought. Before a principle can become a conviction and gather about it enough experiences to support it firmly, the attention is called away to other things, often to principles that apparently or really contradict the former; hence, it is with difficulty that he can get and keep his bearings and grow in firmness. Many an adult who has traveled abroad recalls what a struggle he passed through in order to retain his footing on religious, moral, and social questions. Hence the child, moving from place to place, is inclined to have few firmly fixed notions, just as he has no fixed abode. *Ackermann of Eisenach* declares that there is a difference between city and country children in this connection; on grounds already stated, he says that *children reared in the country develop stronger characters than city children*; the latter

---

[14] F. McMurry, 1893: 64.7.

* Here, then, is the nub of the core curriculum so much discussed in connection with experimentalism a generation later.

dwell in too large and changeable a world to build up an undivided and harmonious or strong personality.[15] * [Italics added.] *

In this manner Herbartians went from matters of practice to generalizations about the culture-epoch theory and back again. They admitted no separation of theory and practice within the system. The most abstract thoughts had their practical educational consequences as a result of deduction. So long as no fault could be found with the reasoning, what more needed to be done? This was rational science.

8. *Pedagogical Method—The Five Steps.* With the curricular content specified by the culture epoch, and with the program organized around a concentrated core, the last step in this complete pedagogical theory called for a method for presenting Robinson Crusoe to the second-grade class. In the final part of his first article, Frank McMurry focused the whole range of Herbartian theory on this practical problem. His reasoning revolved around the famous Herbartian five-step method as developed below:

> As already seen, apperception plays a very important part in the choice of a course of study; it is likewise important in method. To bring it about, it is first necessary to bring vividly into consciousness all the experiences the child has had which pertain to the subject in hand. After they have been thus reproduced, the new ideas should be presented, to be explained by the light of the old and thoroughly apperceived ones. There are thus plainly two steps involved in careful apperception. The old ideas are recalled to consciousness, and then the new related ones presented. These two steps must always be taken in acquiring individual notions. The answer to the second question is that we pass from percepts to concepts by a careful comparison of the percepts and abstraction of the essential characteristics. By such a comparison, the non-essentials are lost sight of. The mind discovers what is commonly true, and dwells upon that alone; i.e., it grasps the generalization or the general truth. Here, also, there are two important steps: first, the act of comparison; and second, the separation of the essential from the non-essential, the mind dwelling upon and formulating the general notion. The comprehension of this notion is to be followed by its application. No matter what the study be, after a rule of law has been reached, the instructor must see that it is applied. This is the fifth necessary step in learning. These steps are all called necessary, because all minds in acquiring knowledge must take them. We all learn in the same general way. So the Herbartians have named these the five formal steps.[16] †

---

[15] F. McMurry, 1894: 65.2.
* It took Mencken in "The Husbandman" to beard the myth of rural superiority some time before Kinsey.
[16] F. McMurry, 1893: 64.8.
† Bell uncovered an expedient general method that worked; Pestalozzi uncovered laws of childhood by introspection and developed the general method of object-teaching; the Herbartians found out how *all minds* learn, and they, too, had a general method for teaching.

Instruction, then, should be conducted in the following steps: (1) recollection, (2) presentation,(3) comparison and separation, (4) generalization, and (5) application. In the Herbartian plan those five steps turned out to be more than a formal division of practices that other workers had found successful over the years. By saying that the steps were all "necessary, because all minds in acquiring knowledge must take them," McMurry revealed the Herbartian view of them as the "actual" steps of mind. Again what began as the formulation of successful practice ended up as pedagogical science derived from a rational science of mind and man. Herbartian rational psychology and philosophy fought toward the fixed notion that mind *must* be this way, and so must pedagogy as a consequence. Once properly fixed in moral purpose, five-step methodology, and theory of apperception, the science was considered proven sound. McMurry formulated that claim in the following paragraph from his address published in 1893:

> This doctrine, to be complete, must fix a definite purpose for the teacher, and show clearly by what means and methods that purpose can be accomplished. If it does that, it might then be called a science, or at least a well-organized system of thought.
>
> There are few men who have given to the world such a doctrine. Pestalozzi has not done it, nor Rousseau, nor Joseph Payne, nor Quick, nor Fitch; Comenius and Herbert Spencer have approached the mere outlines of one; the Herbartians alone have developed such a system in detail, and its essential points are accepted by a considerable body of teachers in Germany.[17]

This was not only a science of scholarship. Regardless of all its theoretical concern, the Herbartian rational system claimed to be a science of classroom practice. Herbartian scholarship pointed toward the possibility of a study of education separate from the needs of immediate practice, but the whole structure of ideas was organized to yield rules which guided practice directly in each particular situation. It was thoroughly practice-centered, yet it drew heavily on established scholarship.

A SCIENCE OF EDUCATION

Affirmed to be rational science, a well-organized system of thought, a theory or philosophy of education, Herbartianism claimed a thoroughness of coverage, an extent of speculation, and a degree of order not previously found in thinking about American public instruction. The speculation, the order of reasoning, and the directives for the conduct of practice were explicitly stated in the doctrine rather than implied in a model practitioner. Theory was not to be fashioned out of the demands of practice or the order of show; nothing less than speculative talk derived from scholarly authority

---

[17] F. McMurry, 1893: 64.1.

would do. By way of establishing the pedigree of such scholarly authority, Charles De Garmo, President of Swarthmore College, offered the following avowal:

> Herbart stands in intimate relation to the great leaders of pedagogical thought, both ancient and modern. With Socrates he accepts the building of moral character as the great end of education; with Plato he holds that intellectual culture is a necessary means to this end; and with Aristotle . . . he regards education as a supplement to the experience derived from nature and the mingling with men in society. His relations to the preceding philosophers are quite as complicated in the field of metaphysics. An extender of one side of Kantianism, he returns to the Eleatics for a correct notion of being, to the Atomists for the notion of the multiplicity of being, to Wolff for "clear notions and well-grounded 'proofs,' " and to Kant for a "science out of notions."[18]

The Herbartians dug deeply into the scholar's bag of ideas and came up with a varied assortment which they arranged in an order that to them seemed systematic. Along with that collection of scholarly thought, many ideas from ordinary living and practical pedagogy had to be fitted to assure that both rational psychology and moral conceptions would be integrated into the system. Writing about this mixture of the scholarly and the practical, MacVannel explained the blending as follows:

> Education as a science is based, according to Herbart, on ethics and psychology. The former points out the goal of education; it sets the problem; the latter the way, the means, and the obstacles to the solution of the problem. This relationship involves the dependence of education on experience, while psychology has its starting-point, not in metaphysics alone, but in experience correctly interpreted by metaphysics.[19]

Based on experience and the "correct" metaphysical interpretation of experience, Herbartian rational science pursued deductions down the educational branch of a philosophy of life. Dealing with the goals of man, with the nature of society and its influence on those goals, with human nature, and with metaphysical matters, they entertained the broadest possible range of issues in the name of educational science. Answers to questions about all of life admitted to talk about education the entire body of speculative philosophy and literature, as well as the cracker-barrel philosophy of Everyman. Scholarship, practice-centered talk, and journalism shaded into one another. Thus, scholarship and casual conversation competed on equal terms in conceptual anarchy. Out of the intellectual jungle created by the indiscriminate mixture of the full range of human thought about the entire scope of life, the Herbartians built a path to practice. That path was

---

[18] De Garmo, 1891: 20.
[19] MacVannel, 1906: 61.1.

an amalgam of scholarly, practical, and journalistic talk. Without a map of the jungle of ideas, they assumed that, because they moved step by step, they must be pursuing a logical course which was the shortest distance from highest aims to the depths of practice.

Eventually they arrived at the practical conclusion of how to teach a particular book to a particular group of children. Having arrived at rules for the conduct of practice with reasons as to why it had to be a certain book, taught in a prescribed manner, at a particular time in the child's life, the Herbartians believed that they had made a logical passage from theory to practice while raising the whole of their rational science to the level of highest scholarship.

Without a map the Herbartians could not judge, however, if their route had been circuitous or not. Theirs was a *logic-centered theory* of education. That the logic turned out to be analogical and mixed, coming from the layman as well as from the scholar, did not matter. In contrast with the feeling-centered "theory" developed around the object method at Oswego, the Herbartians had an explicitly stated rationale. Scholarly authority, step-by-step reasoning, speculation about life, and practical rules went together to form an egghead discipline of education. In place of a standard model who acted out the feelings of his personal philosophy in practice, the Herbartian was an outspoken dialectician. Show had been subordinated to talk—demonstration, to rules and reason.

The Herbartians lifted talk about education out of the arena of narrowly practical explanation and set it free to roam the entire intellectual world in search of a view of the whole of life. Pedagogical talk became conversational philosophy punctuated with scholarship and pedantry. The furthest theoretical speculation about the nature of life seemed to play a part in directing the minute particulars of practice. Occurring, in the United States, at the close of the nineteenth century, it developed during that last period of time in which an educated man could still believe, naïvely, in the universality of the Christian ethic.

Using ordinary conversation about life as the lowest common denominator between scholarly speculation and classroom practice, the Herbartians unified talk about education into a rational science. The long line of logical deduction by which they sought to link speculation with practice helped accent the gap between the scholar's and the practitioner's approach to talking about education. Herbart had been a true scholar. His American interpreters had been practice-centered thinkers. By contrast, instead of building the reasoning which joined the one to the other, advocates of child study began to pay attention to the possibilities of developing a scholar's discipline apart from a practitioner's discipline, with the hope of linking the two in the future.

"If Sarsi wishes me to believe, on the word of Suidas, that the Babylonians cooked eggs by whirling them swiftly in a sling, I will believe it; but I shall say that the cause of such an effect is very remote from that to which they attribute it, and to discover the true cause I shall argue as follows: If an effect, which has succeeded with others at another time, does not take place with us, it necessarily follows that in our experiment there is something lacking which was the cause of the success of the former attempt; and, if we lack but one thing, that one thing is alone the true cause; now, we have no lack of eggs, nor of slings, nor of stout fellows to whirl them, and yet they will not cook, and indeed, if they be hot they will cool the more quickly: and, since nothing is wanting to us save to be Babylonians, it follows that the fact of being Babylonians and not the attrition of the air is the cause of the eggs becoming hard-boiled, which is what I wish to prove."

In its business of discovering proximate causes, Galileo held, science began with observation and observation had the last word. . . .[1]

Galileo wrote his incisive critique of rationalism three hundred years before the Herbartians employed that same method of reasoning to support what they wanted to "prove" about the conduct of educational practice. The culture-epoch theory proved that the curriculum should be organized around a literature and history subject-matter core only if all the Herbartian assumptions were accepted and all the steps of reasoning were credited as valid. The chain between the

[1] Crombie, 1957: 17.

5

Observation and the Pedagogic Attitude: Child Study

speculative theory of apperception and the necessity for following the five steps of instruction in the conduct of classroom practice consisted of similar links. In kind, such proofs did not differ from the parody spun out by Galileo.

The Herbartian line of reasoning came at the end of a long rationalist tradition. That tradition credited an apt analogy with more power to reveal truth about mankind than careful observation could hope to command. Truth beyond observation was uncovered by insight and supported by the logic of common-sense reasoning. Grouping a quasi-scholarly set of analogies around insightful assumptions by means of self-evident reasoning, the Herbartians built a philosophy of life which they called a science of education.

Although three hundred years old, the criticisms of Galileo and Bacon against rationalism were only beginning to be felt in American educational thought at the close of the nineteenth century. In response to "the great Baconian change," G. Stanley Hall launched a program of child observation, description, and reporting in pursuit of empirical science, only to embrace Herbartian rationalism in the form of the culture-epoch theory. E. H. Russell set up a strict program for evaluating the objectivity of child-study descriptions, and then set out to cultivate enthusiasm for children through the same observations that were to be objectively reported. The difference between the grand panoramic unity provided by philosophic speculation and the limited scope of empirical generalizations had not been fully accepted. The scholarly enterprise of building an intellectual discipline of education had not yet been liberated from the task of training practitioners to teach in the public schools. Add to that wedding of academic and practical interests the frequent attempts at popularizing "educational science," and the conditions leading to the future corruption of talk about education emerge.*

The careful description of early child-study programs and the broad speculations of Herbartian rationalism seemed mutually supportive throughout the nineteenth century. Coupled as friends, child study and Herbartianism each picked up traits from the other. The mixture of descriptive and speculative thought which emerged from that interchange produced many and varied claims for an educational science.

The Systematic Study of Children

In addition to the mixture of Herbartian and child-study viewpoints, early steps toward a careful description of human behavior were taking

---

* Standards of rigorous scholarship had to be stretched so that "practical" solutions could be reached, and practice-centered preconceptions were continually buttressed with pseudo-scholarly reasoning. Jargon, pedantry, and journalistic debate could be the only outcome of such procedure.

place in psychological laboratories during the last quarter of the nineteenth century. Within ten years, the scientific study of consciousness had a formal beginning in the following cities: Wundt opened his Leipsig laboratory in 1879, Galton began his Anthropocentric Laboratory in London in 1882, and at the Sorbonne, Paris, the Bedunis-Binet laboratory was organized in 1889. Further, with Ebbinghaus, Kraepelin, Cattell, Jastrow, and Munsterberg doing work on memory, motor skills, and perception during the last decade of the century, education looked forward to progress through the careful description of human behavior. But even before the scientific laboratories and the careful measurement of performance, attention had been given to the careful recording of facts about children. Writing of this early work, C. L. Waddle, formerly head of the department of psychology and education at Los Angeles State Normal School, offered the following chronology:

> The first consecutive record of observed facts of child nature of which we have any information was Tiedemann's Observations on the *Development of the Minds of Children*, published in 1787, unless we except the simple notes made by Pestalozzi concerning his son in the year 1775. These were followed by somewhat similar studies by Lobisch (1851), Kussmaul (1856), and Sigusmund (1859). With the publication of Preyer's *Mind of the Child* in 1881, often spoke of "as model record," a new standard was set for studies of this type and a new impetus given to the interest of people generally in the psychology and physiology of infancy.[2]

But infancy is not restricted to human offspring, although educators understandably hoped to concentrate attention on that species. Many serious students of the psychology or physiology of infancy found the study of other animal offspring more rewarding, since the depth of exploration did not always have to stay within the legal and moral bounds of welfare. In explaining the split that resulted from this difference, Edwin A. Kirkpatrick, Head of the Department of Psychology and Child Study at the State Normal School, Fitchburg, Massachusetts made the following contribution to Paul Monroe's *Cyclopedia of Education:*

> As knowledge of mental development has increased, child-study has become differentiated into two branches of study, Child Study and Genetic Psychology. The latter represents the broader and more scientific phase of the subject, and includes a consideration of the development of mind in animals and in the human race, while the former, though founded on the same principles as the latter, is limited to the consideration of the development of human beings from infancy to maturity.[3]

---

[2] Waddle (C. W. Wadell), 1918: 105.2.
[3] Kirkpatrick, 1911: 56.

In describing the split between students of all infant behavior and those who wanted to concentrate on human infants, Kirkpatrick noted a lessening of scientific scholarship among the latter. Usually, increased specialization yields increased scholarly concentration. In the case of educators interested in the study of children, however, the need for practical guidance in the conduct of classroom teaching forced them to make generalizations which called for speculations beyond scholarly limits. Looking to need primarily, such child-study advocates had to make the available information do even when they recognized it as inadequate.* The genetic psychologist, by contrast, dissociated himself from the demands for usable generalizations so that he could pay close attention to the sources of his information and the extent of generalization that the data would warrant.

Concerned with the maximum possible reliability of his generalizations, the genetic psychologist made progress in observation a prerequisite to an expansion of the range of prediction. As the demand for immediate utility might dictate, educators, by contrast, used available data as a springboard for either philosophic speculation or practical explanation. With different ends in mind, the psychologist viewed the educator as unscholarly, unscientific; and the educator saw the scientist as narrow, impractical, insular. Prompted to defend themselves against appearing to be unscholarly, educators brought the technical vocabularies of other disciplines into their practice-centered talk. *The wholesale incorporation of technical terms without the content and limitations imposed by the parent discipline, however, cluttered talk about education* by dressing the skeleton of a simple thought in unnecessarily elaborate verbiage. Thus, talk about education became more complicated while thought remained unimproved.† In that increased complexity many believed they could see signs of a science of education capable of both scholarly exactness and broad utility for the training of teachers.

The grounds for uniting the research function with the training function of a discipline of education had been well prepared by both the Herbartian view of a rational science and the object-method concept of a felt discipline embodied in a model practitioner. The early developers

---

* This demand, perpetuated today by the continual merger of scholarly and practice-centered thinking in schools of education, inhibits the development of adequate standards of scholarship and encourages practice-centered teachers of curriculum, methodology, and administration to pretend to scholarship which they have not realized. The Ed.D. is the usual degree emerging from the so-called fusing of scholarly and practice-centered interests, and where this degree is granted within the confines of the education department, it seems to mask the unwillingness of education professors to exhibit dissertations for the approval of scholars at large.

† Here may be the condition, half a century ago, that has made it seem scholarly and profitable for educational philosophers to apply the simplest techniques of logical and semantic analysis to talk about education.

of child study had the same intention of keeping observation and description joined with the process of training teachers, as Gordy's account of the Worcester Normal School training process indicated. Writing in 1891, Gordy praised that program in the following description of its activities:

> Pupils are called upon to employ introspection for the purpose of getting a clear idea of the particular mental process or activity under consideration, that they may know it as it is in their own experience, or as it has been, so far as they can recall it by memory. But for a general knowledge of mind they are advised, on the one hand, to study the books that contain the observations and the views of scientific psychologists: on the other hand, to observe the phenomena of mind as manifest in human beings about them. And they are directed particularly to the observing of the minds of children, because this field seems to lie best within the range of their ability, to be of great interest to them, and to have direct practical bearing on their occupation as teachers. Examples of the mental processes, their associations of ideas, their imagination, their reasoning, are asked for by the instructor, and are given in abundance by pupils, out of their own observations and from the supply that is coming in continually, like a perennial spring of water, in the "records" of observations by the school at large.[4]

Training Teachers Through Child Study

G. Stanley Hall, President of Clark University and an outstanding psychologist, has long been considered the "father" of American child study; and he might also be called the uncle of its educational application. He earned this title in at least three ways: through research, as a consultant to educators, and as a popularizer of ideas.

Begun in 1880, Hall's study, *The Contents of Children's Minds on Entering School,* pointed to many deficiencies in both the preparation of children for school and the assumptions made about their capacities once schooling began. This work pioneered the descriptive approach to educational problems so much emphasized by Rice in his 1895 spelling studies. Acting as chief inspiration and active consultant to E. H. Russell, principal of the Worcester Normal School in Massachusetts in 1885, Hall collaborated in the first systematic effort to train prospective teachers by child-study methods. Finally, at the International Congress of Education of the 1893 World's Columbian Exposition in Chicago, Hall delivered an address which opened a period of widespread interest in child study. Therein he pointed to the four major kinds of child study then being conducted: information studies, physical measurement programs, case studies of the

---

[4] Gordy, 1891: 36.8.

handicapped, and measurement of general health. He explained the four areas in this way:

> The history of the scientific study of children began in this country in 1879, when four kindergartens in Boston, acting under Mrs. Quincy Shaw's lead, took three or four children at a time aside and endeavored to find the contents of their mind. The results of this work were published in the *Princeton Review* in 1880. The work showed great gaps, so great that it was dubbed "a study of ignorance of children." It came out that the primers were made for country children, while the great bulk of children are city born. This line of work has been carried on into the college ranks.
> Another line of study is the measurement of children. More children have been measured in the United States than elsewhere, but the results have not been worked over so well here as in Europe. It has been found that children grow tall in the spring, and stocky in fall; further, that different parts of the body have different periods of best growth. . . . A third line of study is exceptional and defective children. "Study the child" is becoming "Study *this* child." The method-enthusiast prides himself on results gained from stupid children; but we must let the bright child set the pace. . . . A fourth line of study relates to health. The modern school is a tremendous engine to drive the child organism. Five hours a day, five days in the week, and nine months of the year—history shows no other such test of child nature.[5]

Yet Hall's speech directed attention more to child study as a scientific movement, as a branch of psychology, rather than to its educational counterpart going on in the normal schools.

THE WORCESTER TRAINING PROGRAM

The first of the four kinds of child study mentioned by Hall, the informational program, became a part of teacher training in the United States in 1885. With the assistance of Hall, Russell introduced the descriptive reporting of child-study observations into the normal school training program at Worcester, Massachusetts. The students at Worcester did not study children in the intense and probing manner used by a Mrs. Shaw. They took a more relaxed approach to observation, as Russell's account revealed. Speaking to the child-study section of an 1889 meeting of the National Education Association, he said:

> The method is very simple, being substantially as follows: Soon after entering the school, students are made acquainted with this feature of our work, and very little effort is required to give them a new interest

---

[5] Hall, 1893: 38.

in children and their ways, partly, no doubt, from the novelty of the thing, but more because the new-comers quickly perceive in the school the presence of such an interest. They very soon feel 'the growing enthusiasm which objective study is so apt to enkindle in youthful minds, and some of them show almost immediately the right apprehension of what is wanted, and the sure tact that will lead to success. Others, of course, lack this, and never make first-rate observers.

The first real task is to correct the prevailing notion, that what is desired is the striking or remarkable sayings and doings of precocious children. It is difficult for beginners to understand that only what is common or habitual in ordinary children is of value. They can hardly believe at first that newspaper paragraphs about children are generally false, and that, even if true, they would be of little use. A second point for beginners is, to refrain from all reflections and comments of their own; to report precisely what they observe—no more and no less—with the accuracy of a photograph. A third precaution has to be much insisted on—that of never allowing the child under observation to know or suspect that he is being observed. Another important thing is to record the observations at the earliest convenient moment.

There is a question how far the beginner should be directed to look for certain specific things in children. I think our experience points towards a general readiness and openness of mind as the most favorable condition. Children are pretty wild game, and must be watched from cover, and approached indirectly. Moreover, their activities go in waves, and with little regularity, so that an observer will generally do best in a waiting and expectant attitude—what sportsmen call "a still hunt." "The best time to catch fish is when they bite" is a homely proverb that applies here. This will answer the question sometimes asked, why our students do not go about this work with more regularity and system. Such a question is natural, but it assumes that the student might almost hold his manual of psychology in one hand and a child in the other, and verify the teaching of the book, item by item. It needs but little experience to show that such a method would work about as well with a child as it would with a beaver or a loon. It is quite possible, however, that a more determinate course than we have pursued would be better.

The pupils are told in a general way in what realms or fields most of their observations will lie: as, for example, the knowledge and ignorance displayed by children, their language and gestures, curiosity, shyness, vanity, lying, etc.; their likes and dislikes, attachments, aversions, fancies, caprices; their favorite stories, songs, and myths, whatever makes them laugh or cry, ideas of the sky, of God, of death, etc.; their abilities as shown in drawing, building, planning, and the like; and above all, their plays and games, social and solitary. No limit is put to the scope of these observations, and no question is raised as to their possible utility.[6]

---

[6] Russell, 1889: 93.3.

Russell and his colleagues cautioned the students against reporting more than they saw and seeing more than was there. In short, they tried to minimize interpretations and maximize description. The observer remained a part of the background, to keep the classroom situation as natural as possible. In addition, by insisting on prompt, differentiated reporting, the program sought to reduce memory loss, temporal distortion, and the confusion of different kinds of observation. In that same address to the National Education Association, Russell described the following technique for differentiating one kind of report from another:

> The next matter is blanks for making the records. These are ordinary half-sheets of note paper, of several different tints, with printed headings covering the following items: The date; the observer's name, age, and post-office address; the name (or initials) of the child observed, its sex, nationality, and age in years and months; and the length of time between making the observation and recording it. White paper is used for such observations as students make themselves; pink for well-attested ones reported by others, yellow for reminiscences of their own childhood; green for mention of whatever they read on the subject; and chocolate for observations that extended continuously over a specified period of time. These tints help in classifying the reports, and they also require the student to reflect upon the precise character of the record he is about to make. The number of records expected from each pupil is purposely left indefinite; it has been found to average not far from two a week for the whole course of two years and a half.[7]

Seeking a wide range of careful observation, in addition to precision in reporting, the Worcester Normal School program sought to apply laboratory-type control to the child-study side of teacher training. But the attempt to attain laboratory control designed to improve objectivity was joined to a subjective reaction that worked against it. Objective observation, the child-study advocates believed, kindled enthusiasm for youngsters. Such enthusiasm had immediate practical utility for students training to be teachers. As observation developed affection, sympathetic understanding, and an acceptance of children, so did added practical utility occur in the process of writing up what had been seen. Russell could afford to ignore the utility of the finished report, since the practical result intended was attitudinal rather than informational. Observation affected attitude directly, and a change in attitude could be expected to influence information. As the observer's attitude changed to one of greater sympathy toward children and their activities, he might become a less objective observer and reporter but potentially a better teacher.

Child study related objective observation to practice through the

---

[7] Russell, 1889: 93.4.

feelings which the teacher trainee developed in the process of looking at youngsters and in writing reports. Instead of a logical or even analogical connection between "theory" and practice, child study short-cut verbal connections entirely. Instead of a rational science, its advocates strove for "felt understanding." The practical goal of creating the proper feeling or attitude in a prospective practitioner took precedence over the explicit formulation of a theory of education. Talk and writing that developed from looking remained primarily practical regardless of the scholarly theory or the careful description that might later emerge from an examination of thousands of reports.

THE WORCESTER REPORTS

Gathering reports at the rate of two a week per student, the Worcester program collected over 20,000 observations in its first ten years. Long, short, simple, and complex reports had been collected without systematic attention to utility or design. From that pile, Miss Ellen M. Haskell, editor for the Graduate Association of the State Normal School at Worcester, Massachusetts, selected 1208 for publication in her book, *Child Observations,* published in 1896. Some selections covered more than a page; others hardly made a sentence. In each, a certain amount of orderliness and restraint could be found, as these two examples show:

> 1. Gertrude. Age 1 year. Gertrude's sister hurt her hand, and ran
>   to her mother to have it kissed. Gertrude saw her, and holding her
>   hand with the other as if it were hurt, extended it to her mother
>   to be kissed.[8]
>
> 1206. Harry. Age, 15 years. Harry heard a ventriloquist. The next day
>   I saw him holding a hand-glass up to his face, and trying to talk
>   as the ventriloquist did, without moving his lips.[9]

Writing the introduction to this book by Haskell, Russell stated that the major aim of Worcester child study was practical. In 1896 he expressed that thought in the following way:

> Taken as a whole, these observations cover a very wide range, not having
> been restricted or directed to particular traits or problems of childhood;
> the aim being, as just stated, not a scientific study of children, in the
> interest of psychology, but an attempt to bring our future teachers into
> closer and more sympathetic relations with them as individuals. In this

---

[8] Haskell, 1896: 42.2.
[9] Haskell, 1896: 42.3.

respect the undertaking has proved highly successful, and it pretends at nothing more.[10] *

Yet such an elaborate system for recording different kinds of observations and the care with which the accumulating body of data was preserved suggest that Russell spoke more accurately about the purpose of the program when he summed it up in the following manner for his 1889 address to the National Education Association:

> First, and chiefly, to give such exercise in the observation of children as is calculated to bring the observer into close and sympathetic relations with them, to awaken and cultivate in those who are to become teachers a reverent interest in all the realities and mysteries of childhood. Secondly, and incidentally, to accumulate a body of well-ascertained facts that may serve in future to enlarge and rectify our knowledge of children, and so help to lay the foundation of a more adequate and pedagogically useful psychology of childhood.[11]

In addition to accomplishing the primary task of training teachers, Russell looked forward to an intellectual discipline of child study based on the data collected through years of careful reporting. The Worcester insistence on careful and objective observation could be explained by the belief that accurate looking was the best way to insure maximum growth in sympathy for children as well as an authentic perception of child behavior. But the care with which the reports were differentiated and the records preserved suggest that the hope for a scientific psychology of childhood which would be as useful to pedagogy as physics had been to engineering commanded considerable attention among these practice-centered normal school dissenters from genetic psychology.

It was probably just such a hope that led Russell to turn tons of those reports over to G. Stanley Hall, who assigned graduate students to analyze them systematically. Russell expressed his hope that such objective observation and reporting would correct certain deficiencies in psychological science. Calling up Sully, Brain, Lewes, Ribot, Preyer, and Hall as supporters of his point of view, Russell expressed that hope this way:

> Their views point plainly to two things: first, the inadequacy of the method of introspection in psychologic study; and secondly, the necessity

---

[10] Haskell, 1896: 42.1.

* This was, then, teacher training by empathy—quite similar to Froebel's suggestion that "thinking love" puts the teacher in the best frame of mind for acting as a mother to the child. Attitude took precedence over content.

[11] Russell, 1889: 93.2.

of observation and experiment, not as superseding, but as supplementing introspection, and giving to the study of mind objective reality and completeness.[12]

Although he might not have understood the scholarship that a science of child study would require, Russell did distinguish between the practical function and the research functions of accurate observation and recording. Observation could be practical on the subjective level, and recording might contribute to an improved discipline by providing more objective information than was then available. The subjective response of increased sympathy for childhood was excellent for teacher-training purposes. The objective record of careful observation contained in the accumulated body of reports might be data for an improved science of child study. Sentiment could be immediately practical in a way that isolated facts could not. On the other hand, isolated facts collected over a long period of time could have scientific value that no amount of sentiment could approach. Yet Russell suffused his whole view of both the practical and the scientific sides of child study with sentiment, as his closing statement in the introduction to Haskell's book indicated:

> Finally, it should ever be borne in mind that the study of children has wider and richer interest than those of psychology or pedagogy or any mere science. . . . I believe it holds the largest possibilities of delight, of increase of knowledge, and of practical utility. Yet its highest ideal, to my thinking, is simply enjoyment of childhood through sympathy and insight, without any ulterior purpose whatever.[13] *

Attracted by the promise of useful sentiment, teacher training had accepted child study as an instrument for developing a sympathetic attitude toward children in potential practitioners. Exploring the possibility of improved scientific understanding, serious scholars of child study began the measurement and fact-gathering tasks with which to found a discipline of infant behavior. Workers at Worcester believed that they had combined the practical and the scholarly aspects of child study into a program of effective practitioner preparation while generating objective reports having scientific value. Genetic psychology, on the other hand, sought to get rid of the reports of amateur observers who had a merely practical and often sentimental interest in child observation. However, Russell's appeal for the "simple enjoyment of childhood through sympathy and insight" in-

---

[12] Russell, 1889: 93.1.

[13] Russell, in Haskell, 1896: 42.4.

* Here, again, is the practice-centered sentiment that made it necessary for serious scholars to dissociate genetic psychology from child study. This same dissociation of scholarship from teacher training must be accomplished today if education is to grow as an academic discipline.

vited just such unscientific sentiment and unscholarly talk about children. In child-study pamphleteering, journalistic talk about education reached its fullest development among professionals.

Students of careful inquiry into child behavior could neither stem nor assimilate the expressions of sentiment about childhood in and out of education. The appreciation of childhood for its own sake was an emotional, not an intellectual, pleasure. As more teachers and laymen began to write and talk about child study from feeling and subjective reflection on their own past, what scholarly and scientific potential early educational child study might have contained quickly died. Practical talk about childhood became emotional talk, and child study forfeited its chance to develop education as an intellectual discipline. Instead, it became a popular journalistic pastime that filled teacher training with every quack notion anyone cared to introduce.

Expanded Horizons for Child Study

G. Stanley Hall acted as a triple-threat promoter of the child-study movement in the United States; as a scholar, he contributed major descriptive papers; as consultant to the Worcester Normal School program, he guided practical training; and as an important speaker at the International Congress of Education in the 1893 Columbian Exposition, he stimulated national and international interest in child study. Of this third aspect of Hall's activity, Waddle had the following to say 25 years after Hall's 1893 speech:

> Not until 1893, at the time of the International Congress of Education, held during the progress of the World's Columbian Exposition at Chicago, was any general enthusiasm aroused for "child-study." At that time Hall addressed a small company of people on the subject, and organized The National Association for the Study of Children. A "Department of Child Study" of the National Education Association was organized the same year. These were followed by the organization of numerous state societies, and many local associations of groups of teachers and parents.[14]

The first of those state societies held a meeting the very next year, 1894. The state child-study society in Illinois had been begun with the organizational help of C. C. Van Liew and Charles A. McMurry. At the same time that they assisted in the development of the first state child-study society, they were busily engaged in launching the National Herbart Society, which was formally established in 1895. Through both Herbartian and state child-study societies, teachers had an opportunity to participate

---

[14] Waddle, 1918: 105.3.

in specialized organizations having a greater unity of viewpoint than could be achieved in the all-inclusive National Education Association.

That the technical aspects of child study and Herbartianism did not fully agree mattered far less than the fact that both strove toward a comprehensive overview of all facets of education nowhere else available. Child study colored the outlook toward all varieties of teaching practice and of child behavior by bathing them in a deeply felt sympathy for childhood as the period of greatest need and greatest potential. Herbartianism linked moral purpose, metaphysical assumptions, and speculations about mankind to the details of practice through a fine-spun net of talk and called the whole pattern a rational science of education. In child study, seeing was feeling, which was believing. For the Herbartians, "saying" led to systematic order, which was science. By many, "feeling" was thought to be the subjective side of "science," and child study seemed to supplement Herbartian doctrine. Together, the two promised a deeper and broader understanding of education than had been previously available throughout the profession. Most important of all, neither view had reservations about giving practical advice about how to teach.

In 1895 the yearbooks of the child-study societies were joined by the magazine *Child-Study Monthly,* which sought to interpret the scholar to the teacher and to the interested layman. The support and continuation of such a monthly commercial publication depended at least as much on the interest it could stimulate as on the scholarly content it presented. Tapping the opinions of scholars and professional leaders, G. W. S. Luckey, originator of the school of education at the University of Nebraska, published an article of interest to educators and laymen in the eighth issue of the first volume of the magazine. Therein Luckey reported that the following three questions were asked of those most prominent in education and in child study:

> 1st. In your experience what seems to be the chief value of Child-study?
> 2nd. What do you consider the most useful lines of advance?
> 3rd. What do you think to be the principal value of Child-study to the teacher?[15]

Among the responses reported by Luckey, the following three came from the most prominent people:

> From Dr. Nicholas Murray Butler, Professor of Philosophy, Columbia College, New York City:
> First. The chief value of child-study seems to lie in two directions: (1) It arouses the teacher to examine and study the mental states of the children before her. This may be called its subjective value. (2) It will in time furnish us with a series of conclusions that will be of practical value in

---

[15] Luckey, 1896: 60.1.

guiding teachers in arrangement of courses of study, methods of instruction, hygienic and sanitary surroundings of school life, etc. This may be called its objective value. . . .

From Dr. G. Stanley Hall, President of Clark University, Worcester, Massachusetts:

First. Child-study brings the teacher into close rapport with the pupil, and establishes that personal bond which brings out the power of the teacher, and especially of a woman teacher. Man may run the school as a machine; his voice, physical strength, and character give him the advantage under present methods. When teaching is a work of love—to know children measures the love of them—the woman's kingdom will come in the classroom.

From Col. Francis W. Parker, Principal of Cook County Normal School:

First. The chief value of child study, to my mind, is to enable the teacher to diagnose the personality of the child, to know something of the child's body, mind and soul. The chief value, at present, of this diagnosis is to find out children who have defects in hearing, seeing or in other motor activities. In other words, the chief value of child study is to call the teacher's attention away from "word Cram" to the child himself. It should follow, then, that if the teacher studies the child she should apply the best conditions for the child's growth. . . .[16]

Butler, Hall, and Parker each emphasized the same subjective value of child study which Russell viewed as primary. And that subjective value had immediate practical utility by making teaching a work of love in a manner similar to that advocated by Pestalozzi in conjunction with his object method. Love was to replace the routinized word *cram* of monitorial method and of Herbartian subject-matter concentration as the unifying force that gave instruction its meaning.

Child study drew much more heavily from the feeling and talk of object method than from the rationale of Herbartianism. Tracing that line of descent, Hall's protégé, William H. Burnham of Clark University, made the following claim for child study as a pedagogical discipline:

Pedagogy based on child study seeks to use all the light that comes from the various fields of psychology, and with that light appropriate all that is best in all the various systems of education. It admits with Pestalozzi the fundamental importance of sense perception. Things before words, the concrete before the abstract, clear perceptions before the working over concepts. With Herbart it maintains also that sense perception is not enough. There must be mental assimilation and the study of casual [sic] relations, but also there must be the expression of thought; and, more than Pestalozzi or Herbart, it places emphasis on the active, the productive, the creative processes in education.[17]

---

[16] Luckey, 1896: 60.2.
[17] Burnham, 1893: 11.

Paralleling the way in which De Garmo praised Herbartianism, Burnham argued for the completeness of child study as a practical discipline of education. Stressing the feeling side of child study as Parker, Hall, Butler, and Russell had done, Burnham directed attention to the subjective elements of classroom practice which could be used for journalistic purposes, with his concern for the "expression of thought," and "the active, the productive, the creative process in education."

Naturally enough, a training program which directed attention at the attitudes and feelings of the teacher-to-be would have things to say about the attitudes and feelings of pupils as well. Russell's disclaimer aside, child study extended to talk-about-education an open invitation to adopt the terminology and the concepts of introspective psychology. "Expression" and "creativity" became key words in the discussion of what instruction could do for the child. Talk of the aims of education soon abounded with the mention of physical, social, intellectual, and emotional needs to be satisfied. (In Ryle's terms, biographical terminology multiplied.) This set the stage for even more journalistic and less scholarly prose.

Unfortunately, needs were not easy to discover, even if they were easy to name. Since they could not be directly observed, they had to be inferred from behavior. But inference is a form of speculation; and once begun, one form of speculation led to other forms. Summing up how such pioneers as Hall were pushed over the brink of philosophic speculation, D. B. Leary, professor of education at the University of Buffalo, wrote as follows:

> The major interest, at least in the mind of Hall himself, has undoubtedly been that which interested Herbart and James—what, namely, is the original nature, what are the unlearned abilities, of the child? Unfortunately, direct observation and experiment were not always the basis for evidence; opinion, hearsay, introspection, and memory often too brightly color the reports. Further, the fields covered often represented a select group of children; moreover, the topics investigated often proved too complex—division was needed. In particular, as Thorndike later showed, Hall's interpretation of the meaning of the order and dates of original tendencies, as well as his application of that doctrine to teaching and to the hygiene of childhood and adolescence, is based rather on speculation than fact.[18]

Scholarship, practical interests, and journalism were mixed so thoroughly that few men even tried to distinguish where one ended and the other began.

---

[18] Leary, 1924: 58.

Severe Limitations

By 1900, Herbartian claims of a comprehensive and consistent rational science had declared the size shoe that would have to be filled by any competing educational theory. Speculation about human nature became a prerequisite to gaining a hearing. But what was necessary for gaining a hearing in professional education was often a reason for ridicule in the rigorous world of the science of human behavior, as the following statement by Waddle suggests:

> Statistical treatment of the data presented often tended to give the appearance of exactness and finality to reports made upon the most intricate problems of child nature by persons ill-prepared to undertake such work. The definitely practical aims which most students cherished encouraged rather than restrained the tendency to hasty generalization. The contention of Barnes that "child study" was not a pure, but rather an applied, science, and the oft-repeated statement of many of the State societies that they had no desire to have their work considered pseudo-scientific, did not wholly succeed in preventing the popular mind from so considering it. This fact tended to alienate the more scientific students, and the popularity of the movement as such waned as rapidly as it had arisen.[19]

Uncovered as amateurs at science, enthusiasts of a practice-centered theory of education, built out of their child-study findings and speculations on human nature, brought discredit to the idea of education as an intellectual discipline. This discredit was heightened by the sentimental reminiscences about children and childhood which filled magazines and some journals, as well-intentioned teachers and sympathetic laymen became the amateur authors of saccharine educational science fiction. Yet, for all this journalistic prose that passed as both scholarship and the substance of teacher training, the child-study movement taken as a whole moved inquiry one step beyond the rationalistic theory which the Herbartians had designed. Waddle described that important step in this way:

> The child-study movement . . . rendered perhaps its most important service in turning the attention of students of education to the study of children, rather than to theories about children.[20]

Such a move away from theories about children and toward the study of children themselves was the first major sign of a general swing

---

[19] Waddle, 1918: 105.4.
[20] Waddle, 1918: 105.1.

away from reliance upon speculation and toward direct observation in the investigation of educational problems. The belief that observation-centered science free from unwarranted speculation would offer the best predictions for the guidance of practice gradually took hold, even if it did not become the primary concern of child study or of training colleges and schools of education.

The pioneers of such an observation-centered science of education made well-established ideas about empirical science available and intelligible to professional educators while pointing out the deficiencies in Herbartian claims for a rational science. In pioneering the idea of an observation-centered science of education, such leaders as Josiah Royce, William James, and John Dewey helped accomplish what child study had begun.

Part 2

Twentieth-Century Confidence in a General Discipline

The truth is, that common-sense, or thought as it first emerges above the level of the narrowly practical, is deeply imbued with that bad logical quality to which the epithet *metaphysical* is commonly applied, and nothing can clear it up but a severe course of logic.[1] *

As the landscape buckles, breaks, and boils up during an era of mountain building, so did the nineteenth century introduce a period of upheaval as both the process and the talk of American education rose above the level of the narrowly practical. Explanations about conducting drill or obtaining obedience within a hierarchical chain of command surrounded monitorial method with no more intellectual content than might be found in the Army's basic-training program. Instruction in how to teach according to the object method added two equally practical components to the normal school programs: demonstration and the discussion of demonstration. But, more important to the eventual development of a discipline of education, the advocates of the object method brought a new kind of talk into the normal school—speculation.

Froebel's concern for the spiritual value of his "symbolic gifts" and Pestalozzi's efforts to arrange the order of instruction according to the mental and physcial

---

[1] Peirce, 1877: 80.
* Generally, the practice-centered educator will avoid such a severe course of logic. Failure to insist on such an exposure may help to explain why so many ministers who seek academic posts take their degrees in education. They can continue to try to do "good" without having to try to define it.

6

Retreat from Rationalism: Scientific Method

nature of the child forced talk about educational matters to include more
than the narrowly practical, even though they did not include a rigorous
logic that cut down on the metaphysics. The object-method training school
at Oswego incorporated practical demonstration and broad speculation
within the same verbal program, but the Herbartians were the ones who
worked on the careful connection between practice and speculation.

From the abstract concepts of the culture-epoch theory and apperception to the concrete practice of teaching Robinson Crusoe in the second
grade according to the five steps of instruction, the Herbartians sought
systematic arrangement. In that effort at building a rational science,
thought soared so far above the narrowly practical that a science of education seemed capable of taking its place alongside other disciplines as an
independent area of intellectual study—as much a science as any other
metaphysical science, such as ethics or theology. Yet, such a rational
discipline of education did not satisfy child-study enthusiasts, who fashioned what seemed to be laboratory methods of observation and the careful
recording of behavior. Descended from a different scientific tradition, advocates of child study pointed to their rapidly growing collection of
semitechnical data on child behavior as the beginning of a discipline of
education. The child-study view of an empirical science of education
achieved a brief coexistence with Herbartian rational science in the work
of such men as G. Stanley Hall; but, as thought about the nature of science
gained clearer expression, the conflict between a rational and an empirical
discipline grew evident. Shading literal statements about human behavior
into literary "fiction" about human nature, rationalism in education, as in
political science, fashioned a most persuasive poetry of what ought to be.

A Rational Discipline

Like the fore and aft anchors of a battleship, Herbartian rational
science was fastened at one end to abstract speculation encrusted with
scholarship and at the other to concrete rules for directing practice. The
Herbartians made the explicit assumption that self-evident Christian
morality comprised the basic aim of social living and, therefore, of organized instruction. The Herbartian view of instruction implied that "the
word"—ideas, abstract understanding—formed the basic unit of learning,
since the stated moral lesson could be found nowhere else. Taking such
assumptions as self-evident, the Herbartians sought to reach practical
certitude through systematic reasoning. Ernest Nagel characterized such
an approach to science in the following paragraph from the *International
Encyclopedia of Unified Science,* originally published in 1939:

> In proclaiming the ideal of science to be systematic knowledge, the
> rationalist tradition has stimulated research and has led to the develop-

ment of science as something other than an indigestible miscellany of dubious facts. On the other hand, the great services of classical rationalism cannot hide the fact that its theory of self-evidence rests upon an inadequate analysis of the methods of science, so that it has frequently blocked the progress of inquiry and, though pledged to the ideal of clarity, has not seldom successfully courted obscurantism. Rationalism made complete certitude the theoretical condition for genuine science, but its belief that the latter was obtainable could be maintained only by neglecting or misinterpreting the approximate and contingent character of statements dealing with matters of fact. The long history of science and philosophy is in large measure the history of the progressive emancipation of men's minds from the theory of self-evident truths and from the postulate of complete certainty as the mark of scientific knowledge. Some of the major turning-points in that history consist in radically diminishing the class of statements certifiable simply by a rational insight into their truth. And some of the most dramatic moments have occurred when the approximate and incompletely grounded character of allegedly indisputable propositions was recognized.[2]

Occurring at the close of a long tradition organized around the quest for certainty, Herbartian rational science claimed distinguished ancestry. Self-evident truth carried its own credentials, and logical deduction stood open to anyone's inspection. Like mastodons of intellectual evolution, the Herbartians could not fathom that the characteristics which had once made them seem impregnable would insure their extinction, now that the climate of scholarship was changing from literary to literal.

The observation of children and the reporting of observation initiated by E. H. Russell at Worcester Normal School announced the beginning of that change of intellectual climate in educational matters. Instead of looking mainly into themselves for insight concerning the nature of childhood and learning, child-study workers were looking at children and striving to minimize preconceptions and to maximize literal reporting. Observation was ready to supplant, revise, and challenge speculation when the orgies of journalistic introspection, sentiment, and fictionalizing finally subsided. Unfortunately, they did not subside.

Earlier the Herbartians had shown the possibility of a systematic and comprehensive discipline of education. The next battle was over what kind of discipline it should be—rational or empirical. Although the work of clarifying the issues involved in that battle passed through many hands, John Dewey, William James, and Josiah Royce were chief among those who made the philosophy of empirical science available for educational application. But before *they* took up the battle, two men had helped bring the skeleton of observational science out where everyone could see it. These men were Thomas Henry Huxley and Charles S. Peirce.

---

[2] Nagel, 1955: 74.

The Spirit of Empirical Method

For several centuries before Americans began to seek after a systematic science of education, philosophers of observation-centered thinking had been formulating the theory of empirical science. Since the philosophy of science was usually conducted in quite technical terms, educationists often remained alarmingly unaware of the intellectual revolution beginning to come to boil beneath their most prized beliefs. By the time that Herbartianism took hold as the theory behind public secondary schooling in America, the philosophy of empirical science had been brought to the attention of workers in all fields. As early as 1854, Thomas Henry Huxley, British biologist and popularizer of Darwinism, provided a clear, if oversimplified, explanation of the process on which observational science based a claim to knowledge. Speaking "On the Educational Value of the Natural History Sciences," he offered the following general formula:

> The subject-matter of Biological science is different from that of other sciences, but the methods all are identical; and these methods are—
>
> 1. *Observation* of facts—including under this head that *artificial observation* which is called *experiment*.
>
> 2. That process of tying similar facts into bundles, ticketed and ready for use, which is called *Comparison* and *Classification*,—the results of the process, the ticket bundles, being named *General propositions*.
>
> 3. *Deduction*, which takes us from the general proposition to facts again—teaches us, if I may say so, to anticipate from the ticket what is inside the bundle. And finally—
>
> 4. *Verification*, which is the process of ascertaining whether, in point of fact, our anticipation is a correct one.
>
> Such are the methods of all science whatsoever. . . .[3]

Given a formula of this kind, the scientific status of a field could be quickly determined. Huxley took the initiative in this way:

> Biology deals only with living beings as isolated things—treats only of the life of the individual: but there is a higher division of science still, which considers living beings as aggregates—which deals with the relation of living beings one to another—the science which *observes* men—whose *experiments* are made by nations one upon another, in battle-fields —whose *general propositions* are embodied in history, morality, and religion—whose deductions lead to our happiness or our misery,—and whose verifications so often come too late, and serve only
>
> "To point a moral or adorn a tale"—
>
> I mean the science of Society or *Sociology*.[4]

---

[3] Huxley, 1854: 46.1.
[4] Huxley, 1854: 46.2.

General in formulation, popular instead of technical in presentation, Huxley's outline captured more of the spirit than the techniques of empirical science. As a poem to the power of empirical method, Huxley's formula had great powers of attraction. It offered simple steps as guides to investigation, and the parallel between biology and sociology inspired the confidence that a precise discipline of behavioral science would emerge. The leap from an observational science of the social process to a descriptive discipline of the educative process was not difficult for the imagination. Huxley's concept of "higher divisions of science" in which "experiments are made by nations one upon another, in battle-fields" had its classroom counterpart in the war against illiteracy and ignorance.

Small classrooms qualified as laboratories in a more precise sense than societies did. Child study had developed methods for careful observation and reporting. An empirical science of education seemed quite within reach, and later advocates of survey and measurement fact-gathering were to claim that it had been grasped. That claim took its strength from the careful observation and recording of facts rather than from any great productivity of general propositions actually or about to be verified. Inquirers into educational matters had begun their first lesson in a much-needed course of logic—how to ask questions which would bring factual rather than speculative answers. That lesson was Peirce's strongest contribution toward strengthening education as a discipline.

Asking Factual Questions

Seldom of interest to anyone but philosophers, technical discussions of the nature of science usually remained confined to scholarly journals and books. Specialists in science itself often lacked the background and training necessary to understand what philosophers had to say about science. But in November, 1877, and in January, 1878, *Popular Science Monthly* published two articles by Charles S. Peirce which brought to a wide audience of specialists and laymen new insights into the kinds of questions which science could entertain.

Although technical in their precision, Peirce's articles used popular and controversial examples with which to make his points. As an illustration of meaningless questions which produce senseless jargon, Peirce analyzed the religious concept of transubstantiation. Coming at a time when Darwinian science was challenging Christian fundamentalism, Peirce's bold move brought the matter of the meaningfulness of certain questions into the public forum. In his January, 1878 article, Peirce raised the issue of what constituted a meaningful question in the following manner:

> Such beliefs (that this or that is wine, or that wine possesses certain properties) are nothing but self-notifications that we should, upon oc-

casion, act in regard to such things as we believe to be wine according to the qualities we believe wine to possess. The occasion of such action would be some sensible perception, the motive of it to produce some sensible result. Thus our action has exclusive reference to what affects the senses, our habit has the same bearing as our action, our belief the same as our habit, our conception the same as our belief; and we can consequently mean nothing by wine but what has certain effects, direct or indirect, upon our senses; and to talk of something having all the sensible characters of wine, yet being in reality blood, is senseless jargon. . . . I only desire to point out how impossible it is that we should have an idea in our minds which relates to anything but conceived sensible effects of things. Our idea of anything *is* our idea of its sensible effects; and if we fancy that we have any other we deceive ourselves, and mistake a mere sensation accompanying the thought for a part of the thought itself.[5]

Peirce recommended the separation, first, of the denotative from the connotative meaning of a word or statement. This step advanced the development of an objective discipline in any field by suggesting that, whatever literary or religious value the emotional side of meaning may have, such subjective feeling is a parasite which distorts the objective silhouette of description and sucks nourishment from the literal meaning of the concept. Second, he insisted that the denotative meaning could be expressed only in terms of sense experience. Condensing these two points in a brief statement, Peirce formulated the following pragmatic principle of meaning:

Consider what effects, which might conceivably have practical* bearings, we conceive the object of our conception to have. Then, our conception of these effects is the whole of our conception of the object.[6]

This is Peirce's pragmatic principle of meaning by which workers in other disciplines justified the amputation of many concepts or parts of concepts. It set a pattern for insisting that the only meaningful questions were those which could be answered in terms of their practical effect, that is, their "conceived sensible effects." Peirce's statement was instrumental in bringing about the reaction against metaphysical ideas which Kilpatrick mentioned in his 1924 appeal for a reintroduction of speculation into educational thought.

That Peirce meant his pragmatic principle to apply only to conceptions about factual matters remained obscure, however, in his 1878 article. Thirty years later, he tried to clear up that matter in the following statement, which appeared in "Pragmatism in Retrospect: A Last Formulation":

---

[5] Peirce, 1878: 82.1.
* Here is one source of the mistaken view that pragmatism concerns itself merely or even mainly with practical matters of the most narrowly utilitarian or expedient kind.
[6] Peirce, 1878: 82.2.

I understand pragmatism to be a method for ascertaining the meaning, not of all ideas, but only of what I call "intellectual concepts," that is to say of those upon the structure of which, arguments concerning objective fact may hinge.[7]

And in that same "Last Formulation," Peirce gave the following expression of the importance of his pragmatic principle:

All pragmatists will further agree that their method of ascertaining the meanings of words and concepts is no other than that experimental method by which all the successful sciences (in which number nobody in his right senses would include metaphysics) have reached the degree of certainty that are severally proper to them today; this experimental method being itself nothing but a particular application of an old logical rule, "By their fruits ye shall know them."[8]

In a scientific discipline the emotional feelings and purely rational concepts which attach to terms, ideas, concepts, and formulations of thought like barnacles on a Cape Cod oyster barge were to be swept off. In his pragmatic principle, Peirce had fashioned the scraping tool for cutting conceptions about objective fact free from extra, non-factual meanings. He would separate the poetry from the science, the literary from the literal.

In the formation of an intellectual discipline designed to provide answers to important questions, any such statement limiting the nature of possible answers automatically prescribed the limits of answerable questions. As the scent of a literal discipline of education became stronger, efforts at limiting the kinds of questions to be raised about educational matters increased. Peirce's pragmatic principle and Huxley's general method of science together became the axe and bed of Procrustes. To be judged a fit scientific discipline, the questions and answers in each area of intellectual inquiry had to be measured against Huxley's general formula. As each question and answer took its place to be measured, Peirce's pragmatic principle sliced away all non-sensible effects. During the early years of the measurement movement, such "nonsense" questions fell from consideration as part of a discipline of education faster than heads during the French Revolution.

Attacks on Herbartian Rational Science

Advocates of child study, such as E. H. Russell and G. Stanley Hall, used the general formula of empirical science in their careful attention to objective observation and descriptive reporting. Educators, such as Thorn-

---

[7] Peirce, 1906: 81.1.
[8] Peirce, 1906: 81.2.

dike—caught up in the measurement and survey movements which developed after 1895 and 1911, respectively—found the task of answering narrowly factual questions extremely demanding and, potentially, completely rewarding. The gains in educational research made before 1925 made the educators confident that if they carefully pursued minute factual data, they would produce a discipline of education comparable in scope to what the Herbartians had envisioned but without the limitations of common-sense assumptions, rational deductions, and dogmatic assertions.

The idea of conducting inquiry about education according to the general method of science and by using only empirically answerable questions did not overcome the claims of Herbartian rational science without a severe struggle. Many found a rational science in hand far better than an empirical science in the bush. To the practitioner unschooled in the differences between what was obvious to reason and what was observed by the senses, the Herbartian system offered what the experts in child study and measurement could only promise. Philosophers of a discipline of education had to put the thoughts of such men as Huxley and Peirce into terms which could be understood by specialists in the various areas of educational thought and practice. In 1888, the philosopher Wilhelm Dilthy performed just such an analysis of the possibilities and limitations of a discipline of education in a paper read before the Academy of Science in Berlin, Germany.

DENYING CERTAINTY

In 1888, Wilhelm Dilthy, professor of philosophy at the University of Berlin, attacked the self-evident moral certitude and the deduced conclusions about human nature which Herbartian thought had made central to a rational science of education. Professional audiences in the United States found Dilthy's attack ably summarized and supported by the American philosopher, Josiah Royce. Three years after Dilthy's paper, Royce wrote an article based on it, which he published in the *Educational Review*. Royce quoted, reconstructed, summarized, and supported Dilthy's paper, "The Possibility of an Universally Valid Pedagogical Science," in the following way:

> Human nature, as a product of evolution, differs from nation to nation, from century to century. Nor is even an abstractly universal formulation of the ethical end of life a useful undertaking. "No moral system has ever yet been able to win universal recognition" (p. 808). The ends of life can only be defined with constant reference to the vital and growing motives and impulses of concrete humanity; and as the latter change so do the ends themselves, with the ethical systems that embody them. Hence the educator cannot hope to have defined for him, with abstract universality, either the material upon which he must always work,—namely,

human nature,—nor the end toward which he must always aim,—namely, the highest moral perfection of his pupil. Both these matters are modified for him by the course of evolution, and by the actual social environment. And yet, with all this necessary limitation, does there not remain a field for the pedagogical science? Yes, answers Dilthy, in case, not the abstract description of human nature, and of the ends of living, but the truly psychological study of the typical forms of human evolution as pursued in the fashion which the historical and biological investigations of modern times have rendered possible. There are a few general laws that hold, not so much as to the content of human nature, but as to the fashion of its organic growth. These biological laws will turn out to have a practical significance. . . . In short, scientific pedagogy, far from telling the teacher finally and completely just what human nature is, and must be, and just what to do with it, will be limited to pointing out what does, on the whole, tend toward good order and toward the organization of impulses into character. "This is the whole province of pedagogy," as a general science. Its application to the conditions of a particular time, nation, family, and child, will be a matter of art, not of science.* And "therefore, no concrete educational questions can be solved in terms of an universally valid science." Such questions will always contain elements of uncertainty, will always require the practical skill of the individual educator, and will always receive answers that will vary with time and occasion. . . . But, on the other hand, it is in vain that the inadequacy of science is made a sufficient excuse for knowing nothing of it. The more inadequate science is when alone, the more need of using it as a beginning when we set about our task.[9]

Royce had placed the full weight of Dilthy's thought across the lifeline of Herbartian rational science. By attacking the possibility of certitude in matters of moral aims, Dilthy had challenged a basic Herbartian assumption. By challenging their interpretation of human nature, he brought the rationalistic science of the Herbartians into question. As one voice, Royce and Dilthy protested the abstract formulation of ethical ends and conceptions of human nature. In place of such abstract formulations, they recommended "the truly psychological study of the typical forms of human evolution . . . pursued in the fashion which the historical and biological investigations of modern times have rendered possible." This would be investigation conducted according to the method of empirical

---

* Before the twentieth century began, Dilthy and Royce could see clearly what normal school-oriented, practice-centered professors of education do not yet realize, namely, that education as a discipline must adopt standards of sense and meaning akin to those needed in behavioral science. Teacher training, with its emphasis on the art of teaching, will have a practice-centered vocabulary and less scholarly standards of sense and nonsense, which would impair serious scholarship on the one hand just as they might facilitate "grasping" the art of teaching on the other.

[9] Royce, 1891: 88.

science, not the rational process of interpreting human nature in analogical terms suggested by a consideration of the cultural stages through which the race was supposed to have passed. Such a science of pedagogy would more nearly resemble a science of psychology than a "science" of metaphysics.

Dilthy and Royce distinguished between a science and the art of pedagogy, as well as pointing out the kind of science to be preferred. By separating the general propositions of scientific inquiry from the art which a practitioner needs to interpret how scientific generalizations might be applied in particular classroom situations, these philosophers would free scholarship from practice-centered talk while harnessing the language of teacher training to the findings of scholars. Royce and Dilthy suggested a different relation between theory and practice and, hence, a different concept of education as a discipline from that which the Herbartians had offered. The Herbartians had assumed that objective information could be systematically arranged within a rationalistic framework and interpreted to supply a convincing demonstration of how to conduct practice. Dilthy and Royce separated the subject matter and generalization processes of science from the more subjective process of interpretation and application. Until this is done in schools of education, the growth of educational scholarship will be hampered by an unnecessary impediment—that of practice-centered demands for immediate application.

SEPARATE DISCIPLINES OF ART AND SCIENCE

In his book of 1901, *Talks to Teachers on Psychology,* William James took up the distinction between the art and the science of education a decade after Dilthy had been interpreted by Royce. James supplemented their view with the following discussion of two parallel but separate approaches to a discipline of education:

> The art of teaching grew up in the schoolroom, out of inventiveness and sympathetic concrete observation. Even where (as in the case of Herbart) the advancer of the art was also a psychologist, the pedagogics and the psychology ran side by side, and the former was not derived in any sense from the latter. The two were congruent, but neither was subordinate. And so everywhere the teaching must *agree* with the psychology, but need not necessarily be the only kind of teaching that would so agree; for many diverse methods of teaching may equally well agree with psychological laws.*

---

* How many more methods could equally agree with even more abstract formulations such as the metaphysics of idealism, realism, scholasticism, or perennialism?

To know psychology, therefore, is absolutely no guarantee that we shall be good teachers.[10]

Thus, James identified the useful part of Herbartian rational science as primarily a set of practical rules of thumb about the art of classroom instruction. James found that the Herbartians, by drawing intellectual support from the rational psychology which paralleled their pedagogics, formalized the successful experience of practitioners into what seemed to be scholarly principles of pedagogy. Such practical principles supplied the framework for what passed as a discipline of education solidly rooted in profound scholarship and as solidly productive of guidance confirmed in practice. The psychological terminology and the rational concepts were mere academic shadows, though used to buttress the claim to a united and mature discipline, a rational science. As in Galileo's example, the Herbartians had known all along what it was that they wanted to prove.

The Herbartian five steps of instruction formalized classroom instruction in a manner which most good teachers could recognize as the distillation of what they had been doing for years. To claim that the five steps should be used in classroom instruction because they represent the stages by which the mind learns was to pattern science after successful classroom practice. Much of the Herbartian rational psychology, therefore, was a matter of developing psychological-sounding ideas with which to support viewpoints long since established as workable, as common-sense, or as both. In this way, the Herbartians maintained a verbal link between their theory and their chosen practice, but they contributed little but jargon to the process of talking about the conduct of practice. As an example of this tendency to manufacture hollow verbalisms, William James analyzed the Herbartian concept of apperception in the following way:

"Apperception" is a word which cuts a great figure in the pedagogics of the present day. Read, for example, this advertisement of a certain textbook, which I take from an educational journal:—

What is apperception?

For an example of Apperception see Blank's *Psychology,* Vol. — of the —Education Series, just published. The difference between Perception and Apperception is explained for the teacher in the preface of Blank's *Psychology.* . . .

The conscientious young teacher is led to believe that it contains a recondite and portentous secret, by losing the true inwardness of which her whole career may be shattered. And yet, when she turns to the books

---

[10] James, 1901: 47.2.

and reads about it, it seems so trivial and commonplace a matter,—
meaning nothing more than the manner in which we receive a thing in
our minds,—that she fears that she must have missed the point through
the shallowness of her intelligence. I think that you see plainly enough
now that the process of apperception is what I called it a moment ago,
a resultant of the association of ideas.

It corresponds to nothing peculiar or elementary in psychology, being
only one of the innumerable results of the psychological process of association of ideas; and psychology itself can easily dispense with the word,
useful as it may be in pedagogics.[11]

Unmasking sheepish common-sense thoughts dressed in the pretentious
wolfskin of technical terminology, James shook the eviscerated skin,
showing that it had been scraped clean of any meaning for psychology
and that its use in pedagogics was due to the emotional connotation which
the idea carried in practice-centered and journalistic contexts rather than
to any descriptive or denotative meaning. Thus, under the sharp criticism
of those who had taken Peirce's injunction seriously, the Herbartian
theory of apperception could be branded nonsense and discarded in the
same sweep that cast the concept of transubstantiation aside.

By discrediting seemingly scholarly talk as hollow verbalism, James
took the "scientific" halo from the rules of thumb and uncovered the
practical principles derived from experience in teaching. Further, James
cast favorable attention on the science of psychology as the source from
which educators might eventually devise a discipline of empirical generalizations. Further, by dramatizing the compatibility of training based on
practical principles and guidance to be gained from such a discipline, he
helped make room for the idea that research in education could emulate
research in psychology in method and power of prediction, without having
to submit to the demands of practice-centered thinking that would stretch
a generalization beyond its elastic limit for the sake of saying something
that the teacher could find immediately useful.

REVERSE IN METHOD

Dilthy and Royce denied the certainty which Herbartians had taken
for granted. James demolished the Herbartians' key concept of apercep-
tion when he revealed its hollow verbalism and exposed the practical
origins of its generalizations. In 1896, at the national meeting of the
Herbart Society, Dewey called upon the Herbartians to reverse their
method. Attacking the culture-epoch theory, he called upon his fellow
society members to abandon their rationalistic method and to adopt the

---

[11] James, 1901: 47.3.

scientific method which Huxley had outlined earlier. Referring to the correspondence which the Herbartians claimed existed between the stages of racial and the stages of child development, Dewey argued in this manner:

> Now in the foregoing I am not questioning the correspondence "in general;" I am simply pointing out considerations which absolutely forbid us to begin from the side of race-development and infer to child development. We must, in all cases, discover the epoch of growth independently in the child himself, and by investigation of the child himself.* All the racial side can do is to suggest questions. Since this epoch was passed through by the race, it is possible we shall find its correlate in the child. Let us, then, be on the lookout for it. Do we find it? But the criterion comes back in all cases to the child himself. If this is admitted by the upholders of the theory, many who have thought they did not agree will find themselves agreeing. But to admit this, is to come near, dangerously near, to making the child the center.[12]

With Dilthy and Royce, James and Dewey pointed out the anachronisms of Herbartian rational science. In addition, James and Dewey went on to suggest how educational theorists might develop a new discipline which would translate the findings of science for application by practitioners.

Relating the Art and the Science

In 1901, Dewey interpreted the method of empirical science in educational terms so as to make the classroom an experimental laboratory similar to the laboratory-type conditions that Huxley had found inherent in the operation of societies. Writing about "Psychology and Social Practice," Dewey explained his view of the classroom as a laboratory in this way:

> Now the school, for psychological purposes, stands in many respects midway between the extreme simplifications of the laboratory and the confused complexities of ordinary life. Its conditions are those of life at large; they are social and practical. But it approaches the laboratory in so far as the ends aimed at are reduced in number, are definite, and thus simplify the conditions; and their psychological phase is uppermost

---

* Exactly the same thing must be said about the supposed connection between such philosophic concepts as Idealism and Realism and the conduct of classroom instruction. Like the Herbartians, the educational philosophers begin from the side of the abstraction and struggle to reach concrete and particular classroom instruction. This alone should identify it as Rationalism. Such rationalism may, like apperception, still have a place in teacher training. It has none in scholarship.

[12] Dewey, 1896: 22.

—the formation of habits of attention, observation, memory, etc.—while in ordinary life these are secondary and swallowed up.* While the psychological theory would guide and illuminate the practice, acting upon the theory would immediately test it, and thus criticize it, bringing about its revision and growth. In the large and open sense of the words, psychology becomes a working hypothesis, instruction is the experimental test and demonstration of the hypothesis; the result is both greater practical control and continued growth in theory.[13]

Dewey's suggestion for a classroom laboratory would make the teacher a part-time laboratory technician, observing and recording the results of particular practical experiments. The science of psychology would provide generalizations which were valid within the framework of that discipline. But these scientific generalizations about human behavior would be *reasons to suppose* that instruction might best be carried out one way rather than another. Such suppositions would be cast in the form of predictions about the conduct of practice. Predictions about the conduct of classroom instruction require an understanding of practice, which the scientist cannot claim, and those same predictions require an understanding of science, which the teacher might not possess. Such a situation called for a third kind of specialist, a *conceptualist,* as William James implied in the following analysis of the gap between the science of psychology and the art of teaching:

> I say moreover that you make a great, a very great mistake, if you think that psychology, being the science of the mind's laws, is something from which you can deduce definite programmes and schemes and methods of instruction for immediate schoolroom use. Psychology is a science, and teaching is an art; and sciences never generate arts directly out of themselves. An intermediary inventive mind must make the application, by using its originality.[14]

Pursuing the same line of thought, Dewey proposed the following triumvirate of psychological theorist, educational conceptualist, and practicing teacher:

> The decisive matter is the extent to which the ideas of the theorist actually project themselves, through the kind offices of the middleman, into the consciousness of the practitioner. It is the participation by the practical

---

* Scheffler seems to have overlooked this side of Dewey's understanding of the classroom when he sought to correct Dewey by saying "the school *ought* to stand apart from life in a basic sense . . . by illuminating a wider world than its limited surroundings and by sustaining those habits of mind which fit it for breadth, penetration, and objectivity of vision." (I. Scheffler, *Philosophy and Education,* Allyn & Bacon, Boston, 1958, p. 269.)
[13] Dewey, 1901: 24.2.
[14] James, 1901: 47.1.

man in the theory, through the agency of the linking science, that determines at once the effectiveness of the work done, and the moral freedom and personal development of the one engaged in it. It is because the physician no longer follows rules, which, however rational in themselves, are yet arbitrary to him (because grounded in principles that he does not understand), that his work is becoming liberal, attaining the dignity of a profession, instead of remaining a mixture of *empiricism* and *quackery*.[15]

Dewey sought to join the objective science of psychology with the subjective consciousness of the practitioner through the agency of a linking science or philosophy of education. In so doing, he provided a many-sided perspective on the problem of establishing an intellectual discipline of education.

First, taking general psychology as his model for objective inquiry and scientific generalization, he did not preclude the possibility of an objective discipline which would describe the behavior of students and teachers in the classroom from the third-person position of a disinterested observer. Improved child-study observation and the generalization which might emerge could yield an objective science of education.

Second, through the imaginative mind of a conceptualist, psychological science could be translated into principles, if not predictions, about how to improve practice. This body of educational theory could be tested in the classroom, not by a disinterested third party, but by a very much interested practitioner. Reports gathered from many practitioners would confirm some principles and refute others. This body of somewhat confirmed principles would help build a linking science, not so objective as psychology, but not so subjective and personal as one teacher's belief as to what worked and what did not.*

Third, each teacher would develop preferences for those parts of the linking science which worked best and which fit in best with his classroom practice. Such a subjective preference, based on having tried out parts of the linking science and its rationale, would be a personal philosophy—first, deeply felt; second, to some degree objectively tested; and third, backed by the authority of the conceptualist, who is at once a translator of science and a synthesizer of personal experience. Such a personally tested belief qualified as a subjective or personal philosophy of education. And, more important, having passed personal, subjective tests, it would have the best recommendation for being tested by others. Passing the personal test of many practitioners, it could be put forth as a

---

[15] Dewey, 1901: 24.1.

* From my own experience, it seems that few indeed are the professors of educational methodology, curriculum, and administration who have such semi-objective backing for the principles they offer potential practitioners.

philosophy which had gained inter-subjective agreement*—certainly a first step on the long, hard road toward objective science.

The coalition of scientist, conceptualist, and practitioner proposed by Dewey aimed at a combination of three approaches to an intellectual understanding of education: observation-centered reasoning, rationalistic theory, and the personal belief or feeling that emerged from practical experience. The bulk of observation-centered reasoning would be left to genetic psychology and any other established science capable of generalizing with stipulated predictability on human behavior. The conceptualist, beginning with those generalizations on the scholarly side and with his personal understanding of practice on the side of the art of teaching, must achieve a synthesis through translation from scholarship, extrapolation beyond scholarly warrant, and interpretation of the collected experience of the profession.

This linking science would require the conceptualist to speculate, or extrapolate generalizations, about human behavior until his reasoning forecast how children might behave under certain typical learning situations. And he would further speculate from his practical experience and guess which areas of science he might most profitably mine, as a scholar, to find potentially useful generalizations—his raw materials. Up to this point, he might have nothing but a deeply felt subjective collection of ideas with no discernible logical order. To communicate his ideas to practitioners, however, this intellectual midwife must produce somewhat scholarly talk; and if his talk has scope, he will develop a coherent theory of education containing parts which the practitioner can test and other reasoned parts which tie the various practices into a conceptual whole, a philosophy. Dewey foresaw an enlightened union of scholarly and practical talk that would inform and help the teacher, thus rendering journalistic talk harmless.

Finally, the practitioner receives this theory of education, with its predictions to be tested in the classroom, on authority of the conceptualist. In turn, the conceptualist as synthesizer has invoked the authority of more or less detailed practical experience; as translator, he invokes the authority of his own scholarship and that of the established science upon which he draws. Trying out some portion of the predictions in an unsystematic way, the practitioner comes to believe or disbelieve in the practical and the speculative aspects of the conceptualist's theory. Having developed his belief in his own classroom, the practitioner tends to feel deeply enough about his personal findings so that his view of the theory

---

* As "consensus" this concept became basic to the Social and Philosophic Foundation of Education at Columbia in *The Improvement of Practical Intelligence,* by Raup, *et al.,* and in *Foundations of American Education,* by Rugg.

will not be severely shaken by someone else's information that the predictions worked out differently for him. The tendency is for the practitioner to feel deeply about the whole philosophy, not about just a part of it. As a consequence of a deeply felt personal philosophy, he seeks to mold his practices into a reflection of those beliefs.

Nevertheless, the observation-centered reasoning, the rationalistic theory, and the personal philosophy to be developed by the scientist, the conceptualist, and the practitioner each incorporated the spirit of observational descriptive science as Huxley had outlined it. Each opposed the reliance on purely reasoned self-evidence, the quackery of hollow verbalisms, and the formulation of expedient principles drawn from personal experience and passed off as deductions derived from scholarly thought. Objective, translative, or subjective thought about education had been pointed toward increased observation.

Building on the better understanding of empirical science facilitated by such philosophers as Huxley and Peirce, other philosophers—Royce, James, and Dewey—made the requirements and the benefits of observational science intelligible to a broad professional audience in America. Enthusiastic about the predictive power which empirical method seemed to insure, those interested in a science of education began to look for it in many forms. Dewey had pointed out ways in which that method could be followed. Just what kind of description the science of education would employ became a subject of much concern during the first decade of the twentieth century. That there soon would be a science of education almost no one doubted.

We may begin with the reminder that, as heirs to the nineteenth century, the institutions that we serve and the attitudes that we honor either passed through, or had their origin in, that century. We do not need, of course, to be reminded that the nineteenth century was an era of great pragmatic triumphs. It is entirely understandable that these triumphs should have led to an amazing confidence in science—taking science in its broadest sense—and in research. . . . It is a surprising and sobering study, this now remote optimism and romantic fervor of the scientist and scholar in the nineteenth century.[1] *

Inspiration from the gains made by observation-centered reasoning in such descriptive sciences as chemistry and botany, confidence that Huxley's method had unlimited application, and determination to prove the existence of a discipline of education set the threefold keynote on which twentieth-century pedagogics opened. Inspiration, confidence, and determination assured energy; and many words could be shot out like electronic impulses to explore thought, returning as strong or weak, accurate or distorted, echoes. As radar proves most necessary when the fog is thickest, such probes sought to trace the elusive and shrouded outlines of a discipline of education. Determining the way in which Huxley's scientific method could be employed might

---

[1] De Witt, 1950: 30.
* Dewey's *Theory of Valuation* (1939) is one of the high points of that optimism in both philosophy and education.

7

Distinguishing Research from Teacher Training

locate such a discipline more precisely, thus enabling it to take a place alongside chemistry, geology, psychology, and sociology as another descriptive science.

Optimism and romantic fervor set the temper of the first ten years of the twentieth century. Conservative and coldly analytic reasoning set in by 1912. And before 1920, Charles H. Judd had announced a pessimism that was an accurate forecast of what Dewey wrote ten years later in *The Sources of a Science of Education*. As an area of thought, Judd announced, education is not one but, instead, several disciplines.

In quite a different mood as the twentieth century began, however, Dewey and James, too, helped generate optimism and romantic fervor concerning a new approach to developing a discipline of education. Better than anyone before them, these philosophers pointed out what a discipline of education was not. By debunking Herbartian rational science, they exposed the shipwreck-rock of observation hovering just below the surface of a calm sea of deductions. To keep teacher training from wallowing between observed data and the art of teaching children, James and Dewey proposed a middleman theorist who would propel scholarship to the shores of practice.

A well-informed scholar, a careful observer, thoroughly experienced in the teaching process, a critical editor of his own thoughts—such a middleman could yield reliable opinions. Dewey himself had done just this. A discipline of reliable opinions, clearly identified as opinions, was a subjective stopgap. Opinions would be confirmed or rejected on the basis of further observation. But even a stopgap literature, frankly branded "considered opinion," implied a discipline that would gradually reduce the area needing subjective interpretation. Such a discipline seemed to wear the gown of science.

By the start of the twentieth century, educationists had become many things. Herbartians flourished in great numbers, attending national meetings designed to advance their science of education through scholarship and speculation. Child study had national, state, and local meetings, as well as popular magazines. In G. Stanley Hall child study had a careful observer turned philosopher. Philosophers of a discipline of education, such as James and Dewey, were following their flair for speculation too. And in the midst of such energetic activity, J. M. Rice had begun the careful collection of descriptive data similar to that soon to be given statistical interpretation. Sparked by such a clash of viewpoints, the task of pinning down the elusive concept of a discipline of education through definition took on zest. In this active climate of measurement, survey, and statistical interpretation, efforts at organizing data to demonstrate the presence of a discipline seemed much like an intellectual peep show —now you see it, now you don't. Scholarly, practical, and journalistic talk were so thoroughly mixed that standards for sifting sense from non-sense remained personal.

Confidence in an Emerging Science of Education

Writing about "Education as a Science" on May 1, 1882, F. A. P. Barnard, President of Columbia, presented an excellent illustration of the interchangeable use of the terms *science* and *philosophy* by Herbartians. Having patted himself on the back for his inaugural recommendation of 1865 that Columbia undertake "properly educating men to the business of education," [2] he went on to lament the slowness with which this request was being fulfilled:

> It is to be hoped that, with the prevalence of better views of the philosophy of education, this great and long-standing abuse may be corrected. It is to be hoped and expected that its reform may be one of the earliest consequences of the inauguration in our country of a systematic course of teaching, of which the science of education may itself be the object.[3]

Systematically arranged teacher-training courses would draw their order from scholarship in philosophy and contribute that order to the practical side of education, yielding principles of how to teach—methodology. Such would be the self-perpetuating, self-correcting virtues of a complete rational science of education that united scholarly and practice-centered talk into one discipline.*

SUPPORTING A RATIONAL SCIENCE

By the 1890's, Herbartian and child-study national societies, as well as the National Education Association, had pumped much talk of a science of education into their journals and teacher magazines. In these publications science, psychology, and philosophy had become so intertwined that the idea of teacher training and a discipline of education had expanded to include almost all areas of human knowledge.† Writing *Education as a Science* in 1879, Alexander Bain, Scottish psychologist, found it necessary

---

[2] Barnard, 1882: 6.1.

[3] Barnard, 1882: 6.2.

* Some professors in schools of education still seem to think this can be done by having educational philosophers and educational psychologists deduce principles of teaching on the one hand, and by having professors of administration, curriculum, and methodology dabble in philosophy and psychology on the other.

† Thus setting up the unfortunate paradox of education professors, who have mastered no one discipline thoroughly, trying to synthesize from several areas, each with its own scholarly debates over what does or does not make sense.

to set some limits to what might be legitimately included under such a title. Advocating "the Prussian National System" (Herbartianism) in the United States, Bain attempted to set the following limits for a science of education:

> I thus propose to remove from the Science of Education matters belonging to much wider departments of human conduct, and to concentrate upon what exclusively pertains to Education—the means of building up the acquired powers of human beings.[4]

Even this did little good, however, since the means of building up the acquired powers of human beings could still include just about anything already incorporated in rational psychology. Speculating about the way the human mind operates, Bain went on to illustrate how rational psychology fitted into the Herbartian view of science:

> To increase the plastic property of the mind, you must nourish the brain. You naturally expect that this result will ensue when the body generally is nourished: and so it will, if there be no exorbitant demands on the part of other organs, giving them such a preference as to have very little for the organ of the mind. If the muscles or the digestion are unduly drawn upon, the brain will not respond to the drafts made upon it.*
>
> Obversely, if the brain is constituted by nature, or excited by stimulation, so as to absorb the lion's share of the nutriment, the opposite result will appear; the mental functions will be exalted, and the other interests more or less impoverished. This is the situation for an abundant display of mental force.[5]

Like four horsemen of an educational apocalypse, physiology, psychology, pedagogy, and philosophy combined to form a rational science seemingly graced with three cardinal virtues: factual authenticity, logical validity, and practical utility. Careful logical reasoning—a primary virtue in philosophy—was joined with the systematic arrangement of ideas to form a science.

Intent on claiming scientific status for the reasoned solution to instructional problems, W. H. Payne, President of Peabody Normal School and former professor of pedagogy at the University of Michigan, would settle for nothing less than a science of educational values. Writing in 1901, he also included the concepts of quantity and quality in the following paragraphs explaining the character and utility of such a science:

> The science of education values is both qualitative and quantitative— qualitative in the exact scientific sense, and quantitative in the same sense

---

[4] Bain, 1897: 4.1.

* Presumably, Bain took as his evidence the widespread knowledge that a big Sunday dinner leads to an afternoon nap.

[5] Bain, 1897: 4.2.

that the temperature of water is quantitative: high or low, as determined
by a thermometer.

It is only this science of values that can furnish rational answers to such
questions as these: On what ground has the study of algebra been made
universal in our high schools? What rational defense is there for the study
of the classics? Such inquiries arise with reference to every subject that
is taught in our schools, and if education is ever to become a rational
art, there must be established a science of educational values, just as
there must be a science of food values before there can be a science of
dietetics.[6]

Payne's science of values and a philosophy of values would be synonymous.
    Huxley and Peirce had sharpened the issue of what kind of science
any discipline might court. Dewey, James, and Royce had brought the
child-study viewpoint to a focus in their model of the middleman theorist
working between opinion and empirically established fact. But educationists such as Payne were writing books and organizing teacher training
along lines laid down by Herbart a hundred years before and interpreted
by the McMurrys, Van Liew, De Garmo, and Barnard—all men of
influence in 1900. Summing up their concept of the rational science basic
to a discipline of education, Samuel B. Sinclair attempted to join the old
with the new. In his 1903 dissertation at the University of Chicago, Sinclair
announced the following résumé of the past, while attempting to make way
for the steps of empirical science as outlined by Huxley 60 years before:

> The generally-accepted definition of science is that "it is a collection of the
> general principles or leading truths relating to any subject arranged in
> systematic order." . . . True science is essentially teleological in char-
> acter; it possesses a systematized body of knowledge, but systematized
> as instruments for the reconstruction of future experience.
>
> I hope to show that educational science possesses a body of systematized
> knowledge arrived at by processes of experimentation, abstraction, gen-
> eralization, etc., but that such educational theory and the mode of its
> genesis must be looked upon from the standpoint of *function*.[7]

The attention paid to defining the science of education during the first
decade of the twentieth century attested to both a depth of conviction
and a penetrating doubt. Convinced that education was or would soon
become a respectable intellectual discipline worthy of the praise-laden
label "science," these same advocates felt the necessity of formulating
and reformulating their definition of that science. Constantly badgered by

---

[6] Payne, 1901: 79.
[7] Sinclair, 1903: 97.

the elusiveness of such a complex task, they seemed to be pleading for attention to their meaning rather than for literal criticism of their expression and formulation of definitions, as if to say, "I know what I mean, but I can't quite say it."

IMPROVING THE DISCIPLINE

Thursday evening, February 28, 1901, the National Society for the Scientific Study of Education held its first meeting. In spirit and in membership the new organization was a continuation of the National Herbart Society which had its official beginning in 1895. Having insisted on the actuality of a science of education, the members of the National Herbart Society seemed intent on labeling themselves a scientific organization. Consistent with the changed emphasis in the new title, "Scientific," as opposed to "Herbartian," the group undertook to re-define science as applied to education. In a "Proposed Plan of Work for the NSSSE," to be found in the *First Yearbook,* 1902, the following definition appeared:

> The scientific study of any subject implies an effort to get at its fundamental principles, and to make as complete and thorough investigation of its problems as specialists in that department can make.[8]

As a statement of intent, this clearly announced that concentrated attention was to be directed at establishing education as a discipline. Adequate as a statement of intent, this left untouched the task of pinning down the meaning of *science*. The society operated on implicit understandings for three years. Then in the *Fourth Yearbook,* M. J. Holmes drew together the opinions of 21 members on the meaning of the "Scientific Study of Education." The following society members were included in that "Report of the Secretary," designed to make such understandings explicit:

> Ezra W. Benedict, J. Stanley Brown, Sarah C. Brooks, W. H. Burnham, Lida B. Earhart, Edgar L. Hewett, Reuben Post Halleck, John A. Keith, H. E. Kratz, Frank A. Manny, F. M. McMurry, M. V. O'Shea, G. D. Pickles, Stuart H. Rowe, Myron T. Scudder, David E. Smith, David S. Snedden, Edwin D. Starbuck, Joseph S. Taylor, E. W. Walker, and Sarah J. Walter.[9]

The 21 explicit statements attempting to define the scientific study of education fell into two categories:

1. The majority spoke about general intellectual rigor and systematic arrangement of thought—Herbartian rational science.

---

[8] C. McMurry, 1902: 63.
[9] Holmes, 1905: 45.

2. A minority looked toward fundamental reforms in the conception of education as a discipline.

Majority Viewpoint—Confirming Rational Science. The list of points set forth by J. Stanley Brown summed up those definitions which explained the scientific study of education along lines previously etched out by advocates of Herbartian rational science. Brown's five points follow:

> (1) A study of some problem so intensively as to reveal greatest weakness in current treatment. (2) Experimentation with a view to discovering a better treatment of the problem. (3) Comparison of results. (4) Abstraction of needless things in solution of problem. (5) Deduction including only essential things.[10]

Such canons of serious academic or intellectual study called for increased rigor in general. In particular, Brown pointed to a dissatisfaction with much of the thinking then current. His steps, as a matter of fact, almost duplicate the five steps of Herbartian method: organization, presentation, separation, generalization, and application.

Frank McMurry moved somewhat closer to including observation as a necessity for scientific study when he defined science this way:

> By scientific method applied to education, I understand the acceptance of some specific problem or hypothesis as the topic to be investigated. Then such a use of the data and logic as will produce conclusions that are convincing to outsiders. The two sources of the data may be books or children.[11]

In the spirit of rational discourse, McMurry supported the power of persuasion over the power of prediction.

Minority Opinion—Reform. In contrast to the opinion of most contributors, Reuben Post Halleck had reservations as to how far education as a discipline could move toward being a science. Out of a deeper concern for the demands of experimental method than had been exhibited by the majority, Halleck voiced his doubt as follows:

> Inductions performed from experiments on different molecules of hydrogen and iron will have a certainty that educators can not hope for, since no two classes of pupils and no two educators can ever be the same in the sense that different molecules of hydrogen are the same. . . . At the same time, concerted effort among educators ought to disprove many prevalent errors in educational induction.[12]

[10] Brown, 1905: 9.
[11] F. McMurry, 1905: 66.
[12] Halleck, 1905: 39.

In opinions such as these, both the minority and the majority voiced their protests against the low level of education as an intellectual discipline up to and including 1905. This negative comment was their testimony to the need they felt for just such an organization as they had—a National Society for the Scientific Study of Education. It might better, however, have been called a society for the strengthening of scholarship about education.

For most of the 21 members who attempted to define education as a science, the idea meant little more than increased rigor. But for David S. Snedden, the concept of education as a science called for an increase in rigor on a scale not yet grasped by many. As a step to unify extremes of rational and experimental approaches to science, he suggested the following:

> . . . Any systematic and careful study ought to be called scientific, provided the investigator can justify his conclusions. Education may suffer from the over application of methods more adapted to concrete sciences, just as it has suffered from too much "dialectic." Let us not worry too much about method, but seek rather to formulate aims in more specific terms than is now the case. We need more work in this direction, and in the direction of agreeing on terminology.* Why not have a committee on terminology which might annually issue a report on suggested definitions, which might be generally accepted when a majority of members agreed?[13]

Snedden perceived that, without definitions and modes of description that were accepted by all, consensus gained on some higher level of abstraction amounted to an exploitation of ambiguity. No matter how functional such an exploitation of ambiguity might be in persuading outsiders, as McMurry suggested, or in indoctrinating teachers, it remained a journalistic device that inhibited genuine scholarship. Such talk about education had no claim to the word "scientific," whether it be interpreted in the rational or in the experimental sense.

The NSSSE never seemed to rest comfortably under the word "scientific." In 1905 a committee on renaming recommended "The National Society of Education." From then on, a succession of coincidences produced the official title of "The National Society for the Study of Education." Guy Whipple, long-time secretary of the organization, described that chain of events this way:

> The same committee advocated that designation again in 1906, but by some curious turn of affairs, the members voted overwhelmingly in favor

---

* Apparently the successes of the several international congresses for stabilizing terminology in botanical and zoological science had not gone unnoticed.
[13] Snedden, 1905: 100.

of "The Herbart Society," with the proviso that the executive committee
might use its discretion to insert "National" or "American" before
"Herbart." Because, by accident, the motion was not offered as an amend-
ment to the constitution, the executive committee refused to act, and the
matter seems to have passed over until 1910, when a revised constitution
was adopted in which the term "Scientific" was dropped and the society
thus took on the name under which it has operated ever since.[14]

Moved with the spirit and intent of its Herbartian membership, the National Society for the Study of Education continued to build an intellectual
discipline of education. As I. Kandel stated in the following summary, such
construction went ahead against stubborn resistance:

> In spite of the discouraging attitude of colleges and universities to the
> study of education, the view was soon accepted that a modern university
> must be an "institution where any person can find instruction in any
> study," and that from the standpoint of the public the scientific study of
> education is as urgent as the study of law, medicine, and engineering. It
> was still necessary, however, and at the beginning of the period no easy
> task, to prove that the study of education included more than the mere
> preparation of teachers.[15] *

Colleges and universities, where unbiased research might best be
pursued, resisted the admission of education as a discipline because of its
shallowness of content. As though reluctant to treat an alcoholic because of
his drunkenness, colleges and universities vainly tried to insist that education attain the sober status of an independent scholarly discipline before
being admitted for improvement. Yet education courses and programs of
professional preparation did become an established part of university and
college offerings before any widespread agreement existed concerning either
the precise meaning of course titles or the boundaries of such overlapping
areas of content as method, curriculum, general pedagogy, and principles
of education.† Possibly more than any other set of publications, the yearbooks of the NSSE gave professors confidence that there was content for
education as a scholarly discipline. Further, the meetings as well as the
publications of the NSSE helped convince professionals that a separate
discipline of education was both possible and desirable. Having established
intent, the problem of what such a discipline might look like remained.

---

[14] Whipple, 1941: 110.

[15] Kandel, 1924: 51.1.

* In terms of getting money and time budgeted for research not supported by
the government or foundations, this still remains a difficult task.

† In this lies the key to the frequent undergraduate criticism that "if you've
taken one education course, you've taken them all."

Mapping Out the Discipline

One of the most careful early explanations of education as a discipline appeared in the first two annual issues of *The School Review Monographs*. Like the publications of the National Herbart Society, these had a brief life span under their initial title. Appearing in 1911, the first issue took up the controversial topics of educational method, theory, and science. Paul Monroe and E. L. Thorndike launched an examination of the crucial issues involved in defining the nature of the study of education. Their articles dealt with "Research within the Field of Education, Its Organization and Encouragement." The following year, the same matters came to further attention under the title "The Present Status of Education as a Science."

TWO AERIAL VIEWS

Appearing together in the 1911 *Monograph,* Thorndike and Monroe spoke with the confidence and vigor of a pride of young lions stalking a marvelous kill. With the first three volumes of his *Cyclopedia of Education* already off the presses, Monroe had drawn together the best thought of the best minds, which had done their best to give meaning to the concepts in which a discipline of education must deal. He had distilled the body of a discipline from the overwhelming volume of scholarly, practical, and journalistic prose that the nineteenth century yielded.

Thorndike, on the other hand, was having considerable success with his application of new statistical techniques to educational problems. With the survey movement just opening up in 1911, Thorndike could see the discipline that might soon emerge from the rigorous gathering and statistical processing of data. His was a prediction of things to come.

An Eclectic Discipline of Education.   The vast editorial task that Monroe undertook in organizing the *Cyclopedia of Education* gave him the tolerance of an anthropologist and the taste of an archeologist. Able to tolerate diversity in method, he saw workers of the past making significant contributions to education as a discipline even though they did not have the same rigor in scientific method advertised by Dewey and practiced by Thorndike. Appreciating the diverse products of all kinds of thinking and workmanship, as the archeologist must, Monroe was able to exhibit these thoughts for what they were worth and call that collection, eclectic though it might be, a discipline. While praising the work of modern craftsmen, he called for a recognition of the craft exercised by other men, at other times, by other means. It was in such a spirit that he wrote the following appeal for cooperative research in education:

Hardly less significant than the general professional purposes of research are the types of methods employed. The consideration of method presents another phase of possible co-operation. As previously suggested, method requires such absolute freedom, that the co-operation demanded is often of a negative character, namely toleration, and an acceptance of other judgments and methods as well as a support of one's own.

The traditional methods of logical investigation which appertained to such scientific study of education as existed in centuries preceding the nineteenth have ceased to receive any great consideration. At the present time the number capable of using such methods with results of any value are so few that they are above the general rule; and the question of co-operative effort hardly extends to them. This statement does not deny that there are many phases of philosophical thought in its relation to the educational systems of the past or to the contributions of the present which are open to investigation. It only calls attention to the common attitude that has rejected—for our own time—the method of introspection, as a means of solution of the actual problems of objective life. A much more serious condition confronts us in the tendency to reject the observational methods of the Herbartian school and of the nineteenth century in general. While this method has served its time, and more accurate methods which are capable of being applied to certain, if not all, of the phases of education considered by the Herbartian schools have been evolved, the question remains, Is the more recent method alone worthy of acceptance? Under the leadership of the advanced German group, and in general of the influence of experimental psychology on education, there had developed an inclination to deny validity to any other method. This group is strong not only in Germany; it is active in England, and has its representatives with us. The comparative method, whether the statistical or so-called census method—the American method as it is termed in Europe—or the historical methods of textual criticism and of institutional comparison, are alike rejected. Possibly the appropriation of the term "experimental" need not concern those who use the various forms of the comparative method; but the observational has not yet been so put out of court that no claim to their use of the term exists. What is needed here is toleration. Especially is it true of the two claimants for the term "experimental." The standard by which all could be judged fairly is that of results. Has the newer phase of the experimental method so justified its claim to be the only method of investigation of educational problems, that all others should be rejected? The test should be not alone that of the problems investigated and the conclusions published; but that of the actual truths established, and their final application of such new truths to current educational practice, either by rejection and criticism or by positive contribution.

Possibly this is not a fair test as yet of any one of these methods. But it will be the ultimate test. Karl Pealson has said that fully 50 per cent of all scientific research is worthless and much of it harmful. Possibly the statement could be made stronger for education. Certainly such a judgment has importance for the future rather than for the past, since research work in education by any method has been very slight.

Co-operation which is possible and is needed here lies in the breadth of view and the sympathy which will welcome and encourage any form of study, with professional value, and any form of research which has scientific character and promises some result. It certainly is folly to waste time and energy in decrying a competitive method when the opportunity for experiments is so limitless and the needs for definite scientific answers to problems are so great. Though it is true that we have the suggestion of the same great scientist previously quoted that what we need is an endowment of an institution for the suppression of unintelligent research, yet it is only out of the variety of endeavor that we can expect in time to select the tendencies which promise the most.[16]

Compilation followed by careful evaluation, Monroe held, constituted the process by which a clear, concentrated, and useful discipline of education might be distilled. In principle Monroe and Thorndike agreed on the approach. In practice, however, Thorndike prove to be less a man of the rationalistic past and more a man of the factual-empirical future.

A Factual Discipline of Education. Monroe viewed the discipline of education as if through a wide-angle lens. Making sure to keep the whole panorama visible at once, he sought for as much detail as possible. Thorndike, locating his subject with a Sherlock Holmes-type magnifying glass, analyzed the parts in as great detail as his available microscopes would allow. Sacrificing the comprehensiveness of a historical, anthropological, or archeological approach, he reached toward the exhaustive and definitive analysis of the systematic botanist or the comparative embryologist. Each clearly visible fact became a pinpoint stitch in what would eventually become a quilted discipline of education. In the following paragraph, Thorndike presented the dimensions of such a task:

. . . the number of useful studies to be made is, for all practical purposes, infinite. An educational survey of one state would seem to be at least as elaborate a task as a geological survey of a continent. The educational life-history of one boy would certainly demand as much time and skill as the biological history of the ants or bees. The results produced eight years hence in the children who entered the New York City schools this fall offer a problem more complex than that of the results of the contraction of the earth. What physical science has to do in comparison with the cosmologies of the early philosophers, the science of education has to do in comparison with the first generalizations of Herbart, Spencer, or Dewey.[17]

---

[16] P. Monroe, 1911: 69.2.
[17] Thorndike, 1911: 102.

The task of data-gathering for a discipline of education had additional complications, which Thorndike continued to point out:

> Complexity, variability, and the absence of proper units and scales of measure are the three great difficulties. For example, so apparently a simple educational achievement as knowledge of two-place column addition involves, besides the forty-five fundamental associations and their reverses, at least nine distinct habits or processes. No one of these is constant in its behavior. Hence each must be measured many times in each individual.[18]

And finally, in the following caution, Thorndike suggested the human limitations which would slow down the development of such a factual discipline:

> The most efficient organizer and manager of scientific work of my acquaintance once said: "If you want to do twice as much work, get four assistants; if you want to do three times as much, get sixteen assistants; if you want to do four times as much, you *can't*."[19] *

Thorndike resembled an intellectual Columbus, confident that the trip would be worth the effort but unsure of what might be discovered. Most of all, however, he would dispel thoughts of a brief and simple voyage. Compared with the task of data-gathering which field workers faced, the first principles of the Herbartians, James, and Dewey were armchair speculations made in comfort.

Set side by side in that 1911 issue of the *School Review Monographs,* these two aerial photographs of a discipline of education made a composite picture of what was available from the past and what should be attainable in the future. Monroe made the best of the past available in his *Cyclopedia of Education* and called that the nucleus of a discipline of education. Thorndike sought the best tools for mining the data continually becoming available. Looking to the time when the bucket of factual data would be overflowing, he saw a discipline of education being forged. Both were scholars free to pursue inquiry without having to answer the narrow, practice-centered questions that see value only in findings that have immediate utility in the classroom.

CLOSER GLIMPSES

Following up the composite aerial view of a discipline of education as seen with one eye to the past and the other to the future, the second num-

---

[18] Thorndike, 1911: 102.2.
[19] Thorndike, 1911: 102.3.
* Here is the answer to those who think a complex problem can be solved quickly merely by making larger sums available for research.

ber of the *School Review Monographs* took a careful look at "The Present Status of Education as a Science." This 1912 volume brought together three specialists capable of identifying the features of educational discipline in smaller segments: V. A. C. Henmon, an educational psychologist from the University of Wisconsin; William C. Ruediger, newly appointed dean of Teachers College, George Washington University; and Chester Parker, important faculty member in education at the University of Chicago. Together, they expressed high confidence in both the actuality and the perfectibility, or at least improvability, of a scholarly discipline of education.

Educational Psychology—V. A. C. Henmon. Still a new division of experimental inquiry in 1912, and not yet in possession of a clear distinction between research and teacher training, educational psychology came in for the same species of criticism and ridicule which educational sociology and educational philosophy have encountered more recently. Henmon characterized the serious critics as contending that educational psychology lacked worthwhile content in terms of both facts and principles. Rather than deny such allegations, he ascribed such conditions of intellectual poverty to the belief that the main purpose of educational psychology is to supply simple rules for teacher-training purposes. Summing up the faults inherent in such a narrowly practical view of educational psychology, Henmon supported the contention of the critics in the following way:

> Just as neither a knowledge of physics, nor merely pointing out possible practical applications of physics, will be especially useful to the engineer confronted by a specific problem, so will neither a knowledge of psychology, nor merely pointing out possible practical applications here and there in school practice, help the teacher much. The result of this attitude was that instead of a direct knowledge of psychology the fundamental conceptions of psychology were presented in manuals of method and psychologies for the schoolroom, in which practical rules supposedly deduced from psychology and simplified for practical guidance were supplied.[20]

Then, going one step further, he cut the support from beneath the prevalent belief that such principles of teaching were the educational application of psychological information and theory:

> As a matter of fact, *these rules of procedure were not deduced from psychological laws at all but were the outcome of successful practical experience interpreted in psychological terms.*[21] * [Italics added.]

---

[20] Henmon, 1912: 43.4.
[21] Henmon, 1912: 43.4.
* This is still the prevailing practice in teacher-training texts. It is this process that multiplies at once both publications and jargon. Still the texts are at least public; the teacher-training course in methods, in curriculum, and in administration are subject to no inspection.

Having pointed to the source of the new jargon, Henmon had identified one reason why less responsible critics had been given to such continual explosions as the following which he included in his introduction:

> In a recent criticism of education as a science, educational psychology was particularly singled out as "a pretentious humbug that has grown like an excrescence on the body educational."[22]

The search for simple, mechanical rules whereby teachers could be trained quickly, in quantity, led to this verbal piracy of general psychology. Henmon did not endorse such efforts by including them as the psychological portion of a discipline of education. In place of such verbal gymnastics and over-simplification in the name of practice, he sought to establish educational psychology as an area of fact-gathering and law-making quite like general psychology in nature but distinct from it in function and focus of attention. In the following paragraph he explained both the similarity and the difference:

> The problem of educational psychology is distinctly different from that of general or genetic psychology. Each has a common object—the knowledge of mind and its laws—but the point of view is different. To borrow a distinction made by Messmer, psychology is concerned with mental processes, educational psychology with mental work. Psychology studies the natural activity and development of minds, educational psychology studies the activity and development of minds, when it is definitely directed to the attainment of certain ends. The one studies the processes that are involved in natural, undirected learning, the other the way in which these processes operate most economically and effectively when directed to the acquisition of the experience embodied in the curriculum. Systematic, constrained mental performance differs radically from spontaneous, uncontrolled activity both in its methods and results. Psychology studies the nature and forms of association; educational psychology the best and most economical methods of forming the associations demanded for a mastery of the knowledge which experience has shown to be the most useful and most essential.[23]

Such a discipline of directed learning would have facts and principles of its own drawn from the same scientific kind of inquiry as conducted in general psychology. With educational psychology as a nucleus, a discipline of education might freely develop.

With Thorndike, Henmon looked forward to the almost infinite number of useful factual studies that could be conducted without worrying about whether these would be called general psychology or part of a discipline of education. Dividing the labor for convenience, he suggested

---

[22] Henmon, 1912: 43.1.
[23] Henmon, 1912: 43.6.

that education focus on the facts and principles of directed learning, as it took place through the curriculum. The object of investigation would thus be the student in school. The classroom would be the laboratory. Other workers might work with the same person at different times and in different settings, and those findings would be pertinent to some other aspect of psychology.

For Henmon, educational psychology was a special branch of the science of psychology and, as such, should follow the same general plan for conducting research as Huxley had outlined almost 70 years earlier. Such a division of labor would make educational psychology a distinct discipline of how men might best apply themselves to attaining certain stated ends—a science of application. From this Henmon concluded that "educational psychology would thus have a specific problem of its own and would ultimately develop its own methods," [24] and "actual school experiments will ultimately be the basis on which the science will rest." [25]

Distinguishing clearly between experimental research and principles of successful teaching cast in psychological terms, Henmon guided educational psychology away from a dependence on its rationalistic past toward what seemed to hold the promise of academic and scientific respectability in the near future.

Principles of Education—William C. Ruediger. Ruediger classified the major divisions of education as a discipline. Finding a place for the fact-gathering advocated by Thorndike and Henmon, he also found space for the principles fashioned from successful experience. Exploring in greater detail, Ruediger coordinated the views of past and future which Monroe and Thorndike had personified separately the year before. Looking at *education* as a term comparable to *medicine, engineering,* or *architecture,* Ruediger classified three major aspects of such concepts:

(1) The concepts stand for vast fields of practice, professions, where the results of science find application for the direct benefit of mankind.

(2) Education as a profession has a theoretic side which rests on and embraces many sciences.

(3) The pure sciences order facts and principles on the basis of logical similarities and relations.[26]

The artful practice whereby mankind benefits directly from the actions of other men represented one side of the concept "education." But education as a scholarly discipline was a theoretical, not a practical endeavor; such a

---

[24] Henmon, 1912: 43.7.
[25] Henmon, 1912: 43.7.
[26] Ruediger, 1912: 89.1.

theoretical discipline eventually rested on logical similarities and relations, both derived from an examination of facts and imposed on the selection of facts as worthy of consideration. Thus, Ruediger spoke of the eventual basis for an entire discipline of education in the same terms which Henmon used to emphasize the similarity of method between educational psychology rightly conceived and experimental general psychology. All four—Henmon, Ruediger, Monroe, and Thorndike—would use the methods of experimental science, but each would be distinguished by his choice of observational area. The uniqueness of a discipline of education would be its organization. Pure sciences make logical relations available to applied sciences. Applied science makes useful relations available to practice, so far as possible. A discipline of education would be a supra-applied science which drew together the material in several applied sciences and organized them for use in teaching. Speaking of this hierarchy of application, Ruediger made the following statement:

> What is true in the professions generally, is true also in the profession of teaching. So far as teaching has a theoretical aspect, this aspect is represented by a group of applied sciences, and these in turn are closely related to a group of pure sciences.[27]

Research in the pure sciences was not only distinguished from the beneficial activity of practice: in the case of teaching, it became twice removed. Between pure science and practice the applied sciences and the discipline of education had intruded. And that discipline of education resembled the linking science of education which Dewey and James had mentioned earlier.

In place of Dewey's middleman theorist, Ruediger suggested an explicit discipline; but the function was the same, namely, to make the findings of established science useful to the teacher. Thus, it continued to be quite simple to equate the study of education with "the mere preparation of teachers," as Kandel put it. [28] The established sciences supplied the raw material, the applied sciences processed those materials, and the discipline of education distributed them to teachers for application. But Ruediger had a new wrinkle, to wit, feedback. He explained this additional source of new raw material as follows:

> That there is a relation of content between the pure and applied sciences cannot be denied, but this relation is largely a reciprocal one. The applied scientist may indeed turn to the pure scientist for principles, and even for facts, just as the pure scientist gets many of his facts and problems from the practitioner, but before the applied scientist can make adequate use of the data so obtained he must reorganize them and test their application. The latter step frequently not only involves experimentation,

---

[27] Ruediger, 1912: 89.2.
[28] Kandel, 1924: 51.2.

but leads to new problems that fall to the lot of the applied scientist for solution. Indeed, an applied science should certainly progress no less through the researches prosecuted in the related pure sciences.[29]

Much after the manner prescribed by Henmon, the applied sciences and the discipline of education as an inter-disciplinary science of application would each gather its own facts and offer its own generalizations. Such facts and principles would be produced by the discipline of education, to be fed back as plasma into its veins, giving the body of content new raw material unobtainable from any other source.

But in assessing "The Present Status of Education as a Science," Ruediger owed allegiance to all sources from which a discipline of education might obtain valuable content. Summarizing the full scope of such a discipline, he offered the following conclusion:

> Educational progress on the side of the curriculum and the course of study, and *pari passu* in the principles of education, can be contributed to from the following four sources at least: (1) by a historical study of the relation of the school and society; (2) by utilizing the advances continually being made in the pure sciences; (3) by generalizing from existing educational practices; and (4) by formal experimentation and quantitative measurement.[30]

By analyzing each of the four sources, he characterized the state of the discipline in 1912. Acknowledging the importance of past thinking, he had the following praise for historical study and generalization from past and existing practices.

> When we look upon the content and practice of education as they were no farther back than at the time of Basedow and Pestalozzi and then look upon them as they are today, we are fairly struck with the amount of progress that has been made. This progress has been made less, no doubt, through formal experimentation and measurement than through informal trials and successes and through the generalizations and descriptions made on the basis of existing practices by the insight of educational leaders.

> Education is a practical art as well as an applied science. It ranks in this respect with agriculture, government, navigation, and business. In all these fields practice rests at present only in part on scientific laws and principles held consciously. But all successful practice undoubtedly does rest upon such laws and principles, and it is the duty of the scientist to make them explicit. He should study the practices about him and generalize from them. *It is in this way that by far the most of our principles of education and of teaching have been obtained.* Nor should this method of inquiry

---

[29] Ruediger, 1912: 89.3.
[30] Ruediger, 1912: 89.6.

be disparaged. Social life is the primary laboratory for the social sciences and it is abundantly in place for the scientist to make use of it as such.[31] [Italics added.]

Looking forward in time, Ruediger foresaw the dependence on generalizations from present experience giving way to a discipline of education developed through laboratory classrooms. Confident that the kind of discipline which Henmon foresaw in educational psychology would spread beyond method and administration, Ruediger offered the following optimistic prediction:

> Educational theory is now in possession of a number of quantitative studies, but these appear to fall entirely into the domains of educational psychology, educational method, and school administration. In the principles of education, as here defined, only general studies have so far been made. But there is no reason why the effects of different curricula, ideals, and the like should not be subjected to statistical study and mathematical measurement. The report of the University of Chicago Elementary School as given in Dewey's *School and Society* approaches this, and as laboratory schools in connection with teachers' colleges and departments of education get more common we can expect much more in this line. It is more difficult to measure precisely the social influences of education than to test methods of instruction, and so far the facilities for making such measurements have been but meagerly available; but the laboratory schools that are now being established will bring in this opportunity and we may rest assured that our college teachers of education will take advantage of it. It would be well indeed if every school system of considerable size would set apart one of its schools as a model or laboratory school with a well-trained educational expert in charge. Scientific progress in education would then begin to have the chance that its importance deserves.[32]

By 1912 Ruediger could see Thorndike's type of quantitative study steadily displacing the qualitative generalizations from practice which comprised the bulk of education as a discipline at that time. In this respect, Ruediger held the same view of the future imminence of a quantitative discipline of education as that maintained by the third author writing on "The Present Status of Education as a Science," S. Chester Parker.

Educational Methods—S. Chester Parker.   In addition to stating his confidence in the imminence of a quantitative science of education, Parker catalogued the debt that a discipline of education owed to generalizations made from successful experience and from common sense. Diverging only slightly from the four-part division of the study of education supplied by Ruediger, Parker presented his categorization under the following heading:

---

[31] Ruediger, 1912: 89.7.
[32] Ruediger, 1912: 89.8.

Principles of Method Divided into Four Classes
According to Origin

For purposes of discussion, current principles of educational method may be divided, from the standpoint of source or origin, into four groups, as follows:

1. Those principles which have become current as the result of a long historical tradition which is characterized by more or less systematic a-priori analysis and argument.

2. Those derived from more recent developments in general psychological theory, such as the work of James and Dewey.

3. Those which are corollaries of the results of experimental psychology.

4. Those which have been reached by direct experimental and statistical investigation of actual schoolroom processes.[33]

Where Ruediger and Henmon spoke of the a priori principles which made up the majority of educational theory at that time, Parker took the pains to list a considerable number of examples. Beginning with Rousseau, he listed the following eight principles from *Emile*:

1. Methods of instruction should aim at many-sided maturing and training of the individual. (Emphasized by Pestalozzi as "Harmonious training of the faculties" and by Herbartians as "many-sided interests.")

2. Methods of teaching should be adapted to the maturing of the child's instincts and capacities. (Especially emphasized by the Froebelians.)

3. Real experiences (with things or persons) should be the starting-point of instruction. (Developed primarily as Pestalozzian object-teaching.)

   a) Hence, home geography should be the starting point of geography teaching. (A direct connection from Rousseau through Salzman, Pestalozzi, Karl Ritter, Arnold Guyot, Colonel F. W. Parker to the Frye geographies of today.)

4. Children learn through motor activity which should not be wasted in random play, however, but should be connected with observation, reasoning, and expression, especially drawing. (Emphasized by Basedow, by Pestalozzi, to a limited extent, by the Froebelians and Dewey.)

5. Premature memorizing of words and symbols without understanding is pernicious and spoils the child's judgment. (Emphasized at first by Pestalozzians, but soon degenerated, revived by Herbartians and Froebelians.)

6. The ability of children to reason about matters within their comprehension justifies emphasis on the investigation of small problems of ap-

---

[33] Parker, 1912: 77.1.

plied science. (This principle was long neglected. It was emphasized somewhat by Froebelians and especially by Dewey.)

7. The study of social relations should be approached from the industrial standpoint. (Emphasized somewhat by Basedow, Petalozzi, and Froebel; recently given special emphasis by Dewey.)

a) Robinson Crusoe should serve as a central core for a study of problems in applied science, and as a basis of approach to the study of industrial and social relations.

8. The child's present interests and curiosity should activate instruction in the early years, and his appreciation of the utility of the school processes in later years. (Emphasized by Basedow and the Herbartians and Froebelians; now being emphasized in the reconstruction of the upper-grade teaching and high-school mathematics.[34]

From Practice-Centered Talk to Journalistic Slogans

Parker found Pestalozzi responsible for the objective oral method of ₁nstruction and also for the principle of proceeding from the simple to the complex. To prove that the method had not disappeared, Parker pointed to the simple-complex approach embodied in contemporary reading instruction: some teachers began with single letters or with simple sounds. On further examination, the objective oral method turned out to have the following significance:

> . . . the Pestalozzians carried out, independent of the influence of Herbart, the elaboration of oral instruction which has come to be identified in the minds of many persons with the steps of preparation and presentation in the Herbartian formal steps. Warren Colburn went even farther, and in the preface of his *Intellectual Arithmetic*, published in Boston in 1821, formulated what he called the method of "analytic induction," which parallels the Herbartian steps. Inasmuch as Colburn's book was widely used in America until after the middle of the nineteenth century, it is fair to assume that many American teachers were acquainted with the process represented in the Herbartian steps before these were popularized in the nineties.[35]

Parker credited Froebel for two advances: the emphasis on motor expression and the concern for participation in a cooperative social situation.[36] The Herbartians, in turn, sponsored the formal steps of instruction and the principle of correlation. [37] After such a list of examples, Parker

---

[34] Parker, 1912: 77.1.
[35] Parker, 1912: 77.3.
[36] Parker, 1912: 77.4.
[37] *Ibid.*

brought forward the following conclusion along the same lines mentioned by the three former authors:

> *Such traditional a priori principles constitute the largest part of contemporary principles of method.* Only a few examples have been given, but the list could easily be prolonged until the stock of current principles was almost exhausted.[38]

Parker's demonstration that the educational thought of that time consisted largely of a priori rules couched in psychological and philosophic terms directed attention to the status of education as a rational discipline. But, as with Henmon and Ruediger, this conclusion did not keep him from realizing the potential of a new kind of discipline that had been already achieved in part. Such an intellectual split-vision enabled Parker to give credit to older approaches without losing sight of how much of the future was already implicit in the present. Turning from a priori sources to observed evidence in the following manner, he affirmed his confidence in what the discipline of education was becoming:

> Even if we follow Thorndike, and eliminate from a possible "science of educational methods" the first two sources which were discussed above (a-priori traditional and general psychological) it is easy in connection with the third and fourth sources (experimental psychology and direct experimental and statistical investigation of methods) to demonstrate that such a science has "arrived" and is with us "essentially," as Huxley said of biology in 1854. Hence if the question were narrowed to read, "Is education an experimental science which uses reliable methods of control and secures precise measurements of results?" we may prove that it has reached even this stage of development in connection with certain of its problems; and no better evidence need be cited than such studies as those of Courtis on arithmetic. . . .[39]

Final Fate

The 1911 and 1912 issues of *School Review Monographs* boldly announced that the discipline of education was an accomplished fact. Although such a discipline had much to contribute to the training of teachers, all authors indicated that the discipline did not owe its existence merely to that function.

Monroe, Ruediger, and Parker openly stated that the great bulk of the discipline came from a priori thinking rooted in successful past practice and less rigorously controlled inquiry than science was then demanding. With

---

[38] Parker, 1912: 77.5.
[39] Parker, 1912: 77.6.

Thorndike and Henmon, these authors unanimously looked forward to a rapid expansion of empirical investigation and information. They foresaw that careful observation and guarded generalization would gradually move the main body of content of a discipline of education away from a dependence on a priori sources to a reliance on the same sources of scientific thinking as Huxley, Peirce, Royce, James, and Dewey had advocated years before. What in 1911 and 1912 authors could not take into account was the fact that a change in the kind of content being gathered would lead to a change in the kind of organization necessary to give it meaning.

A discipline in which the same, or at least very similar, a priori generalizations permeated all the various branches could be quite comprehensively mastered by one man, and such a scholar could offer a unified synthesis of the field as a whole. Identifying 1910 as the pivotal year * in which such an exhibition of genius became clearly impossible, Kandel explained from the perspective of 1924 what scholars writing twelve years earlier could not have been expected to see. After making a comparison of the simple list of courses offered at Teachers College, Columbia, in 1898 with the enlarged program of 1906, he went on to say:

> Five years later it became possible to consider seriously the problem of research within the field of education. Hitherto the various studies were isolated and unconnected subjects within the larger field. After 1910 the field gradually became so wide and its subdivisions so highly specialized that no student could be expected to master them all. The rapid development of facilities for the graduate study of education leading to advanced degrees may be said to have begun at that time. . . .[40]

In 1918, six years before Kandel's recapitulation and six years after the articles by Henmon, Ruediger, and Parker, C. H. Judd clearly formulated the problem facing education as a field of inquiry. In his book, *Introduction to the Scientific Study of Education,* Judd argued, along the same lines later taken by Kandel, against the idea of viewing education as a single discipline. His reasoning went as follows:

> The science of education aims to collect by all available methods full information with regard to the origin, development, and present form of school practices and also full information with regard for social needs. It aims to subject present practices to rigid tests and comparisons and to analyze all procedures in the schools by experimental methods and by observation. It aims to secure complete and definite records for all that

---

* One is reminded of Virgina Woolf's statement that in 1910 human nature changed.

[40] Kandel, 1924: 51.4.

the school attempts and accomplishes. The results of school work are to be evaluated by rigid methods of comparison and analysis. To direct studies of the school the science of education must add full studies of the social life of which the school is a part and of the individual nature which is to be trained and molded through the educational process. . . . This program is so comprehensive in its scope that it becomes evident at once that the science of education is a composite science requiring the cooperation of many investigators. In its formulations it may deal in a broad way with general problems, or it may break up into numerous subdivisions appealing to the specialist.

It would therefore be more accurate to describe it as a group of specialized studies rather than a single discipline.[41] *

Judd and Thorndike shared the same vision of the enormity of the research task involved in merely gathering the factual data with which to describe educational practice. Viewing such practice as a social activity too broad to be studied as a whole, they recognized the need for coordinating the findings of numerous specialists working in all manner and variety of distinct areas of investigation. Just as the study of man as a biological organism depended on the development of special sciences, such as anatomy, endocrinology, neurology, and genetics, so would the study of man as a learning organism in a social setting depend on the appropriate division of the labors of investigation—as between educational psychology and educational sociology.

For Judd, a science of education was almost as overwhelming an enterprise as a science of all of life or a science of social institutions. Any attempt at understanding such an expanse of social activity and individual behavior—involving at least two of society's major social institutions, the school and the home—which did not draw on the full spectrum of available specialties he considered virtually worthless. In place of talk about a unified science of education, Judd called for a disciplined approach to the study of the teaching-learning activity in all its aspects. And it had to be the scholar's kind of discipline which put "knowing about," in the sense of factual data, ahead of "knowing how," or practical application. The numerous specialized studies would begin as separate areas of empirical investigation. Judd believed that such separate specialties could cooperate with one another and eventually be coordinated into a composite science of the educational process. It was in this way that he approached the concept of education as an intellectual discipline.

---

[41] Judd, 1918: 50.
* Each of these men saw a science of education developing apace with knowledge in each of the behavioral sciences, and they had unqualified optimism that a golden age of psychological and sociological science was not far off.

Summary

In line with the 2,000-year-old tradition of rationalism, the Herbartian view of education as an intellectual discipline combined a shrewd sense of workability with the dialectician's gift for casting a priori generalizations in the terms of contemporary science. Educators, having been led to expect that particulars of practice should be deduced from systematically organized theory, quickly adapted the newer terminology of experimental psychology as a cloak to provide a new outline for old generalizations drawn from generations of successful practice. Underneath such camouflage, practice remained the basic source of, as well as the *raison d'être* for, the ideas designated as the content of education as a rational discipline or science. It was such a practice-centered view of education which Brown and McMurry defended in the *Fourth Yearbook* of the National Society for the Scientific Study of Education, published in 1905.

In 1911 and 1912 Monroe, Thorndike, Henmon, Ruediger, and Parker stripped away the camouflage from education's rational science and exposed the a priori generalizations on which it depended. Parker and Ruediger went further and suggested that talk based on practical experience, on established beliefs still untested, and on rationalistic speculation be separated from observation-centered reasoning. Thus, practice-centered talk could be used in teacher training wherever needed without contaminating the observation-centered reasoning basic to the empirical discipline of education which seemed to be emerging from measurement and survey investigation. Under such an arrangement the immediate practical task of training teachers would have access to whatever generalizations seemed most useful; it would be frankly expedient and eclectic. The long-range scholarly task of developing an intellectual discipline of education which would first supplement and eventually supplant practice-centered talk would be just as frankly observation-centered. Freed from the demand for hasty overgeneralizations framed for the sake of giving emergency aid to practice, observation-centered reasoning could attempt to emulate the established descriptive sciences. Ideally, observation-centered research would enlighten teacher training by continually reducing the number of a priori generalizations as well as by extending new generalizations in their place.

In the decade before World War I, the problems of observation-centered research and of practitioner preparation became unmanageable. On the one hand, research had begun to splinter into fractional disciplines. By 1910, according to Kandel, the subdivisions became so numerous and so specialized that no student could be expected to master them all. On the other hand, teacher training had been assigned the task of providing practitioners for schools that were rapidly assuming the burden of all manner of social service and of helping that "army" of practitioners to provide improved instruction.

Sensitive to these new dimensions of practitioner preparation, Judd saw the need for initiating scholarly investigation into all areas of social activity relevant to this new conception of the role of the public schools. In effect, Judd, and Thorndike too, had warned researchers that *the factual description of public schooling seen as a major social institution would have to cover more ground than all that descriptive science had examined before Darwin.* And to cover such a wide range of investigation, it became necessary to divide and subdivide areas of inquiry into segments of special study appropriate to the tools and techniques of research as well as to the interests and capacities of researchers. Thus, Judd described educational science as composite—composed of a group of specialized studies rather than a single discipline.

Thorndike, Henmon, Ruediger, Parker, and Judd all agreed that the future of education as a discipline, or as a group of specialized studies, lay in a careful cultivation of observation-centered reasoning uncluttered by the a priori generalizations so familiar to Herbartian rational science and so much a part of teacher training. * Only Monroe registered a protest against the premature abandonment of the old tools before the new ones had been fully tested and perfected. All six of these authors took it for granted that the careful accumulation of factual data in an atmosphere free from the demands of immediate practical application would be encouraged and accelerated so that a composite science of descriptive and predictive content would eventually be developed. Each had faith in the cumulative effectiveness of fact-gathering pursued with diligence, care, and a scholarly interest in knowing about things. No one, except possibly Monroe, anticipated that the cause of a discipline of education based on observation-centered research might come to harm at the hands of practice-centered rationalists convinced that such factualism had failed to supply guidance for the conduct of instruction. In 1911 and 1912, observation-centered research seemed to be the royal road to a discipline of education while the practice-centered generalizations of teacher training seemed destined, one by one, to be made unnecessary or obsolete. Two decades later, however, a priori generalizations and practice-centered research had begun to displace observation-centered research as the basis for a different kind of educational discipline. The failure of factualism had left the vision of education as a discipline quite confused again. Factualism failed, first, for want of a language within which

---

* This insistence on uniting scholarly and practice-centered talk may well be responsible for the scarcity of genuine scholars in education departments and in teachers' colleges. Rare is the man who can mix the two and retain scholarly integrity.

fact-finding could take place without producing more dispute over terms than agreement over findings. It failed, second, for want of a theory that would account for the most commonly observed, diverse aspects of classroom behavior. Looking back two centuries, Whitehead cautioned both empiricists and their critics when he said:

> We here hit upon one of the dangers of unimaginative empiricism . . . of all people in the world, Newton fell into it. Huyghens had produced the wave theory of lights. But this theory failed to account for the most obvious facts about light as in our ordinary experience, namely, that shadows cast by obstructing objects are defined by rectilinear rays. Accordingly, Newton rejected this theory and adopted the corpuscular theory which completely explained shadows. Since then both theories have had their periods of triumph. At the present moment the scientific world is seeking for a combination of the two. These examples illustrate the danger of refusing to entertain an idea because of its failure to explain one of the most obvious facts in the subject matter in question. If you have had your attention directed to the novelties in thought in your own lifetime you will have observed that almost all really new ideas have a certain aspect of foolishness when they are first produced.[42]

Those who would strive first to control youngsters so as to enable the bureaucratic system of public schooling to develop an efficient routine fought a cold war against "permissivism" and "progressive education." Those who would provide enough elbow room in the classroom so that spontaneous interests could enliven learning with the introduction of novelty fought with equal vigor against the harsh "authoritarianism" of "undemocratic," "traditional" school procedures. Each group reached deep into its bag of emotional tricks to call up public and professional support in the name of everything dear. Journalism inundated scholarship, and neither side left room for the other to admit that each had something less than half the truth.

---

[42] A. N. Whitehead, 1959: 112.

In a more real sense than was ever dreamed by Sir Joshua Fitch in 1900, the schools and school systems of the country have become the experimental stations of a vast array of organizations for the study of education; and experimentation by trial and error methods are being replaced by experimentation under the control of scientific method.[1]

Up to this point the term *empiricism* has been used to designate the general, anti-rationalistic direction taken in the gathering of data by direct observation. Now it becomes necessary to identify a halfway point along the path to an empirical science, namely, factualism.

In the factual stage separate pieces, or small clusters, of data have significance only as isolated items of information. For example, the careful cataloguing of stellar movements by Tycho Brahe constituted a discrete collection of facts by means of which Kepler derived the principles of sidereal motion. Kepler developed an intellectual framework which unified Tycho Brahe's information; but until Kepler did this, the information resembled bricks and lumber to be used in a building not yet designed. Thus, factualism may be characterized as antecedent to observation-centered reasoning. It consists in data-gathering before reason has been fruitful in discerning a comprehensive design implicit in the data itself. Linnaeus went through this process, as Darwin must have aboard ship.

---

[1] Kandel, 1924: 51.3.

8

The Failure of Factualism

Between 1912 and 1924 observation, description, and factual reporting of the kind introduced by child study expanded like an explosion in
teacher training as a practice-centered attempt to produce talk which was
somewhat scholarly but which had immediate use.

The idea of education as an academic or subject-matter discipline
passed through the intellectual puberty rites of careful analysis about 1912.
Anticipating the ritual, Royce, James, and Dewey had set the ground plan
for education as an empirical science. Herbartian advocates of a rational
science mistook the adolescence of systematic deduction for adult behavior.
In 1911 Monroe and Thorndike corrected this oversight by pointing out
the full range of observation and deduction that characterizes a discipline
from infancy to maturity.

The actual rites were administered publicly by Henmon and Parker
in 1912. In *School Review Monographs* they exposed the past practices to
careful criticism while outlining the demands which the future would impose.
Attesting to the heavy dependence of present content upon a priori generalizations, each author also affirmed his belief that future behavior would
be different.

In 1912 the increased rigor in fact-gathering that had developed
under the careful guidance of serious students of child study offered support to that belief. By 1918, when Judd characterized the study of education
as a series of separate disciplines joined primarily by a common concern
for the same social institution, the evidence was overwhelming. Any effort
to return to a simple rational science of education was as impossible as
turning an advanced industrial society back into a succession of self-sufficient
rural communities. In the case of education, the difference had been made
by the shift of concern from the investigation of individuals to the investigation of groups. General psychology, child study, and educational psychology
offered much valuable data, but the scope of coverage resembled pinholes
in a wall map of the United States: where they touched, they penetrated;
but each hole stood out alone, and a lifetime of poking would not connect
them. Therein lay the theoretical paralysis of factualism.

The investigation of group performance, begun in 1895 by J. M. Rice
and extended greatly by the survey movement after 1911, promised coverage on the scope insisted on by Thorndike. And at the same time, the data
promised to become unmanageable unless systematically interpreted and
catalogued. Three of the most important contributions to making that data
available for use have been Paul Monroe's *Cyclopedia of Education,* the
Yearbooks of the NSSE, and Walter S. Monroe's 1941 *Encyclopedia of
Educational Research.* Together, they sum up the change that took place
with regard to the content of the study of education from the time when
it was just emerging as a separate discipline in 1895 to the period of 1941,

when it was being gathered into a supra-subject called the "Foundations of Education."

Competing Approaches to Research

The two possible patterns of research available for developing a discipline of education were both established before 1900. Following general psychology in the tradition of detailed scientific investigation, the serious students of child study had begun to gather extensive data about individual cases. Looking toward the establishment of a scientific discipline of child study, these students moved in the direction of a discipline of education based on *narrowly controlled observation* resembling laboratory research.

Pursuing inquiry in a different direction, J. M. Rice attempted to gather objective information covering a huge population of students in order to establish standards of expectation. In his 1895 project, Rice pioneered the achievement-testing and survey movements. These inundated the various areas of educational inquiry with such a supply of data that cataloguing generalizations and studies for use became a necessity rather than a convenience. In contrast to the controlled atmosphere of laboratory research, the methods introduced by Rice took a *broad field survey* approach to the development of a discipline.

BEGINNING BROAD FIELD SURVEYS

In February, 1895 J. M. Rice, editor of the *Forum,* began a ten-month study designed to show "what our teachers have accomplished in spelling, and what, therefore, may be reasonably demanded of our schools in this subject." [2] His over-all aim in testing nearly 33,000 children [3] was best expressed in the following part of his 1897 article, "The Futility of the Spelling Grind":

> I endeavor to prove that the first step toward placing elementary education on a scientific basis must necessarily lie in determining what results may reasonably be expected at the end of a given period of instruction. If we have no definite notions in regard to what our teachers ought to accomplish, our ideas must be doubly vague as to how much time needs to be devoted to each branch. And as long as this remains unanswered, no well-founded opinion can be given concerning the possibility of broadening the course of study without detriment to the formal

---

[2] Rice, 1897: 87.2.
[3] *Ibid.*

branches—the point around which the entire question of educational reform revolves.[4] *

Confining his study to performance in spelling, Rice restricted attention to the objectively observable product of student performance. In place of an exhaustive examination of individuals in search of reasons why performance went up or down, Rice concentrated on one aspect of performance and extensively explored it by testing many classroom groups. In attending to the collection of the simple facts of performance without a search for causal factors, Rice collected considerable data. In so doing, he set a pattern of scholarly data collection which fit in well with the survey techniques and statistical processing of information soon to get under way. Such an approach made it possible for researchers to look forward to gathering information about the social institution of education on the nationwide scale called for by Thorndike. This information, gathered directly from the field under actual teaching conditions, held considerable appeal for some researchers. It was just such an appeal which Thorndike found attractive in the year when the survey movement was beginning. He spoke of it in the following terms in the 1911 issue of the *School Review Monographs*:

> What makes quantitative work in education easy is the ease of securing material. Any town would provide this entire society with matter for study for all our lives. We need not wait for comets, nor travel to mountains, nor pay for rare earths, nor construct elaborate apparatus. Although expensive educational laboratories, museums, clinics, hospitals, experimental schools, expeditions, and the like are of very great service, no one of them is a *sine qua non* in the present state of the science.[5]

MORE CONTROLLED OBSERVATION

Although not claiming the laboratory approach to the study of education as a *sine qua non,* both James and Dewey favored the laboratory approach, since it paralleled developments that had just shown such marvelous results in general psychology. The experimental school which Dewey conducted at the University of Chicago suggested that a quasi-laboratory approach offered much in terms of (1) original data from careful observation, (2) experimentation in application of generalizations from psychology, and (3) the practical training of a conceptualist capable of building a linking science between psychology and teaching.

---

[4] Rice, 1897: 87.1.
* Rice began to gather much needed data. Thorndike likened the task of describing what was happening in the schools to a geographic survey of a continent; yet, half a century later, Conant had to state that no generalizations could be made about American public schooling. Shall we have only international *geophysical* years?
[5] Thorndike, 1911: 102.2.

Another prominent psychologist, Otto Munsterberg, explored the possibilities of a laboratory approach to the study of education in an article for *Educational Review* published in 1898. Beginning with the following statement of what a discipline of education must do for itself, he concluded with an opinion of how the task might best be accomplished:

It [education] cannot expect to find every necessary psychological and physiological information always ready-made.* As no science is merely a collection of scraps, psychology as such cannot examine every possible psychological fact in the universe, but must select just those which are essential for the understanding of the psychical elements and laws. This choice in the interest of psychology differs of course fully from the choice of psychical facts which education would select for its own purposes. Here the science of education must take the matter in its own hand and must work up, with all the subtle means and methods of modern psychology, those psychological phenomena which are important for the special problems; the most intimate relation to the psychological laboratories is here a matter of course. In what form education will fulfill this demand may be of course at first itself a matter of educational experiment. Some believe in special psycho-educational experimental laboratories, some believe in special experimental schools, and recently the proposition was made for the appointment of special school psychologists attached to the superintendent's office in large cities. In any case the work has to be done; the psychologist as such cannot do it, and the teacher cannot do it, either. For the psychologist it would be a burden, for the teacher it would be a most serious danger; the student of education alone can do it. Of course even these adjuncts of superintendents, and these principals of experimental schools, must never forget that their work refers always only to the one half, which is misleading without the other half—to the causal system, which must be harmonized with the teleological one.

Personally I consider the psycho-educational laboratory as the most natural step forward. Such laboratories would be psycho-psysical laboratories, in which the problems are selected and adjusted from the standpoint of educational interest. All that has been done so far in our psychological laboratories for the study of attention, memory, apperception, imagination, and so on has had, in spite of the seductive titles, almost never anything to do with that part of these functions which is essential for the mental activities in the classroom. While the individual teacher, as we have seen, has to keep away from our psychological laboratories because our attitude is opposed to his,† the student of education ought to keep away from us because, in spite of the same attitude, we have too seldom problems which belong to his field. It is a waste of energy to hunt up our

---

* Nor did education find psychologists interested in inquiring into educational matters; hence, educational psychologists had to carve out a domain, lately coveted.
† The scholarly-detached versus the practical-moral attitudes.

chronoscope tables and kymograph records for some little bits of educational information which the psychologist brought forward by chance; sciences cannot live from the chances of work which is intended for other purposes.* When in the quiet experimental working place of the psycho-educational scholar, through the steady co-operation of specialists, a real system of acknowledged facts is secured, then the practical attempts of the consulting school psychologist and of the leader of experimental classrooms have a safer basis, and their work will help again the theoretical scholar till the cooperation of all these agents produces a practical education which the teacher will accept without his own experimenting. Then the teacher may learn psychology, to understand afterward theoretically the educational theory he is trained in, but he himself has not to make education theory and not to struggle with psychological experiments.[6]

Indeed, the work had to be done. The psychologist, forced to choose problems in the interest of his own discipline, was fully occupied. The teacher, involved in instruction, could not fulfill his practical function if he were to become an observer as well. Before 1900 an understanding of educational problems had been a collection of scraps from other areas of inquiry. The method was to be that of psychology or, more generally, the broad outline of scientific method that Huxley had characterized. It only remained to pick the instrument—psycho-educational laboratories, experimental schools, or school psychologists. All were, to some extent, attempted.

School psychologists were few and hard to train, however, and in their stead teachers were substituted as guidance counselors who acted either as amateur psychiatrists or as psychotherapists or psychometricians who made referrals. As the load of practical service increased, and the level of talent demanded for guidance work declined, the possibility for research disappeared. In turn, the experimental schools struggled with the problem of implementing new programs and gathering data; but, since children were not guinea pigs, and since devotion to the practical task of teaching commanded more attention, attempts to have teachers conduct research failed too. Further, the instructional staff of experimental schools soon became critic teachers responsible for student-teacher training. Everywhere practice-centered demands crowded out scholarship. Research was left to advanced-degree students, who found the university laboratory school a convenient place to initiate minor controls without going through the formal channels of a public school board. The degree of control instituted during a doctoral study also marked the sole extent to which such

---

* Thus a discipline of education will not grow out of advances in behavioral science alone.

[6] Munsterberg, 1898: 73.

experimental schools approached the ideal of the psycho-educational laboratory which Munsterberg advocated.

The laboratory approach to narrowly controlled educational research never developed the possibilities which Munsterberg saw for it. The broader field survey, not the psycho-educational laboratory, was the source of the proliferation of data which necessitated cataloguing.

THREE-DIMENSIONAL EXAMINATIONS

Looking back across *Twenty-Five Years of American Education* in the quarter-century memorial volume of readings dedicated in 1925 to Paul Monroe by his former students, Jesse B. Sears summarized the "Development of Tests and Measurements." Charting the historic stepping-stones whereby laboratory research emerged as generalizations useful in classroom practice, Sears mentioned the following key figures:

> One can see Galton's early studies of nature and nurture passing through his own laboratory into that of Cattell, where more evidence and finer methods of measurement were added, and thence to Thorndike, from whom they have issued as generalizations on the technique of instruction and as effectual means of measuring the results of instruction, and later, of the capacity to receive instruction.[7]

Then he went on to trace the rapid development of tests which enabled investigators to gather extensive information in surveys and research projects designed to tap the inexhaustible reservoir of data available from the schools. In the following paragraph he provided the chronology of test development progressively expanding the volume of data:

> This idea of mental testing was soon taken up in this country. In the school for subnormal children at Vineland Dr. Henry Goddard introduced the 1905 tests in the latter part of 1908. Later he tested 2000 normal children, and in 1908 prepared a revision of the Binet-Simon scale. A second revision was made by Kuhlman in 1909-12 in connection with his work in the Faribault, Minnesota, school for sub-normal children. In 1912 Terman and Childs revised and extended the scale, and in 1916 the Stanford revision appeared.[8]

Again 1912 stands out as a year of accelerated growth. It was also the middle year for the publication of the first major compendium of educational thought, Monroe's *Cyclopedia of Education*.

---

[7] Sears, 1924: 96.2.
[8] Sears, 1924: 96.1.

Standardization of Concepts

Paul Monroe, with the assistance of departmental editors and more than one thousand individual contributors, attempted in five volumes to define and explain the major concepts operating in American education at the beginning of the twentieth century. The first two volumes of *A Cyclopedia of Education* appeared in 1911, the third in 1912, and the last two in 1913. The full *Cyclopedia* carried 3,655 pages of text and over 7,000 subject entries or topics. The following list of departmental editors reads like a *Who's Who* of famous contributors to the improvement of education as a scholarly discipline and as artful practice: *

Editors	*Positions*
1. Elmer E. Brown	Commissioner of Education of the United States
2. Edward F. Buchner	Professor of Education and Philosophy, Johns Hopkins University
3. William H. Burnham	Professor of Pedagogy in the School of Hygiene, Clark University, Worcester
4. Gabriel Compayré	Inspector General of Public Instruction, Paris
5. Elwood P. Cubberley	Head of Department of Education, Leland Stanford Junior University, Stanford
6. John Dewey	Professor of Philosophy, Columbia University, New York City
7. Charles H. Judd	Director of School of Education, University of Chicago
8. Arthur F. Leach	Charity Commissioner of England
9. J. E. G. De Montmorency	Barrister at Law, London, and Assistant Editor of the *Contemporary Review*
10. Wilhelm Munch	Professor of Pedagogy, University of Berlin

---

* No educational jury before or since has had such a fine set of credentials and such distinguished accomplishments.

11. Anna Tolman Smith	Specialist, Bureau of Education, Washington, D.C.
12. David Snedden	Commissioner of Education, State of Massachusetts
13. Henry Suzzallo	Professor of Philosophy of Education, Teachers College, Columbia University
14. Foster Watson	Professor of Education, University College of Wales

These departmental editors undertook the evaluative task of distilling a pure body of educational thought. Superfluous and redundant concepts had to be drained off to avoid contamination. Hazy meanings and vague abstraction had to be filtered for maximum clarity. Then the final ingredients had to be arranged for both the scholar and the practitioner. Within the text, the concept of education as a discipline underwent this exacting critical analysis from several sides, but the two most direct explanations came from Edward H. Cameron and John Dewey under the headings "Experimental Pedagogy" and "Experiment in Education."

EXPERIMENTAL PEDAGOGY

An Associate Professor of Psychology at Yale University, Edward H. Cameron offered his explanation in this form:

> Experimental pedagogy, therefore, implies an opposition to a pedagogy of a more theoretical character based upon some philosophical system or preconception of the aim of education, and upon the casual observation of educators.

> Although experimental pedagogy follows the lead of psychology in both its methods and its results, it relies also upon results of all the sciences whose facts have significance for education, such as anatomy, physiology, anthropometry, pathology, logic, ethics, and esthetics.* It borrows facts from all these fields, but regards them from an entirely different point of view; namely, that of education. It is therefore an independent science. While experimental pedagogy is dependent for its facts to some extent upon all of the sciences mentioned, it is chiefly indebted to investigations of the physical and mental life of the child, such as are afforded by child psychology and physiology, and the pathology and psychopathology of the child. The child thus becomes the object of exact investigation, and pedagogical principles and methods are decided on the basis of scientific observation of their effects upon his training and development.[9]

---

* Here is the idea that Rugg, and after him Brameld, was to expand into the Foundations of Education concept, analyzed in Chapter 11.
[9] Cameron, 1911: 12.

In keeping with Henmon's thinking of 1912, Cameron's view of education as a discipline is a more exacting version of child study. With the child as the object of exact investigation, the psycho-educational laboratory suggested by Munsterberg would be the ultimate setting for insuring maximum precision.

EXPERIMENT IN EDUCATION

John Dewey, concerned with both the academic and the practical conception of scientific method in the study of educational problems, put the idea of laboratory schools in the context of the kinds of disciplines to be developed. He distinguished between a practical and a scientific discipline in the following way:

> The function of experimentation in education falls into two more or less distinct and more or less over-lapping rubrics: (1) that conducted for practical, and (2) that conducted for scientific purposes. . . . What is needed in order to make this specific and casual type of [practical] experimentation more available for the science of education is (1) more careful and exact observation of the conditions and effects of such changes; and (2) systematic arrangement for the registration and communication of the results obtained. In other words, a large part of this practical experimentation is now scientifically useless* because (1) no pains are taken to record the antecedent state of affairs into which the change is introduced, and to isolate the special consequences which follow from its introduction; and because (2) the results are not recorded and published in such systematic form as to secure cumulative and co-operative results.† . . .
>
> Educational experimentation in the narrower sense refers to changes made not so much for the sake of improving specific and detailed results as for the sake of throwing light on some educational problem. These two types of experimentation, however, inevitably blend or shade into each other. . . .
>
> Scientific experimentation must itself be subdivided into two kinds, according as it is more specific or more general: (1) a body of data regarding the observations, the memories, the habit-forming, etc., of school children is already accumulating, through suitable adaptations of the methods of the psychological laboratory. . . . In short, laboratory experimentation, or adaptations of the technique of the psychological laboratory, will show what methods in current use are most effective under conventional conditions; they will not test the relative worth of the conventionally

---

* As was the case with child-study observations.

† The growth of journalistic talk multiplied terms, created slogans, built up jargon, and in general made it impossible to be sure what terms such as "enriched" or "activity" or "life experience" meant.

current type of education as compared with some suggestive reformed type. (2) For the latter purpose, special experimental schools are absolutely indispensable. Their results are less quantitative, seemingly less accurate, and less scientific, just because they are dealing with matters educationally much more important. However, this does not mean that the two types of experimentation are opposed to each other, but that they should supplement each other.[10] *

Dewey's distinction between the less rigorous practical experimentation carried on by teachers trying out new methods in the classroom and the exacting requirements of psychological inquiry indicates that the idea of education as a discipline remained open to a wide range of interpretation. As with Monroe, Thorndike, Henmon, Ruediger, and Parker, or with Munsterberg before them, the kind of research to be advocated depended on the kind of discipline anticipated. Dewey saw the need for as broad a range of experiments and observations as could be recorded, with some care as to antecedent conditions, and systematically catalogued for cumulative and cooperative understanding. He had confidence that terminology could be defined and standardized.

THE ACHIEVEMENT

Published in five volumes from 1911 through 1913, the *Cyclopedia* was organized in those years which Kandel identified as the twilight of education as a unified discipline. After 1910 the fragmentation of inquiry into numerous areas of specialized study made it impossible for one student to master them all. But those who edited the various departments under Monroe's direction were men who had come to maturity late in the nineteenth century, when one man could master much, if not all, of the material pertinent to education as a field of study. And he could rise, as a result of that mastery, to the stature of a giant, as Dewey did.

Combining practical experience with extensive scholarship, many of the departmental editors had figured prominently in generating the very concepts they were distilling for inclusion in the *Cyclopedia*. Coming at the close of the long epoch of conceptual giants and at the beginning of the new era of fact-gathering worker-bees, Monroe's *Cyclopedia* crystalized the most important ideas of educational giants in their purest form at the moment of richest maturity. These five volumes still constitute more

---

[10] Dewey, 1911: 26.

* In view of Dewey's willingness to accept less quantitative practitioner judgments as evidence of instructional success, it seems unfortunate that he is most frequently characterized as inflexible on the point of the kind of proof he would accept as meriting attention. In fact, the kinds of evidence he would allow as an indication of the success or failure of a line of social action seem almost sentimental when contrasted with the attitude of later positivists.

than a dictionary of important terms; they are a key to the educational significance of the major ideas active throughout the nineteenth century. As a scholarly dictionary of key concepts and terms, the publication helped strategically to stabilize usage and to clarify meaning in the manner Snedden had wished for in 1905.

Considered against a background of the primitive state of such social sciences as anthropology * and sociology in 1912, the *Cyclopedia* seems to contain within it the whole of education as an intellectual discipline. Careful in terminology, comprehensive in scope, uncompromising, the *Cyclopedia* is a model of what can be accomplished in the name of educational scholarship.

By stabilizing the language for talking about education, both with regard to the terminology employed and to the meaning of complex content, Monroe's *Cyclopedia* cut across the trunk of education as a rational discipline and exposed the rich cross section of content with which it entered the twentieth century.

Less spectacular, but of equal importance for the insights it offered into the change that took place in the concept of education as an intellectual discipline, is the longitudinal view of the research and publications of the National Society for the Study of Education made by Guy Whipple a quarter of a century later.

Summary of Longitudinal Research

As a continuation of the National Herbart Society, the NSSSE— later the NSSE—published its early yearbooks during the rise of the idea that education as a discipline should resemble the empirical sciences. For a time, as Parker[11] and Henmon[12] implied, talk about a science of education almost took precedence over actual research. In the early yearbooks of the NSSSE, opinion constituted the great bulk of the contents. But with the beginning of widespread psychological testing and the start of the survey movement in 1911, the public schools began to take on an experimental aspect.[13] About the same time, according to Guy Whipple, secretary for the NSSE, that society began to undertake more scientific types of inquiry.[14]

---

* Sir James George Frazer's classic amalgam of literary scholarship *The Golden Bough* (1890) remained the most outstanding work in cultural anthropology at that time.

[11] Parker, 1912: 77.5.
[12] Henmon, 1912: 43.4.
[13] Buckingham, 1941: 10.
[14] Whipple, 1938: 109.1.

THE THIRTY-SEVENTH YEARBOOK

The yearbooks of the National Society for the Study of Education provide an excellent longitudinal view of the year-to-year development of important areas of educational opinion, research, and concept formation. In particular, Part Two of the *Thirty-Seventh Yearbook* of the NSSE, published in 1938, has presented a subject-matter summary of that longitudinal development under the title, "The Scientific Movement in Education." The areas covered and the men responsible for a résumé of the research done are as follows:

Content Areas	Authors *
1. School Surveys	C. H. Judd
2. Educational Administration	J. C. Reavis
3. Education of Teachers	E. S. Evenden
4. Curriculum	W. Peik, C. Cushman, G. Fox
5. General Methods	A. I. Gates
6. Special Methods	
6.1 Handwriting	N. Freeman
6.2 Reading	W. S. Gray
6.3 Spelling	E. Horn
6.4 English Usage	E. H. Greene
6.5 Mathematics	G. Bushwell and E. Breslich
6.6 Natural Science	S. R. Powers
6.7 Social Studies	H. E. Wilson
6.8 Practical Arts	J. M. Brewer
6.9 Music and Art	W. L. Uhl
6.10 Home Economics	C. M. Brown
7. Classification, Promotion, and Marking of Pupils	A. O. Heck
8. Individualization of Instruction	S. A. Courtis
9. Discipline and Control	R. Strang
10. Guidance in Education	M. R. Trabue
11. Higher Education	F. J. Kelly
12. General Methods (Contributions of the Society)	G. M. Whipple
12.1 Historical, Comparative, Documentary	N. Edwards

---

* With a few notable exceptions, these were not the giants but the workhorses of educational scholarship.

Content Areas	Authors
12.2 Social Survey and Community Study	C. Marsh
12.3 Statistical Analysis and Comparison	K. J. Holzinger
12.4 Laboratory Experimentation	G. T. Buswell
12.5 Classroom Experimentation	Walter S. Monroe
12.6 Case Study	W. C. Olson
12.7 Educational Diagnosis	L. J. Brueckner
13. Specific Techniques of Investigation	
13.1 Examining and Testing Acquired Knowledge, Skill, and Ability	R. W. Tyler
13.2 Testing Intelligence, Aptitude, and Personality	C. Watson
13.3 Observation, Questionnaire, and Rating	L. V. Koos
14. Scientific Knowledge about	
14.1 Psychology of Learning	J. F. Dashiell
14.2 Individual Differences	F. S. Freeman
14.3 Mental Growth and Development	G. D. Stoddard
14.4 Mental Hygiene	M. Sherman
14.5 Organization of Society and Social Pathology	W. Wallas
14.6 Economics	H. F. Clark
15. Science and Philosophy	
15.1 A Priori Speculation vs. Pragmatic or Empirical Enquiry in Aims	J. Dewey
15.2 Province of Scientific Inquiry	F. N. Freeman

Each item occupied a separate chapter in the book. And, more important, each chapter accorded with Judd's view of a series of separate disciplines. Any connection among the areas of research summarized is either historical or due to common association with a major discipline such as psychology. Further, the great number of areas included as separate disciplines of education in which extensive research had taken place fell within the three areas of quantitative research identified by Ruediger in 1912: method or curriculum, administration, and psychology.

The chapter on "The Contributions of This Society to the Scientific Movement in Education with Special Reference to the Trends in Problems and Methods of Inquiry" done by Whipple provided an excellent longitudinal summary of the stages through which work on providing content for a discipline of education had passed. Grouping the accomplishments of 36 years under 18 categories, Whipple described the first five years of the Society's publications (1901-1906) as "Personal Opinion about General Principles and Theory." [15] Overlapping the first period and extending into the late 1920's, he called the second "General Principles and Fundamental Theory Arrived at by Discussion and Pooling of Opinions by Several Persons." [16] Switching from time periods to topical categories, Whipple next listed four categories concerned with specific issues—appraisal of yearbook content, historical summaries, literary analysis, and the present status of current practice. He concluded with a "Survey of Present Status or Practices on a Comprehensive and Quantified Scale." [17] Therein he noted a change of pace in the research pursued under the idea of education as an independent area of study:

> New machinery is employed—the questionaire, tables of distribution, graphs, and the like. Furthermore, in the best illustrations, the data are used as a basis for comparisons and interpretations that greatly enhance their value. In other words, the survey of present practices is not an end in itself, but a preliminary step to larger undertakings. Take, in illustration, the study of "Industrial Education" (11, I, 1912), which bears the subtitle "Typical Experiments Described and Interpreted," . . .[18]

Among the topics in Whipple's classification of the work of the Society, the one including the quantified survey movement came closest to describing the kind of scientific progress Thorndike had prescribed.

WHIPPLE'S RÉSUMÉ

Charting the full range and direction of the Society's work, Whipple offered abbreviated overviews of the 18 categories into which he had originally classified that work. His summary generalized about the stages through which the Society had gone during its 36 years of history:

> (1) a stage characterized by a predominance of individual opinion or of pooled opinion, becoming probably progressively more expert;*
> (2) a stage characterized by the injection of quantification and featuring assemblages of data in historical summaries, analyses of reports, surveys of practices, outcomes, of questionnaires, and the like;†
> (3) a stage characterized by insistence upon refinements of statistical method, upon measurements, scales, and standardization, culminating in

---

[15] Whipple, 1938: 109.2.
[16] Whipple, 1938: 109.3.
[17] Whipple, 1938: 109.4.
[18] Whipple, 1938: 109.4.
* Carrying out the nineteenth-century pattern set by the giants.
† Beginning of the measurement movement.

recipes, practical rules, remedial devices, and numerous instructional and administrative recommendations; *

(4) a stage characterized by the appearance of new techniques, like the interview, visitation, the case study, less precise but in a way more comprehensive and more ambitious than the methods of the third stage; †

(5) a stage characterized by attempts to formulate objectives more recondite than factual acquisition, to analyze the learning processes for skills, attitudes, and sentiments regarded as potentially teachable, and to lay out the instruction accordingly in a given field of subject matter longitudinally throughout the school grades; e.g., in arithmetic, geography, science; and possibly, ‡

(6) a stage characterized, rather curiously, by a return to a considerable extent, to the approach used in the first stage. . . . it seems to me . . . to be conditioned by the attempt to attack new and broader problems for which at present we lack precise techniques of investigation, in which case the resort once more to expression of opinion is just an accident.[19]

Whipple's total view of the scientific study of education resembled a bell-shaped curve extending over a 40-year period which began in 1902. It began on the line of speculation and opinion. During the second decade of the century, it rose with the increase and improvement of psychological testing tools and the growth of statistics. Reaching the high point of scientific development in the areas of curriculum or method, administration, and psychology shortly after 1925, it fell back down toward the line as educators began to speculate (1) about problems which could not at that time be tested with the same kind of rigor, or (2) about the virtues of returning to a rational science which provided unity through philosophic deduction.

The separate areas of inquiry on educational problems covered in the *Yearbook* catalogue the major achievements of the measurement and survey movements. Both began and prospered under the belief that the separate areas of inquiry might eventually lead to broad scientific principles and theories that would illuminate the unity just beneath the surface.

Hope of a unified discipline of education worthy of being called a science held out past 1925, but by 1937 it had given way to the belief that the study of educational problems had merely passed through a stage in which the methods of science had been applied to numerous individual problems. The full insularity of factual information about schooling can be gathered from the 1941 publication of the *Encyclopedia of Educational Research*. Lacking a conceptual framework, the editor could only select topics whose authors typically presented isolated data in a manner which

---

* Thorndike's influence diluted by practice-centered interests.
† Mirroring the growth of clinical psychology.
‡ The increased concern for practice-centered conclusions.
[19] Whipple, 1938: 109.5.

suggested that separate facts ranked equally with meaning-giving concepts. The isolated factual studies and the teams of surveyors produced no giants capable of synthesizing the data so as to uncover basic patterns that cut across separate lines of inquiry.

Separate but Equal Data

Published in 1941 under the editorship of Walter S. Monroe (no relation to Paul Monroe), the *Encyclopedia* attempted to draw together "a critical evaluation, synthesis, and interpretation of reported studies in the field of education" [20] for the benefit of "students in teacher training institutions, teachers, supervisors, administrators, professors of education, and even interested laymen." [21] Monroe estimated that 100,000 studies had to be synthesized into approximately 1,000,000 words.[22] In the 1,344 pages of text, the number of studies reviewed by the 189 contributors came to "several times more than the 7000 actually listed" [23] in the bibliographies.

The *Encyclopedia* extended the work done by Whipple and the *Thirty-Seventh Yearbook* into a more comprehensive definition and illustration of the factual dimension of the study of education. Thus, in the preface Monroe made the following statement of the purpose of the work:

> . . . the final list of topics is the product of many influences and represents the results of a persistent attempt to effect a comprehensive outline of the field of educational research. It is, however, doubtless imperfect. At the present time any determination of the boundaries of the field of educational research must be arbitrary. There are no authoritative criteria on which to base decisions regarding how far to go into such related fields as psychology, statistics, sociology, architecture, and political science. Another difficulty is created by the lack of adequate specification of what constitutes research in the field of education.[24] *

Lacking explicit criteria of what constituted scholarship in the field of education, the *Encyclopedia* itself reflects the implicit standards that had gained wide acceptance by 1940. Monroe and his editors were cautious and careful men. As a field of inquiry, education had suffered numerous accusations from academic quarters. In the past, under the influence of rational science, speculation had run wild, yet it had passed as scholarship

---

[20] W. S. Monroe, 1941: 71.1.
[21] *Ibid.*
[22] *Ibid.*
[23] W. S. Monroe, 1941: 71.3.
[24] W. S. Monroe, 1941: 71.2.
* The case is still unchanged, yet someone must have the courage to be a critic and say "this is research" and "that is merely publication for promotion."

among the Herbartians. The sentimental ramblings of child-study journalism had been even more humiliating. In the organization of course work
for the training of teachers, anecdotal comments and a priori generalizations still accounted for considerable content.

Monroe and his associates charted a safe course toward scholarship.
They included only detailed factual studies—the more quantified, the better. Their inclusions seemed to be quite in line with the kind of research
going on in the behavioral sciences generally. What was not so apparent
was that such a collection of minute information, lacking a general framework for coherent interrelation and interpretation, bore a greater resem-
blance to the accumulation of a million fathom readings by Mississippi
riverboat captains than to any careful scientific investigation. Taken without reference to longitude, latitude, time, sun, stars, or fixed position on
the shore, some of the facts resembled marks made on the side of the boat
and others were as useful as crosses painted on the water.

In point of fact, the measurement and survey movements produced
considerable data quite similar to river fathom-readings. First, the primary
value of a sounding is that it enables the captain to anticipate how to
maneuver his ship through new waters or over a shifting bottom—such
a utility is immediate and practical. Second, a collection of soundings taken
with excruciating care for their quantitative accuracy but unrelated to
points on shore or in the sky can only suggest possible maximum, minimum, and average depths at the time the soundings were made. Although
such a pile of fathom readings offers testimony that many vessels must
have sailed successfully from Memphis to New Orleans and back again,
they hardly constitute a scientific study of the Mississippi river bottom
even if they represent the only data available.

Piled up like fathom-readings out of countless logbooks, the reported
research in the *Encyclopedia* documented the state of education as an intellectual discipline at the close of the pre-World War II period—a
museum of once useful information largely disassociated from the context
in which it had meaning. The social institution of schooling had been
divided into separate pools for careful sounding, but no one had designed
a fixed frame of reference against which to record the meaning of the
recorded data. Further, within each sub-discipline, factual information
often remained unconnected. The rule was discontinuity. Yet the fault
was not Monroe's, nor could it be considered a flaw in the scholarship of
his editors. As an encyclopedia of conducted research, it is part of education's body of lasting scholarship.

Fearful of the excesses of theory construction that had marred the
past, the only avenue to what passed for scientific objectivity seemed to
be the separation of specialties and an equality among facts and among
concepts. The *Encyclopedia* catalogued the separate, but equal, states of
data and of ideas at the very moment when educators had begun to in-

stitute a program of teacher training designed to force the integration of factual data within a philosophic framework—the "Foundation of Education."

Contrast of Opposites

The rational science which filled *A Cyclopedia of Education* with the major ideas of nineteenth-century educational thought lacked objectively gathered data. The *Cyclopedia* caught the spirit and content of those vital ideas and offered them a fertile field in which to await the planting of seeds of factual information. In 1912 confidence in the triumph of education as an empirical science seemed assured. It was just such confidence that prompted Bird T. Baldwin, director of educational research at the University of Texas, to declare that the scientific discipline was already an accomplished fact. Responding to Ruediger's article in that same 1912 issue of the *School Review Monographs,* Baldwin made the following claim that the empirical science of education could and should divest itself of rational science:

> To recapitulate very briefly: we have come to a stage of development in our field when it is necessary to differentiate between the philosophy of education and the scientific principles of education, since the subject is not merely a critical discussion of facts and principles gathered from other sciences; neither is it merely a profession. It is an empirical science with its own data, its own viewpoint, its own problems and situations, its own history, and its own practices and opportunities for experimentation.[25] *

Although Baldwin's claim seemed premature in the context of Henmon's, Ruediger's, and Parker's more conservative positions, the situation 12 years later seemed to confirm his optimism. Writing in 1924, Sears gave the following testimony to the advances in investigation which had captured Baldwin's imagination earlier:

> It would not be correct to say that all this rapid headway has been made without mistakes. A few important controversies have arisen on rather important points; and those who know most about the movement are surest of the tentative character of many of the tests and formulae that have been used widely and with confidence by many workers; but that the movement represents the largest quarter century of work that has ever

---

[25] Baldwin, 1912: 5.

* If it seems untenable to defend education as an empirical science, it might seem more defensible to suggest that it is potentially an area of scholarly inquiry worthy of support and encouragement and in need of being liberated from the practice-centered demands of teacher training.

been done in education, no intelligent person can doubt. The student of statistics may be going too far with some of his theories to suit the mathematician; psychologists may disagree as to just what intelligence is or to just what mental tests measure. . . . Granting all these things, however, we must point to the solid achievement in the way of accomplished reorganization, in the way of available facts about the schools, in the way of a large amount of scientific literature on education, and in the confidence and forward look of the leading men in the field today as the real meaning of the measurement movement in education.[26]

Indeed, the investigation which the *Encyclopedia of Educational Research* catalogued in alphabetical order offered effective proof of the extent to which factualism failed to improve talk about education. Practice-centered fact-gathering dominates each page. The amount of observation-centered research directed toward the immediate aim of knowledge-for-its-own-sake and the long-range goal of increased predictive power remained small because inquiry had seldom been guided by an over-all conceptual framework in which the findings turned out to be either part of the large puzzle into which other findings had already been fitted or key pieces in a new puzzle not yet begun. The over-all effect of such a disproportionate share of practice-centered factualism is that what might have been parts of a large puzzle got lost in a haystack of chopped-up facts.

The dominance of practice-centered factualism produced an eclecticism of unmanageable, because unimaginable, proportions. The facts neither confirmed nor refuted any idea, theory, or objective point of view, because they were not gathered in relation to a framework of explicit concepts. At best they suggest some possible description of a particular activity. Instead of being the objective investigations on which observation-centered reasoning could be based, they turned out to be the first attempts at making a felt point of view explicit. Far from being facts in the usual sense of the word, they were undefined tokens of a new way of speaking about education—a way that might eventually lead to a language of objective description.

Viewed as factual research from which the pattern of educational theory should emerge after the pinpoints of data had been plotted, factualism failed. Even if the findings of such practice-centered inquiry were given the status of scientific fact, it seems that education lacked the persistence, endurance, and funds to produce a pattern from such curiosity-collecting tactics. The market for sensational guesses always seemed to attract far more attention than the need for carefully qualified statements. The factualism of the measurement and survey movements increased the diversity of talk and the disparity of information to the point where no

---

[26] Sears, 1924: 96.5.

man could touch all the content and detect any inherent pattern or imagine with sufficient breadth to conceive a scheme into which it could all be fitted and ordered.

As factual research, the data confounded through contradiction. Only the mechanical systems of library cataloguing or alphabetical arrangements were adequate for comprehensive coverage. Built to include contradiction, such mechanical order was the antithesis of conceptual order, since it was imposed independently of meaning. For all its scholarship, far from being a first step toward organizing a science of empirical research in education, the mechanical order and conceptual disarray of the *Encyclopedia* testify to the diversity of practice-centered problems that have commanded most attention.

As experimentation in a new way of speaking about education, factualism could be called the prenatal heartbeat of a science of education or the exploratory phase prerequisite to the growth of a technical language capable of describing practice in objective terms. Seen as an anthology of factual talk, the *Encyclopedia* ceases to be a compendium of unmanageable information and becomes a further attempt to standardize ways of talking about observation. But, since the *Encyclopedia* was edited with the idea that it was to be a compendium of data, it performs its standardization function quite by accident, and thus proves inferior to the *Cyclopedia* which preceded it by 30 years.

The *Cyclopedia of Education* sought to define certain *key concepts* used in education; and to that end the editors explored the relationships, contradictions, divergences, and agreements among ways of talking about education. The *Cyclopedia* remains a scholar's map to the nineteenth-century world of educational thought, and it has the unity of being a work written in the language used by giants accustomed to communicating with one another in scholarly terms. Preceding the measurement movement, the *Cyclopedia* was a book of *ideas* in which the difference in style among authors remained subordinate to the interchange of thought commonly understood. By contrast, the *Encyclopedia of Educational Research* collects insular reviews of disconnected findings into a volume which defies the distillation of any commonly understood body of ideas yet maintains a certain uniformity in the manner of talking about those findings.

Between the 1913 and the 1941 catalogues, Whipple's 1937 summary plotted a curve. The personal opinions of rational science, lacking factual backing, fell off into disuse. Further, the factualism of measurement and survey investigation fragmented scholarship about education into isolated reports. Without the guiding framework of concepts, which only expert personal opinion could have supplied in such early days of factual inquiry, each area of investigation became a bottomless pit absorbing all data without raising the level of understanding.

The *Cyclopedia* was a scholarly move toward standardizing talk about education on the broadest levels of conceptualization. If it had been continued as Monroe suggested, it might have led to the design of a framework within which factual research could have been cumulative in its proof or disproof of a theory of education. The *Encyclopedia* has opened the possibility of standardizing descriptive talk about practice in such a way that future factual research might be cumulative, because each reported observation could be stated in a known relationship to each other observation. In the sense that it is an exploration into how to describe practice in objective terms capable of comparison with other descriptions from other workers, times, places, and perspectives, it represents a step toward independent scholarship, as pointed out by Huxley, Peirce, Royce, James, Dewey, Thorndike, Paul Monroe, Henmon, Ruediger, and Parker. Each of these men looked toward a future when more and more human behavior would be described in the manner of empirical science. The philosophers of a discipline of education among them saw that the key to such a body of theoretical generalizations depended on a language of objective description capable of giving a thorough account of schooling as a major social institution. Narrowly personal accounts of practice useful in explaining methods of instruction, as well as broad speculation about philosophies of life useful in building attitudes toward children, both had to be distinguished from objective description and observation-centered research. The findings summarized in the *Encyclopedia* represent a long-term effort to minimize personal and speculative talk and to maximize objective description. It stands as a catalogue of accounts of ways of describing practice in more or less objective terms, but not as a report of accomplished objective description and observation-centered research. The *Encyclopedia* is a source book of the language of educational measurement. It shows how much this usage stands in need of standardization, whereas the earlier *Cyclopedia* is a source book of nineteenth-century ideas expressed in the academic language as it had been standardized at the end of that century.

Long before the *Encyclopedia* reviewed efforts at objective description, however, talk about education felt the impact of practice-centered research designed to improve teacher training directly. In separate educational categories—curriculum, administration, guidance, and method— anecdotal talk based on present and past experience evolved useful generalizations. Common-sense questions were often answered in the vocabulary of scholarly authority. Speculation about life and about the classroom had been decorated with content from academic authority. This meant that the qualitative difference between scholarly and practice-centered talk had been obscured, and, as a consequence, that the distinction between education as an intellectual discipline and as content with which to train practitioners gradually disappeared. Impediments in the way of clarifying standards of scholarship, of course, cast shadows in which journalistic talk could roam with respectability.

In 1912 Thorndike, Henmon, Ruediger, and Parker anticipated the growth of a discipline dependent on observation-centered reasoning and directed toward the uncompromising pursuit of information about all elements of schooling and the teaching-learning process. They expected the a priori generalizations drawn from personal opinion and past experience, so much in evidence at the time, to atrophy from disuse and blow away. But when the extensive pursuit of factual data failed to yield generalizations which would join the various specialties into the kind of composite science which Judd had forecast in 1918, simplifications and overgeneralizations from psychology began to be mixed with both the anecdotal and the speculative content of teacher-training courses.

All areas of professional preparation repeated the same philosophic disputes as a prelude to the presentation of technical data carefully selected to support a point of view chosen on a priori grounds. While measurement and survey research was conducting experiments in the use of descriptive language, teacher training was absorbing the very vocabulary of that experiment. All such talk claimed some basis in observation and some status as theory. Talk had become theory, regardless of its source, its purpose, its significance, its meaning, or its method. In such a climate of intellectual anarchy, journalistic prose often gained more attention than the less interesting conclusions of careful scholarship.

In a recent address before the National Educational Association, President Butler of Columbia University said:

> "Two generations ago it became patent to the people of this country that mere scholarship was not a sufficient preparation for teaching, and schools came into existence whose object it was to prepare teachers by a study of method. That was a desirable, indeed a necessary, reform if the schools were to increase in efficiency beyond the point they had then reached. But I am clear that that movement has now gone too far, and the teachers of method have now become enamoured of method for method's sake. They have forgotten that method is a means and not an end, and their fine-spun analysis and long-continued preparation is like placing a great, huge vestibule before a very small and insignificant house. It makes education wasteful in a very high degree."

Perhaps this is the most general, as well as the most serious, of all the charges brought against the normal school. It is said to be "top-heavy" in theory; that its courses present a great body of theory which does not find concrete embodiment in the normal school itself nor in the actual school work of normal teachers; it wastes its energies in striking the air.[1]

In the first years of the twentieth century, speculation about object method and deduction from Herbartian rational science filled normal school teacher-training

---

[1] Illinois Faculty, 1903: 31.

9

Talk Taken
for Theory

programs with vastly more talk than demonstration. Concern for the symbolic and spiritual significance of object-teaching sent thoughts about primary school instruction into the outer space of metaphysical abstraction. Herbartian deduction showered all parts of secondary-school practice with logical fall-out. In a program designed for the practical job of training teachers, the term "theory" became an epithet for the kind of talk having the least utility.

Butler and the Illinois faculty declared that normal school programs were top-heavy with theory in the barren, interim year of 1904, that is, after the rhetoric of Herbartian rationalism had been recognized as senile but before observation-centered reasoning in the measurement and survey movements had reached puberty. Henmon, Ruediger, and Parker had not yet explored the distinction between observation-centered research and practice-centered training as the basis for developing education as an intellectual discipline. Monroe's *Cyclopedia,* with its standardizing effect on the rhetoric of teacher training, lay almost a decade in the future. There was not wide anticipation of Thorndike's vigorous appeal for careful description before speculation on a limited scale. According to Whipple, education as an intellectual discipline consisted primarily of opinion and self-evident logic aimed at persuading the teacher to conduct practice in certain ways. Educational theory consisted of practice-centered dialectic, which was supposed to supplement demonstration, exercise of skill, and observation of children. It was a rhetoric which persuaded teachers to attempt to teach according to such general methods as object-teaching and the Herbartian five steps.

By standardizing the preparation of teachers, the method of instruction, and the attitudes of the prospective practitioner, the normal schools hoped to establish a minimum level of competence and performance. For this they had two instruments: talk and show. Practice teaching, child-study observation, and demonstrations *showed* the student how to teach and invited him to show his skill and point of view. *Talk* explained, filled out, and supplemented show. Initially, show had been obviously practical, and talk had been as obviously necessary. As the length of normal school training increased and the amount of show remained constant, the proportion of talk increased. As it absorbed the vocabulary of emerging behavioral science, acquired footnotes from classical literature, and attended to philosophic questions, such talk became respected as theory.

Only the difference between talk and show remained obvious when normal school training mixed up a batch of educational theory. Talk about methods, curriculum, administration, the common branches, elementary schools, secondary schools, and institutions of higher learning absorbed the dialectic which passed as educational theory the way a paper towel soaks up water, letting it go with the slightest squeeze. Theory compounded theory, and all that Butler and the Illinois faculty could see was a talk-heavy curriculum of teacher training. Demonstration lessons and practice teaching (show) had clear practical significance, at least.

Show, Talk, and Rhetoric in the Normal School

Elisha Tiknor suggested the idea of the normal school in 1789.[2] It had a simple conceptual base, namely, that standardizing the methods of instruction and the teacher's command of content should raise the level of performance and assure a respectable minimum of professional competence.* As a social institution, however, the normal school became a crucible in which current ideas were compounded with successful experience to be distributed as a prescription for daily use in the public schools. Analyzing the ingredients of that prescription, J. P. Gordy wrote his book, *Rise and Growth of the Normal School in the United States.*

Writing in 1891 as the normal school concept reached toward the end-of-the-century peak, Gordy depicted the full scope of the institution before it was absorbed in the teacher's college movement and later underwent partial eclipse when universities began to take teacher preparation seriously. Issued by the Government Printing Office, Washington, D.C., Gordy's analysis covered five stages, in which the balance between talking and showing gradually shifted toward the dominance of rhetoric that Nicholas Murray Butler found so objectionable. The stages can be categorized as (1) mechanical, (2) exposure, (3) demonstrative, (4) observational, and (5) verbal.

1. MECHANICAL STAGE—MONITORIAL METHOD

The Lancasterian monitorial system produced quick and decisive results against absolute illiteracy. Drill in the skills of reading, figuring, writing, and memorization of content was efficient in a mechanical way. Obedience achieved under a military chain of command reflected the same mechanical solution to the problem of order. Simple in concept and cheap in operation, the monitorial method severely influenced the normal schools which began in the period when that approach to teaching dominated major city systems.

Gordy's criticism focused on two "misconceptions" of the monitorial method which have not yet disappeared from teacher training:

---

[2] Gordy, 1891: 36.10.

* Monitorial method must be kept in mind lest the difference between yesterday's minimum and today's make it seem that the normal school accomplished no good at all.

(1) that teaching consists in imparting bits of factual knowledge; and (2) that to impart such knowledge, one need know only as much as is to be imparted.[3] Such a view of teaching as the imparting of information under a mechanical system of memorization, drill, and obedience had led to the rigid standardization of lessons. Drill the monitor in the content he has to learn; give him absolute authority within the chain of command; and have him extract the memoriter product from his students.[*] Thus you have trained a teacher. When the normal schools began, their first concern was to provide a broader exposure to the same common branches of learning taught in the academies.

2. EXPOSURE TO COMMON BRANCHES

To make certain that the graduates of normal schools had at least as much command of the subjects they were to teach as monitorial tutors, it was necessary to expose them to the common branches. To avoid competition with the liberal arts colleges and the academies,[†] this exposure took, as Gordy explained, the following form:

> . . . there was quite a unanimity of opinion among the educators of Massachusetts as to the theory upon which the course of study in the normal schools should be based. As their special object was the preparation of teachers for the work of the common schools, they agreed that these schools could best accomplish that object by giving their pupils a special professional knowledge of the subject they were preparing to teach, as well as of pedagogics.[4]

Exposure to the common branches was to be of a special type, to provide a professional knowledge of the subjects to be taught. Instead of repeating the exposure they passed through in the public schools, the teacher-trainees were to be confronted with these subjects in their most usable, rather than their most academic, forms. Such a professional organization of content necessitated talk about the teaching of the common branches, talk that would fit well with the other kind of talk about education—pedagogics. So the pattern went: showing led to professional, practical talk; practical

---

[3] Gordy, 1891: 36.2.

[*] Such standardization of the whole classroom routine haunts teachers, who see the move toward standardization of content as a return to such iron-handed authority.

[†] In general, liberal arts colleges and academies encouraged only their poorest students to become teachers, and now we complain about the low level of education of teachers and see neither irony nor justice in the situation.

[‡] Shrewd professionals, these educators did not want the secondary-school level of work as presented in the normal schools directly compared with the academic work in the colleges.

[4] Gordy, 1891: 36.4.

talk merged with pedagogics, sometimes practical and sometimes not. Pedagogics was theory, and talk about how much pedagogics and professionalized common branches to include became more theory. Educational theory multiplied like amoebae (in stagnant waters).

3. DEMONSTRATION—PRACTICE TEACHING

The program at the Oswego Normal School greatly reduced in two ways instruction in common branches. At first, only experienced teachers were admitted to training in the object method. Their command of the common branches could be taken for granted. Second, much of the instruction in the object method was an exposure, a showing of things rather than a talking about academic subject matter.

Teacher training in the object method at Oswego, through observation and the demonstration of skill through practice teaching, carried showing to its peak. The method showed students objects; observation showed prospective teachers how to show students objects; and practice teaching forced the student teacher to show the critic teacher his skill at showing students objects. Oswego was the center of the most practical kind of teacher training.

But showing led to talking, and this led to pedagogics. Practical teacher training was surrounded with Froebel's speculations about the symbolic significance of objects. Pestalozzi's talk about the place of affection and acceptance in the classroom, as well as his principles of how mind operates, filled in the spaces between "showings" at Oswego. Before 1880, talk threatened to outdistance showing as normal school professors sought to convince one another that they were academic people.

4. OBSERVATION OF CHILDREN

Child study formalized the observational side of practice-teaching programs. That formalization added two different kinds of talk to the program of the normal schools. The first was a growing body of quasi-scientific data recorded at Worcester Normal School and other carefully conducted child-study centers. The second kind of talk came from the success of these observations in creating an attitude of interest and acceptance of a wider range of child behavior than had been considered previously. Discussing this broadening function of child-study observation, Gordy offered the following personal observation:

> Principal Russell says that his graduates say, after experience in teaching, that they find no feature of their preparatory work more directly beneficial, especially in dealing with exceptional children, than this training in the observation of children.[5]

---

[5] Gordy, 1891: 36.7.

But this extension of Pestalozzian affection for children brought the emotional effect of observation into the talk about teaching carried on in the normal schools. A "feeling" for children became part of the understanding of them. The heart had to share billing with the head in the discussion of educational problems.* It was not enough to have an understanding of how to teach; knowledge of practice had to be accompanied by a desire or attitude that would breed a commitment, if not a dedication. "How teach" was now accompanied by "why teach." And the amplification of the response "because kids are wonderful" eventually had to lead in the direction of child nature and the good life.

5. VERBALIZATION

Before the journalistic talk of childhood distorted verbalization about teaching into an emotional mockery of reason, more logical minds introduced many long-standing philosophic questions into normal school training. Showing had led to talking, and talk about teaching could not long avoid deeper issues which scholars and laymen alike had never settled.†

Elementary public education had become established throughout the nation by 1880, and secondary education showed all indications of comparable coverage in the near future. After the quasi-philosophic and psychological terms were dropped, Pestalozzi and Froebel could be credited with setting forth a common-sense view of the learning process which began with the showing of objects. Herbartians, modernizing a trend well established in monitorial practices, favored the "word" over the object as the key to learning and knowledge. Certainly merchants of learning had eventually to face the philosophic issues implicit in defining knowledge. Advocates of a nationwide social institution called universal public schooling had to formulate their objectives. Value questions inevitably came up in normal school programs. All these aspects of philosophic verbalization about education Gordy found in the program, for example, of the normal school at St. Cloud, Minnesota. Concluding with his own formulation of the purpose of the normal school, Gordy defended such verbalization in these terms:

> In stating the philosophy of method, the natural course is to start from the method and reason back step by step until the facts of consciousness are reached, upon which, in the last analysis, it is reached. In stating the

---

* Such injunctions as Froebel urged (thinking love), combined with the sentimental feelings for childhood raised by child study, probably did much to accelerate the development of journalistic talk in education.

† Which is not to admit that scholars and laymen talked about those questions in the same terms or even in terms that were readily translatable from the scholar's tongue to one which the layman could understand.

method of philosophy the natural course is to take the opposite direction, starting from the facts of consciousness, to reason step by step until we have found a firm basis for science and the activities of everyday life. Hence, inasmuch as the normal school exists for the purpose of making better teachers; inasmuch as it "is to train teachers in the art of knowing and expressing knowledge," in the art of being, it must, in order to work intelligently, be in possession of the science of knowledge. This fact constitutes it a technical school of university grade, and the highest in a possible series of schools in a system of education, since it assumes to inquire into the very grounds of all forms of knowledge, and must thus bring into review the purposes, processes, and results of all other schools. In a word, it is a school of philosophy.[6]

By just such assertions and counter assertions, the verbalization stage of normal school development flourished. By taking up questions of purpose, knowledge, and valuation on the technical level of philosophy and by pursuing *answers* on the common-sense level of cracker-barrel philosophizing,* all phases of curriculum, method, and administration acquired the heavy appearance of scholarship which gave little evidence of directly practical results. Theory, while remaining practice-centered, had become quite useless in the normal schools, and Butler, among others, lamented this.

Triumph of Rhetoric

Gordy's account of nineteenth-century normal school growth documented the dominance of "talk" over "show" during the period when the first teachers' colleges began to develop. His quotation from the charter of the New York College for the Training of Teachers at Albany, founded January 12, 1889, captured the emphasis placed on the verbal side of teacher preparation. He cited the following as evidence of the direction soon to be followed by the normal schools:

. . . that the elements of a secondary education are not to be taught at the proposed college, but are to be required of candidates for admission; that the object of the college will be to give instruction in the history, philosophy, and science of education, in psychology, in the science and art of teaching, and the methods of teaching the various subjects included under that head; that a school of practice and observation will be main-

---

[6] Gordy, 1891: 36.11.

* Architecture, for example, seems to be an area in which the most profound questions frequently arise yet architects seem to persist in the naïve belief that these questions can be answered in quite common-sense, even conversational, terms without an examination of how philosophers have dealt with those same matters. This affords them the luxury of not reading.

tained in connection with the college, and that a course of instruction and practice of not less than two years is to be organized, the completion of which to the satisfaction of the trustees and faculty of the said college may entitle the candidate to the degree of bachelor of pedagogy.[7]

Talk, or theory, had become so important that it received formal recognition in the degree of bachelor of pedagogy. The teachers' college, with this degree, became an intermediate step between normal school teacher training and programs of professional preparation in university departments of pedagogy. Educators felt that they had a discipline on hand that contained scholarly content.

The 1889 Albany charter, Gordy's book of 1891, and the several university departments of pedagogy begun by then all preceded the greatest flow of educational rhetoric that the nineteenth century produced. It issued in full force from the national organizations for the spreading of Herbartian rational science and for the popularization of child study.

Seeing the discipline of education as a rational science, the Herbartians pumped what they took to be logical deductions into the training program for secondary-school teachers which was then developing. Herbartian philosophic talk proved to be fraught with detailed guidance for the conduct of practice, once the rhetoric of conviction made the assumptions acceptable. Further advancing the disease, child study's rhetoric of emotional attachment for children gave elementary-school teacher preparation a journalistic pallor. Reminiscence, scraps of information, and human-interest stories were all brought together to help create the right attitude toward children.

From two sides the rhetoric of conviction converged on teacher training, leaving talk about elementary and secondary education doubly split. Object method emphasized the primacy of things, while Herbartianism advocated the supremacy of the "word" in literature and history. In addition, the Herbartians argued for a logical understanding of child behavior through theories like the culture-epoch or apperception. Child study advanced the belief that an appreciation of children must be felt before it can be understood. To the detriment of education as a subject of study, both reduced scholarly and practical talk to a journalistic common denominator.*

In the presence of controversy, rhetoric triumphed; and by 1900, the rhetoric of normal school training was being accompanied by teacher-training programs in colleges and universities. Demonstration and practice

---

[7] Gordy, 1891: 36.9.

* It must be admitted, however, that as a plan for social action, this rhetoric had a practical effect. It did persuade teachers to attempt to implement certain general methods. Much of what is said in time of war, for example, is best forgotten when peace is achieved. So it is with teaching.

teaching, so strong at Oswego, failed to develop as they might have, since so-called "theory" carried the prestige of seeming academic and scholarly.

Search for Quality and Breadth—University Professional Training

Monitorial programs kept losing tutors faster than they could train good ones. Normal schools began to train teachers at a time when the rapid development of the public schools produced new openings at a frightening rate. Quantity preceded quality in teacher training before the Civil War. The post-Civil War object-method training program at Oswego held out for quality and got it. That famous normal school produced a good share of the leadership that, in manning the new normal schools, sought a balance between rapid preparation in the face of expanded western demand and the sense of quality, if not scholarship, that they had been trained to respect. By 1900 the insistence on higher quality of professional preparation had begun to gain noticeable power. Looking into that power struggle from the vantage point of 1932, Jessie M. Pangburn provided the following insight into the supply-demand problem in her book, *The Evolution of the American Teachers Colleges:*

> There was always a supply of teachers of a sort. The shortage was in the ranks of the professionally trained teacher. The number of persons untrained or partially trained, though legally certified and available for manning the schools, was more than sufficient to fill the positions, and the result was a "competition of the unprepared" which kept wages low and tended to retard educational progress.[8]

As the institutions of teacher preparation made consistent gains in the quality of talking and showing during the nineteenth century, the standard or ideal of professional training rose up to orbit around those programs at untouchable altitudes. Plotting the ideal of 1897, J. J. Findlay set the following goal for those involved in the training of teachers:

> I desire to indicate, not so much to specialists in pedagogy, as to teachers and administrators who are interested in training colleges, how large is the field of investigation which the study of education opens up. He who would serve the whole of it must be a psychologist and physiologist, and at the same time he must understand the problems of local and national politics. His acquaintance with the various branches of science and art must be thorough enough to enable him to philosophize upon their nature and their functions. And, in order to make his knowledge fruitful, he must have gained a practical experience of the life and ways of the child and of the school society.[9]

---

[8] Pangburn, 1932: 76.1.
[9] Findlay, 1897: 33.

Findlay invited the trainer of teachers to philosophize about almost everything in the name of education. Butler's complaint about normal schools being top-heavy with theory suggests that teachers in those schools accepted the invitation but failed to elevate their talk to the levels of either philosophy or pedagogy. Thus, the student preparing for a career in teaching suffered. Just how fully he suffered and was excluded from the very institution which might have given him some of the training he needed inspired Charles De Garmo to write a severe protest.

PROFESSIONAL HANDICAP

President of Swarthmore College, active founding member of the Herbart Society, student of philosophy and of education, De Garmo in 1892 outlined the serious gap between normal school training and university professional programs:

> No co-ordination of the normal school and the university in the training of teachers now exists. This condition of things is owing chiefly to two causes: first, because normal-school graduates are not admitted to the universities on their diplomas; and second, because the pedagogical work in the universities is not, as usually organized, distinctly different from that of good normal schools. With a total lack of credit on one side and a general lack of educational facility on the other, it is not strange that there should be such a complete disjunction of the two classes of institutions in the training of teachers. . . .

> The first idea that came in with the chairs of pedagogy seems to have been that the university should make up to the student in some degree his lack of normal-school training, so that the first work along these lines was elementary, and not unlike that given in normal schools. Such elementary treatises as Page, Quick, Fitch, Compayré, were freely used. The result has been that to many persons the term "pedagogy" has become synonymous with the contents of these books. So long as university work in pedagogy bears this character, it will contain nothing for the trained normal-school graduate. Furthermore, however strong the personal influence of the professor of pedagogy may be, he has small chance of imbuing men with the spirit of education, of developing in them the pedagogical consciousness in everything they do, so long as their instruction in content-studies like biology, physics, economics, history, is given by men whose standpoint is anything rather than pedagogical. Two changes, therefore, seem to be necessary before any real, desirable co-ordination of normal schools and universities in educational training can take place. First, the pedagogical work of universities must be radically changed; and second, normal-school graduates must be freely admitted to it on their diplomas. . . .

> Turning now to the normal-school graduates, we find them excluded from the university as a class, because they have not had the traditional college preparation in languages. After teaching a few years, they wake

up to find themselves confronted by a dead wall to further progress, on account of the elementary character of their training, and too old to begin the work that others are doing before the age of sixteen or eighteen. The result is that most of them stop growing, settle down into routine work, or drift off into other callings. Now, if educational departments such as have been indicated can be established, the star of hope once more rises for the normal-school graduate. His facile skill as a teacher, his initial enthusiasm acquired at the normal school, his maturity and his earnestness of purpose, far more than counterbalance any loss he may have suffered from a lack of drill in language. The education department, not being dependent upon linguistic training in its students, or responsible for its absence, may freely and with credit to itself admit normal school graduates to its undergraduate course upon equal terms with those who come to it from lower university classes.[10]

The gap between the minimum practical preparation of the normal schools and the stiff academic requirements for university entrance swallowed precisely those teachers who might approach the professional ideal suggested by Findlay. Further, the failure of university training programs to do more than repeat the elementary content of the normal schools meant that those who did jump the gap to gain university entrance were not receiving the kind of cultural upgrading that other areas of that institution could provide.* On the one hand, the universities resisted professional education programs; and, on the other, those which admitted them kept the content so impoverished as to pretend that they did not exist. This snobbishness toward the superiority of academic training over useful professional content stirred John Dewey to write the following appeal in 1901:

> It is no longer possible to hug complacently the ideal that the academic teacher is perforce devoted to high spiritual ideals, while the doctor, lawyer, and man of business are engaged in the mercenary pursuit of vulgar utilities. But we have hardly reconstructed our theory of the whole matter. Our conception of culture is still tainted with inheritance of the aristocratic seclusion of a leisure class—leisure meaning relief from participation in the work of a workaday world. Culture, to use the happy phrase of one of my colleagues,† has been prized largely as a means of "invidious distinction." If I were to venture into what might appear to you the metaphysical field, I think I could also show that the current idea of culture belongs to the pre-biological period—it is a survival of the

---

[10] De Garmo, 1892: 21.
* Of course, they could only hope to get into education departments in the first place. The liberal arts professors were busy holding up "high standards," such as two languages, so that they could later point to the low quality of liberal arts learning to be found among public school teachers.
† Dewey and Thorstein Veblen were both members of the University of Chicago staff in 1901.

time when mind was conceived as an independent entity living in an elegant isolation from its environment. . . . It is flat hostility to the ethics of modern life to suppose that there are two different aims of life located on different planes; that the few who are educated are to live on a plane of exclusive and isolated culture, while the many toil below on the level of practical endeavor directed at material commodity. The problem of our modern life is precisely to do away with all the barriers that keep up this division. If the university cannot accommodate itself to this movement, so much the worse for it. Nay, more; it is doomed to helpless failure unless it does more than accommodate itself; unless it becomes one of the chief agencies for bridging the gap, and bringing about an effective interaction of all callings in society.[11]

Outlining the case for professional training in general, Dewey protested against the same gap that De Garmo had identified eight years earlier. In line with Findlay's appeal for breadth in teacher training, De Garmo and Dewey insisted that professional educators be given the benefit of cultural learning as well. Each realized that the ideal of the professionally competent practitioner demanded a general as well as a special education. The specialist serving people needed an understanding of the concepts and forces inherent in the past, present, and future of the society he performed in as well as peak proficiency in his specialty. Further, De Garmo and Dewey quickly perceived that the only place such a combination of general and special education could be achieved was in the university.

DEWEY'S PLAN

Dewey had specific suggestions about how the university should go about realizing the ideal of a cultivated and competent teacher. Four years before his outburst against the invidious distinction separating academic and professional learning, he submitted a lengthy plan to William Rainey Harper, President of the University of Chicago. Embodying the essentials of a modern school of education, it amplified several portions of the program outlined for the New York College for the Training of Teachers. Written January 6, 1897, ahead of its time in conception, the proposal was committed unpublished to the archives of the University of Chicago. The plan suggested the following organization of teacher training:

The various lines of work which are naturally included within the scope of a University Department of Pedagogy may be reduced to a few main heads. We have

1. What may be termed for convenience, Educational Physics and

---

[11] Dewey, 1902: 25.

Physiology, dealing with the whole plant of educational work and the adaptation of that to the physical being and welfare of the pupils.

2. Educational Sociology which concerns itself with the organization and administration of the educational system, both in relation to other social conditions and institutions and in its own external mechanism and workings.

3. Educational Psychology which deals with all matters appertaining to the adaptation of the school resources and the subject matter of the curriculum to the child. Its problem is how, out of the plant and school system described above, to get the maximum of result from the standpoint of the individual pupil.

4. We have the subject matter of general pedagogy occupying itself with the theoretical considerations regarding the nature, ends and aims of educational work and the intellectual organization of curriculum and methods corresponding thereto.

5. Educational History dealing both with the systems which have actually obtained at various times and in various countries, and also with the development of the theory of education as such.[12]

The fourth main head, general pedagogy, received this additional notice:

This is the head which receives most attention, and in some cases, exclusive attention, in the existing status of Pedagogy in colleges. It deals with the philosophy of education as such and the question of educational aims and means.[13]

Sensitive to the preponderance of "talk" over "show" in his own plan, Dewey went on to explain the necessity for this:

In the above nothing has been said about work in the actual training of teachers as it is assumed that for the most part, at least at the outset, the whole stress must be thrown upon the cultural side rather than upon the professional.[14] *

The physics, physiology, psychology, sociology, and history of education which Dewey grouped around general pedagogy were the bars of a cage strong enough to restrain the most ferocious Abominable Snowman of

---

[12] Dewey, 1897: Appendix, pp. 319-322.
[13] Dewey, 1897: Appendix, p. 321.
[14] Dewey, 1897: Appendix, p. 322.
* The problem of upgrading the education of teachers had been at the bottom of normal school developments, and it remained foremost half a century later, in this plan by Dewey.

the "educationist" genus. Surrounded by the factual, descriptive content of educational physics, physiology, psychology, sociology, and history, the claims of professors of general pedagogy were checked on all sides by available knowledge. Held within the tight restraints of academic philosophy and serious critical reflection, such course work would be forced into the direction of scholarship. No longer could a methods teacher jump behind the shadows of rhetoric and speak with the hollow voice which made him seem to be everywhere at once.

Such talk about education as Dewey proposed would be a scholarly, respectable organization of available information for enlightenment and use. Careful reflection upon reliable experience and academic philosophy would be the catalysts by means of which a middleman-conceptualist could generate theoretical propositions for consideration by practitioners. This would be a scholarly, respectable kind of general pedagogy which would be continually refined by the feedback from practitioners who tried to implement the concepts.

The State of Teacher-Training Theory

In the last two decades of the nineteenth century and the first two decades of the twentieth, the great body of educational theory went under several aliases. Among them, *general pedagogy, philosophy of education, educational method,* and *principles of education* were the most frequent titles for such talk about teaching. Complaints about the excess of theory flourished. The infrequent plans to contain that talk within the limits of available information and to tame it with the whip of scholarly discipline often had no more effect than Dewey's neglected memo. Nevertheless, although the descriptive content Dewey assigned to his five main heads did not become universally popular, the titles of three of his divisions did. Those three popular aliases for general pedagogy were *educational philosophy, educational sociology,* and, in some respects, *educational psychology.*

CHAOS OF CONTENT—THE PRINCIPLES OF EDUCATION

In 1912 Ruediger severely criticized the fact that major universities with departments of education showed no agreement whatever concerning the meaning of courses in one way or another dealing with principles of education. To illustrate his point, in his *School Review Monographs* article he described abbreviated outlines of the course announcements and catalogue descriptions of 25 major institutions. The institutions he cited were Chicago, Cincinnati, Colorado, Columbia, Cornell, George Washington, Harvard, Illinois, Indiana, Iowa, Kansas, Leland Stanford Junior University, Minnesota, Missouri, Nebraska, New York, Ohio State, Peabody College, Pittsburgh, Texas, Virginia, Washington State, Wellesley, Wisconsin, and Yale.

Course titles from these institutions were most frequently "Principles of Education" and "Philosophy of Education"; but "Study of Education" and "Educational Sociology" also appeared. The descriptions of these courses included the following variety of subjects or approaches to education: general problems, history—in its biological, psychological, sociological, and vocational phases—ethics, methods, hygiene, child study, religious points of view, brain localization, nervous system, evolution of morals in the race and in the child, play, formal discipline, physical education, evolution, what knowledge is of most worth, appreciation, interest, habituation, problems of social welfare, sociology, psychology, and the basis for a scientific theory of education.

General pedagogical theory, clearly, had spread out to touch, but not scratch, the broadest reaches of human knowledge. In its effort to touch everything, it frequently penetrated nothing. Under different course titles and in different university departments of pedagogy, the talk in such professional programs duplicated the pattern of half a century's development in the normal schools. Butler complained about it in 1904 with reference to the normal schools. Ruediger documented the cancerous spread of the malady in university departments of education by 1911. Summarizing this condition and the evil consequences which resulted, Ruediger voiced the following familiar criticisms of teacher training and the state of educational theory:

> Restricting ourselves now to about one-half of the college courses in the principles of education, it appears to be true that all conceivable topics in educational theory are hopelessly intermingled in them. If the title, "Principles of Education," is meant to stand for some definite and coherent phase of educational theory, these outlines of courses certainly do not show it. Apparently this title is still used by many teachers of education as a blanket phrase. Save that the material is educational, no uniform principle of selection is apparent. It would be difficult to find any topic in educational theory that is not included in one or more of these outlines, and the topics of but few of the outlines correspond to any considerable degree. In this list there are apparently as many different courses in respect to content as there are persons giving them. This shows a greater primitiveness in the organization of educational theory, if not the content as well, than one would have reason to expect.

> The effect of this heterogeneous array of topics under the title "Principles or Philosophy of Education" (and other educational subjects and even the relation between subjects appear to be little, if any, better) has a number of harmful effects. It serves to disgust more students than many teachers of education realize. The average college student wants something definite; he rightly wants to cover a relatively distinct phase of

subject-matter in each study that he pursues, and when he finds himself in a subject that apparently possesses no limiting principles of selection and no logical sequence of topics, he is frankly disgusted.

Now when this student goes to another educational course he is likely to find many of the same topics again treated—*and treated in a primary way*—that he has had in the principles of education. This adds to his disgust, for it not only leaves him bewildered but it wastes his time. Allowing for all adequate correlations, it would no doubt still be well within the mark to say that from one-fourth to one-half of the student's time in teachers colleges and departments of education is wasted, and this all through lack of organization. This is undoubtedly the most regrettable result that follows the present chaotic state of educational theory.[15] *

Conceived expressly for the purpose of improving the intellectual content of a discipline of education for use, the educational theory presented in professional courses lacked even such prerequisite ingredients as organization. Internal content of courses in general pedagogical theory was disorganized, and such discontinuity prospered within programs of professional preparation in both university departments of education and normal schools. In short, the state of course offerings in principles of education (across the full range of major universities in the country) could only be described as chaotic, and there is no reason to suspect that the situation has changed.

Such a condition could not have been further from the organization which Dewey's plan suggested. Opinion dominated information, persuasion dictated to description, and journalistic rhetoric accounted for the bulk of educational theory. Talk, indeed, took precedence over show, but it was the talk of popular conversation and journalism instead of the talk of scholarship. Thus, the virtue of scope dissolved before the vices of disorganization and superficiality. For depth, theory depended upon the quality of experience and insight which the talker brought to the classroom rather than upon the product of serious academic reflection. The organization was personal rather than logical and, as a consequence, ephemeral and subjective rather than cumulative and objective.

Although it is a truism that all theory must be talk—in the broad sense of thought, it must be spoken or written communication—it is not nearly so self-evident that all thought, all speech, and all writing on education should be considered theory. The identification of educational

---

[15] Ruediger, 1912: 89.5.

* And until explicit standards of scholarship gain wide acceptance among professors of education, this situation will not be remedied. Lacking such standards and such scholars, some good can be done by insisting that the content of such courses be made public, at least within the ranks of university professors at large.

theory with all "non-show" aspects of teacher training and the identification of the study of education with the preparation of practitioners had brought the idea of education as intellectual discipline into academic, practical, and popular disgrace. From this it has never recovered despite achievements in factual research and despite the useful organization of psychological theory for instructional purposes.

THE BEGINNINGS OF ORDER—EDUCATIONAL PSYCHOLOGY

For his 1912 article in the *School Review Monographs,* Henmon sent an inquiry "out to some of the larger institutions in which educational psychology was offered." [16] Reporting on the diversity revealed by the almost unanimous returns, he concluded:

> The variation in content of the courses is very great. At least five types of introductory courses, called educational psychology, can be distinguished:
>
> 1. Principles of teaching based on psychology, in which psychological conceptions are applied to educational practice. Concrete and practical problems arising in school work are interpreted in the light of psychological principles.
>
> 2. Psychology of the various school subjects—an analysis of the mental processes involved in reading, writing, spelling, arithmetic, etc., with the practical applications to teaching.
>
> 3. Selected topics from genetic psychology and child-study, with a view to tracing in broad outline the normal mental development from childhood to manhood.
>
> 4. Selected topics from general psychology which are treated in greater detail than in the general courses with specific application to school practice. This course differs from the first type by the greater emphasis on psychological facts than on their application to the art of instruction.
>
> 5. Psychology of learning—an analysis of the various forms of learning and the factors conditioning the learning process.
>
> This classification is admittedly rough, but indicates that educational psychology obviously means rather different things in the different institutions.[17]

---

[16] Henmon, 1912: 43.2.
[17] Henmon, 1912: 43.3.

Rough as it might be, Henmon's classification indicated that the educational psychology courses of 1912 were marvelously uniform when compared with the chaos in Principles of Education courses that Ruediger exposed. Based on general psychology, equipped with the tools of empirical research and the skills of statistical computation, educational psychology could organize content for application in the classroom and check to see how it worked. Communicating through the more precise elements of the technical language of psychology, the talk in educational psychology courses had some claim to being called theory. Of all approaches to organizing content for use, educational psychology courses promised to contain the least conversation and the most objective information.

The stability of educational psychology as an area of professional training had come in part from an early emphasis on objective information and the skills for the gathering, as well as interpretation and reporting, of such data. Tracing "The Development of Tests and Measurements" in 1924, Sears pointed to Thorndike's place in the establishment of such scientific skills and understandings as a part of professional training in this way:

> In [1902–1903] a Teachers College, Columbia University bulletin announced a course by Professor Thorndike as follows:
>
>> "Education (or Psychology) 108—Practicum. The application of psychological and statistical methods to education. *The course will deal with* means of measurement of physical, mental, and moral qualities, including the abilities involved in the school subjects, and rates of progress in various functions: the treatment of averages; measurement of relationships; *etc.*"
>
> It is clear from this announcement that educational measurement, as we now understand it, had at that time become a definite possibility in the mind of Professor Thorndike. In view of the outcome of the work which he thus initiated it seems proper to refer to the year 1902, and to Teachers College, as the time and place of the formal launching of the present movement in educational tests and scales.[18]

Going on to chronicle the appearance of similar courses at Stanford in 1911-1912, the University of Chicago in 1912-1913, Minnesota in 1915-1916, and Indiana University in 1917-1918, he concluded with the following summary:

> According to a survey of catalogs for 233 institutions of higher learning (*Journal of Educational Research,* November, 1920) most of the state

---

[18] Sears, 1924: 96.3.

universities, half of the state normal schools, nearly half of the non-state universities, and a fair number of other types of schools offered courses in educational measurements in the summer of 1920. Educational measurement has thus become a standard course in most departments, schools, and colleges of education.[19]

Such courses in skills of measurement represented a standardized content and product, which other areas of professional training could not even approximate. With research distinguished from practitioner preparation, courses in test construction and statistical computation took on a specialized utility in the training of investigators. Talk about how to conduct practice gave way to concern for the investigations of practice. Research, in turn, promised to yield objective information about practice which could compete successfully against mere opinion or generalization from past personal experience. Under such circumstances, course work throughout educational psychology embodied the unity which a concentration on description could provide. The experiments with descriptive talk had been begun, and 40 years later it would emerge in the *Encyclopedia of Educational Research*.

Alerted to the importance of information in any improvement of talk about education, Henmon suggested a balance of opinion, description, and prediction in educational theory. Principles or philosophy of education would discipline opinion about the aim or ends of schooling. The sciences, especially those of the behavioral group, would describe actual conditions. And educational psychology would predict and verify the means or methods by which the aims could be most efficiently achieved.[20] If Henmon had had his way, all roads would have pointed toward scholarship.

As the school became a major and comprehensive social institution of public welfare, and as the sciences of human behavior began to look at people collectively, that had been said of educational psychology at the close of an era of intense concentration on the individual child began to apply to educational sociology.

FEELING, FACT, AND FICTION—EDUCATIONAL SOCIOLOGY

In describing the content of courses in the principles or philosophy of education from an examination of the 1911 catalogs of 26 major colleges and universities, Ruediger included the following item:

COLUMBIA, (Suzzallo) 1911. Educational Sociology. A systematic presentation of the relation of education to society, being a special applica-

---

[19] Sears, 1924: 96.4.
[20] Henmon, 1912: 43.5.

tion of modern sociological knowledge to the problems of social welfare as achieved through educational activities. The relation of social conditions to school aims, functions, values, organizations, curricula, and methods will be noted.[21]

Writing in that same year, for publication the next, Ruediger apparently knew his man. Failing to take Suzzallo's course title at face value, he correctly classified the content as philosophy of education. Writing in 1924 of the past quarter-century, William H. Kilpatrick confirmed Ruediger's classification in this statement:

> . . . there came in the first half of our period . . . a pronounced reaction against "metaphysics." One result of this was to lead Professor (now President) Henry Suzzallo in 1909 to propose, in effect, to abandon the name "Philosophy of Education" and substitute instead of that "Educational Sociology."[22]

During the first decade of the twentieth century, general pedagogy had been replaced by Principles of Education as a course title. "Principles" gave way to "philosophy." Educational Sociology was only the latest of a long line of title changes by means of which institutions attempted to escape briefly from the reputation of professional dogmatism. Yet the change in title did reflect a change in emphasis. Rational educational psychology had been a philosophy of the individual. The talk included in educational sociology was a rational philosophy of the group and of social welfare—social philosophy.

Although different in outlook, object method and Herbartian rational psychology had helped make nineteenth-century talk about education a reflection of beliefs about the individual. The moral man of Herbartian moral aims, the culture-epoch theory, the growing social science, and the political-economic climate were made over in the twentieth century. Talk about education became a reflection of ever-increasing concern over the role of the individual in a complex, industrial, urban society struggling to keep elections meaningful without crippling those holding major offices. The "moral man" gave way to the "good citizen."

The spirit of this change could not be escaped. In 1917 the Riverside Series of professional textbooks, edited by Elwood P. Cubberley of Stanford University, published W. R. Smith's book called *An Introduction to Educational Psychology*. Writing more like a lay minister than a scholar, Smith made the following appeal for a dogmatism and indoctrination in the name of social education:

---

[21] Ruediger, 1912: 89.4.
[22] Kilpatrick, 1924: 54.2.

Education must be emotionalized. Thus to the individual educational end must be added the social end. It is not enough for the individual to know what to do; he must want to do it. Motive must be developed no less than skill. This is inseparable from group training. . . . Moral education requires not only the development of correct ethical insight, but training into moral habits of action. Social education alone can result in proper social reactions. Social habits are as important as individual habits, and they can be acquired only in the social group.[23] *

Rhetoric and opinion, at best cracker-barrel social philosophy, delivered by men not professionally trained in philosophy, filled courses in principles of education, educational philosophy, and, after 1911, educational sociology.

The slow pace of development from dogmatism to description in educational psychology can be gauged from Smith's second book for the Riverside Series. Written 11 years later, in 1928, *Principles of Educational Sociology* offered the following comments on the status of the field in comparison with educational psychology:

This psychological bias is evident in all phases of life, but it is particularly strong in the field of education, where applied psychology has made its largest contribution and where sociology is still in the stage of theory rather than that of detailed analysis and experimentation.[24] †

In that same year, many of the suggestions for the organization of educational sociology gained expression at the meetings and in the yearbooks of the newly formed, and short-lived, National Society for the Study of Educational Sociology. One of the leading voices belonged to David Snedden. In the second yearbook of that society, published in 1928, he proposed a ten-step answer to the question, "What Is Educational Sociology?" The two steps which follow covered the core of his viewpoint:

　　A.　Sociology is the general science of (usually) human social groups, social relations and processes, social forces, and social functions and values. Some—perhaps much—of education and, above all, public education is designed to improve human relations, make human societies more efficient, raise the level of social valuations, strengthen individual

---

[23] Smith, 1917: 98.

* Contrast this plea with Dewey's examination of the use of information in choice-making, as set forth in *Theory of Valuation,* and you have some idea of the spread between scholarship and journalism within the bounds of professional acceptance and philosophy of education.

[24] Smith, 1928: 99.

† Those who remember what passed as theory in sociology before 1930 have little cause to be intolerant of the state of educational theory—as can be said in some measure of economics, political science, and clinical psychology.

men and women for their social functions, and, generally, enhance human welfare.

B. Educational sociology, then, is the assemblage of all the reliable knowledge (including techniques of increasing, ordering, and applying such knowledge) which can be derived from sociology (and its ancillary or member sciences) and which can be used in educational practice as well as in controlled advances in that field of work.[25]

Snedden's hopes for educational sociology used educational psychology as a model. Both should become descriptive, predictive, and experimental. Both could capitalize on the same courses, developing measurement and statistical skills for computation. Both should begin with an account of "what is," supplementing one another with individual and social points of view.

Yet, not all educational sociologists were content with describing "what is." In 1932, Willard Waller, associate professor of sociology, Pennsylvania State College, injected a fictional element into the field. In the preface to his popular book, *The Sociology of Teaching,* he described a new kind of educational sociology:

But if one is to show the school as it really is, it is not enough to be unprejudiced. It is necessary to achieve some sort of literary realism. I think of this work, therefore, as an adventure in realism. To be realistic, I believe, is simply to be concrete. To be concrete is to present materials in such a way that characters do not lose the qualities of persons, nor situations their intrinsic human reality. Realistic sociology must be concrete. In my own case, this preference for concreteness has led to a relative distrust of statistical method, which has seemed, for my purposes, of little utility. . . . The work is, in one sense, a systematic application of the concepts of sociology and social psychology to the social phenomena of school life. . . . The purpose of the book . . . is to give insight into concrete situations typical of the typical school. . . . Whatever seemed likely to give insight has been included, and all else, however worthwhile in other respects, has been excluded. *A certain amount of fictional material has been included.* This must be judged as fiction; it is good fiction, and it is relevant to our point, if it is based upon good insight. A number of atypical cases have been included because of the illustrative value of such material.[26] *

---

[25] Snedden, 1929: 101.

[26] Waller, 1932: 106.

* This novelist's conception of fictional verisimilitude often leads to the conclusion that art is a better reflection of "reality" than limited scientific descriptions could ever be; thus, the literary explanation serves in place of literal description. Literary accounts have a tendency to be "heroic," bigger than life, it seems, and to suggest that the "ideal" is just around the corner.

Supplanting fact with feeling, Waller sought a "true" educational sociology, superior to the limited findings of science. This would be a description of the way things "really are."

Theory as Talk

Each new area of special educational content had two major battles to fight—the one for distance, the other for order. As an intellectual discipline, the specialty needed distance or detachment from the demands of immediate usefulness in practical application. In the early stages of development, the premature demands for application forced opinion to masquerade as fact in the clothing of technical terms borrowed from other better-established areas of inquiry. Misappropriated without the conceptual content and the specific limitations imposed in the parent discipline, such talk about education could only mask ordinary ideas displaying themselves as theory. Such journalistic talk invaded education as a subject of study like an unfilterable virus—almost unnoticed.

Liberation from the demands of immediate application would enable factual research to continue with the task of developing a language capable of describing practice in objective terms. Now it seems likely that such data-gathering was more pre-scientific experimentation in ways of talking about measurement than a direct contribution to the objective description of public education as a major social institution. Such full-time attention to the development of knowledge-for-its-own-sake helped advance the scholarship capable of improving techniques of reporting. The development of technical concepts and precise terminology should have evolved from the careful filtering of a vast quantity of reporting as well as by conscious design. Once given a language effective in describing practice objectively, the task of careful research foreseen by Thorndike could begin systematically. In this way, it seemed, education would become a respectable scholarly discipline and possibly one of the behavioral sciences.

As professional training, talk about education needed two kinds of order to become more useful. One involved the internal order of content; the other called for external stability in the content assigned to such categories as principles of education and educational psychology from institution to institution.* Ruediger had clearly demonstrated the correctness of the widespread belief that talk about principles of education bore a relationship in name only from university to university. *Principles of education, educational philosophy,* and *general pedagogy* were used as

---

* Although these are not yet accomplished and still needed, there may be some comfort in the fact that no standardization in requirements for drivers' licenses has yet been achieved from state to state.

synonyms, not because they stood for any common body of content, but because each was sufficiently broad to include anything. Theory in professional training had no concrete referent beyond the fact that it was talk, not show. Theory meant talk, and talk meant theory, in university departments of education as well as normal schools and teachers' colleges. Such a state of affairs probably contributed considerably to the dismay which Pangburn expressed in 1932 in the following way:

> Differences in quantity and organization of the constituent elements in the curricula of the several schools (normal, college departments of education, and University departments of pedagogy), and the operation of the elective principle have combined to yield a national system of teacher training which is bewildering in its complexity.[27] *

The internal organization of content within professionalized disciplines exhibited similar complexity and disarray. Educational sociology compressed the cycle of growth undergone by educational psychology. Beginning as a combination of social philosophy of American life and general pedagogy of group instruction, it mixed speculation with methodology for the practical purpose of making instruction more sociable. Scholarship of sorts pressed "principles of sociology" into educational services to justify the classroom practices which were to be deduced from them.

Meanwhile, back at the ranch (in the state colleges and universities), efforts were being made to replace speculation and methodology of group instruction with sociological information of a carefully descriptive nature on the one hand, and to supplement it with the literary "realism" of Waller's social science-fiction on the other. Educational psychology had moved toward a descriptive stage as a professional area embodying considerable objective content derived from the parent discipline. By 1928 educational sociology was attempting to follow that same path toward becoming a linking science based on an objective science such as Dewey had suggested in 1901.

The vocabulary, grammar, and substance of talk about education boiled as the speculation and methodology of rationalism, devised as a dialectic, ran headlong into the factualism of the measurement and the survey movements (which were, it seems to me, an experiment in scholarly ways of talking about classroom conditions and practices). Describing the results of that running battle, from the time that object method, Herbartianism, and child study began it, to the point where Dewey was about to begin another major engagement over the sources of a science of education, Cubberley wrote as follows in 1925:

---

[27] Pangburn, 1932: 76.2.
* No more so than undergraduate education from university to university, however.

The philosophy of the educational process, as we have it in its best expression today, has been a matter of evolution, and the change is as yet by no means complete. During the past half-century the changes have been so rapid that almost every decade has seen the evolution of a new point of view. In consequence there are many teachers in our schools to-day whose work is guided by an outworn educational philosophy. Still more, one finds here and there both entire school systems and teacher-training institutions which are being conducted in accordance with a working philosophy which has been outgrown and discarded by progressive workers elsewhere.[28]

Philosophic talk, presented as teacher-training course work, balanced delicately on changing points of view. With equal tenuousness, these hung on the reports of measurement and survey findings, soon to be confounded by equally authentic reports made from new and unanticipated points of view. The absence of leading concepts to be tested throughout many investigations left individual reports with little intellectual significance. Highly suggestive studies, such as those concerning self-selection of food in children's diets, encouraged broad speculation that set forth *laissez faire* as a principle of curriculum construction. Gathered with no criteria for separating relevant observations from irrelevant ones, the reports approached the validity of a tourist's impressions on the day he ventured forth without a guide. In the absence of landmarks to indicate the places from which the observer looked from one occasion to another, the reports could not be easily correlated with one another. Under such a handicap, organization of facts for use in teacher training required the user to supply the ideational content and the significance to be attached to each finding or some collection of them. Organization for use often became personally ordered obsolescence, and the countless experiments in ways of looking at practice and of talking about observing youngsters implicit in those seemingly contradictory reports went unrecognized.

Educational psychology, educational sociology, and educational philosophy developed at different rates; and, within each, various stages could be found, depending on who had organized it. By 1925 educational psychology had achieved the greatest amount of order and unity as both a linking science or practice-centered discipline for teacher training and as a scholarly research discipline which tested theories about how well children learn under certain controlled conditions. In this situation, the educational sociologists struggled to follow their psychologist colleagues in minimizing both speculation and immediate practical concern for methodology of instruction. As inheritor of the estate of general pedagogy, educational philosophy continued to include journalistic talk that had risen to

---

[28] Cubberley, 1925: 18.

the level of good essay writing. Often its scholarship was a kind of research into the academic support for journalistic ideas. Within courses and among universities, the organization of these quasi-practical, quasi-research disciplines remained quite personal. In speculating about life and instruction, educational philosophy became involved in practice-centered talk of questionable utility. In attempting, for example, to translate the reported findings of unguided observers into a linking science for un-informed practitioners, educational philosophy talked in terms of ques-tionable scholarship. It was just such scholarly deficiencies which prompted George Axtelle, professor of educational philosophy at New York Univer-sity, to write the following comment in the Spring, 1956, issue of the *Harvard Educational Review:* ". . . professors of education are themselves commonly illiterate philosophically, and command little more than the gross oversimplifications they communicate to their students." [29]

Meanwhile educational sociology and educational psychology as-sumed that the factualism of the measurement-survey movements had provided objective, though severely limited, descriptions of practice. Trans-lating these works of unassessed worth into principles to be communicated to practitioners seemed to be the next legitimate step in working toward the science of education which seemed just around the corner. The disputes which arose over which facts should be used and which should be ignored forced the educational course work into the philosophic dispute as to which ways of describing practice were to be considered objective observations. In such disputes, the inadequacy of the descriptive language came out accidentally, and the triumph of one kind of description over another proceeded without system. The dispute remained on the level of which facts were to be accepted rather than penetrating to the basic question of what constitutes a language of objective description.

Building the world views of realism, idealism, and instrumentalism through speculation about the nature of reality, educational philosophy turned away from the job of helping the descriptive side of educational sociology and educational psychology evolve an effective language for talking about what "is." Controversy over which speculative scheme was best for teachers to believe in obscured the problem of how little was known about the social institution in which they would practice. Finding how Plato and Aristotle could be made to support the conclusions of coffee-cup philosophy * became the "scholarship" of the practice-centered talk. Everyone became a "philosopher." Courses in methods, curriculum, and administration all had to have "a basis in philosophy." Administration became "democratic." Democracy had to be discussed in terms of freedom,

---

[29] Axtelle, 1956: 3.

* As Professor D. Bob Gowin of Cornell so aptly put it: "onecupmanship."

and this led to the questions of free will, determinism, and so forth. That such speculation short-cut the task of description too frequently escaped notice. Had the sheer demand for teachers been less, the problems of research and a definition of scholarship might have taken precedence over teacher training.

Educational social science was evolving a descriptive language by trial and error while entertaining the belief that it was placing the mortar of theory on the factual bricks of empirical science. Educational philosophy spent much energy trying to turn the brass of journalistic speculation into platinum-plated scholarship. Talk about curriculum, administration, and methodology remained randomly eclectic and unaware that the unorganized combination of factualism, speculation, and personal opinion was not educational science. Into this growing chaos stepped John Dewey, determined to set things right by clarifying the meaning of education as a science with a 1929 version of his 1901 distinction between objective, translative, and subjective science.

The most striking single movement in education of the present decade has been the development of more scientific tests and measurements. At first this brought few problems to the philosophy of education, but more recently two lines of questioning have been raised. The published results of the application of the Army Intelligence Tests to upwards of a million men during the World War have been interpreted by some to call in question the possibility of running society on a democratic basis. . . . As democracy is a perpetual experiment, it would be as unfortunate for anything to lessen interest in equality of opportunity for development as to lower faith in warranted endeavor. That theories of society and programs of action must of course square with the facts no true modern will deny. The philosophy of education must and will take its facts from whatever source they come, but it will insist first that reported facts be real facts and second that no narrow or hasty interpretation of the facts shall determine action. For the time, at any rate, we face in this a serious problem.

The other difficulty raised by tests and measurements is more technical. As was inevitable, the measuring of achievement began with the matters that lent themselves best to measuring, which so far has generally meant the more mechanical of educational outcomes. As was further inevitable, these measures have been put to work in the service of accepted theories as to the educative process. The results along both lines have been in many places to hamper a broader and more human type of educative procedure which had begun to grow up in answer to other lines of development. . . . We find in them a conflict be-

10

Belief As
a Discipline

tween two aspects of education, that having to do with the aims and values and that having to do with means and achievement. Such a conflict according to our conception comes before the philosophy of education.[1]

The talk that passed for theory in teacher training made university departments of pedagogy, teachers' colleges, and normal schools the last secular academic roosts of the nineteenth-century man who philosophized on all of humanity, society, and life. Even while confidence in the findings of the measurements and survey movements continued to rise, teacher training maintained more intimate contact with the general pedagogy of the past century than with the behavioral sciences of the present one. Paul Monroe's *Cyclopedia* had made the concepts of rationalism available in authoritative form. But the factualism of contemporary research did little more than inject some information and foster the wholesale absorption of psychological and sociological terminology into course work and professional publication.

Recast in the vocabulary of psychology and sociology, talk of general pedagogy had been prepared for the conversational philosophizing occasioned by World War I (Is the world safe for Democracy?), the Russian Revolution (What is the role of the common man?), and the 1929 stock market crash (Has capitalism failed?). Over that same decade, the welfare function of the public schools in the United States expanded enormously. Job preparation during a depression, minimal nutrition through school lunches, programs for the handicapped and low-ability youngsters, all received attention in the schools. Concurrently the institution of public schooling itself grew so large as to defy objective description with the limited resources being devoted to the task. Growing on a foundation of local control, the differences among schools increased at the same time that the differences among regions and between rural and urban groups decreased.

By 1930 the issue had become whether education as a research discipline and as talk for professional training would emulate either the tortoise, by attempting the careful observation and description of existent conditions, or the hare, by building speculative utopias of how things should be. It was so difficult to be literal and extensive in inquiry that the temptation to be literary and comprehensive held great appeal.

For education to grow as a discipline, the jargon created out of the technical terms misused in coffee-cup conversation would have to give way to precise, reliable, descriptive terms which could be used with a minimum of ambiguity and vagueness by a majority of scholars in the reporting of observation as well as in the communication of ideas. Such tools of de-

---

[1] Kilpatrick, 1924: 54.1.

scription would permit education to focus on the examination of its present condition as the proper function of both research and training. The sentimental wish for a better world expressed in the vague abstractions of the "intellectual" would have to be transformed into patience with limited information and diligence in the dismissal of overgeneralization. Talk about education had been intellectualized but it had not become scholarly. Those responsible for teacher training seem not to have realized that there was a difference.

In the long run, the romance of the panoramic vision of future social possibilities won out over the realism of a detailed description of present performance. Replacing the general pedagogy of the nineteenth century, educational philosophy followed the appeal to prescribe what ought to be rather than describing what is. Somehow it seemed enough to condemn existing conditions—a frequent practice in journalism. A description of what "is" must be concrete and limited to what investigators have had time to observe, but a prescription of what ought to be is limited only by the powers of imagination, so long as it is not hampered by a sufficiently detailed knowledge of existing conditions to encourage the speaker to frame his thought in terms of what seems possible. Dealing in unfettered abstraction, the philosophy of education reached out to touch almost everything in its efforts to keep up with the expanded social consciousness developed after 1920. But the only language capable of making quick crossings over the vast reaches of intellectual space covered by such theories of education was the journalistic talk of conversational philosophy. Just how far such talk would have to stretch without breaking, Chapman and Counts delineated in their book of 1924, *Principles of Education*. Naming the four corners of the intellectual universe that needed charting, they wrote:

> There is particular need today for varied formulation of a philosophy of education—formulations which, in the light of educational and psychological research, take into account the development of science, the revolution of industry, the rise of democracy, and the integration of the peoples of the world.[2]

Description or Justification in a Discipline

As the rising tide of the measurement movement crossed the descending wave of Herbartian rational science about 1912, confidence in the power of and the possibilities for an empirical science of education soared. By 1925, as the measurement movement reached the crest of its rapid

---

[2] Chapman and Counts, 1924: 13.

growth and struggled to maintain a plateau, authors such as Kilpatrick, Chapman, and Counts had begun to revive interest in the rationalistic side of education as a discipline.

The success of research and confidence in an empirical discipline of education had promoted an overconfidence which Francis E. Peterson summarized in his *Philosophies of Education Current in the Preparation of Teachers in the United States.* Looking back from 1933 across that period of self-satisfaction, he wrote:

> Science became a watchword in education; there was talk of a science of education; and the scientific method was enthusiastically heralded as a veritable panacea of our many educational ills. Increasingly, it came to be regarded as a method which was applicable no matter what the nature of the problem, and capable, in well-nigh every case, of furnishing a solution.[3]

But such intellectual boosterism soon began to sound hollow and then arrogant. Originally, the rapid growth of factual information had suggested that education would become first a descriptive science, then a predictive one, and finally a comprehensive discipline. As a descriptive science, it would contain careful and complete descriptions of all aspects of present practice. From description, the prediction of effective and efficient teaching methods would be possible. Finally, matured by validated predictions, the discipline of education would develop suffusing causal theories.

After 1925, however, it became apparent that most workers underestimated the difficulty of comprehensive description. Impatient with the available factual information, disappointed by the absence of suffusing hypotheses controlling investigation, needing some comprehensive theory on which to base professional training, educators began to look favorably on the rational processes of a philosophy of education. In addition, confidence in the growing factual reservoir had led to pressure to have the aims of education at least stated in measurable terms and, most profitably, in terms presently measurable if not already measured. The equal and opposite pressure was to speak about aims in qualitative (as opposed to quantitative) terms. Creativity and freedom were such qualities.

By 1925 the revolution in education as a research discipline had been matched by an older revolution in practice. With an appeal for the handling of things in an atmosphere of affection, the object method had opposed the routinized drill, memorization, and obedience of monitorial training. Opposing the formality of Herbartian concentration on the moral lessons of history and literature, child study urged an attitude that would accept wider ranges of behavior in an effort to evoke creative activity

---

[3] Peterson, 1933: 84.1.

and emotional expression. This more humane approach to teaching had by 1925 made some inroads on practice in the name of progressive education, but it remained an infant area of professional training.

An empirical discipline of education had hopes of minimizing the a priori assumptions and generalizations from past experience on which Herbartian rationale had constructed deductions which directed practice. But as a discipline of empirical research, educational theory would have to follow the collection of observable information and not wander off into philosophic talk about the coming social order and what ought to be. Talk of democratic classrooms, creative expression, and improved social attitudes offered little, indeed, that was observable for quantitative measurement in the first place, and it spoke of these goals as products to be realized in the future from a new kind of practice. The question of what kind of discipline of education to encourage depended on whether the primary purpose was to be a philosophic *justification* of a particular new and untried approach to the conduct of practice, or a *description* of the observable elements of practice. Description would demand logical organization of content and the primary development of subject-matter content into a discipline of education. Justification of practice would breed reasoning capable of persuading practitioners to use certain practices and to aim for a certain set of goals. It would be moralistic rather than descriptive, and, since the justification of practice implied conviction on the part of the practitioner, there would be a temptation to employ journalistic talk to get it. But even when supported by scholarship, justification, belief, and persuasion fall more to the lot of philosophy than to that of science.

At the same time that the measurement movement began to lose headway as a basis for building a discipline of education, many faculty members of Teachers College, Columbia University, had taken up the leadership of the case for philosophic theory. Chronicling the unity of viewpoint among that philosophy-struck cast of professional educators, Peterson presented the thoughts of Counts, Lepley, and Raup in the following mixture of commentary and quotation:

> We do not discredit science, but merely point out that the scientific method has been carried to extreme and unwarranted lengths, quite beyond the legitimate scope of science as such. Of recent years a reaction has set in; and it is this opposition—not to science, be it said, but to what are considered the excessive claims made for the scientific method, in education as well as in other fields—that has become the real point at issue in the controversy represented by this category: Counts has said on this point:
>
> ". . . Many prominent educators seem even to believe that there is no educational problem which is incapable of objective solution. They contend, moreover, that insistence on the employment of any other method

is to waste time and obscure thinking. . . . They consequently demand facts, and yet more facts; . . . They, however, never define very clearly just what they mean by facts, and how facts are to be distinguished from ideas. Because of this distrust of speculation there are great university departments of education in the United States in which no general course in educational philosophy or the general theory of education are offered. The Americans thus hope to make Education an exact science and remove its problem from the realm of dispute.

"This complete absorption in educational science, however, is beginning to relax. Many able students of the question . . . argue that, while facts are absolutely essential to the solution of an educational problem, the same facts with different sets of values lead to different solutions. In other words, they maintain that the facts must be brought into harmony with some theory of what is good and beautiful, and must be definitely related to some particular order of society."

It is herein held that there is no inherent conflict between science and philosophy. . . . Lepley set forth the similarities and differences between the two methods, with a division-of-labor relationship referred to above when he said:

". . . Philosophy is thus concerned more exclusively with a criticism, theoretical constructions, interpretation, and suggestion. . . ."

It is not an outright objection to science which is the crux of this category. Essentially, it is an emphasis upon the need of recognizing certain limitations of the scientific method, and there are large areas in the realm of human phenomena in which objective procedures are not applicable. . . .

Raup stresses the importance of developing further what he terms "the wider range of thought." Raup said:

". . . We have been trying to crowd the whole of vital human thought through the cold and cramped channels of the method of exact science. . . . We are coming to realize that human thought eventually forges out its beliefs and decisions, not in the coolers of exact science, but in the crucible of vital, interacting human desires and preferences."[4] *

---

[4] Peterson, 1933: 84.2.

* With the possible exceptions of confidence in the miraculous powers of Santa Claus and the Easter Bunny, adults continue to believe more in line with what they want (immortality, help, summary solutions) than with what daily and scientific experience leads them to expect. Dewey continued to believe that this state of affairs could be changed and that people could be taught to bring their wants in line with their knowledge.

Science in a Discipline of Education

Quite contrary to Raup, Counts, Kilpatrick, and Lepley, the philosophers of a science of education who wrote for the *School Review Monographs* of 1911 and 1912 had foreseen a different future. Monroe, Thorndike, Ruediger, Henmon, and Parker helped distinguish between the findings of observational and experimental research as opposed to the a priori assumptions and generalizations from past experience organized to provide rational support for successful or preferred practice. The older rational philosophy or science had been displaced by the new empiricism. In Monroe's *Cyclopedia* of those same years, John Dewey spoke of two kinds of experimentation native to that new science that held out hope for an improved discipline of education: (1) "that conducted for practical, and (2) that conducted for scientific purposes." [5]

Dewey welded those two approaches to experimentation into a new approach to the idea of a discipline of education in his 1929 book *The Sources of a Science of Education*. This book offered considerable guidance to Teachers College faculty members and helped strategically to shape the idea of the foundations approach to a professional discipline of education.

Before writing his 1929 book, however, Dewey wrote an article in 1928 which amplified his idea of the practical nature of educational research and the philosophic nature of the intellectual content of a discipline of education. The article, "Progressive Education and the Science of Education," supplements the book; and together they provide the basic rationale for replacing the idea of an empirical science of education with the concept of foundational fields.

ENCOURAGING THE AMATEUR RESEARCHER

By 1928 the spread of progressive practices had been well facilitated by the journals, professional organizations, some normal school, college, and university training programs, and general occupational gossip. It was just such a state of affairs which prompted Dewey to ask the following rhetorical questions in his 1928 article:

Can we be content if from the various progressive* schools there

---

[5] Dewey, 1911: 26.
* In such contexts as these the term "progressive" had a practice-centered utility, referring to programs with the characteristics Dewey sets forth. Both the advocates and the critics of such practices hastened the decline of the term by neglecting to specify the practices associated with it. Today it is a journalistic word entirely.

emanate suggestions which radiate to other schools to enliven and vital-
ize their work; or should we demand that out of the cooperative under-
takings of the various schools a coherent body of educational principles
shall gradually emerge as a distinctive contribution to the theory of
education?[6]

Affirming the desirability of a distinctive contribution to the theory of
education, Dewey calculated that the starting point of that contribution
lay in the generalities which all programs of progressive practice had in
common. He catalogued those common elements of practice in this
manner:

> All of the [progressive] schools . . . exhibit as compared with traditional
> schools, a common emphasis upon respect for individuality and for in-
> creased freedom;* a common disposition to build upon the nature and
> experience of the boys and girls that come to them, instead of imposing
> from without external subject matter and standards.† They all display
> a certain atmosphere of informality, because experience has proved that
> formalization is hostile to genuine mental activity and to sincere emo-
> tional expression and growth.‡ Emphasis upon activity as distinct from
> passivity is one of the common factors.** And again, I assume that there
> is in all of these schools a common unusual attention to the human fac-
> tors, to normal social relations, to communication and intercourse which
> is like in kind to that which is found in the great world beyond the school
> doors;†† that all alike believe that these normal human contacts of child
> with child and of child with teacher are of supreme educational im-
> portance, and that all alike disbelieve in those artificial personal relations
> which have been the chief factor in isolation of schools from life. So
> much at least of common spirit and purpose we may assume to exist. And
> in so far, we already have the elements of a distinctive contribution to
> the body of educational theory: respect for individual capacities, inter-
> ests and experience; enough external freedom and informality at least to
> enable teachers to become acquainted with children as they really are;
> respect for self-initiated and self-conducted learning; respect for activity
> as the stimulus and centre of learning; and perhaps above all, belief in
> social contact, communication, and cooperation upon a normal human
> plane as all-enveloping medium.[7]

---

[6] Dewey, 1928: 27.1.
* Elbow room, not anarchy, remember.
† Recall how hard object-teaching had to fight against monitorial method for
this.
‡ Herbartian (Prussian) formalism was the target here.
** Studies in the attention span of children and child-study observation had
confirmed Pestalozzi's "rule": activity is a law of childhood.
†† Class lessons, equalitarianism, and American distaste for aristocratic pre-
tensions add up to a concern for what could loosely be termed a democratic
classroom atmosphere.
[7] Dewey, 1928: 27.2.

Recognizing that such qualities do not lend themselves easily to quantitative measurement in the manner of achievement testing, Dewey affirmed his belief that, in the long run, the careful observation of qualities had more to offer. He made his case for such a clinical science of education in the following way:

. . . quality of activity and of consequence is more important for the teacher than any quantitative element. If this fact prevents the development of a certain kind of science it may be unfortunate. But the educator cannot sit down and wait till there are methods by which quality may be reduced to quantity; he must operate here and now. If he can organize his qualitative processes and results into some connected intellectual form, he is really advancing scientific method much more than if, ignoring what is actually most important, he devotes his energies to such unimportant by-products as may now be measured.[8] *

Anticipating objections, he further stated:

Whether this be called science or philosophy of education, I for one, care little. . . .[9]

Dewey was concerned with the careful collection of clinical observations on the qualitative factors of classroom practice in public schools. He expressed his recognition of the difficulty and the value of such a body of content when he wrote:

A series of constantly multiplying careful reports on conditions which experience has shown in actual cases to be favorable and unfavorable to learning would revolutionize the whole subject of method.† This problem is complex and difficult. Learning involves, as just said, at least three factors: knowledge, skill and character. Each of these must be studied. It requires judgment and art to select from the total circumstances of a case just what elements are the causal conditions of learning, which are influential, and which are secondary or irrelevant. It requires candor and

---

[8] Dewey, 1928: 27.3.
* The parallel would be that if poets had waited to have their feelings confirmed there would be no poetry. Teachers had to get on with improving the art of teaching. The account of one good classroom artist, he might have reasoned, was worth more than all Rice's data on something so inconsequential, though measurable, as spelling. But because parents so seldom take note of how much youngsters may learn by going to school, inability to spell is taken as evidence of widespread neglect that still goes unnoticed. They remain unconvinced that monitorial drill in spelling failed in its day. Possibly, moralists that we are, it isn't the spelling but the drill we care about, preferring to believe that a return to the technique of drill will bring back the good old days before juvenile delinquency.
[9] Dewey, 1928: 27.4.
† Such reports still would revolutionize methods if methods teachers could be made to heed them.

sincerity to keep track of failures as well as successes and to estimate the relative degree of success obtained. It requires trained and acute observation to note the indications of progress in learning, and even more to detect their causes*—a much more highly skilled kind of observation than is needed to note the results of mechanically applied tests. Yet the progress of a science of education depends upon the systematic accumulation of just this sort of material. Solution of the problem of discovering the causes of learning is an endless process. But no advance will be made in the solution till a start is made, and the freer and more experimental character of progressive schools places the responsibility for making the start squarely upon them.[10] †

Teachers in the progressive schools must, in addition to their instructional duties, keep a careful and objective mental anecdotal record of all classroom activity. From that record of what activities lead to what results, this teacher should be able to infer the principles in operation and suggest the causes of learning. The work of many such teachers would yield a clinical discipline of education in which the intellectual content would provide reliable information about how to best achieve the qualitative goals of progressive education. Such a discipline might be called educational method, or principles of education, or educational theory, or philosophy of education, or a science of education. Whatever it might be called, it would provide generalizations from successful practical experience. In fact, it would be general pedagogy developed collectively rather than as the opinion of one man or a string of historical authorities. And the terminological reform for such cooperation suggested by Snedden in 1905 has not yet been accomplished.

In Dewey's plan for a clinical discipline of education, the professional practitioner committed fully to the instructional process must have a split vision in order to see it objectively with the third eye of the mind. The practitioner who chose this way to teach because he believed in the qualitative goals that it should achieve would be expected to give a somewhat unbiased report as to his own professional competence and success and the degree to which the approach of his choice had been successful. Committed to making his program work, he must be critical of its limitations and not overimpressed by its success. Objectivity in such a circumstance is like objectivity in an automobile accident. The more serious the accident, the less chance one has of getting accurate data: often the drivers can't give an objective view because the limitations of their perspective, guilt, and fear prohibit it. Even an innocent bystander cannot be heavily relied upon. In such a clinical discipline there would be no innocent

---

* It requires time and fewer than 150 students a day in English classes.
[10] Dewey, 1928: 27.5.
† Action research.

bystanders; the professional teacher would be an amateur researcher and the classroom a quasi-laboratory situation.

This clinical discipline of education would, however, include research conducted for practical purposes. Although Dewey cared little whether it was called method, principles, theory, science, or philosophy, this 1928 approach to intellectual content amplified the "practical experimentation" he described in his 1912 article in Monroe's *Cyclopedia*. As amateur inquiry conducted for practical purposes, it would achieve two major results: (1) the principles and theory would be induced from this careful child-study-like observation of behavior, and (2) it would be reported and interpreted by a sympathetic professional practitioner.*

Coming from practice, such theory would not be separated from actual classroom instruction. Rather, it would be in part a description and in part a generalization of practice. Made by a sympathetic teacher trying to be as objective as possible, the theory, as well as the practice, would be guided by the same suffusing practical goal. As classroom instruction would be designed to bring about social change, so would such educational theory be designed with the idea of achieving social ends as a basic assumption. Midway through the article, Dewey stated the practical goal of both instruction and theory when he wrote:

> If you want schools to perpetuate the present order, with at most an elimination of waste and with such additions as enable it to do better what it is already doing, then one type of intellectual method or "science" is indicated. But if one conceives that a social order different in quality and direction from the present is desirable and that schools should strive to educate with social change in view by producing individuals not complacent about what already exists, and equipped with desires and abilities to assist in transforming it, quite a different method and content is indicated for educational science.[11]

Classroom practice would be directly geared to transforming society. Generalizations from practice would yield a clinical discipline of education capable of providing an intellectual understanding of how to transform society. Such a clinical discipline of education would be like a discipline of psychiatry. Teachers acting as clinical psychiatrists of classroom activity would develop generalizations about how they changed human behavior, and these generalizations could be built into an intellectual understanding of practice. In a similar manner, practicing faith healers could produce a clinical discipline of "medicine"—quite practical and possibly not scientific. Even so, however, a practical clinical discipline of education, such as

---

* It would be grass-roots theory, inductive in a sense, and in source the opposite of the "foundations of education" approach to theory taken at Columbia.
[11] Dewey, 1928: 27.4.

Dewey appealed for, would have been a substantial improvement over much of the professional training of 1928. This clinical approach to developing practice-centered talk has had its greatest success in providing the intellectual content of curriculum, administration, and methods texts and courses.

DISCOURAGING THE PROFESSIONAL RESEARCHER

Technical talk about a science of education had passed through an important transition by 1929. The idea of a science of education achieved prominence as a unified discipline when, before 1900, the Herbartians parlayed systematic order into claims for a complete rational science. A decade later, Thorndike pointed up the Herculean but necessary task of description which had to be undertaken as a first step toward the kind of science that Huxley had foreseen for sociology.

In 1912 Parker used the studies of Courtis in arithmetic to show that mature empirical science had arrived in some parts of the study of education. By the time of World War I, Judd could see independent disciplines of education corresponding to the various scientific specialties required for extensive inquiry into the various sectors of the social institution of schooling. And by 1928 efforts were being made by men like Snedden to see that educational sociology would follow its sister specialty, educational psychology, in the direction of becoming a descriptive-predictive discipline having research reciprocity with the parent science.

Technical talk about a science of education had evolved to the point of considering the scientific aspects of the various educational specialties. Non-technical talk had remained static in its confidence in a unified discipline and merely transferred allegiance from Herbartian rational science to Huxlean empirical science. Much of what Dewey had to say in his 1928 article was non-technical talk about a science of education. Such a clinical discipline of education built up by professional teachers, but amateur researchers, could still be more carefully worked out than most of what passed as educational theory. Then such improved talk could be called *theory, principles, method, philosophy,* or *science of education.* In his 1929 book, however, Dewey concerned himself with technical talk about a science of education, or, more precisely, with the place of established sciences in the study of education.

In *The Sources of a Science of Education,* Dewey asked two questions: (1) *Is* there a science of education? and, (2) *Can there be* a science of education? [12] Before answering "no" to both, he restated the questions in more technical terms this way:

---

[12] Dewey, 1929: 28.1.

The question as to the sources of a science of education is, then, to be taken in this sense. What are the ways by means of which the function of education in all its branches and phases—selection of material for the curriculum, methods of instruction and discipline, organization and administration of schools—can be conducted with systematic increase of intelligent control and understanding?* What are the materials on which we may—and should—draw in order that educational activities may become in a less degree products of routing tradition, accident and transitory accidental influences?[13]

Dewey made a twofold approach to a science of education. First, he proposed to see how public-school practice could be best arranged to provide the pupils with "intelligent control and understanding." This was the teachers' moral commitment to students and to society—a practitioner's responsibility. Such an attempt to fuse the moral commitments of practice to the scholarly side of a discipline would be comparable to trying to build a science of physics by organizing the manufacture of automobiles in a way to produce both maximum intellectual understanding and maximum dividends for stockholders. Some understanding of metals and mechanics and economics might emerge, but any discipline developed from attending purely to efficiency in manufacture would hardly resemble physics as science knows it. Second, he wanted to find out what available subject matter could be put to use to improve instructional practice. Such a science of education must be restricted to the translation and application of research done elsewhere, as the engineer translates the findings of physics for application in the construction of cars. The translation and application of research to industrial use is the peculiar art of the engineer. The engineer and the teacher were seen as practitioners of such "arts."

It is in this sense that Dewey stated that in any opposition of science and art, he would have to join those asserting that education is an art.[14] Amplifying this comparison between engineering and education as arts of application, he went on as follows:

But there is no opposition, although there is a distinction. We must not be misled by words. Engineering is, in actual practice, an art. But it is an art that progressively incorporates more and more science into itself, more of mathematics, physics, and chemistry. † It is the kind of art it is precisely

---

* This is the long line of connection from theory, to middleman interpreter, to practitioner, and finally to instruction itself. The hazards of such a series of intellectual transactions are uncountable.

[13] Dewey, 1929: 26.2.

[14] Dewey, 1929: 28.3.

† An opposite trend would be the exploitation of confusion by obscurantists in literature. They rebel against developments in logic and assert that other kinds of meaning they cannot describe, but profess to display, are more important for furthering human understanding.

because of a content of scientific subject-matter which guides it as a practical operation.[15]

After the manner of medicine and engineering, then, educational science must come from a practical and an intellectual source, as follows:

> Two conclusions as to the sources of educational science are now before us.
> First, educational practices furnish the material that sets the problems of such a science, while sciences already developed to a fair state of maturity are the sources from which material is derived to deal intellectually with those problems. *There is no more a special independent science of education than there is of bridge making.* Second, material drawn from *other* sciences furnish the content of educational science when it is focused on the problems that arise in education.[16]* [Extended italics added.]

Classroom practice would act as a source of educational science by exhibiting the problem and testing the solution. Established science would be an intellectual source of the science by providing the subject matter from which a solution could be intellectually devised. Such a process would call for a three-way partnership of practitioner, conceptualist, and scientist. The scientist would build the intellectual content, as he has always done. The practitioner would record the problems and the results of testing the solutions proposed, as in Dewey's 1928 article. The middleman conceptualist, familiar with practice and science, would also assist in identifying problems and suggesting what research the scientist might undertake. The middleman's main function, however, would be to propose solutions to practical problems out of his knowledge of science. These he would give to the practitioner for testing and for use in the improvement of the art of teaching.

In this way, the intellectual content of education, although not so far along as the content of engineering or medicine, progressively would reach out to include that material from the established sciences which could be understood and put to use. Such a symbiotic discipline of education is nourished by translation and exists for application. Like an osmotic filter, it draws in minerals from the sea of facts and passes on those which the organic practice of education needs for growing purposes. Although such a discipline absorbs facts and can even produce factual material of its own, it does not contain the prerequisites of independent existence. Dewey stated those prerequisites in this way:

---

[15] Dewey, 1929: 28.3.
[16] Dewey, 1929: 28.7.
* Thus, there is pure science, the middleman interpreter who tells how it might be applied, the practitioner who applies it, and the act of teaching thus improved.

> The history of physics proves conclusively that measurements and cor-
> relations, no matter how quantitatively exact, cannot yield a science except
> in connection with general principles which indicate *what* measurements
> to conduct and *how* they are to be interpreted.[17]

In the absence of guiding principles which suggest where to look and what
the findings mean, what began as prospecting quickly turned into scrap-
collecting. Educational research, Dewey implied, consisted of a huge pile of
factual scraps picked up in the belief that they might eventually prove
useful but, actually, getting rustier day by day. Scraps do not make a
science.

Dealing with what does make a science, Dewey stated the following
minimal condition for a science of education:

> This could happen only if some way had been found by which mental or
> psychological phenomena are capable of statement in terms of units of
> space, time, motion, and mass. . . . Nor have we as yet any *other* general
> hypotheses in the light of which to know what we are measuring and by
> which we can interpret results, place them in a system and lead on to
> fruitful indirect measurements. . . . A period of groping is inevitable.
> *But the lack of an intellectually coherent and inclusive system is a positive
> warning against attributing scientific value to results merely because they
> are reached by means of recognized techniques borrowed from sciences
> already established and are capable of being stated in quantitative form-
> ulae.*[18] [Extended italics added.]

Such an attribution of scientific value to more careful fact-gathering leads
to the following error:

> Failure to perceive that educational science has no content of its own
> leads . . . to a segregation of research which tends to render it futile. The
> assumption, if only tacit, that educational science has its own peculiar
> subject-matter results in an isolation which makes the latter a "mystery"*
> in the sense in which the higher crafts were once mysteries. A superficial
> token of this isolation is found in the development of that peculiar termi-
> nology called "pedageese." Segregation also accounts for the tendency . . .
> to go at educational affairs without a sufficient grounding in the non-edu-
> cational disciplines that must be drawn upon, and hence to exaggerate
> minor points in an absurdly one-sided way,† and to grasp at some special
> scientific technique as if its use were a magical guarantee of a scientific
> product.[19] ‡

---

[17] Dewey, 1929: 28.4.
[18] Dewey, 1929: 28.5.
* Reliance on metaphysics as the basis for a rational science.
† The emphasis on student-teacher planning that led Walter S. Monroe to say
that "direct assignments have no place in the project method."
[19] Dewey, 1929: 28.9.
‡ Statistical and questionnaire-survey research.

Far from the stature of an independent science, a discipline of education,
Dewey concluded, can never exceed the quality of the parent disciplines
from which it must draw. * And, Dewey added, those disciplines exhibit
the following characteristics:

> . . . the outstanding fact is that the sciences which must be drawn upon
> to supply scientific content to the work of the practitioner in education
> are themselves less mature than those which furnish the intellectual
> content for engineering. The human sciences that are sources of the
> scientific content of education—biology, psychology, and sociology—
> for example, are relatively backward compared with mathematics and
> mechanics.[20]

Added to the difficulties of inheriting information from the relatively undeveloped behavioral sciences, the discipline of education faced the human
limitations of translation, interpretation, and communication. The best
translation cannot pretend to improve on the intellectual content of the
original. All it can hope to do is to be as faithful as possible to the original,
carrying over its spirit into the new practical tongue and capturing its
meaning with a minimum of distortion. But the difficulties of translation
made up the simpler half of the problem, as Dewey indicated in this summation:

> The net conclusion of our discussion is that the final reality of educational
> science is not found in books, nor in experimental laboratories, nor in
> the classrooms where it is taught, but *in the minds of those engaged in
> directing educational activities.* Results may be scientific, short of their
> operative presence in the attitudes and habits of observation, judgment
> and planning of those engaged in the educative act. But they are not
> *educational* science short of this point. They are psychology, sociology,
> statistics, or whatever.[21] † [Italics added.]

Translation, alone, introduced the problem of faithfulness to the original.
Interpretation of science for improved understanding of the conduct of
classroom practice added the problem of scholarship in terms of scope of
coverage, evaluation as to reliability, relevance, and significance. Translation and interpretation could be put into books, but the content of such
books still had to be put into heads, to become educational science. They
had to be communicated to the minds of practitioners who could—and it
was a short step to "would"—use them. This was Dewey's view of

---

* While giving assent to this conclusion, Harold Rugg expected the foundations of education actually to exceed the parent discipline and to create an
original discipline. (See page 208).
[20] Dewey, 1929: 28.8.
[21] Dewey, 1929: 28.6.
† This would be one more answer to the question, "What is educational philosophy?" (See *Harvard Educational Review,* Vol. 26, No. 2, Spring, 1956.)

a philosophy of education. Less scholarly men than Dewey used more journalistic means to accomplish this, leading to indoctrination and propaganda.

To the objective problems of translation and interpretation Dewey added the subjective problems of communication. Faithfulness of translation and reliability of interpretation had to be matched by fidelity of reception and accuracy of understanding. The broadcast had to be understood to complete the communication.

Dewey had not disposed of a science of education so much as he moved attention away from the idea of an objective discipline to the translation of scientific data into subjective "attitudes and habits of observation" which would control practice. *

In the absence of a research discipline for the objective description of education as a contemporary social institution, and for want of a teacher-training program based on such comprehensive factual information, Dewey sought unity in belief achieved by philosophic speculation which gave meaning to available information. Instead of pointing out how educational research could become a separate and more scientific descriptive discipline, he put the job of careful description off on the established sciences, which, then as now, directed their attention elsewhere than to children in classrooms.

Using the facts of established science as fuel to be fed into the furnace of the practitioner's belief, he relied on two factors for the development of a teacher-training discipline: first, he counted on the scholarly skills and verbal precision of the middleman conceptualist to offer facts to the mind and to supplement them with the enriching qualities of his own experience and point of view; and second, he relied on the fact that the prospective practitioner was a living, moving person who had been given both direction and momentum by a cultural environment.

Somehow, out of his own personal view of life, the practitioner would add to the organization and the meaning with which the conceptualist had tried to infuse the data. And both conceptualist and the potential practitioner would supplement one another, because they were both a product of the same broad cultural heritage. This was the subjective basis for a unified discipline of teacher training implicit in Dewey's proposal of 1929.

Four Stages of an Educational Discipline

Dewey's 1928 article suggested that a collection of personal reports about successful progressive practices made by teachers in the field would

---

* Note Peirce's concern with how the Assassin moved his followers to fight. ("The Fixation of Belief," *Popular Science Monthly*, Nov., 1877, p. 14.)

add a fourth dimension to his objective, translative, and subjective approaches to a discipline of education. The objective stage of dependence on established science for factual information and reliable generalization would remain weak so long as psychology and sociology continued to offer information about education as a by-product of research done in other fields. The translative stage demanded considerable scholarship in the findings of science, and this would infringe on the amount and scope of contact with practice the middleman theorist could achieve. Thus, in effect, Dewey's 1928 article would have provided the conceptualist with a broader view of practice by having practitioners report their observations in much the same manner that child-study observers reported under the Worcester program. Assuming that a language of objective description was available, Dewey concluded that such a growing body of practice-centered reports would supply an intellectual content which would become part of the linking science.

Such reporting would bring the practitioner one step toward becoming a middleman theorist himself, and this would make the transition from objective information to subjective belief an almost uninterrupted flow. The cold facts of science would be mixed with the more personal reports of progressive practitioners, suggesting a framework on which to hang the facts. Tentatively arranged on a framework of reports collected from many practitioners viewing their own activities from roughly the same "progressive" point of view, the loosely arranged body of content would be digested by a middleman theorist and compactly ordered into compelling and communicable talk. Taken as four parts in the process of building a unified discipline of teacher training, the steps would be as follows:

1. *The Objective Stage.* The objective stage would be received intact from established science, having as much descriptive accuracy and predictive power as experts in empirical research could supply. In terms of the present outlook, the developments in behavioral science have been disappointing by comparison with 1920 expectations.

2. *The Clinical Stage.* In the clinical stage, the reports would be made by amateur researchers committed to a general philosophic point of view. These would be introspective reports on particulars of practice made by teachers. Though less objective than the content received from the first stage, these would have the advantage of being derived from direct and extensive attention to existent practice. This stage seems to have failed as badly as child study, despite efforts of local groups such as the Southeast Michigan Core Curriculum Conference.

3. *The Translative Stage.* Stage three—translative—would be a personal distillate of one man's point of view—a more or less amateur philosophy of education. Judging from a survey of dissertations, it seems

to me that this stage has shown a failure in scholarship at the advanced-degree level—possibly aggravated by the Ed.D. degree.

4. *The Subjective Stage.* Finally, the subjective stage would consist in the personal understandings and feelings retained by the practitioner, a personal philosophy, a belief, a feeling—possibly, a faith. (Some would argue that the general education level of teachers has seldom been sufficient to enable them to do more than accept or reject what they are spoon-fed.)

In calling the subjective stage the only educational science, Dewey diverted attention away from the development of a formal intellectual discipline and directed it toward the development of attitudes in practitioners. Attitudes would be directly useful in the moral task of altering actual practice. In place of the homely adage, "Each man needs a faith to live by," Dewey's concern with attitudes substituted the professional expression, "Each teacher needs a 'philosophy' to teach by." Marketing a personal philosophy of education embodied in the disposition of a practitioner, he could afford not to care whether it was called *method, principles, theory, science,* or *philosophy.* But following the practice of escaping the connotations of terms associated with past talk and belief, when Dewey's proposal took concrete form, it was called *the foundations of education,* the topic of the next chapter.

A good singer makes others follow his tune, and a good educator makes others follow his ideal.[1]

As early as 1897 John Dewey set forth his idea that the basic intellectual content for teacher training should come from established sciences outside the family of educational research disciplines. In his 1897 memo to William Rainey Harper on the organization of a fully equipped department of pedagogy, Dewey nominated physiology, biology, psychology, and sociology as likely sources. His 1901 concept of a linking science of education, developed by a conceptualist,* placed the full responsibility for the development of primary concepts to be given educational application upon the established sciences. The 1928 paper advocating the descriptive reporting of successful progressive practices added the element of clinical research, whereby educators would supplement the data of science but in no way supplant it. And finally, in 1929, Dewey reaffirmed his view that education must take its data and intellectual content from outside sources and organize them into their most useful form.

In such an approach to teacher training, the sciences would mine the raw materials, the conceptualist would manufacture prefabricated units of thought,

---

[1] Yutang, 1938: 59.
* No standards of scholarship, except those implicit in a Ph.D. program, have been set, and these have been altered by Ed.D. programs which often keep approval of the dissertation entirely within the education school faculty.

11

A Moralistic Doctrine: Foundations of Education

and the practitioner would build a "philosophy" to his own specifications in the do-it-yourself tradition. As raw materials such as lime, clay, iron, and silicon must be processed to make such building materials as cement, brick, steel, and glass, so would the data of science be processed for potential use in the classroom. As the raw materials determine the kinds of processed materials available for building, so do the processed materials influence the kind of structure possible. But in teacher training, as in manufacture and architecture, the middleman theorist and the practitioner would be invited to experiment with new ways of using old materials. Invention, not the scholarship of careful translation and interpretation, proved to be the underlying motivation in the elaboration of the subjective personal philosophy of education which practitioners developed around Dewey's concept of experimentalism.

Dewey wrote *The Sources of a Science of Education* in 1929 as the factualism of measurement and survey research had begun to lose forward thrust. Pushing against factualism in a head-on collision, Dewey's colleagues at Columbia University had come out against the arrogance of claims that an empirical science of education had all but been realized and that observation-centered reasoning would solve any problems that were, indeed, solvable. The philosophy-bent conceptualists at Columbia quickly institutionalized Dewey's plan in a way that removed well-established scientific information and generalizations from teacher training. They assumed that professional standing and staff membership assured a level of scholarship which could be taken for granted.*

Where Dewey had foreseen an accomplished personal belief in the mind of a practitioner capable of exercising it in practical situations, the Teachers College program added a note of social obligation. The social foundations of education, assuming a rock-bottom basis in established science on the part of the middleman theorist, set out to accomplish a moral commitment in the mind of a practitioner determined to teach so as to direct social change. The subtle shifts from *including* objective science to *taking it for granted,* from *providing* processed materials for a personal belief to *supplying* those materials which would insure a particular social belief, from accomplishing a belief that *could* be used to achieving a determination so that the belief *would* be used, changed Dewey's subjective discipline or personal philosophy into a subjectively held moralistic doctrine. And it seems almost impossible for a moralist to remain

---

* It seems to me that weak professors thwart inquiry into the "sense" of what they teach, and that this intellectual featherbedding continues, thus assuring the least capable of tenure and the power to drive more able men away. The power hierarchy, in some schools of education, seems to fear research and those who do it.

entirely scholarly, especially when he wants to see his program implemented in his lifetime.*

Neither Dewey nor his colleagues foresaw that the challenge of speculative invention would crowd out interest in objective description. Yet the taste for generalization, tightly circumscribed by observed data, is better cultivated in a scholar's study, sound-proofed against the clamor for findings which have immediate utility, than from a podium in front of practitioners seeking help in the conduct of classroom instruction.

With regard to the established sciences and the objective intellectual content to be gleaned from them, the foundations program resembled an active family too busy to care for its cellar. Eating, sleeping, and entertaining on the main floor, no one thinks of the basement except when it leaks, when it holds an indispensable item in storage, or when the furnace goes out because someone forgot to order fuel. In such a family it might even be possible to raise a generation of grandchildren who never set foot in the cellar yet believed themselves fully acquainted with the whole structure.

Concerned with the social viewpoint to be communicated to practitioners, the Teachers College advocates of the foundations of education raised a generation of middleman teacher-educators† who at best took their science second hand. Dewey had designed a foundations concept with the concrete content of observation-centered reasoning as its cellar, but the original specifications of *that* foundation were constantly being weakened through the steady addition of the loose sands of social philosophy inadequately sifted.

Conversational Origins

In 1896 United States Commissioner of Education W. T. Harris suggested the social foundations point of view when he observed that "education is founded of (sic.) sociology." [2] And by "sociology" he meant "the science of civilization; the science of a combination of men into social wholes." [3] Especially in 1896, such a science of civilization would be

---

* It is similar to expecting a politician to remain entirely honest and still get elected. (The reason young people are so often attracted to political viewpoints on world federalism is that they can afford to be idealistic and uncompromising because they have no chance of gaining power soon—a kind of adolescent idealism.)

† These were the middleman theories that Axtelle had in mind (p. 177) when he said, "Professors of education (sometimes) command little more than the gross oversimplification they communicate to their students."

[2] Harris, 1896: 41.

[3] *Ibid.*

rational philosophy. The observation and description of tribes and societies had hardly begun. Yet even rationalistic philosophy felt the pressures of a growing social awareness in all manner of thought. Psychology had been too long focused on the individual. Social psychology and social philosophy, as well as pedagogy of the group, were attempting to broaden horizons of interest beyond the particular, and often peculiar, youngster on which child study had focused attention.

A quarter of a century later, social consciences twinged as intellectuals re-examined a system of universal public education that might have contributed to the insularity which left the charter of the League of Nations unratified. The depression made social consciousness almost a household item. Communism and art made it an intellectual necessity.

During the pre- and post-crash years of frenetic prosperity and courageous poverty, the conceptualists on the faculty of Teachers College, Columbia considered the problem of the nation's welfare and the care of its people. In his book, *The Foundations of American Education* (1947), Harold Rugg recalled that group and the atmosphere in which the basic social philosophy of the Foundations of Education Program was being formed. His recollections took the following form:

> The new study of society launched by Veblen, Turner, et al., was bearing fruit—in education as well as in government. In the 1930's the new educational organ on the social front was *The Social Frontier* and the new organization was the John Dewey Society for the Study of Education and the Culture. Both of these new instruments were fashioned by a little nucleus of professors of the social foundations of education at Teachers College. One by one after 1926 I had watched the new members of the group join our staff—Counts, Childs, Raup, Watson, Brunner, Newlon, Clark, Johnson, Cottrell, and others. As early as 1927 we formed our little Discussion Group around Dr. Kilpatrick as chairman. It served us on the social-educational frontier as Peirce's Metaphysical Club served the young intelligentsia of Cambridge sixty years before and his similar one, those at Hopkins in the '80's. Regularly from 1927 to 1934, intermittently from 1934 to 1938, and again for several years after war began in September, 1939, we have held our bimonthly dinner-discussion meeting, canvassing informally, without programs planned in advance, the roots of every phase of our culture. In hundreds of hours of friendly argument we dug to the social foundations of education. Even by 1932 we had become a cohesive group, taking our stand together for the general conception of a welfare state, agreeing fairly closely on the constituents of the democratic principle.[4] *

---

[4] Rugg, 1947: 90.7.
* To use Stevenson's distinction: more likely an agreement in attitude than in belief; hence, an opinion insensitive to logical or informational refutation.

As Rugg, here, frankly pointed out, the unplanned, informal, after-dinner discussions of philosophy-minded educators formed the real source of the Teachers College foundations program. In place of the documented scholarship akin to the objective side of Dewey's sources of intellectual content, the Teachers College group substituted coffee-cup conversation about a welfare state and the principles of American democracy. In comfortable communion with professional peers, it would not have been polite to ask for references or to analyze utopian speculation for its basis in fact.* From 1927 to 1934, that group compounded conversation until a standardized doctrine had begun to emerge and their vocabularies had become almost interchangeable.

In 1934 the first formal offerings in the Foundations of Education appeared. Consonant with the darker days of the depression in 1938, the offerings were renamed "Social and Economic Foundations." And in 1943 that was shortened to "Social Foundations." [5]

Organizational Beginnings

Further insight into the origin and organization of the foundations program at Columbia has been provided in an informative letter from R. Freeman Butts, then director of the division of Foundations of Education, Teachers College, Columbia University. Butts responded to an inquiry by Professor Cowley of Stanford. In this letter, dated October 2, 1957, Butts gave the following informal account of the program as he saw it develop from 1935:

> The origin of the term, I believe, grew out of the social and educational setting of the late 1920's and early 1930's. The two most influential aspects of the setting were (1) the *depression* and the world-wide economic and social crisis, and (2) the great *specialization* in professional and liberal arts courses.
>
> (1) The social crisis led to the belief that we needed courses that would deal with social issues and education. Education needed to study the main trends in society, the critical issues that faced society, the ways in which education is affected by these trends and issues, and the role that education could and should play in society. The emphasis was not only upon knowledge of what had happened and was happening but also upon the normative study of what education should do to play its part in solving the social crisis.

---

* Rugg's likening of the Columbia meeting to Peirce's Metaphysical Clubs seems to be a bid for scholarly status.
[5] Lawrence, 1951: 57.1.

(2) Course offerings in most higher institutions had become highly specialized as a result of rapid increases of knowledge and the use of the elective system. The idea thus grew that we needed course offerings and administrative arrangements that would bring several different fields together. This is an interdisciplinary idea. Educators should see society as a *whole* and see education as a *total enterprise* in relation to the society and culture.

So *foundations courses* were designed to overcome the specialization represented by separate courses in the history of education, philosophy of education, psychology of education, sociology of education, comparative education, and educational economics. This effort drew upon the survey or integrated course ideas that were being developed in Contemporary Civilization at Columbia and elsewhere. Some courses were actually taught by panels of instructors representing different fields. I suppose this reflected the general ferment in college education that was being expressed in such places as the Wisconsin Experimental College, Minnesota General College, etc., etc.

Also, the *departmental organization* was revised to bring together faculty members who were jointly concerned with the foundations of education. We set up two departments:

(1) The Department of Social and Philosophical Foundations brought together those who were teaching

> Sociology of education (We have added anthropology)
> Educational economics (We have added political science)
> Social psychology
> History of education
> Comparative education (We have added international ed.)
> Philosophy of education (We have added religion)

(2) The Department of Psychological Foundations brought together those who were teaching

> Educational psychology
> Developmental psychology
> Remedial reading and the psychology of school subjects
> Tests and measurements
> Educational research and statistics
> (We have added the "Psychological Services:")
>
>> group procedures and development
>> adjustment and personality
>> vocational guidance and personnel psychology
>> counselling psychology (including rehabilitation counselling)
>> clinical psychology

These two departments were brought together in the Division of Foundations of Education. The directors of the Division have been William H. Kilpatrick, Jesse H. Newlon, George S. Counts, and Arthur I. Gates.

In recent years I believe there has been more emphasis upon the scholarship, research methods, and empirical study represented by the university disciplines and somewhat less upon the crisis outlook and the social or reconstructive role of education.

I have never felt that the term "foundations" has been thought of so much as meaning the underpinnings upon which the superstructure of education is built. I have felt that it has meant rather the *basic* study of society and human behavior as they relate to education in the sense of *fundamental* or *essential*. The emphasis is upon the fundamental ideas, concepts, scholarship, and theory essential for understanding and improving practice and techniques.

The term has also had a combination of meanings with respect to professional and liberal or general education. Some think of the foundations as essentially a general education for teachers to give them an understanding of society and human behavior that may have been neglected in their liberal arts education. Others have thought of the foundations as the common corpus of professional knowledge necessary for all educators to have no matter what their specialized task in education may be.

I believe that *both* of these elements are important, and I like to think of the foundations as the bridge or linkage between the university disciplines of scholarship and the professional training for specialized jobs. It is thus *both* general *and* professional. Greater stress upon the foundations of education makes the essential difference between an undergraduate normal school and a professional college of education. It also marks the difference between a purely academic graduate school of arts and sciences and a truly graduate school of professional education.

Basic Conception

In 1938, Guy Whipple foresaw the speculative cast of educational thought when he predicted a return to individual and group opinion in the literature of the National Society for the Study of Education. He generously ascribed the return to expressions of opinion to the professional habit of entertaining problems beyond the scope of scientific measurement. The attempt to see society as a whole and to place public education as a key institution within it raised just such issues.* But conversation which

---

* With considerable respect for the coverage and initiative of such men as Rugg, one can still paraphrase a song of that period: educators rush in where scholars fear to tread. Practice-centered thinking is impatient to put the findings of scholars to use. Like salesmen who exaggerate the merits of their product, middleman educational theorists have frequently stretched their "right to be sure" so far as to rupture it. Yet it remains for the reader to choose among works exhibited under such headings as "educational theory" and "conceptual research."

stretched imagination to suggest a panorama of society-as-a-whole could not slow down to distinguish between prediction currently beyond the reach of measurement and speculation forever beyond the possibility of observation. Too often all questions were met and handled on the same rationalistic grounds.

As is the case in much lecture work, a good deal of the after-dinner conversation which spawned the Social Foundations Program at Columbia passed from the middleman conceptualist to the practitioner without being formally recorded or carefully documented. But one member of the Teachers College staff, Harold Rugg, set out to convert the residue of that talk into an orderly argument. In his book, *The Foundations of American Education,* published in 1947, Rugg gave his interpretation of the worth, basis, content, and uses of the concepts implicit in those early conversations.

THE IDEALS

As Dewey had done in 1929, Rugg concluded that there could be no science of education because of the absence of a unique body of primary concepts.[6] Confirming his agreement with Dewey about the nature of the outside sources for the intellectual content of educational thought, Rugg went on to outline his view of the foundations of education in the following way:

> Education is an art and a technology which employs the primary concepts of other bodies of subject matter which are established sciences:
> —from physics: energy, the field . . .
> —from biology: growth, integration, individual differences . . .
> —from psychology: experience, the Self, the problem, personality, movement . . .
> —from culture and society: democracy, freedom, control, equality, the sustained yield . . .
> —from esthetics: expressional act, felt-movements, form . . .
> On these and other sciences the educationalists, working as technologists and artists, can now build a Great School. But shall they aspire also to create a Science of Education? No.[7]

Immediately, however, Rugg's inclusion of aesthetics as an established science suggests both peculiar usage and a departure from Dewey's view of the foundations of education. Dewey had identified the sources of intellectual content as physics, physiology, sociology, psychology, and biology —factual sciences in the usual sense of the word. In that usual sense,

---

[6] Rugg, 1947: 90.8.
[7] Rugg, 1947: 90.9.

aesthetics is classified as philosophy, humanities, or criticism—certainly not as science. It stands in contrast to the literal, factual, observation-centered sciences as a literary discipline in which subjective feeling, rational argumentation, and a personal point of view combine to yield a unique expression of opinion concerning normative judgments. With this literary approach to the expression of considered opinion, aesthetics can entertain questions as broad as Tolstoy's "What is art?" This same essay technique could be adapted to the question, "What is democracy?" In addition to broadening the sources of content to include aesthetics and morality, Rugg also favored the less quantitative sides of psychology and biology.

By 1934 course work in educational psychology harbored most of the informational gains made by the earlier spurt in measurement. By the end of World War II, it had become the teacher-training fortress for what-ever remained of observational-descriptive-predictive reasoning from the period of confidence in an empirical science of education. Meanwhile, portions of educational sociology had begun to part with the philosophic past, giving the educational social sciences a stability somewhat improved over conditions for principles of education courses in 1912. A foundations program, however, which proposed to deal with society as a whole, the welfare state, and democracy had to get away from the piecemeal, micro-scopic factualism of literal observation. Social issues had to be approached in the macroscopic manner of literary essays, at best, and of after-dinner conversation most frequently. But the idea of education as an intellectual discipline had just emerged from a period of intense concern for a science of education based on observation-centered reasoning. Consequently, the proposal of a humanistic, rationalistic discipline of education would not have survived just comparison with Herbartian rational science.

To facilitate a macroscopic approach to social problems, Rugg re-placed the objective science of Dewey's sources for intellectual content with those aspects of behavioral science which viewed human and social problems in the panoramic terms that Whipple had foreseen as the coming trend in educational thought. Rugg proposed just such a substitution in this passage from his book:

> In the generation between the opening of Dewey's Laboratory School and the publication of his *Human Nature and Conduct,* an experimentalist psychology of intelligence and problem-solving thinking was developed and largely adopted by progressive educators. In the more conservative teacher-education institutions, a much more limited "connectionist" (Thorndike) psychology of habit was made the psychological course of study. In a few schools and colleges a curious mosaic of the two theories was taught. But it could not be said at any time that American education was founded upon *a* psychology. Such agreement as there was bore down heavily on intelligence, problem-solving thinking, and habit; but through-out the half-century the schools and teachers colleges have lacked a psy-

chology; witness the abysmal psychological ignorance of the doctoral candidates in education—little less than an academic scandal.*

And during all this time rich and indispensable, but largely unused, makings of a psychology were available in the work of a score of pioneers from Peirce and James to Allport, Sheldon, and Lewin. In the chapters of my book I have documented five examples:

- —The dominant role in the human act of feeling-as-body-response as developed by Peirce, James, Lipps, Watson and others.
- —The confirmation of the feeling-as-body-response emphasis from the psychology of esthetics, and the emergence of the concept of "movement" in a new psychology of meaning and expression.
- —A psychology of persons and personality which emphasizes the role of the temperamental traits—from the researches of William Stern, Gordon Allport, and others.
- —A "constitutional" psychology in which physique and temperament are primary and intelligence secondary—from seventy-five years of physiological studies.
- —The faint suggestion of a field-force-energy psychology emphasizing the role of psychic energies—suggested by Lewin's all too brief work.

All these are organic rather than connectionistic. All stress feeling and body-response and build on the powerful interpretative role of movement.[8]

Each of these "unused makings" of a psychology which Rugg proposed as foundational elements of professional training was an embryonic intellectual discipline. Quite contrary to the established sciences which Dewey recommended as foundational content, each was the suggestion of an area in which a science *might be* developed. Dewey had said that the intellectual understanding of educational problems must wait for content to be developed in the established sciences and then to be translated for educational use. Rugg had no intention of waiting for these nascent areas to mature. He proposed that educators lead the way where experts hesitated.†

Even so, however, a foundations program based on the content of the new areas of psychology would have preserved the scientific spirit of

---

* But such men did become the middleman conceptualists in many teachers colleges. And they could get their degrees in education without even having to perform for anyone outside the education faculty—a double standard of scholarship. This does not mean that the work done for an Ed.D. is always inferior to that done for a Ph.D., but it means that it *can* be inferior.

[8] Rugg, 1947: 90.1.

† Thus violating an implicit conservatism enforced by such arbiters of scholarship as dissertation committees and readers. The more underdeveloped the area of inquiry (anthropology, for example), the less room for originality and experimentation *in basic method.*

what Dewey had proposed as an objective source. Just how much of a
change in spirit Rugg proposed came out in the following statement:

> One of my major theses is that the design of education requires *four* foun-
> dations—psychology, sociology, esthetics, and ethics—not two or three!
> And a good school cannot be built on a psychology of intelligence, prob-
> lem solving, and habit alone; its program of education will fail unless it
> springs out of the fullest use of feeling and expression.
>
> In this area of the culture also, the lives and work of the Men of the
> Consensus have documented my thesis. All are *expressional artists,* irre-
> spective of the special mediums in which they cultivate their scene, and
> of their academic classifications—philosophers, psychologists, sociologists,
> land reconstructionists, architects, painters, poets, dancers, teachers. All
> employ the creative act. *Each one is striving to say what he sees, feels, of
> life in his unique way. . . . To say, moreover, what his people feel, their
> way . . . and to say it rigorously with form. . . .* Thus I have acted on
> the conviction that it is in the lives and works of producing artists—not
> of the pedagogues of art or philosophers of esthetics—that one finds the
> educational cues for the creative process. The educator must go to this
> primary source, for *these* are the Force People. Expressive art is the art
> of Forces—of felt-relations—and the body is the primary expressional
> instrument of feeling. Thus our findings for the new Esthetics confirm
> those of the new Psychology. Feeling and body-response are primary.[9]

Feeling and expression—creative art and intellectual invention, the work
of the force people—would be the ideational and emotional ingredients
of a new interpretation of society-as-a-whole and of education as one of
its major institutions. The foundations would extend across the full range
of emotional expression and intellectual understanding by integrating art,
aesthetics, and ethics with new movements in the established sciences.
*Instead of a discipline which lived by translation and transfusion from
objective data and observation-centered reasoning, Rugg hoped for the
inventive and expressive power to match the creative output of the parent
disciplines with an educational original.* Despite his rejection of the idea
of a science of education, he did hope for a unique and original discipline
for education as a subject of study.

The new foundations of education as proposed by Rugg would not
be so sober as the basement of bricks from established science as Dewey
proposed for the objective stage. Rugg's foundation would be more like
a gourmet's continuously renewed soup. Begun with a basic stock drawn
from newer trends in the behavioral sciences, enriched with all manner
of creative arts, and spiced with aesthetics, ethics, and morality, the soup
would be held at an intellectual simmer. Further, replenished with the

---

[9] Rugg, 1947: 90.2.

left-overs of dinner-table conversation, it would be cleared each semester by skimming off the residue absorbed by the raw-egg of criticism.

Nourishing as such a potpourri of professional preparation might sometimes be, Rugg's foundations of education lacked the stability of being firmly tied to the objective sections of established science. The original antecedents of Rugg's foundation concept, like the original stock of a gourmet soup, would gradually become so diluted that the objective flavor it may have once possessed would be undetectable.* Thus, gradually the line of descent would grow so complex as to be untraceable.†In the development of a new discipline of teacher training out of a synthesis of all knowledge after the models provided by the men of force (creative artists), translation would have to give way to invention. It was in such a creative sense that Rugg spoke of aesthetics as a science. In that same sense, he said of ethics:

> While the makings of a new psychology, sociology, and esthetics are now at hand to serve as foundations for a new education, the building of a new ethics has lagged far behind. The principle of cultural lag was evidenced again, social institutions lagging behind changes in the productive material culture and psychological and moral factors changing even more slowly. . . . We know now that this statement can be made only in the framework of the Structure of Power of the emerging society.[10]

Whatever the "Structure of Power of the emerging society" might be, it seems to have been Rugg's speculative view of how society would develop. And in building a foundations of education program around such a speculative concept through the synthesis of creative expression from all the arts, the professional educator would once again be an amateur rushing in where experts refused. Not especially trained in the scholarly problems of discipline construction, and without broad and extensive internship in the sciences or the creative arts, the worker in Rugg's foundations of education would have to substitute courage for command, with the likelihood of producing professional dogma through intellectual arrogance.

Rugg, like Dewey, had expected to find that courage in pioneers on

---

* In trying to become one of the "force people," advocates of the foundation's viewpoint faced the danger of partisanship about education as extreme as a painter's partisanship for his brand of "modern art." Dealing in concepts having social-philosophic significance, instead of form and color, this partisanship and the efforts to be "forceful" seemed more like propaganda. At least it became moralistic.

†Yet the attempt to trace out the antecedent for some of the commonplace ideas passed as doctoral-level research, giving an atmosphere of scholarliness to the commonsensical and further obscuring the differences among scholarly, practical, and journalistic statements.

[10] Rugg, 1947: 90.3.

the faculties of the progressive schools. Just as Dewey hoped that practitioners of classroom instruction would help build a clinical discipline of education, Rugg anticipated that forward-looking teachers would supply intellectual leadership in the study of the new foundational disciplines.*

A careful look at several public schools and teacher-training faculties in 1942 and 1943 curbed his optimism and brought forth the following lament about the impoverished state of the intellectual and the applied sides of the foundations concept:

> *I found no study of that new sociology going on among the faculties of the schools. . . .* Much random improvising activity there was—but no study of the *first principles of esthetics and design. . . .* I found no single faculty consciously building a developmental program from the nursery school to adulthood on a psychology of the person. *And no faculty systematically studying the new psychology today. . . .* A new morals and the vague structure of a new ethics have been evolving in our society, but still are not being utilized in even the best of our schools.[11] †

Rugg contended that the activity programs of progressive schools failed to mature into a study of American society because the practitioners who were directing learning had no view of that society as a whole or even of its major parts.[12] Too busy with administrative and instructional tasks to institute on-the-job study, they needed an opportunity to achieve such understanding through a professional training program organized around the psychological, social, aesthetic, and ethical foundations of American civilization and education. But to provide such understandings, teacher-training institutions would have to be changed completely. In the following paragraph from his article published in a 1951 issue of *Educational Theory,* Rugg emphatically stated the extensive change needed:

> *Our institutions tend to be trade schools rather than centers for the discovery of new ideas. We are concerned with the "know-how" rather than the "know-what." With the formula rather than the First Principle and the equation.* Yet the whole history of modern science should teach us

---

* Though neither Dewey nor Rugg can be accused of being merely practice-centered, this does suggest that they looked on education-as-a-subject-of-study as something that would quite naturally emerge from the intellectual interest and concern of practitioners. The exclusion of normal school students from university entrance, as pointed out in 1892 by De Garmo (p. 161), had been overcome; but a huge gap had opened up between the scholarship in academic programs, such as philosophy, and professional-degree programs. It seems odd to find Rugg expecting public school teachers and teacher-training faculties to be well informed in the scholarship of psychology, sociology, and ethics.

[11] Rugg, 1947: 90.5.

† Rugg confirms the suspicion that practice develops more out of expedience and local conditions than from scholarly findings in psychology.

[12] Rugg, 1947: 90.4.

that we shall not succeed in producing properly designed and organized teacher-education programs *until we first succeed in developing a sound theory of society, of the nature, behavior, and expression of men, as foundations of education. . . . This means that our teacher-education institutions must stamp out their traditional trade-school temper and become centers of ideas.*[13]

Teacher-training institutions were not to be centers for traditional ideas translated from established science. Rather, by means of the foundations program, they would be centers for the synthesis of all information and of creative expression pertinent to the invention of a "sound theory of society, of the nature, behavior, and expression of man." *

In effect repeating Gordy's 1891 view of the normal school as a school of philosophy, Rugg called for a social-philosophic core of thought as the heart of professional training. But, since even experts in any one of the foundational areas of thought—psychology, sociology, aesthetics, and ethics—have found it impossible to generate a theory which commands the degree of unanimity achieved by, say, the general Darwinian hypothesis in the biological sciences, this sound theory of society would have to be *created* by professors of education. Yet few professional educationists achieve a philosopher's training in aesthetics and ethics or a scientist's training in psychology and sociology. Even fewer qualify as scholars of all four areas, and shallow are the teams which achieve consensus on such a broad range of ideas. As much as it prepared the way for sound scholarship, as he intended, Rugg's proposal invited amateur scholars at less reputable teacher-training colleges to continue the coffee-cup conversation and after-dinner philosophy which the Columbia faculty had found so congenial, so productive, and so profitable.

The Illinois Social Foundations of Education Program

By 1950 the appeal that Rugg made for a change in teacher preparation had influenced at least six professional programs, beyond course work at Teachers College, Columbia University. These institutions with foundational programs were the University of Illinois, University of Florida, Ohio State University, San Francisco State College, the teachers college at Troy, Alabama, and Eastern Washington College of Education at Cheney, Washington.[14] A scholarly and extensive fulfillment of Rugg's idea of a founda-

---

[13] Rugg, 1951: 91.

* Max Lerner's *America As a Civilization* suggests both the great complexity of the task which Rugg outlined and the literary, rather than literal, approach necessary for any kind of synthesis that seeks to encompass so much. And it took a journalist to do it.

[14] Lawrence, 1951: 57.2.

tion program was carried out by the largely Columbia-trained foundation staff of the University of Illinois. In 1947, the year of Rugg's publication, the College of Education at the University of Illinois began a reorganizational study of their graduate program. Three years later, it put many of Rugg's suggestions to work. The following year, 1951, Archibald W. Anderson, Kenneth D. Benne, Foster McMurray, B. Othanel Smith, and William O. Stanley wrote *The Theoretical Foundations of Education* as an explanation of the major ideas behind the new program at the University of Illinois.

CONTENT AND MEANING

The actual program described in the booklet could provide "minimum course offerings in only three foundation fields: the historical, philosophical, and social."[15] The report examined a fourth foundational area also: comparative education. A complete program would also include educational aesthetics and educational sociology.[16]

In order to avoid confusion, the authors distinguish between educational sociology and social foundations by defining the former in these terms:

> Educational Sociology, as a scholarly discipline, applies the methods of sociological study to the institutions of deliberate education, and to the interrelations between educational and other institutions.[17]

They defined social foundations this way:

> Social foundations, as a field, is concerned with those aspects and problems of society which need to be taken into account in determining educational policy, especially as this policy concerns the social role of the school, and in determining broader social policies which affect educational policy.[18] *

As used in the Illinois program, the term "social foundations" referred to one of the four theoretical foundations—historical, comparative, philosophic, or social. Collectively, the Division of Psychological Foundations and the Division of Theoretical Foundations included the full scope of the idea that Rugg had put forth for the improvement of teacher preparation. Together, these divisions had the following responsibility:

---

[15] Anderson, 1951: 2.2.

[16] *Ibid.*

[17] *Ibid.*

[18] Anderson, 1951: 2.1.

* In this way they designated one as a preparation for scholarship and the other as a body of practice-centered thought.

. . . the development in teacher training institutions of common viewpoints with respect to the over-all task of public education, common intellectual tools for the analysis of this task, and common commitment to
the improvement of the teaching profession.[19] *

DESIGNED FROM NEED

The Illinois program exhibited four equal theoretical foundations:
historical, comparative, philosophical, and social. The first two were
resources for finding out what others did at different times and in different
places. But the work of developing a common point of view toward the
child, the school, the role of the teacher, and American society would be
done in the latter two. Together, these four foundations were to satisfy
practical, professional, and social needs.

PRACTICAL UNITY

Arguing that the theoretical foundations should supply the practitioner with an understanding of his function as a teacher, the authors
made the following case:

1. Professional education is properly determined by the requirements
of the teaching function.[20] †
2. No agreement on that function now exists.[21]
3. The teaching function should be defined in terms of the development
of the child.[22]
4. Ultimately, the education of the child, or even the way in which the
child will be understood, is a function of the conditions, the problems,
the beliefs, the aspirations and the ideals of a particular people.‡ Hence,
the ends and purposes of education can neither be determined nor understood apart from a study of the culture in which the school is located.[23]

Beginning by defining the ends of education, the Illinois faculty assumed
that the understanding of "the conditions, the problems, the beliefs, the
aspirations, and the ideals" of the American people had progressed to
the point where middleman theorists could formulate similar views of the

---

[19] Anderson, 1951: 2.3.
* Here, then, is the practice-centered emphasis.
[20] *Ibid.*
† Not by the available information (presumably, this goes without saying, but
it shows the practice-centered concern).
[21] *Ibid.*
[22] Anderson, 1951: 2.4.
‡ Making such understanding a philosophic kind of inquiry rather than a
psychological one.
[23] Anderson, *op. cit.*

child, the teacher, the school, and American society that would not be at odds with available description and observation-centered reasoning. This speculative extrapolation of the few limited generalizations which found widespread support in psychology and sociology would set out a point of aim for practitioners—doubtless, a moving target.

PROFESSIONAL UNITY

The Illinois authors gave this account of the complexity that specialization in the various divisions of teacher training had created:

> The teaching profession, like the public, is now segmented both horizontally and vertically. Horizontally, the profession is divided into specialized groups representing subject matter departments and various other types of specialized educational work. Vertically, it is further divided into elementary, secondary, and collegiate levels, accompanied by invidious distinctions in prestige and financial reward. Moreover, vertical segmentation is further complicated by a professional splitting, at each of these levels, into administrative and teaching groups with different degrees of status and authority. In a very genuine sense, all these distinctions represent proper and necessary divisions of function. In the absence of a common orientation to the educational task, however, these differentiations in function have often degenerated with narrow and vested interests with limited distorted views of the over-all job of education, and into unfortunate and harmful cleavages in authority and status. This condition has seriously hampered the development of professional unity and of a common professional conception of the educational task.[24]

This absence of professional unity was paralleled by intellectual disunity as well.

Factualism, which took objective description for granted in the reports of measurement and survey investigations, provided administration with a set of factual studies separate from those in curriculum and guidance. Sometimes different, sometimes contradictory in nature, these studies could not be effectively coordinated to reveal a consistent thread of information throughout the various specialties without such editing as to result in an arbitrary selection of findings to support a foredrawn conclusion. Utopian models of the ideal practitioner fashioned on personal experience produced conflict among interpretations of the role to be played by the teacher, the guidance counselor, and the administrator, as well as yielding conflicting stereotypes of each role. The disparity in what was taken to be factual information encouraged a divergence in attitude toward how to perform in practice. The emphasis on practice-centered thinking joined with the various divergences to encourage splitting educa-

---

[24] Anderson, 1951: 2.3.

tional psychology into two divisions, one for elementary-school preparation and one for secondary-school preparation, with the question of separate sections in educational psychology for the junior high and the junior college sometimes receiving serious attention.*

SOCIAL UNITY

Need extended beyond the correlation of talk in the various specialties and a comprehension of the teaching function. The need for practical and professional unity of viewpoint made up part of a plenary problem, which the authors characterized in this way:

> A confused culture, marked by deep-seated conflicts and tensions, not only means war and internal strife, it means warped and maladjusted personalities. . . .†
> Education, in the last analysis, is always a form of statesmanship; and never more so than in a period of rapid and profound social change. . . . This fact . . . clearly indicates that the responsibility for the *common* program of professional education designed for all types of educational workers, without regard for their particular specialty, rests primarily with those disciplines which are usually referred to as the foundations of education.[25]

The program in theoretical foundations would itself be a form of statesmanship which both pioneered in creating professional unity and set standards for others to emulate. Beyond making the University of Illinois College of Education a model to be copied by other teacher-training institutions, the program would be an implicit recommendation for everyone to develop comparable social conceptions to maximize his efficiency in the American experiment. The more important the role and the more famous the player, the more vital the need. And beyond being a model for the prominent and the professional, the Illinois foundations program was a testimony to the future when every student of education would bring with him to the public schools a unified social belief. That unified social belief would consist of the following parts:

> A grasp of the organic and reciprocal relationships between school and society, and of the major problems created for public education by the present social conditions and conflicts in American society. Centrally, this

---

* This division extends even to educational philosophy; but, at bottom, it seems to represent the last-ditch efforts of normal school people, who would maximize drill and construction of models in methods courses despite cries of "Mickey Mouse."

† Practice-centered thinking does not necessarily mean narrow concern for classroom instruction alone.

[25] Anderson, 1951: 2.5.

grasp involves the information, insights and skills required to: (a) appreciate the powerful educative effect of cultural arrangements; (b) analyze the social realities and democratic ideals of our society; (c) confront these two aspects of American life in a sympathetic, but critical and realistic, appraisal of both our institutional structure and our moral evaluations; and (d) use the results of this appreciation, analysis and confrontation in the formulation and testing of an intelligent conception of the social function of public education in America.[26] *

To restate the case, few if any full-time scholars combine a thorough training in the anthropology of American culture with an expert's background in social and moral philosophy. Nor are they able to test a conception so broad as "the social function of education in America." The people teaching such foundational courses would, moreover, not be full-time experts in anthropology, philosophy, and measurement. Thus, to achieve the projected coverage, conversational speculation would have to take the place of exact scholarship. And the practical, professional, and social unity achieved would be the unity of tent-like speculation rather than bead-like connection. Thus, the theoretical foundations would spread a tent of abstractions over the separate areas of teacher training. This practice-centered cover subsequently became the content of educational theory seeking scholarly acceptance as the substance of a discipline of education, at least as far as textbooks, journals, and dissertations were concerned.

The kind of unity needed to improve education as an academic discipline could be gained, however, only by painfully examining of all facts which pretended to be objective reports, not by lumping them indiscriminately under a canvas of abstractions. Each alleged fact would have to be graded for importance and weighed for value, and then placed in line with others like a bead about to be strung. In that way, the best available reports might be strung by a thread of thought into a theory, thus moving inquiry beyond factualism.

The theoretical foundations spread the tent of rational social philosophy over the separate educational disciplines in the belief that professional unity would result from such a conceptual *tour de force*. But it was not intended to be the intellectual unity of facts strung together in a theory. It was a psychological unity of common attitudes and beliefs, as indicated by this statement:

Up to the present time, however, the most successful use of experimental methods has occurred in the physical sciences. Consequently, many

---

[26] Anderson, 1951: 2.6.

* It is interesting to wonder how many professors anywhere in any university in the United States could do this for himself, much less teach it to primary- and secondary-school teachers.

able and sincere persons have identified experimental method exclusively with the canons and techniques employed in these sciences. Obviously, this interpretation of experimental method is too narrow for the present purpose. "Foundations" study involves more than the verification of descriptive principles. It entails . . . the validation of normative rules, the formulation, criticism and reconsideration of educational decisions and policies, and, as an integral part of all these processes, the reconstruction of beliefs and attitudes. There is a serious controversy over the question of whether or not normative principles, including basic ethical principles, can be scientifically verified and established. . . . But there is little room for doubt in the case of the problems of practical judgment.* Decision and policy making in education, as in other forms of human endeavor, obviously entail considerations and methods that are not ordinarily included within the pale of science. The same thing may be said of the reconstruction of attitudes and beliefs. The reconstruction of attitudes and beliefs may be—indeed, in the absence of crass indoctrination, must be—accompanied and guided by reason and evidence, as policy and decision making may take into account all of the discoverable facts and all of the established scientific generalizations bearing upon the question at issue. But in all these cases, the results, and the processes by which these results are reached, are also shaped and influenced by other factors and considerations. The fact is that the formulation of policy, the making of decisions, and the reconstruction of attitudes and beliefs, viewed from the standpoint of the participant, are not exclusively scientific or even intellectual processes.[27] †

As the informational source basic to the conceptual job of reconstructing social aims, the data of factualism and the observation-centered reasoning of the measurement movement resembled muted trumpets in a band playing mood music under whose spell decisions would be made. Broad abstractions were the melody. Decision-making and policy-formulation, the Illinois faculty maintained, were best influenced by the total mood created in the foundation courses. Objective data constituted but one instrument and had to follow the tune. The melody abstractions (general ideals) were the key to the creation of a mood for decision making. In the following terms the authors explained how the melody functioned:

. . . the power of general ideals to stir the imagination and the loyalty of men has been fully attested.‡ It is unduly cynical to attribute this power solely to the hypnotic effect of empty but glittering phrases.** On the con-

---

* Most of these men worked with Raup on *The Improvement of Practical Intelligence.*

[27] Anderson, 1951: 2.8.

† As is the case with practice-centered thinking whether in be in education, law, engineering, medicine, or agriculture.

‡ World War II was still fresh in mind.

** The postwar concern with general semantics seems more relevant here than thoroughgoing logical analysis.

trary, much of the appeal of ideals is due to the fact that they have embodied genuine human aspirations and desires. And they are the heart of any society. For it is the sense of common ends and standards, together with the feeling of unity and brotherhood created by this sharing of hopes and interests, which transforms a mere population into a living community. The poetic and ritualistic celebration of these pillars of society is natural and important.[28]

Accompanied by the rational content of common-sense logic, general ideals had the power of an emotional charge hidden in connotation. The general ideal was the sugar-coated capsule encasing vitamins which strengthened belief. The "poetic and ritualistic celebration" of such general ideals added to the emotional charge or impact which they could generate. Talk designed to change attitudes and reconstruct beliefs contained all the elements of oratory in which what is said means far less than the effect it has on the hearer. These seem elements of a literary approach to understanding. Journalistic expression thrived on such elements. Correspondingly, scholarship atrophied. Further, an accomplished discipline that must be realized, not in talk, but in the minds of practitioners, places its major emphasis on the resulting subjective effect. This effect achieved in the mind was the locus of Dewey's educational science. Attitudes to be reconstructed, beliefs to be inspired, are effects to be achieved within people. It was just such subjective, personal, practitioner-centered ends which Brameld later set forth in these terms:

> We may hope that many young teachers will thus begin their professional careers with the rudiments at least of *clear commitment* to the "ideal Superego" of the democratic "charter"*—a goal that they can defend because they have reflected seriously upon it, because they have experienced something of its institutional embodiment in their own education, and because they have *come to believe* that to strive for human freedom will be worth both the hardships and rewards of their chosen life-work.[29] [Italics added.]

The Trend

From Dewey through Brameld, the tendency has been to build an emphasis on subjective belief into an instrument for achieving specific

---

[28] Anderson, 1951: 2.7.
* In one decade, Rugg's "Structure of Power in the Emerging Society" seems to have become "ideal superego" of the democratic "charter." Here is one more instance of the terminology of Freudian psychology turned into pseudo-scholarly jargon and used as if self-evidently meaningful. In this way, journalistic prose took the fore, often in the guise of scholarship.
[29] Brameld, 1957: 8.2.

personal commitment among practitioners. Accomplished in tne mind of the practitioner, Dewey's educational science depended heavily on objective, clinical, and translative stages of preparation. For Dewey, the non-scientific, nonintellectual, literary elements remained minimal. By adding the creative expression of the men of force to the construction of a theory of American society as a whole, viewed in the framework of the struggle for power, Rugg added two ingredients: (1) emotional content and (2) such broad speculation that careful scholarship had to be forsaken for conversational talk which took objective information for granted. In addition, he directed attention to the specific concept of the welfare state and the principles of democracy. The dogmatic nature of the belief to be achieved can be judged from the following assertion by Rugg: ". . . democracy is the only proper government for family, school, community, nation, or world; the people together distill judgment and decisions out of their collective experience."[30] Moving ahead, the Illinois faculty elevated the poetic and the ritualistic celebration of general ideals to a key role in the reconstruction of attitudes and beliefs. They expected through their program to influence decision-making. The objective, clinical, and translative stages of Dewey's foundations concept were treated as being vastly subordinate to the particular subjective ends to be achieved by literary means. When little is known about how decisions that accord with democratic principles and with a concept of the welfare state are made, there is no difficulty in being generous with all possible means for making them.*

Another Voice

The generosity which Rugg and the Illinois faculty displayed toward the content of foundations programs Theodore Brameld amplified in his book, *Cultural Foundations of Education,* published in 1957. Interested in the use of anthropological information in teacher training, Brameld expressed his views that virtually all available avenues to influencing belief should be incorporated into foundation courses. In addition to the foundational areas mentioned by Rugg and the Illinois authors, Brameld asked for "the study of the fine arts and applied arts, of the great religions, and of the philosophers as these affect and are affected by the dynamics and patterns of culture."[31]

---

[30] Rugg, 1947: 90.6.

* This practice-centered emphasis and the neglect of careful scholarship has further strengthened the normal school conviction that the only way to train teachers is through direct exposure to practice teaching and the continuance of methods courses where students build up scrapbooks of teaching materials and recipes. Here is the teacher-training equivalent of training nurses almost entirely through hospital service.

[31] Brameld, 1957: 8.1.

This literary combination of the scientific and the poetic, the descriptive, and the emotive was to provide the direction in which attitudes and beliefs fundamental to decision-making were to be reconstructed. Planted in the minds of practitioners, certain general ideals would provide below the level of consciousness a dispositional unity in the public schools that would emerge as consistency in policy formulation. It would, as Brameld put it, be a subjective commitment to the ideal superego of the democratic charter. By emotional and intellectual means, the foundations of education would cultivate belief in a particular social doctrine which prescribed how man should relate to his fellow man. Gentle and general though the prescription might be, restrained and restricted as the emotional and intellectual persuasion might be, the foundation-of-education approach to teacher training had become oratory for a moralistic doctrine. Social reconstructionism became its most virulent form. Journalism emerged as "educational theory."*

The academic world tends to pride itself upon maximizing clear, explicit, intellectual understanding, all the while analyzing overgeneralizations and dissecting hollow abstractions. By celebrating the poetic and ritualistic side of general ideals, the foundations programs, however, tended to maximize the emotional and unscholarly side of instruction. Such direct pursuit of commitment and belief made the foundational courses resemble a minister's sermons rather than a professor's lectures.

The Inspiration of General Ideals

The foundations approach to teacher training, impelled by concern for what children, schools, practitioners, and society needed, was future-, not present-, oriented. A quick glance at the skills exhibited by even competent teaching-technicians convinced such architects of the foundations concept as Rugg that new beliefs about man and society, rather than improved technical skill or knowledge of content to be taught, held the key to reorganizing instruction, the teaching profession, and, ultimately, American society. The sum total of available skills could not hope to achieve the utopian vision that Rugg, the Illinois faculty, and Brameld nursed. Even talk about this vision-to-be-believed-in had to transcend the language of observation, since these philosophies of the future dealt with general ideals to be realized.

The difference between such future-oriented teacher training under the foundations idea and the present-oriented training of an engineer is summed up operationally in the distinction between the view of the teacher

---

* Education is not the only field guilty of this error. Political science and literary criticism have also known this illness.

as a statesman and that of the engineer as a proficient technician or applied science researcher. Through the use of objective, descriptive talk, the engineer can be trained to be an efficient catalyst in the production of material goods. A Communist or Fascist engineer can still be an expert in the construction of rockets. A contractor can assemble technical talent and be confident that the sum total of skills assembled will be sufficient to put up a bridge that will carry the intended load. In such fields, the concept of the competent practitioner does not greatly exceed the sum total of a specified set of special skills. Engineering envisions a scientist-technician-practitioner, not an artist-statesman.

Picturing the teacher as an artist-statesman, the foundations program had to concentrate on cultivating temperament on top of technical skill. Technical competence had to be capped with the feelings, beliefs, attitudes, and emotional commitment which enabled specialized ability to rise above itself and to reach for a new integration of understanding and performance that is more than the sum total of what has come before —that is, creative. The foundations program was built to provide an internal something which could not be made explicit through talk or show but which would dispose the practitioner to act in a preferred manner.

Such poetic talk capable of influencing right action thus amounted to a modern teacher-training application of the Herbartian belief that exposure to literature was an important way to produce right-minded and right-willed citizens. And only through such poetic talk could a theory of the child, the teacher, the school, the family, the community, and American society be developed and put together into a unified doctrine. The sum total of objective information available could not come near such scope. The sum total of technical-teaching skills available would not add up to the ideal practitioner motivated by such a doctrine. The artist-statesman-teacher had to be inspired to be artful, to be committed to a particular social doctrine in order to be statesmanlike, and to be skilled to organize the technical details of instruction so that the two qualities of temperament could be focused on the student.

A utopian vision held that the artist-statesman-teacher consisted of more than the sum total of skills shown in practice. It would be easier to identify such a "savior-like" teacher in retrospect than to recognize him before he performed his miracles. But, clearly, whoever would be such a savior must be inspired. In a similar manner, the view of American society-as-a-whole and of the doctrine of democracy consisted of more than the sum total of objective, clinical, and translative talk that could be based on a mixture of descriptive science and reports of practical experiences. In such a practice-centered context the concept of democracy is like the concept of heaven: people will agree on its importance, its worth, the possibility of attaining it, the necessity of attaining it, and even how to gain it, without ever having seen it and without being able to describe it or to define it. But, clearly, whoever would attain it must believe in democracy.

By mixing poetic expression with objective description, the foundations program hoped to maximize potential for somehow achieving inspiration and belief while holding distortion and indoctrination—propaganda and proselytizing—to a minimum. But, in concentrating on the positive task of achieving inspiration and belief, Rugg, the Illinois faculty, and Brameld seemed not to realize that an equal amount of effort, or even more, would be required to keep distortion and indoctrination out. In building a moralistic discipline, they and their followers failed to realize that talk about education, considered as a teacher-training discipline, possessed only as much value as its lowest common denominator. It is the weakest scholarship and the last accurate description, not the most deeply felt coffee-cup conversation nor the most imaginative speculation, which determines the strength of a chain of thought. Journalistic elements kept intruding, and there was no standard of scholarship to be used as a filter to sift them out.

The mixture of artistic expression and scientific information with which foundations programs compounded doctrine to influence belief took a knowledge of existent conditions for granted. The failure of factualism had led many educators to object to the idea of an empirical science of education, but the extensive pursuit of measurement studies and survey projects, with their volumes of reported findings, had inspired widespread confidence that the job of carefully describing the public schools in objective terms was well under way. Even Rugg's dedication to the new sciences of feeling and body response betrayed a deep conviction that the basic job of description was well in hand and that the foundation program must anticipate how to meet the needs of the future, which could be reliably foreseen by looking at how descriptive knowledge of the present was being used in the "creative work" of "the people of force," as Rugg called them.

Failure to realize that the measurement and survey movements, as well as the sciences of feeling and body response, were experiments in ways of describing the present, rather than a reservoir of objective facts, led the advocates of the foundations program to a misplaced emphasis. Believing their speculation to be the extrapolation of known data, they gave considerable attention to imaginative speculation about how things ought to be, instead of checking up on reports about how things are. The manufacture of new talk about how things ought to be in the future, without a careful analysis of the reliability of old talk about past and present conditions, cultivated a twin distortion. What passed as educational scholarship became attacks on straw men who never were, in the defense of phantoms who would never be. Both the "bad guys" and the "good guys" belonged to the myths of useless "theory," with nothing to check the journalistic tendency to reduce all issues to black and white polar opposites—traditionalism versus progressivism, democracy versus authoritarianism. Instead of pioneering the construction of a language for objective description of educational practice through the careful analysis of the reports which claimed status as facts or observation-centered reasoning, the foundations of education went out to generate social-science fiction.* Assuming that each middleman conceptualist had a thorough training in the objective, clinical, and translative stages, its advocates gave primary attention to creating inspirational doctrines. Entertaining, stimulating, and even moving as those literary doctrines sometimes were, the lack of attention to well-established information made them resemble tableaux of intellectual shadows more than monuments of ably sculptured scholarship. At their worst, such doctrines were the humorless burlesques of an amateur mime. In sum, the foundation movement strove to establish *education as a literary discipline* operating between the exacting scholarly and logical demands of philosophy and the careful, detailed attention to literal description prerequisite to empirical science.

---

* At best, it reached a level some distance below the kinds of essays that Orwell wrote, and which deserve to be called serious commentary on important social issues.

Part 3

General Methods
and Concepts
of a Discipline

. . . the mere concept of activity *in general* no longer has any definite educational value. It did have when it stood in marked contrast with quiescence and passive absorption.* But we have now reached a point where the problem is to study in a discriminating way from a variety of points of view various modes of activity, and to observe their respective consequences when they are employed. Otherwise an activity program will be in danger of being a catchword used to justify all sorts of things of diverging value . . . . in the abstract this activity may be boisterous, rowdy, thoughtless, blindly emotional, passionate, mechanical, and perfunctory. . . . Activity may consist of a succession of more or less spasmodic, because brief and interrupted performances, or of a consecutively developing occupation evolving over a long period.[1] †

Dewey urged that the consequences of involving pupils in the construction of projects and the solving of problems be observed, recorded, and evaluated so that the literal significance of these activities could be determined. He urged that educators look carefully at the conditions of practice and the consequences of instructing. He did not favor the tendency to settle for agreement on the general method. He wanted the specifics of how it worked in the classroom reported

---

* Many concepts have limited utility for a time but do positive harm to further inquiry when used beyond a certain context.
[1] Dewey, 1934: 29.
† Dewey's critics quite frequently overlook the concern he shows here.

12

Two Frameworks for Classifying

in as much detail as possible. Middleman theorists seeking to justify a particular general method did not always follow Dewey's example.

In the Civil War of American public schooling, the "Dirty Rebel" and the "Damned Yankee" have been Traditionalism and Progressivism. Under such battle slogans a variety of lesser dichotomies have developed after the fashion of the pejoratives common to much "yellow journalism." A listing of terms associated with the polarization of general methods which has passed as part of both teacher training and a general discipline of education would include the following:

Traditional (Old)	*Progressive (New)*
drill-dominated	problem-centered
lecture-oriented	project-oriented
teacher-regulated	group-regulated
information-centered	value-centered
competition-controlled	cooperation-controlled
college-directed	welfare-directed
fear-governed	appreciation-governed

In at least two important respects, such dichotomies, martialed in defense of a polarized general method, give false impressions. First, the dichotomy itself suggests an exclusiveness which is, in fact, not present. Neither camp can claim the exclusive practice of, or complete insulation from, any of the attributes listed. Each characteristic has that relationship to its counterpart found in the Aristotelian expression, "No form without content, no content without form." Similarly, method without content has no meaning. Second, the category "Traditional" or "Progressive" suggests a unity of value—a denominator common to all members—not evident. On this point, Harold Weisberg of Brandeis University has set the score straight in his original paper for Scheffler's book of readings, *Philosophy and Education*. After a detailed analysis of the concepts of Tradition and the Traditionalist, he concluded:

> To argue for a sense of tradition means, really, to argue for some specific values embedded within traditions, on specific grounds. There is no "tradition," only traditions. Traditions conflict with and contradict each other. There are traditions of some practice or another but no traditon *uberhaupt.* . . . If what I have been arguing is correct, the issue of "traditionalism" vs. "experimentalism" in education is to be construed in a radically different light. . . . The questions which should concern educators are specific ones and include a variety of traditions.[2]

Indeed, each of the six specific traditions which set forth a general method of instruction must be examined. This is taken up in the next chapter.

---

[2] Weisberg, 1958: 107.

But Weisberg's caution that no single tradition can be fruitfully inspected as the categorical opposite of either Traditionalism or Progressivism deserves emphasis. Predicated on just such a false dichotomy, the disputes over Progressivism and Traditionalism incorporate contradiction and internal conflict within the fundamental concepts used to characterize practice. Small wonder that one concept becomes the garbage heap for everything not claimed as a virtue by the other. Inclusive of contradictions from the start, the concept of traditionalism assumes the powers of a giant. Against such a malevolence, it becomes necessary to build the very model of a saint. With myth creating myth, what began as a controversy of unmatched pairs grew into a contest between a Demon and a Santa Claus, with no one questioning either's existence. The plurality of conceptions and practices gathered under one hollow tent eventually forces its opposition to incorporate a comparable diversity. Instead of answering questions about education, such false dichotomies erect journalistic structures which must be condemned as unsound and demolished individually and collectively by such critical analysis as Weisberg performed.

Properly, for his purposes, Weisberg analyzed the general concept of tradition. In his search for the borders of clear meaning, his continent is normal usage. He stated that meanings must be extracted from particular traditions, but he did not take up the task.

The justifiable distinctions with which to replace false dichotomies so current in talk about education must be sought in such specific educational traditions as Monitorial Method, Herbartianism, and Experimentalism. Yet even false dichotomies would not survive if they did not have some verisimilitude. As prejudice operates through exaggeration which can be passed off as representative of the group under attack, so does false dichotomy usually have an element of truth underlying its distortions. The problem becomes how to isolate that element in as pure a form as possible. To do this, it is necessary to examine two aspects of major traditions: the practical side (general methods) and the intellectual side (general disciplines). Two tools are needed.

A Tool for Analyzing Practical Traditions

Isolating warranted distinctions from several educational traditions, like separating cream, demands a minimum of contamination. In this respect, a neutral framework for reporting the major elements of those traditions resembles a pasteurization vat. Ultimately the outcome depends on what is poured in, but at least the container can be clean to begin with and big enough to accommodate the input yet small enough to be manageable.

Although earlier educators such as Quintilian or Comenius could give the bulk of their attention to methods and content of instruction, those who followed Froebel and Pestalozzi could not turn away from the psychology of the individual learner. In addition, American concern for schooling as a major public institution brought in another branch of consideration. Each major American educational tradition had to deal with all three elements of education: the individual, instruction, and the institution. A way of classifying each tradition as it relates to a general method of instruction can be built from three categories best designated by the following prefixes:

1. *intra*—within, inside
2. *inter*—among, between, together
3. *super*—above, beyond, over, more than

Combining these three prefixes with the three elements mentioned above yields the following framework for description*:

FRAMEWORK FOR CLASSIFYING A TRADITION IN TERMS OF ITS GENERAL METHOD		
	Individual	Instructional	Institutional
intra (within, inside)	The psychology of the learner and how he learns, behaves, feels, or thinks	The structure and activities within a particular course, subject, or program	Internal operation of the school
inter (among, between, together)	The sociology of the classroom and the school—how students mix, mingle, interact, and adjust	The connections between subjects, such as English and social studies, or the interrelations among activities throughout the school	The relation of the school to other institutions such as the Church or the Supreme Court (described by Dewey in his 1897 Memorandum to W. R. Harper —Appendix)
super (above, over, beyond, more than)	Developments in the person which include more than his mental ability or his relationships with others	Outcomes of instruction extending beyond the sum total of courses given—such as love of learning	How the school functions with regard to the society as a whole

In the course of the development of American education, some categories in the chart have received more attention than others. Some traditions have had little or nothing to say in certain of the nine categories described above. However, this framework does offer a neutral, comprehensive, yet simple basis for describing and comparing the six major practical traditions in American education.

---

* Just as it is appropriate to talk about intramural athletics, intercultural communication, and supernatural powers, so would these distinctions lead to the recognition of different levels of discussion and different kinds of concepts.

USES OF THE FRAMEWORK

Eventually the diagram will be put to work condensing the descriptions of the six practical traditions into summary statements which represent their most important central tendencies. This rounding-off of ideas for the purpose of close juxtaposition short-cuts many involved arguments, quite possibly worthy in their own right, and runs the risk of mis-diagnosing the main conceptions of the movement. If successful, however, it offers a comprehensive, though not scholarly, overview of the key general methods and related conception of practice operating throughout the development of American public school teaching. From such a panoramic sweep, the peaks and valleys should stand out more clearly and the need for journalistic caricature may be lessened. Dichotomous ways of talking about general methods of instruction can be set aside, and it may not be necessary to grant academic status to parts of a general discipline of education that give support to such dichotomies.

Even so, however, such a display of the further reaches of practice-centered thought remains within the bounds of education as, at best, a literary discipline.

A Tool for Analyzing Education as a Subject of Study

"Education" is, and should be, a term as comprehensive as "life" or "experience." The great educational theorists have used it to refer to nothing less than teaching-and-learning in all its possible manifestations, exemplifications, and ramifications. Even when they discuss something as narrow as spelling or handwriting, the larger conception dominates their thought. And any less ambitious approach to educational problems quickly degenerates into a fussy preoccupation with trivia. But teaching-and-learning is an aspect of nearly all experience, not a "subject" separated from other "subjects" by well marked boundaries.[3]

"Science" and "art" fit on the same level of abstraction with all-of-life suggested for "education" in the epigraph above by Professor Black. Yet certain easy divisions emerge in a discussion of science or of art which have no ready parallel in education. Science, for example, separates into physics, biology, and psychology; art divides into literature, painting, sculpture, and the dance. How shall education be divided: primary, secondary, higher, adult, public, and private; or, from another side, administration, teaching, method, and curriculum? The twentieth century has continued to

---

[3] Black, 1956: 7.

deal with education summarily while taking precautions against the wholesale discussion of all of science and all of art. The use of literary, rather than literal, approaches to building the intellectual content of education as a subject of both teacher training and academic study has fostered the belief that there is a general discipline of education.

How can such a broad-as-life concept of "education" be handled? In an important sense, it cannot. As a first step toward making it manageable, however, William K. Frankena, of the philosophy department of the University of Michigan, divided it as follows:

> At once a distinction must be made between education as a process and education as an academic discipline. In the former sense, education is the process by which society makes of its members what it is desirable that they should become . . . either in general or in so far as this may be carried on by what are called "schools." In the second sense, education is the discipline which studies this process in one way or another, its findings being reported and passed on in professional courses in schools of education.[4]

In such a dichotomous sense, all not included under "schooling" would be part of the discipline. This brings the divisions theory and practice to mind. Yet consideration of Frankena's second sense of the term "education"—an academic discipline—suggests some important questions, such as:

1. What does the discipline include?
2. What does it exclude?
3. What are its leading ideas, concepts, and theories?
4. What is the basic framework of the discipline within which all disputing theories operate?
5. How have the ideas, concepts, and theories been developed?
6. How do they relate to practice?
7. On what basis are they organized?

Such questions inquire into the nature of education as a discipline. Yet, as the whole of this study demonstrates, in areas of thought where talk about education stretched to ambitious proportions, so much must be included that the discipline can be neither simply defined nor comprehensively catalogued. This situation was well summed up in a half-humorous statement made by James Feibleman about education in general:

---

[4] Frankena, 1956: 34.

"No matter how elementary the contents of education may be the presentation of it is bound to be complex!"[5]

Grasping Education as a Discipline

There must be a qualitative difference between an intellectual discipline and mere verbalization, on the one hand, and between an intellectual discipline of education and the practical preparation of teachers, on the other. The frequent complaint that teacher training is too much centered on recipes or methods of *how* to instruct suggests that such practical explanation and the demonstration of technique could be multiplied indefinitely without achieving "discipline" status. Yet explanations of how to teach are part of one or another "theory" of instruction. Practical training for public school work incorporates various theories of curriculum, administration, and instruction. Such theories contain propositions stated on various levels of abstraction appropriate to such recognized disciplines as psychology or biology.

Those involved in building literary explanations of use in teacher training have been inclined to consider such practice-centered theories the content of a general discipline of education. Many other members of the academic community have attacked this content as a body of verbalizations about schooling which is not worthy of "discipline" status because of its scholarly defects. Further, no stable body of content has yet been set aside as the basic body of either a discipline of education or the material for professional training.

The longitude and the latitude for plotting the nature of education as a discipline must come from history and reasoning, respectively. Any framework for describing such content must be big enough to include any parts discovered through the careful analysis of actual programs yet small enough so that the categories suggest the working outline of what such a discipline might be like. The historical framework must include the full range of parts in an order which facilitates the charting of development.

In such a large project as charting an outline of the development of education as an intellectual discipline in the United States alone, however, the historical framework cannot be so detailed as to preclude over-all summation and the perception of movement. The reasoned framework must set forth the potential meaning of education as an intellectual discipline; the historical framework must reveal which possibilities were realized, and thus provide a chart sketching whatever evolution has taken place.

---

[5] Feibleman, 1956: 32.

THE REASONED FRAMEWORK

"Theory" and "practice" seem to be the wrong terms with which to handle an investigation into the nature of education as an intellectual discipline. First, practice—the schooling process that the discipline in one way or another studies—is no longer being directly discussed. A theory-versus-practice dichotomy represents an insistence on the big-as-life view of education, in which efforts to break the concept down into graspable parts are overruled. Second, the word *theory* has both automatic status and highly diversified meanings from its usage in physics, criminology, political science, and design, for example. Again, as the whole of the fore-going chapters indicate, the task of defining theory for use in the discussion of education as a general discipline would be almost as difficult as that of defining the discipline itself.

In place of the practice-theory duad, *the six categories of the reasoned framework which follow* are broad enough to describe the potential content of an educational discipline without assuming that the actual content has achieved a level of organization that qualifies it as method, rules, principles, or theory.

1. *The Media.* From previous discussion, "talk" and "show"* represent a beginning point for the discussion of the methods, rules, principles, and theories that have been put forth as ingredients in a discipline of education, or as instruments for the training of teachers. *Talk,* the spoken and written word, may attain a level of organization similar to theory in economics, or it may remain forever on the intellectual level of conversation. *Show,* the demonstration of skills and techniques or the performance of practice-teaching routines, can supplement talk by way of illustration. *Show* and *talk* offer a genuine dichotomy with which to begin an examination of education as a discipline: *show* operates through active demonstration, and *talk* employs verbalization. These two media, talk and show, seem lowest common denominators of teacher training and of a discipline of education.

2. *The Central Elements.* The principal ingredients of talk and show were condensed from the major conceptions of the schooling process in the United States and the principal kinds of programs for training teachers, as examined in Part I. Four ways of employing talk and show seem evident:

1. Straightforward description.

---

* As common-sense beginnings, these have no more hidden meaning than "show and tell" in kindergarten (the reader must pardon the laboring of these phrases).

2. Logical argumentation.
3. Imaginative speculation.
4. The creation of feeling (such as evoking an attitude of sympathy for childhood directly through the first-hand observation of children).

Although these seldom appear in pure form, each of these four approaches emerges now and again as a central tendency around which talk or show has been organized. Such elements grow easily into such two-part adverbs as "description-centered," "logic-centered," "speculation-centered," and "feeling-centered."

3. *The Means of Perpetuation.* Both the way in which the content of a discipline has been gathered and the way in which it is dispensed offer insight into its nature. Much of what has been said in the major traditions of teacher training has been criticized for being pedantic, conversational, or obvious. Yet each is merely an excess of one of three main approaches to the accumulation of useful content: scholarship, which gleans what others have found out; common sense, which draws equally on the wisdom and the ignorance of tradition; and observation, which checks things first-hand.

4. *The Primary Purpose.* Scholarship, common sense, and observation can be disinterested, in a worldly sense, or they can be deeply involved in everyday affairs of practical living. Disinterested inquiry has sometimes been called knowledge-for-its-own-sake, or it has been taken to mean a primary interest in the advancement of knowledge itself. Deeply involved investigation differs from the pursuit of knowledge for its own sake by having its focus clearly fixed on what has to be improved now. The bulk of scholarship, common-sense reasoning, and observation used either as investigation or as course content has been deeply involved in such practical tasks as improving instruction, administration, curriculum, method, or guidance.

5. *The Product.* Investigation into the schooling process and the passing on of findings in teacher-training courses results in the total product which Frankena called the "academic discipline of education." Judged as a whole, that product has at different times been:

1. An accumulation of data,
2. An eclectic body of content,
3. A body of provincial doctrines, and
4. A set of personal beliefs.

6. *The Philosophical Focus.* And finally, the product can be classified as being primarily (a) generalizations made in advance of observed information (rationalism), (b) observed information without comprehensive generalization (factualism), or (c) generalization carefully based

on information gained through observation and description (empiricism). Thus, the six parts of the reasoned framework can be arranged as follows:

Media	Central Elements	Means of Perpetuation	Primary Purpose	Product	Philosophical Focus
	Description		Advance Information	Accumulated Data	Rationalism
		Scholarship			
Talk				Eclectic Content	
	Logic	Common Sense			Factualism
	Speculation			Provincial Doctrine	
Show		Observation			
			Improve Practice	Personal Belief	Empiricism
	Feeling				

Such an arrangement facilitates the simple but graphic tracing of developments in each of six efforts to build practice-centered traditions.

Let us begin with continuity and conceive in the field of human psychology a scale on which are distributed all kinds and aspects of human behavior. At the low end mere body acts; at the upper end appears the highest functioning of self-conscious personality. A little above the bottom would come the behavior of the body cells. . . . Higher up would come such complicated bodily functions as digestion, breathing, and heartbeat. Higher perhaps would come such appetites as hunger, thirst, sex, and the like. . . . Between these and the highest would come many habitual acts and other functions which serve human needs but are not directed with very definite conscious thinking. Finally, at the top of the scale, come the highest instances of intelligent purposing, critical thinking, and moral conduct.[1]

In *Selfhood and Civilization* (1941) Kilpatrick sets out his causal hypotheses in process terms which Ryle later labelled "mythical causal hypotheses": intelligent purposing and critical thinking. In this instance Kilpatrick was writing as if he could describe literally the hierarchy of mental activities which would give support to the conception of practice known as "experimentalism." He had no idea that he might be dealing in psychological fictions given the appearance of substance by verbal magic. Only in retrospect do such doctrines show up as deficient in literal meaning. The Herbartians believed as fully in the literal significance of their theory of apperception and their

13

---

[1] Kilpatrick, 1941: 55.

General Methods
from Six
Practical Traditions

concept of the cultural epoch as Darwinians do in the theory of evolution. Indeed, such is the way with beliefs. The religious doctrines of primitive groups amuse us as inventive analogies, but there is little amusement in Christian circles when the resurrection of Christ is likened to primitive beliefs. Only the revelations of "primitive people" can be called hallucinations. Some ideas seem clearly fictions, but others seem as clearly literal. Many ideas which have governed how teachers look at children and at classroom instruction seem fictitious now, but in their day they were taken to be accurate accounts of child nature, and they led to implementations as deadly serious as the ritual sacrifices in primitive tribes.

Much with a philosophic flavor similar to the speculation embarked on by Kilpatrick in the quotation above has been piled around the original statements made by Froebel, Pestalozzi, Herbart, and Dewey. Men like Bode, Kilpatrick, and Childs made careers by extrapolation from the original. Yet, with regard to its meaning for actual classroom practice, the bulk of what passes for educational philosophy, educational psychology, and educational sociology seems to surround the five major conceptions of practice like surplus fat.* The issue between Hutchins and the Experimentalists, with its metaphysical dispute over the nature of man and reality, meets opposition from Peirce's pragmatic principle of meaning when latter-day Experimentalists do not doubt the value of classical literature and Perennialists incorporate extensive activity projects and vocational training into their schools. It is hard to know what "practical consequences" follow from one belief as against another. The philosophic disputes suggest "reasons to suppose" that this or that might follow. But each dialectician finds his own reasons to suppose this or that. By contrast, the general methods represent a concept which the working teacher can carry with him.

Here, then, in simplified form are the four nineteenth-century conceptions of practice and two from the twentieth century: monitorial method, object-teaching, Herbartianism, child study, experimentalism, and the current academic emphasis. Together, they set forth the generalized models of practice-centered thought taken from the scholarship of their day. As concerns practice itself, all but the current academic emphasis offer a general method thought to be usable in most classroom situations. This evolution in conceptions of practice may be the basic content of education as a subject of study.

---

* The five general methods, monitorial, object-teaching, Herbartianism, child study, and experimentalism, make it seem that an understanding of practice is at hand. The generalizations drawn from academic disciplines such as psychology make it seem that a general discipline has been developed. The trick is to have the generalizations from behavioral science support the general methods. Here Philosophy of Education is usually employed.

1. MONITORIAL METHOD

Practical in the narrow sense, the techniques of instruction assembled under monitorial method expressed a need for economy and control in education. Exploring both a wilderness in the West and the jungle of overseas trade, the new nation had few dollars and scant attention to spare for that unappreciated natural resource, the ordinary youngster.

Using boys as instructors and as disciplinarians kept dollar costs low. Inexperienced boys could not, however, have the background in subject matter or in practical judgment attained by a partly trained adult. Instruction had to be packaged in convenient units: first, for mastery by the tutor; then, for presentation to the novice; further, for drill and memorization; and, finally, for examination and approval. Since boys could not exercise adult discretion about the quality of a performance, some standard that required little judgment had to be found.

Clearly, any boy could distinguish a faulty performance from a perfect one with a minimum of judgment. Perfection became the measure of adequacy, and those kinds of achievement which could be assayed for flaws in the most mechanical manner became the primary concern of instruction. Routinized drill, memorization, and repetition all focused on the achievement of a flawless performance. Learning was defined in terms of whatever training would result in the acceptable mastery. Instruction held first place, with consideration for the individual far behind, and with concern over the total function of the school as a social institution almost out of sight.

Since boys had no mature understanding of the management and control of younger boys, instruction had to take place within the context of obedience, thus adding a military-like hierarchy or chain of command to the natural tyranny that emerges when one youngster is given authority over others. Monitorial method accepted obedience as a prerequisite for beginning instruction and conceived of the individual in terms of the force needed to control him. Since boys extracted obedience from their charges in whatever way they could, the concept of discipline became a matter of the results achieved rather than how they were obtained. The end, not the means, received primary consideration because the techniques had to be developed *ad hoc*.

Given the requirement of having boys act as teachers, the excessive routinization of instruction and militarization of control followed as the simplest and most practical principles for the organization of monitorial method. Mechanized instruction and military control at the command of unsupervised youngsters were tools to be used but not to be improved. Each generation of tutors inherited a post, a class, and a set of rules to operate by as best as he could. He had neither the background to evaluate the rules before acting on them nor the opportunity to alter them afterward. The practical, descriptive, and a-theoretical nature of monitorial method was accented by the fact that the rules-of-thumb given to tutors were devised by adults and were not subject to test by those who made them or to revision by those who used them. This completed the concept of the school as a military-type institution in which orders were carried out but not questioned. Its main concepts can be arranged as in the accompanying tabulation.

MONITORIAL METHOD AS A GENERAL METHOD		
Individual	Instructional	Institutional
intra A child is naturally disruptive and thus must be controlled first, to be trained later.	Drill, memorization, and perfect recitation led to mechanical techniques of instruction.	The school developed as a military-type hierarchy in which obedience to authority and responsibility within the chain of command were paramount.
inter Group discipline maintained through obedience of each member allowed efficient organization for drill and memorization.	With attention given to individual units of instruction to be mastered by each group, subjects remained discrete and separate.	
super The child was seen as a small beast.*	Fixed standards. Regents.	

---

* Lest the characterization of the child as a nasty beast seem irrelevant to contemporary educational thought, this statement from Gilbert Highet's popular book, *The Art of Teaching,* must be considered as an example of a literary approach to what others have attempted to understand in a more literal way:

"They (children) are quite unlike adults. They are so different that it would be easier to understand them if they looked like animals. You know how a baby, before it is born, passes through the main stages of evolution. It begins by looking like an amoeba, goes on to look like a fish, resembles a big-headed monkey for some time, and ends up at birth looking remarkably like a little red blind clutching grimacing ape. I have often thought that in its first fifteen years of life it passes through another series of animal existences. Boys of nine and ten, for instance, are very like dogs. Watch a pack of them hot on the scent, yapping, running and jumping, bouncing aimlessly around full of unexpendable energy, kicking one another or breaking down a door as carelessly as a dog nips at its neighbor's flanks or bursts through a hedge. When they are really enjoying the chase, all their teeth and eyes gleam and their breath and laughter go 'huh, hugh, huh' like a leash of fox-terriers. Girls in their middle teens are like horses, strong, nervous, given to sudden illnesses and inexplicable terrors, able to work remarkably hard if they are kept firmly in hand, but really happiest when they are thinking of nothing particular and prancing about with their manes flying. Both dogs and horses are amiable creatures and can be domesticated, but it is a mistake to treat them as though they were human. It is also a mistake to treat horses as though they were dogs, or dogs like horses.

Monitorial practices harmonized with the prevailing common-sense notion of youngsters as small beasts to be trained for minimum literacy and to be housebroken through firm discipline. The common-sense view of child nature seems secondary to the practical demands which led to mechanization of instruction and militarization, but even the common-sense view attended primarily to the outcomes of training and the control achieved by harsh discipline. This reinforcement between the common-sense view of child nature and the practical demands of monitorial instruction resulted in a single-minded emphasis on drill, memorization, and control. Occurring at the beginning of the American experiment in public schooling, the impact of this as a *general method* would be difficult to overemphasize. Even when the harmony between the two was disturbed by a competing view of child nature imported with object-teaching, the practical emphasis on drill and obedience remained strong. Here was a general method that one might expect from a military male orphan asylum.

2. OBJECT METHOD

The crude psychology of childhood which divided attention between the results of instruction and the process of learning entered American pedagogy through object-teaching. Yet that rational psychology arrived less as a theory of child behavior than as an elaboration of proven techniques of instruction. Pestalozzi's insights into the mind of man and Froebel's Protestant social psychology were cemented to personal experience with ordinary youngsters in and around the classroom. As practitioners, their indisputable area of genius, Pestalozzi and Froebel selected

---

"So, if you are interested in teaching, do not even expect the young to be like yourself and the people you know. Learn the peculiar patterns of their thought and emotions just as you would learn to understand horses or dogs —or other animals (for there are all kinds of different animals implicit in children; the very small ones are often more like birds)—and then you will find that many of the inexplicable things they do are easy to understand, many of the unpardonable things easy to forget.

"How can you learn this? Chiefly with experience. . . ." (Highet, 1950:44.)

In this fine example of anti-theoretic intellectualism, Highet did not have to add "psychology notwithstanding." He merely took it for granted that his "insight" was to be preferred to the prevailing notions in psychology and in education. Too frequently the misanthropic outlook of those who are more at home with words than with people makes them poor candidates for public school teaching no matter how well they did in their liberal arts studies. Understandably, they employ their power with words to assail the professionals who judged them unfit to work with children. The other half of the matter is that the professionals who judge who is fit to teach sometimes have such a narrow view of how teachers should behave with youngsters that they exclude those whose outstanding mastery of a field of study has equipped them to succeed in unorthodox ways. Academic mastery is a necessary but not a sufficient condition to merit the opportunity to teach.

the rules of how to teach best from that practical wisdom that had collected like sediment from Quintilian to Comenius. They interpreted them in terms of the home they made for youngsters. First and foremost, they had turned their homes into schools in which they could give the child their full attention in all phases of living. School was a "real life" situation in a unique sense.

With rules in hand, Pestalozzi and Froebel undertook the task for which they had less systematic preparation—speculation about human nature. Such speculative talk about the individual had to be glued to the rules of thumb for teaching in order to assure practice the guidance of theory.

Froebel reduced the objects handled in classroom instruction to a specific set of geometric blocks, but their role was instrumental in a learning process in which the final outcome was some kind of spiritual awareness. The general method of having youngsters come in contact with objects counted chiefly as the means by which the individual became aware of what all of life was about. How the particulars fit into our over-all conception of the American school curriculum can be seen by the accompanying diagram, "Synoptical Table of the Gifts and Occupations Showing the Connection Between the Kindergarten and School" (Mme A. de Portugall).[2]

As adopted in the United States, Pestalozzi's object method concentrated less on the particular objects to be handled for spiritual awareness and abstract understanding and more on the knowledge of what the world was like. Instruction in each area of subject matter benefited from the body activity and sensory feelings aroused in working with objects. To support this view of general method, Pestalozzi reasoned that learning became more facile and efficient as instruction took account of the inner workings of the individual. Those inner workings so necessary to efficient learning benefited by a catalyst—sympathetic understanding from the teacher.

Both Pestalozzi and Froebel modeled their concept of the school as an institution after the home and family. In writing *Mother Play,* Froebel presented the mother as symbolic of all social virtues as well as instrumental in the early acquisition of these characteristics. Pestalozzi made little distinction between how youngsters were to be treated in class or out of class in their dormitories, dining rooms, and social activities. Even though the specific mechanics of how parental, personal, and social activities in the home influenced the child remained obscure, educators did not doubt that the atmosphere created there had a lasting effect. That same atmosphere filled the whole general method, as the accompanying diagram suggests:

---

[2] Wiggins and Smith, 1896: 114.

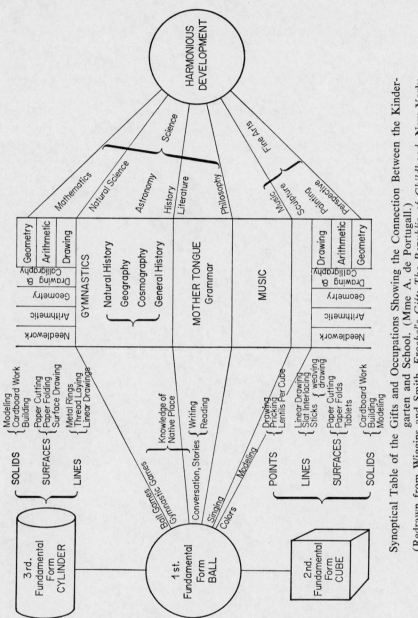

Synoptical Table of the Gifts and Occupations Showing the Connection Between the Kinder-garten and School. (Mme A. de Portugall.)

(Redrawn from Wiggins and Smith, *Froebel's Gift: The Republic of Childhood.* New York: Houghton, Mifflin and Co., 1896.)

OBJECT METHOD AS A GENERAL METHOD		
	Individual	Instructional	Institutional
intra	Sensory experiences arouse feelings within the individual which give qualitatively different kinds of understandings upon which future learning could build and draw.	Contacts with particular objects must provide the basis for an understanding of abstract concepts in any field.	The classroom is similar to the home. The teacher provides sympathy and acceptance to stimulate interest and inquiry.
inter	The broad range of normal behavior must be allowed. Provision for interaction between youngsters is important.	The connection between objects and abstract concepts must be made clear.	
super	The youngster appeared to be a plant drawing understanding from sensory contact as a leaf draws nourishment from sunlight.	The child must achieve an understanding of what the world is *like* and what it is *about* in terms of forces, concepts, and ideas underlying sensory experiences.	

By looking into himself and at his relationships with others, the Pestalozzian, a representative individual in a normal society, sought a window through which to witness mental and social processes at work in their natural habitat. Descriptions of inner operations became the explanations of why instruction conducted in the object-teaching way worked and why other kinds of instruction would not do so well. Each new generation of teachers was encouraged to revise the rules and renovate the rationale. Such change signalled the emergence of the teacher as a professional with a voice in talk about instruction, but it also marked a shift in the nature of educational talk from a direct to an indirect concern for practice. It veered practitioners toward amateur philosophy and it shunted professionals toward the belief that they were building a general discipline, at once useful in training teachers and profound in its contribution to understanding individuals, instruction, and the institution of public schooling. Lacking standards of scholarship, these professionals saw literary generalizations from various areas of thought being cemented together to form a general discipline of education both broader and more practical than previous philosophic systems.

Monitorial practice employed expedient rules of thumb and executed them like military orders. Coming from administrators who did little or no teaching, these rules generated almost no feedback; and the directness of talk about practice deteriorated. A slackening of attention to specific content to be achieved in the classroom accompanied the recognition that instruction could lead to many kinds of learning, only some of which were included in skill mastery, drill, and memorization. Interest in the behavior of pupils, and especially in those inner workings of their minds, suggested new ways in which the outcomes of instruction could be talked about. Instead of translating talk about the inner workings of the individual into terms observable as the consequence of instruction, the aims of instruction were specified in terms of the inner workings of the mind.

Such biographical phrases as "need fulfillment" and "student interest" became ever more prominent in talk about general methods of instruction. Formerly, under monitorial method, talk about education had remained untheoretical and thus did not lose its connection with practice. Through the speculative tendencies of talk about object method, the efforts at building a theory of how the child worked inside himself forced talk about practice to adopt the subjective vocabulary of personal biography. The connection between theory and practice remained close only because talk about both employed the same rhetoric. In fact, practice had been cast adrift; and no one seemed to notice until the Herbartians appeared. Alarmed at such chaos, the Herbartian rational science sought to establish a genuine rather than a rhetorical connection between talk and practice, on the one hand, and yet to build a more systematic theory than object-teaching had erected. In short, it built a more complex general discipline of education to explain a simpler general method of teaching.

3. HERBARTIANISM

Never widespread beyond the northeastern cities of the nation, monitorial practice had weakened with age and abuse when object-teaching made its bid to become the dominant instructional technique in the new elementary schools being built all over the country. In contrast, object-teaching had neared full strength, both in the extent of actual influence and in the development of a rationale, when Herbartian practice appeared in force about 1890. A head-on collision in the public schools would have been inevitable if both programs had been on the same track. Object-teaching had remained concentrated in public elementary instruction, however, and Herbartianism made its early gains in public and private secondary instruction. The conflict, therefore, developed first among the concepts talked about. On the level of instruction itself, the battle broke out a generation later, but when the circumstances had been reversed. Herbartianism, deeply lodged in public secondary instruction by then, became the force resisting the new expression of the object-method viewpoint, which sought institutional form under the heading of Experimentalism. The attempt to set Herbartian general methods atop Pestalozzian elementary teaching and to call the monster a unified system of public schooling caused difficulties.

In 1890, however, the Herbartians were the innovators; and they needed a powerful thesis—more powerful than object method. A mere revival of monitorial method would not do. The attention of object-teaching to method and material objects at the expense of emphasis on more abstract learnings left an opening which Herbartianism filled with strong partisanship for the moral lesson to be learned from literature and history. But primary concern in building the rationale went, not to such content achievement but, rather, to the all-embracing goal it facilitated—moral character. Conceived to be the result of all proper instruction, moral character formed the tent within which other questions about education had to be arranged. Its fabric was maximum ambiguity. Here the Herbartians set up their general discipline as a cover for their general method.

"Moral character" served the Herbartians as a unifying concept both because of its ambiguity and because of the consensus it commanded. This paradox was the fulcrum on which Herbartianism balanced as the century changed. Just ambiguous enough, "moral character" allowed anyone to bring in his own particular variations of the Christian ethic without becoming a dissenter. Though vague, as with the definitions of "democracy," such phrases as "Christian ethic" and "moral character" commanded consensus from the layman even though he could not, and did not, define their content. In those days before modern anthropology, when ordinary citizens sought some common bulwark against atheistic implications drawn from evolution, such general terms cemented together religious thought which would otherwise have been helplessly diversified in a pluralistic society. Moral character and the Christian ethic stood for the common viewpoint. Even though unspecified, moral character stood for behavior to be expected of all men of good will regardless of their particular faith or immediate circumstances. And Herbartianism promised it as the product of a general method of instruction.

Coming after the concern of object-teaching for child interest and teacher sympathy, the Herbartians could not merely reassert simple monitorial obedience. "Interest" had to be included, but it did not have to retain its earlier meaning. Taking it out of the context of sympathetic acceptance in a home situation and placing it next to will and obedience effectively altered the concept. In the name of morality, interest became a debt owed to both the teacher and the content. The school was not a Pestalozzian "home," but an institution set up by the state.

Whether newly arrived or settled for generations, Americans carried the European indoctrination in obedience to authority deep in their basic family units, even while revolting against it as a form of civil government. Next to the family itself, the school had become the most personal living place for an ever-increasing number of Americans. Although the Herbartians did not see the school as an extension of the family, benevolent paternalism provided the concept of obedience which they expected throughout the school. The teacher—a father surrogate—served as moral model; and this role absolved him of the object-teaching demand for "motherly" sympathy. Instead, he had to extract obedience (disguised as interest), often by being stern.

The *proper* presentation of the right material at the *propitious* moment by an *informed* person would *create* interest, Herbartians reasoned. This ideal combination failing, the child who saw the worth of the material presented would mobilize his will and take an interest. On the other hand, when the teacher had taken precautions in selection, preparation, and presentation of material, the student who showed no interest brought suspicion upon himself. Except in cases of gross error in selection, negligence in preparation, or incompetence in presentation, the student *owed* interest in the name of what was best for him. And, as every Herbartian knew, interest appeared as the enthusiasm with which the student did what the instructor wanted him to do—a desirable beginning for moral character based on conformity to established standards. *Will* was the internal mechanism upon which interest depended when spontaneous generation failed, thus making it an indispensable element in the ultimate product—moral character. In practice, interest and will came out as obedience to authority; but, even so, the Herbartians had been brought to the recognition that something went on inside the child. To explain those internal happenings, they had apperception and the culture-epoch theory.

With the concept of apperception and the culture-epoch theory, the Herbartians generalized about the development of human nature and about how the mind learned. Yet a general method of instruction—not speculation—continued to be the Herbartian center of gravity, and each broad generalization merged into a method or technique and focused into a particular practice to be employed in the classroom. The stages of human development charted in the culture-epoch theory explained the process by which man and children became civilized, responsible, moral agents. The stages of that process indicated which lessons from literature and history would fit the stages of development that the child passed through from the beginning to the end of school as he moved from being savage to becoming civilized. A logically organized curriculum with specific content designated for each year resulted.

In similar manner, the theory of apperception outlined the general steps by which the mind learned, thus pointing out how teaching must be done—preparation, presentation, examination, generalization, and application. This reinforced a whole battery of practice: the well-organized content lecture, backed by an extensive lesson plan set within chronological grade placement and a pattern of prescribed courses of study for each year.

The Herbartians put numerous monitorial commitments to work in modernized dress. Even when the terminology resembled that of object-teaching, the spirit remained opposite. Herbartian pedagogy, stripped of its elegant rationale, stood for the following:

1. The primary importance of abstract thought, such as *ideas* about justice and virtue attained from literature and history.
2. The power of lessons from literature and history to change behavior.
3. The necessity of obedience to authority in both content learning and moral training.
4. The importance of order in all aspects of learning: first, the orderly presentation of lessons according to the five steps; second, the order of the content to be learned as determined by scholars; third, the order of the curriculum from first year to final grade; and finally, the internal order of a controlled will and, thus, a directed interest, resulting in obedience.

Diagrammed, it reads as in the accompanying chart.

HERBARTIANISM AS A GENERAL METHOD		
Individual	Instructional	Institutional
intra 1. Interest would be triggered off by content which fit the stage of development the child was in; and if it didn't, the child should use his will to force interest. 2. Mind learns according to five stages of apperception.	1. Content must be presented according to the five stages of mind. 2. A child who has failed to master necessary background cannot go on to the next lesson or the next grade.	As in a well-run Boy Scout Camp, benevolent paternalism is necessary and best. Like a scout master, the teacher is a model of skill, knowledge, and moral character. Too much familiarity leads to contempt.
inter 1. Each age group has its appropriate stage of development and, thus, grade grouping provides homogeneity. 2. Stages of child development parallel stages through which the race has passed.	1. The curriculum must be organized according to stages of the development of the race. 2. Each year's work should be concentrated around a literature and history core of content.	
super The child, a social embryo destined to develop according to a known pattern, must be guided in a moral direction.	Social evolution will develop ever more cultured and knowledgeable civilizations, and the schools can accelerate this progress.	

Herbartian thinking opposed object-teaching in at least two ways: first, the Herbartians kept their concepts directed at the practical, moral, and content commitments; second, their attention gravitated toward more specific rules of thumb. The Herbartians sought to understand a child's nature in relation to techniques for injecting content into him and for imposing control on his behavior: interest and will, mobilized as conscious and subconscious obedience, would impress the lessons of literature and govern their use in life. With interest and will assured, the rest of learning needed to be arranged only for maximum efficiency. The question of exactly how the lessons from literature and history influenced moral behavior was answered in terms of the current psychological mechanisms. The assertion of a causal connection between abstract ideas, obedience to authority, and the moral goals of all education had to suffice.

In answer to questions about how child nature operated, the explanations provided by object-teaching showed no more depth of causal understanding than did those of the Herbartians. But this search for answers was carried over into a new educational program, at once more narrowly focused on child behavior and more given to talking about practice in terms of the feeling and inner workings of the pupil—child study. Froebel's "thinking love" sometimes became a substitute both for knowledge of content and for skill in such "trivial" things as maintaining discipline.

4. CHILD STUDY

Herbartian paternalism went beyond the organization of content by scholars for the future benefit of the pupil and society. It demanded that will and interest be exhibited by personal orderliness, obedience, and effort. The classroom atmosphere abounded in constraint. Quite different in temper, object-teaching insisted that, whatever the organization of content specified by scholars, it must be preceded by personal physical contact with appropriate objects or involvement in related activities if learning were to be optimum. This handling of objects and this concern for activities attendant to learning were to be viewed within a non-constraining atmosphere. Without abandoning order, it was hoped that the teacher would provide sympathy for the youngster and acceptance for his fumbling efforts. In this way, the child could engage in many different activities, all quite normal to exploration. In place of constraint, they sought elbow room.

In 1890, however, as child study grew in strength, public schooling programs had not yet grown to include so many pupils that continuity between elbow room at the elementary level and constraint at the secondary level seemed a serious problem. Both points of view continued to gain momentum.

Added to the Pestalozzian habit of introspection, the observation and reporting of child behavior seemed a catalyst, first, in transforming teacher attitudes toward children and instruction; and second, in providing information and insights into child nature which would both advance and clarify understanding of how students felt, learned, and behaved. Observation and reporting would result in a "reverent interest in all realities and mysteries of childhood," as Russell put it. The teacher would become *sympathetic* toward youngsters (reinforcement for object-teaching) and *accepting* of an even broader range of normal child behavior.

Child study insisted that, to be understood, children must be observed, and that, to be maximally meaningful, observations must be objectively reported in terms of behavior. Occurring at the very opening of the survey and measurement movement, such rigor seemed to point to a whole new conception of talk about education. But, in fact, the rigor and the reporting went for naught, since the major purpose of observation and reporting was a practical, not a scholarly, one: the stimulation of teacher sympathy for students and the acceptance of a broader range of normal behavior in the classroom. By using terms appropriated from the discussion of how the internal mechanisms of child nature were supposed to operate, child-study advocates couched their talk about education in the terminology of attitudes and feeling states. Thus the whole emphasis on objective reporting of observed behavior was negated by the move to carry the discussion of practice into the inobservable world of processes that were supposed to go on inside the child. Yet the new terminology seemed "scientific."

Burnham spoke entirely in terms of internal processes when he claimed that child study placed emphasis on the active, the productive, and the creative in education. In such talk about instruction, the teacher with the appropriate attitude of sympathy and acceptance would release the child's creative potential. Instruction would hover around the expressive, the internally governed, the curious, but, most of all, the whole child. Attitudes of sympathy and acceptance marked that vague general method called "permissive instruction."

To eliminate the insistence on obedience so basic to Herbartian paternalism, child study introduced a self-governing principle which overcame the appearance of disorganization introduced by an increase in physical activity; it also took the question of order into a discussion of processes operating inside the youngster. The worst external chaos in the classroom might be a reflection of the most peaceful internal order within the child. Appearances could not be trusted. Committed to the principles of beginning with careful, objective, diversified observations, child study nullified this by petitioning teachers not to be deceived by simple accounts of what they had seen. If observation marked the beginning of reporting, reports of inobservable internal states marked the results, even though the program at Worcester warned against such interpretation. Grafting Freudian concepts to pedagogy, child study reached for a general discipline. Charted, the basic concepts fill the diagram as shown in the accompanying tabulation.

CHILD STUDY AS A GENERAL METHOD		
Individual	Instructional	Institutional
intra The child is viewed as an active, expressive organism which suffers and fails to grow naturally under unnecessary restraints or imposed order.	There had to be an increase in physical activity in the classroom and encouragement of the expression of personal opinion and feeling.	1. School should be permissive like a home or nursery. 2. Teachers should be as autonomous as gardeners who tend different flowers in different parts of the world.
inter Freedom of self-expression would lead to self-control and do away with the necessity for artificial restraints.	Activities such as project work, handling things, and discussing things of personal interest, were to lead to such creative expression as is developed in music and painting.	
super The hope was for a creative, self-regulated youngster who would become intensely involved in his work. The child, like a flower, needs the right climate and soil.	Creativity, self-regulation, and involvement would characterize all instruction and would foster growth of the "whole child" (emotional and physical development would be added to intellectual growth). Allowed to unfold like petals on a flower, the child's creative expression will exhibit the same natural beauty. Thus, he was to be a kind of natural artist.	Personal and social growth through self-expression.

The Herbartians used "will" and "interest" as causal mechanisms. In the same manner, child study spoke about the internal workings of mind, understanding, and growth in terms which served as interchangeable tokens in talk about the process of learning and the consequences of instruction. But the point is that both Herbartian and child-study advocates spoke about what happened inside people and what caused behavior changes as if anyone could "see" these internal events and causal connections. They were "obvious" and, hence, understood for the naming— interest, will, activity, or creativity.

Assembling a brief for formalism in both content and control, the Herbartians employed terms from the rational psychology and the philosophy of individualism. Child study adopted terms from the equally individualized genetic and experimental psychology just emerging. But in the twentieth century, as bureaucracy invaded both business and government, and as the revolutions in communication and transportation expanded daily associations, psychology became social. In such a milieu, Experimentalism appropriated the vocabulary of child study and expanded it into a new terminology of group behavior: "active" became "interactive," "objective" turned social as "inter-subjective," "productive" came out "cooperative," "expressive" became "collective," and "creativity" changed, like an emerging butterfly, into "consensus." The language of individual effort and accomplishment became group talk of communication and agreement. Individualistic or social, the processes so designated were too frequently thought to be understood for the naming, whether referring to the institution, the instruction, or the individual.

5. EXPERIMENTALISM

After 1915, both elementary and secondary schools sped toward the inclusion of the great majority of youngsters, regardless of background, preparation, ability, or facilities. To have something for everyone became an insistent demand as numbers and diversity of youngsters increased. Answering for the elementary school, child study said in effect: "Worry less about the content to be given to all and more about the expression to be obtained from each." Yet this outlook aggravated the problems of content continuity and transition from elementary to secondary school, a problem which became important in direct proportion with the ever-growing number of students completing elementary school and gaining admission to secondary school. The Herbartians, however, had solved the continuity problem for secondary schools and offered recommendations for unifying the whole curriculum: organize content daily by the five-step method, monthly and yearly around the core of concentration, and throughout according to child-development stages as identified by the culture-epoch theory. There it was: the practices which would make room for diversity lacked continuity, and those so provident of content continuity could not accommodate the diversity in abilities that were already present and bound to increase. The consequence—civil war in public education.

Elbow Room in Teaching. After 1920, the need for a program that would accommodate all normal children began to dictate how achievement and continuity would have to be defined. Awareness that academic content, no matter how well presented, could not reliably or continually stimulate effort was added to the realization that continuity, no matter how logical, did not guarantee retention, and that mere retention had precious little to do with performance outside school. The absence of a proven program which would achieve results broadly credited as worthwhile encouraged widespread trial-and-error experimentation, with the hope that new techniques of instruction could be found that would arouse the interest that generates effort in the classroom and beyond. As teachers searched for the activities and the involvement that would assure mastery and secure further effort, they found that they and the students needed more freedom of intellectual and physical movement than Herbartianism or even object-teaching allowed. To do something for all those children and to have them do something for themselves required more elbow room. Some constraints had to be removed, and it took no deep philosophic insight into the nature of democratic society or profound psychological knowledge to know it—even corn needs room in which to grow. With children working in groups, elbow room is necessary.

Academic carping set aside for a moment, Dewey's 1928 characterization of progressive practices illustrated in each statement one or more of the following traits to be directly or indirectly associated with elbow room, or spontaneity:

1. The intensity of the revolt against formalism.
2. The emphasis on child-study expressionism.
3. The need for freedom for the child to work in.
4. The fact that the school program was for everyone.
5. The formulation of object-teaching and child-study recommendations into new generalizations about social processes.

Arranged from the general to the more particular and back to the comprehensive again, those elements of progressive practice provided an excellent glimpse of the spirit of practical elbow room as follows:

1. Increased freedom.
2. An atmosphere of informality.
3. Respect for individuality.
4. Disbelief in artificial personal relations.
5. Enough external freedom and informality to enable teachers to become acquainted with children as they really are.
6. Emphasis on activity as distinct from passivity.
7. Building on the nature and experience of the child.
8. Not imposing external subject matter and standards from without.
9. Respect for self-initiated and self-conducted learning.
10. Respect for physical activity as the stimulus and center of learning.
11. Formalization as hostile to genuine mental activity and sincere emotional expression and growth.
12. Belief in social contact, communication, and cooperation upon the normal human plane as the all-enveloping medium.
13. Attention to the so-called human factors.

Each guide to practical elbow room kept a corollary ready for a quick-draw attack against signs of constraint. That the generalizations and their corollaries served as effective weapons that did not require extensive qualification or explanation reflects the simple and direct nature of the beginning of this revolt against constraint. Increased freedom, informality, respect, communication, and cooperation had to do primarily with the "atmosphere" of practice. In a sense, atmosphere is to the group what attitude is to the individual. Numerous practical activities, such as having children in charge of regulating the shades in the classroom, could be implemented quickly to show movement toward increased freedom. Any number of incidents, such as standing for recitation, could be raised as evidence of constraint.

"Atmosphere," like "reputation," involves two difficulties: it is not a matter of getting one, but rather the kind and the extent. Such phrases as "increased freedom and activity," "building on the child's interests and experiences," "satisfying needs," and "encouraging social contacts" each carries with it those same questions: precisely what kind and to what extent or degree. Without such specification, the phrases remain almost wholly ambiguous. Certainly elsewhere the statement of an intention to hunt must be followed by a specification of whether it will be rhinoceros for trophy or starfish for photographing, before any decisions about equipment can be made.

The great failure of the literature of professional education is that, for the greater part of the twentieth century, it has done everything to exploit this ambiguity and almost nothing to explicate it. In search of agreement among practitioners instead of a clarification of specifications, the authors of articles in professional journals and textbooks consistently and steadfastly declined to specify what experiences should be offered, what interests should be considered, what needs should be satisfied. Practical talk thus lost substance and could only rearrange words in search of more felicitous ways of saying the same thing. Rhetoric, no matter how literate, cannot make a practical discipline, although it can give the impression of being part of a general discipline to the semiliterate and technically trained.

Continual and extensive reliance on ambiguity does not occur without reason. No sooner is it decided that a particular activity is to be encouraged than a new question follows: "Why this one and not some other?" To this, the only substantial answer requires empirical evidence of the consequences of employing one activity in instruction as against alternatives. But such evidence cannot be found. And, if it could, further evidence would be required to indicate the amount of time students should spend on such an activity as wilderness camping as against writing letters to congressmen. In the absence of evidence, only the acceptance of general answers as if they provided specific direction can avoid such embarrassment. Hence the prominence of literary explication as justification of general methods, such as problem-solving and the project method.

The Project Method. The attendance revolution brought into the classroom increased variety of ability, of ethnic origins, of socioeconomic background, and of levels of aspiration. With variety in all things the rule rather than the exception, heterogeneity, being inevitable, seemed desirable—even democratic. Like the city and the army, the school became a melting pot. But pitting youngsters of obviously different capabilities against one another or against a fixed standard of excellence seemed no fairer than the tortoise competing against the hare or both against the clock, Aesop notwithstanding. Just as something had to be made available for everyone, so did each youngster have to have a chance, preferably an equal chance, of succeeding.

Problem-solving, the *activity movement,* and the *project method* are all terms applied to the general method designed to provide some activity in which all could participate and from which most could benefit. Outstanding among those who championed facets of this new methodology were John Dewey, William H. Kilpatrick, and Walter S. Monroe. Chief among the critics were William C. Bagley and Ross Finney. At the height of interest in the new methodology, in 1934, the National Society for the Study of Education brought out a yearbook exploring the activity-movement concept. Seven years earlier, H. B. Alberty had prepared a much more careful conceptual analysis of the ideas basic to the movement in a little-noted monograph released by The Ohio State University. From these sources, the general method involved can be assessed.

Kilpatrick. With the concept of the project method, Kilpatrick thought he had made a major instructional breakthrough. He then quickly sought to link the general method with democracy through the idea of self-fashioned purposes. His own words illustrate well the kind of common-sense social philosophy widespread in the professional journals, at meetings, and in teacher-training courses just before, during, and immediately after World War One:

> We scorn the man who passively accepts what fate or some other chance brings to him. We admire the man who is master of his fate, when with deliberate regard for a total situation forms clear and far-reaching purposes, who plans and executes with nice care the purposes so formed. A man who habitually regulates his life with reference to worthy social aims meets at once the demands for practical efficiency and for moral responsibility. Such a one presents the ideal of democratic citizenship.[3] *

Then, to connect such talk about forming purposes and democratic citizenship with pedagogy, he reasoned:

---

[3] Kilpatrick, 1918: 53.1.
* A good example of journalistic prose—persuasive if not informative.

As the purposeful act is then the typical unit of the worthy life in a democratic society, so also should it be made the typical unit of school procedure.* We of America have for years increasingly desired that education be considered as life itself and not as a mere preparation for later living. . . . Education based on the purposeful act prepares best for life while at the same time it constitutes the present worthy life itself.[4]

The democratic citizen, like the figure in the poem *Invictus*,† is master of his fate and captain of his soul. He achieves this command by learning to plan and to execute his own purposes. The school provides him with systematic training in such planning and execution of "good" purposes. Certainly any school which can get maximum immediate and maximum long-range benefit from one and the same practice must be the most efficient possible. It is in just this poetic-utopian way that Kilpatrick expected maximum benefit to flow from the adoption of what he called the "project method" as the basic model for all instruction. He wrote:

> The contention of this paper is that wholehearted purposeful activity in a social situation as the typical unit of school procedure is the best guarantee of the utilization of the child's native capacities now too frequently wasted. Under proper guidance purpose means efficiency, not only in reaching the projected end of the activity immediately at hand, but even more in securing from the activity the learning which it potentially contains. Learning of all kinds and in all its desirable ramifications best proceeds in proportion as wholeheartedness of purpose is present. With the child naturally social and with the skillful teacher to stimulate and guide his purposing, we can especially expect that kind of learning we call character building.[5]

Having stated his basic attitude toward deportment and organization, he attempted to categorize the kinds of learning which would be encouraged under project-method instruction:

> Let us consider the classification of the different types of projects: Type 1, where the purpose is to embody some idea or plan in external form, as building a boat, writing a letter, presenting a play; Type 2, where the purpose is to enjoy some (esthetic) experience, as listening to a story, hearing a symphony, appreciating a picture; Type 3, where the purpose is to straighten out some intellectual difficulty, to solve some problem, as to find out whether or not dew falls, to ascertain how New York outgrew Philadelphia; ‡ Type 4, where the purpose is to obtain some item

---

* This seemed self-evident to a generation of teachers.
[4] Kilpatrick, 1918: 53.2.
† It is not unreasonable that professors and teachers would be moved by the same ideas that the public found so well stated in a popular poem.
[5] Kilpatrick, 1918: 53.3.
‡ Professional quarrels grew up as to whether types 1, 2, and 4 were not "problem-solving" too.

or degree of skill or knowledge, as learning to write grade 14 on the Thorndike Scale, learning the irregular verbs in French.[6]

Simplified, Kilpatrick's four types of projects can be listed as:

1. Construction (writing a letter probably belongs as an example of Type 4).
2. Appreciation.
3. Puzzle-solving.
4. Skill and information mastery.

But for Kilpatrick, the kind of learning mattered far less than the spirit permeating it. This becomes clear when the concept of spontaneous organization received serious consideration under the heading of cooperative planning. In emphasizing this stage of spontaneous organization, Walter S. Monroe voiced an attitude toward instruction which grew in popularity among teachers just before and during the depression.

Monroe. Certainly, if "wholehearted purposeful activity in a social situation" were to become "the typical unit of school procedure" regardless of subject matter to be taught, than a general atmosphere of elbow room rather than constraint would have to pervade all classes. But for a pupil to "plan and execute his own purposes," the spontaneous organization necessary to capitalize on interest and cultivate enthusiasm had to become equally pervasive. Eight years after Kilpatrick's initial statement, in the middle of the "Roaring Twenties," Walter S. Monroe returned to this theme in the following attempt to distinguish the concept of project method from problem solving:

> A variety of definitions have been proposed for "project" as the term is now used but the one formulated by Kilpatrick (1921) appears to be most helpful. He defines a project to be "any unit of purposeful experience, any instance of purposeful activity where the dominating purpose, as an inner urge (1) fixes the aim of the action, (2) guides its process, and (3) furnishes its drive, its inner motivation." [7]

The references to "inner urge" and "inner motivation" indicate how seriously educators sought to establish spontaneity as the principal basis for the organization of instruction. How far this emphasis on spontaneous organization went in the thinking of responsible educators can be gleaned from what Monroe went on to say about the essential difference between problem-solving and project methods. About the project method he said:

---

[6] Kilpatrick, 1918: 53.4.
[7] Monroe, 1926: 70.1.

No assignments are made. Instead the pupils are given an opportunity to do things they want to do.* This does not mean that they are allowed to do as they please and are subject to no restraint nor direction. Spontaneous proposals by the pupils which do not appear to lead to highly educative activity may be discouraged or even vetoed by the teacher. On the other hand the teacher may stimulate *purposing* by the pupils and even suggest projects† but direct assignments have no place in the project method.

The phrase "problem method" has been used to designate a type of instructional procedure which is sometimes confused with the project method. There is, however, a fundamental difference. Under the problem method the exercise is assigned; under the project method it is proposed by the pupils. The actual activities of the pupils and the outcomes, both mental and material, may appear to be the same but the teacher's point of view is different.[8]

The spontaneity that cooperative planning permits, not the nature of the work itself, distinguishes project method from problem-solving, in this analysis. The difference was procedural, organizational. Describing how this reliance on spontaneity changes the whole curriculum, Monroe wrote:

> . . . the project method and a fixed curriculum are incompatible. . . . the adoption of the project method as the typical instructional procedure will usually make it impossible to follow a prescribed curriculum.[9]

Stating it from the teacher's point of view, he said:

> The concept of the project method implies that the pupils are to realize their purposes with a minimum of assistance from the teacher. . . . A teacher employing the project method will seldom if ever be able to plan in advance the particular projects that his class will undertake. Instead he must utilize the purposes exhibited by his pupils.[10] ‡

Throughout their discussions Kilpatrick, Monroe, and other leaders of what later became known as the "activity movement" stressed elbow room in deportment and spontaneity in organization. A full appreciation of the kind of learning implied by such an approach to deportment and

---

* Hence the legitimacy of the cartoon with the disgusted students asking the harassed teacher, "Teacher, do we have to do what we want to do today?"
† The distinction between "motivating" and subtly "intimidating" eluded most teachers.
[8] Monroe, 1926: 70.2.
[9] Monroe, 1926: 70.3.
[10] Monroe, 1926: 70.4.
‡ Notice that the move to minimize planning content in advance occurred when the expansion in personnel and clientele made it more difficult to be sure that teachers and students were mastering the increased body of factual knowledge accumulating in all areas of inquiry.

elbow room received widespread attention much later. One of the documents responsible for the extensive examination and explanation of this aspect of instruction was Part II of the *Thirty-third Yearbook* of the National Society for the Study of Education, which gave full attention to the activity movement. But in 1927, the year after Monroe's statement and seven years before the *Yearbook,* H. B. Alberty at Ohio State University undertook a scholarly analysis of the project method.

Alberty. From the very beginning of his analysis, *A Study of the Project Method in Education,* published in 1927, Alberty admitted that the new methodology had a legitimate complaint against the excesses of drill, memorization, text-worship, and unintelligible abstraction so often associated with didactic, or lecture, instruction. Practice had too often crystallized into meaningless repetition and stultifying drudgery, he affirmed, as follows:

> The pupils learn symbols; words, without having back of them meaningful experiences. They "learn" to recite definitions from the textbook glibly, without having the slightest notion of the real meaning. The girl who took the prize for remembering that a "noun is the name of an animal, thing, or quality, as horse, hair, justice" and then wondered what "horse-hair justice" really was, is one case in point.[11]

In explaining how projects could provide meaningful experiences, advocates of the new methodology often spoke of "real life activity." Just as a thing itself has a kind of "reality" which a photograph lacks, so did the activity of building a house, or even a model of one, represent a real-life experience only described in books. "Direct" experience was seen as better than vicarious experience. Direct contact made symbol memorization unnecessary without impairing understanding. But terms like "real-life activity" were mixed with slogans like "learning by doing," and both were blended with problem-solving and project method to yield much glib talk about instruction under the general heading of "the activity movement." Here, again, a specific approach was generalized as a model for all instruction to follow.

In an effort to disengage sense from nonsense in the kind of talk about instruction which Kilpatrick engaged in and with which he gained so much acceptance among teachers, Alberty reviewed the development of the various concepts involved. He reported that the educational use of the term "project" began when R. W. Stimson, an agent of the Massachusetts Board of Education, "applied it to a plan of 'part time work' in the Vocational Agricultural High School of Massachusetts." [12] Describing such a project, he wrote:

---

[11] Alberty, 1927: 1.1.
[12] Alberty, 1927: 1.2.

If it is desired to teach the boys how to raise potatoes the plan is to have him actually select a plot of ground, prepare the soil, select and plant the seed, and eventually harvest his crop under actual farming conditions. This provides for what later became known as the concept of "real-life activity," "natural setting" or "social situation." [13]

Initially, then, "project" referred to work done away from school and only partially under the direction of school authorities. Taking it a step further, Alberty reports that Stimson looked favorably upon the fact that in 1912 twenty-five boys earned $5102.30 from their projects and that Dennis asserted that "an agricultural project to be of value, must be of economic importance." [14] Not only did youngsters learn from doing, but they did well in the bargain. In this interpretation of project—that it must have economic importance—this real-life activity came as close to being a business enterprise as a school-sponsored program could become.* Initially it had specific practical meaning.

Tracing the extrapolation of the concept of project method from its original meaning as a work activity, Alberty credits G. M. Ruch with equating "project method" with "problem-solving" along lines suggested by Dewey's ideas about reflective thinking. Alberty supported this merger of ideas in the following manner:

> *The problem method becomes completely merged with the project method.* One may say that the stages above indicated (1. a situation calling for adjustment. 2. defining a purpose to adjust it. 3. casting about for solutions. . . . 4. carrying out plans . . . 5. judging success or failure. 6. feeling satisfied or dissatisfied.) are practically synonymous with Dewey's analysis of the complete act of thought, and any activity which might properly be called thinking becomes a project.[15] †

Ruch and Kilpatrick fought against more limited interpretations of "project method" advocated by such leaders as Snedden, Randall, and Moore. Ruch wanted to broaden the concept so that, to use his words, "the project can be fully utilized in all fields of classroom instruction" [16]— a general method.

In order to make the concept over so that it would fit any kind of instructional situation, Kilpatrick dissociated "project" from any particular

---

[13] Alberty, 1927: 1.3.
[14] Alberty, 1927: 1.4.
* Except for such "character building" activities as having youngsters sell Curtis magazines from door to door.
[15] Alberty, 1927: 1.5.
† Whether the complete act of thinking were characterized by Herbartians, Dewey, or Kilpatrick, it still served as the basis for belief that a general method of teaching could be patterned after the general plan by which mind worked.
[16] Alberty, 1927: 1.6.

kind of activity or learning outcome. Thus, terms like "real-life activity" and "natural or social setting" lost their literal meaning as references to a certain kind of activity. How such phrases took on a wholly figurative meaning Alberty explains in this way:

> In the beginning of the use of the project method the basis for the determination, however, was an objective one. One had only to analyze the "project" itself to determine whether or not, independent of any consideration of the learner, it was a "real-life activity." With the new extension proposed by Kilpatrick, it avails us nothing to examine the project, because that method of procedure could never reveal whether the activity was "wholeheartedly purposeful."[17]

Criticizing such an alteration of meaning, he stated:

> Now, upon the arrival of the new definition of the project [Kilpatrick's], the confusion grows because the criterion of what constitutes a project becomes entirely subjective.[18]

And finally, condemning such talk, he concluded:

> We can raise no objection to Kilpatrick gathering together all the valuable principles of the "new education" under the concept of "wholehearted, purposeful activity proceeding in a social environment," but we can legitimately inquire why he should have called the concept by the name of project method. Why call it by any new name?* Why not call it just what it is—wholehearted purposeful activity? This would have served to unite such activities as uttering a prayer, making a dress, and watching a Fourth of July celebration, under one head—though it is hard to see why anyone should want to unite such various activities.[19]

Originally projects had been concrete, and particular kinds of activity had been carried on in natural, not school, settings. Growing potatoes on the farm was one kind of project. As the activity movement developed, men like Kilpatrick connected the sense which such projects made with such slogans as "We learn by doing." If idle hands be the devil's playground, busy hands become the teacher's workshop. But in emphasizing the half-truth that children do, indeed, learn many things best by doing them rather than by reading about them, educators ignored its equally valid corollary, namely, that people often understand least what they do most familiarly. Men love but fail to understand their emotions; they argue but remain

---

[17] Alberty, 1927: 1.7.

[18] Alberty, 1927: 1.8.

* For the purpose of convincing teachers that there was a workable general method involved somewhere in that mixture of practice-centered and journalistic prose.

[19] Alberty, 1927: 1.9.

illogical; and some people, we are told, have children yet know nothing about procreation. What had begun as a generalization from practice had become subordinate to a general method and the rationale that supported it.

The work of Comenius, Pestalozzi, and Froebel impressed on American educators the realization that sensory experience often provides an excellent platform from which to launch concepts. Playing with blocks starts youngsters toward an understanding of volume which words could not duplicate. Here was the three-dimensional application of the phrase, "One picture is worth a thousand words." In their enthusiasm, advocates of the new methodology often mistook the beginning point for the destination. Later, in vocational-training programs, educators often ignored the fact that a youngster could become proficient in rebuilding an automobile engine without ever encountering the concept of combustion. In such an oversight they were as much in error as the teachers of the nineteenth century who, emphasizing poetry, kept the concepts of love, honor, and beauty so abstract that youngsters never realized how they might apply to their home, business, or dress.

Figuratively, the need for "something which everyone could do well" regardless of his ability led practice toward block-building and away from examining the concepts behind construction. Reasoning went about as follows: Everyone could handle concrete objects and benefit from the sensory experience in a way that most could not "grasp," or benefit from, high-level abstractions. Regardless of ability, all youngsters could be started at the same primitive level of sensory experience by being led to work on simple projects which they could build. Able youngsters would soon move on to more abstract understandings. The less able could still be kept interested and occupied with manipulative activities, and they would continue to profit. Whereas, if the less able were forced to work with abstractions they could not understand, nothing would be gained and much lost. Youngsters would fail in their lessons and eventually drop out. They would lose interest, become restless, and raise problems of control.*

To the advocates of the new methodology, projects which offered the opportunity for physical activity, social contact, and the exercise of manipulative skill were necessary. It did not seem unreasonable to begin all instruction with some such activity or to recognize that many youngsters might not progress beyond such activity. It is from just such a starkly practical analysis as this that Alberty concluded that projects diverted

---

* Too often able youngsters did not progress beyond more accomplished activities, and the "understandings" hoped for failed to develop, leaving the youngster skilled in some manipulative activity yet uninformed. This, too, has its counterpart among grammar teachers who admit that the youngsters frequently use nouns properly yet lament their inability to define them. Shop teachers who would emulate teachers of grammar might spend most of their time in teaching definitions of hammers and saws.

attention away from the learning it was expected to accomplish in the same way that the candy coating on a pill makes the child forget that it is medicine. In the following analysis of the project method as oblique or indirect teaching, he proposed this practical definition emphasizing its *ostensive* characteristic:

> *Oblique Teaching:* It should be noted that the project which the teacher set up (in the original sense of project method as found in Agricultural Education and Home Economics) really aimed at the same thing (acquisition of knowledge, skill, etc.) which he tried though sometimes unsuccessfully to accomplish by "book learning," but he proceeded in a very different maner. He set up a procedure which called for an activity which, from the pupil's point of view, did not aim at learning at all; it aimed at the accomplishment of some *other* result which was of value to him.* For example, his aim would be to *raise* a prize calf, not to *learn* to raise one. This leads to the definition which we wish to propose.
> The project method in education is that teaching procedure which aims at securing learning (i.e. the acquisition of knowledge, habits, skills, ideals, etc.) *indirectly* by means of activities which have the following characteristics: 1. the goal which is supposed to dominate the pupil and lure him on to the accomplishment of the end, is not the *learning* sought by the teacher, but is some concrete result or accomplishment. 2. The learning essential to the satisfactory completion of the activity is always *instrumental* to this goal. That is, what ever learning is achieved is a by-product of the activity and is not directly arrived at by the pupil.[20]

By disengaging the concept of project from talk about "real-life activities," "natural setting," "inner-motivation," "typical unit of the worthy life," and "democracy" Alberty attempted to restore its practical meaning. He saw that the project led to a *direct* kind of sensory experience which often had incalculable merit as a beginning point from which to capture student interest and build certain skills. But he also saw that, in terms of more abstract understandings, such as a geometric concept or the causes of the Civil War, projects such as building a model of Fort Sumter, no matter how much fun in themselves, represented an *indirect* approach to something beyond the project.†

---

* This change in focus was often seen as necessary to gain interest; hence, student-planning was put forth as motivation disguised as "purposing." Correction of this error sought to overcome the manipulative aspect of such motivation by referring to "genuine interest" and "real-life activity." Later, educational philosophers practiced analytic or linguistic philosophy by pointing out the redundancy involved. This manufacture of pseudo-scholarship might better be set aside in favor of the historical examination of the sense of statements in contexts.

[20] Alberty, 1927: 1.10.

† The emphasis on such indirect learning in getting youngsters to plan and to do projects, in turn, led to the mistaken view that mastery of subject-matter content by the teacher could be minimized in favor of procedures or techniques which were part of the general method called "project method."

Captivated by the fact that projects provided activities that everyone could do reasonably well, find satisfaction in, and learn "something" from, advocates of the new methodology often convinced themselves that everything could be taught by projects. From that conclusion it was only a short step to the belief that everything could be taught *best* that way. Such a conviction led naturally to slogans which implied that only the (physically) active child learned. Hence, no projects, no learning. What they overlooked was that a pupil could handle blocks indefinitely and not encounter the concept of volume. "Discovery" is not inevitable, often it is not efficient, sometimes it is not likely, and in some instances it might not be possible.

Projects and Practice. Alberty pointed out clearly that, as general methods of instruction, the project method and the problem-solving method differed only insignificantly. Both methods, and the activity movement as a whole, emphasized ostensive activity in the classroom and minimized concern for didactic instruction. Further, Alberty explained that the early development of the project as an activity associated with vocational agriculture took place as a specific instructional technique. In its earliest form, the project had promise of developing as a generalization from actual practice. Instead, however, of being a grass-roots generalization synthesized from the common elements found in actual practice, the project-method concept fashioned by Kilpatrick was merely the subjective counterpart of the steps of scientific method described by Dewey: adjustment, purpose, imagination, execution, assessment of worth, and evaluation of satisfaction. From such a subjective general conception of instruction, Kilpatrick directed much of his attention to the "self-other process" in psychology and its implications for democracy.

Monroe came closer to making specific recommendations for practice when he stated that the project method implied cooperative planning, and that reliance on pre-planned sequence had to be abandoned. It was precisely such specific conclusions for actual practice which got the project method into some of its greatest difficulties. Indeed, specific directives for instruction could be pronounced. Their workability was another matter. The profession had 2,000 years of collective experience behind the Herbartian formulation of the five steps but only 20 of trial and error in the use of projects.

As long as the general conception of practice offered by Kilpatrick got little closer to classroom behavior than the generalization that "the purposeful act" should be the typical unit of school procedure in a democratic society, discussion remained safely abstract and ambiguous. What began sensibly enough as a recognition of the importance of elbow room and spontaneity in the classroom soon grew pretentious. Talk about education climbed the ladder of abstraction from "typical units of instruction" and "the purposeful act" to psychological doctrines of permissiveness, self-other, phenomenalism, and gestalt. From psychology the route led to philosophy of human nature, moral character, social welfare, freedom, democracy, and the metaphysics of experience. Belief in the typical unit of instruction frequently made it seem unnecessary to look at instruction further.

The project method did not, however, develop in a vacuum. In part, it grew out of a reaction against the direct, didactic lecture given standing as a general method by the Herbartian five-step method. But even when the Herbartians got hold of it, there had been a long history of its use and, in the present, the contrast between direct and oblique lessons has been restated as "the old versus the new."

The Old Methodology. The direct nature of didactic instruction has been given quite clearly by Gilbert Ryle in his book *The Concept of Mind*. He wrote:

> Didactic speaking and writing . . . is talk in which, unlike most of the other, what we tell is intended to be kept in mind. . . . Now didactic discourse, like other sorts of lessons, but unlike most other sorts of talk, is intended to be remembered, imitated and rehearsed by the recipient. It can be repeated without losing its point, and it is suitable for retransmission by word of mouth or in writing. Lessons so taught can be preserved, as lessons taught by demonstrations and examples cannot be preserved; they can therefore be accumulated, assembled, compared, sifted, and criticized. . . . Intellectual progress is possible just because the immature can be taught what only the mature could have found out. [21]

The difference between direct and indirect learning stands out. The didactic nature of monitorial instruction and the Herbartian program can be reconstructed from this statement, and the fitness of such activity for recording on tape or for performance on television indicates its relevance to contemporary developments in the current academic emphasis. But the general method which gave didactic activity the standing it enjoyed when the project method was proposed by Kilpatrick emerged in its most specific form from Herbartianism. Taking the theory of apperception as a literal account of human thought processes, Herbart patterned the five-step method of instruction directly after the steps of apperception which he affirmed. Even when the theory of apperception as passed down to teachers was discredited by scholars like William James, the five-step method of didactic instruction remained in favor as a general method; and when the Herbartian formulation gave way to the five steps of scientific method, the belief that some general method of didactic instruction could be found remained strong. The lecture method itself often acted as the illustration.

Especially as the youngster went further on in school, the lecture became ever increasingly the dominant method of instruction. Academic

---

[21] Ryle, 1949: 94.1.

subjects of the kind encountered in liberal arts colleges lent themselves well to the lecture method. Also, the amount of reading that had to be done increased in the higher grades. The lecture and the textbook in academic subjects provided the instruments for direct didactic instruction. Of all, the Herbartians built the most comprehensive general method of direct instruction. The Experimentalists focused on the oblique teaching described by Alberty as implicit in the project method. Still, the Experimentalists could argue that they were teaching how to make choices directly, whereas the Herbartians, who proposed that awareness of moral principles would emerge from a study of history and literature, were oblique and indirect.

In this way, talk about education expanded beyond the practical issue of whether or not simple projects or didactic-telling were the best general methods for instruction. The practical classroom issues became part of a change in outlook that extended from prison reform to child rearing.

Expanded Talk. During the 1930's the search for equal partnership in the home had heavy impact on child-rearing practices and husband-wife relations. Businesses had to listen to labor's complaints, and personnel-management programs expanded. In such a climate, educational elbow room made indelible changes in the practical routine of schooling. Youngsters had more to say and a greater variety of things to do than ever before. In the schools, something for everyone became fact, but not without cost.

Diversity in abilities and the sheer numbers of students both had expanded so fast that trial-and-error experimentation had not been able to provide comparable improvement in techniques for instruction. But sheer quantity, and diversity in ability and background, could not justify the exclusion of some students from school, since the trend was toward maximum inclusion. Nor could the inevitability of decline in the quality of instruction be admitted. Somehow, practice had to be buttressed against a recognition of decline in the quality of accomplishment with words if not with facts. Since the formulation of working principles through trial and error could not be hurried appreciably, and since something had to be said, talk about how to teach took on many of these journalistic characteristics:

1. Denial of decline: youngsters spell better now than ever before.
2. Attention to what *should* and not to what *could* be: ends (goals) must be discussed and agreed upon before means (methods) can be judged appropriate.
3. A preference for the general and abstract over the concrete and particular: practice unguided by philosophy is blind, and a philosophy not rooted in metaphysics is adrift.
4. A dismissal of what *is* with a loaded word: Traditionalism!

5. Expectation that the teacher's attitude is sufficient to change student performance: "Belief is the fuel and the radar of action." The committed teacher is the communicating teacher. A proper attitude toward youngsters is more important than mere technical competence in method or knowledge of subject matter.

6. A re-defining of accomplishment: social adjustment, effort, growth as measured against past performance, anticipation of what kind of future citizen the child will become.

7. Suggestions of general strategies which the practitioner must make operational: core curriculum, unified studies, broad field programming, fused course (all integrating content while achieving "significant guidance objectives" through an "enriched curriculum").

8. An untestable general method: five steps of scientific method as applied to information problem-solving, intelligent decision-making, the building of new values, critical thinking.

9. A comprehensive moral tone: the whole child, the adaptable personality, the well-adjusted child, the creative individual, the well-rounded person, a balanced personality, a contributing member of society, a good citizen, education for democracy.

10. Hollow phrases: "Play must be an element in the good life." "All education is training in leadership."

Such statements did not advance practice so much as they aggravated dissatisfaction with established techniques of instructing and served as blanket permission for indiscriminate trial-and-error experimentation in classroom procedure. As the need for some stopgap to fend off a decline in instructional quality increased, rashness in experimentation often turned to riot and innovation. Without evidence to offer in support of such innovation, the only defense was journalistic talk. The language of education exploded with loaded phrases about the individual, instruction, and the institution of public schooling. Possibly the best way to illustrate that fusion of practice-centered and journalistic thought is to employ some of that language in the accompanying chart.

Possibly no other professional literature provides so complete an account of the liberalism of the 1930's as does the talk about Experimentalism. Gestalt psychology, permissive child care, non-directive counseling, equalitarian organization, diversified authority, cooperative planning, relative values—central attitudes of the prewar decade—emerge from statements about the individual, instruction, and the institution. The terminology represented a vast amalgam: explanation of needs, motivation, and achievement were set in the matrix of the social psychology of groups

EXPERIMENTALISM AS A GENERAL METHOD		
	Individual	Instructional	Institutional
intra	Meeting his *felt needs* and tapping his *genuine interests* would provide *intrinsic motivation* and enable him to achieve *genuine emotional expression* within the bounds of *self-imposed* discipline. (Basic concept)—Satisfy his biological and social needs.	*Psychological organization* of content will replace logical and chronological organization as the *need* for a particular skill or body of information in the solution of a problem suggests the child is *ready* and *motivated* to master it. (Basic concept)—1. Useful and functional learning. 2. Self-initiated learning.	The scientific method of solving *real problems* in the classroom, among the *staff,* and involving the citizenry would make the school democratic. (Basic concept) —*Democracy.* Thus, the school was a miniature democratic community.
inter	The increased activity of project work would provide a stimulus and an outlet for *creative* expression. Group work would facilitate *social adjustment.* The student would build a better picture of himself by seeing himself reflected in the responses of others toward him. (Basic concept)—*Cooperation.*	All knowledge is initially of equal worth, but some knowledge is more relevant in any particular problem. Project work employing content and skills as needed would reveal all knowledge as *interdependent,* thus overcoming *artificial compartmentalization.* (Basic concept)—Project work activities provide best learning.	Serving *the whole community,* the school would become a model service institution and both an example of and a training ground for *intelligent democratic participation* in solving social problems. (Basic concept)—*Social problem-solving.*
super	*Cooperative planning* would give experience in *decision-making,* thus teaching him at once *responsibility for his choices, cooperation, tolerance* for the views of others, and the value of *consensus. Decisions* made in pursuit of desirable goals would enable him to build *functional* or *operative values* and improve his *moral behavior.* Thus, the individual had the crucial facets: he was (1) a "needs system" searching for answers and satisfaction, (2) a critic of all a priori moral rules yet a socially responsible lawmaker constantly rebuilding institutions to maximize welfare. This has been summarized in the concept of "responsible citizen" or social critic.	The *interest* generated by problem-solving would extend beyond formal schooling and compartmentalized content and lead to *self-initiated learning* and *critical thinking* about problems through the systematic use of scientific method. (Basic concept)—*scientific method and science of values.**	The school serves the society best by training the next generation to *rebuild* its own set of values so that they emerge as adults prepared to embark on *peaceful revolution* through *social reconstruction.* (Basic concept)—*continuous peaceful revolution.*

* Dewey developed the scholarship behind this in his *Theory of Valuation.*

but were biased in favor of the cultural relativism so important in anthropology, philosophy, and literary essays. * Further, the unity-of-science movement and the efforts toward a science of values appear in the project method and in the concept of solving moral problems by the scientific method (at once an over-arching moral aim and a methodological answer to the Herbartian five steps of instruction).

The unemployment of the depression rings from each effort to cut back on academic subjects in favor of learning that will insure almost immediate earning power, security, and eventual welfare. This factor, coupled with the increased importance of science in a technological society, provided a combination nearly fatal to already encrusted foreign languages and to humanities subjects grown complacent and even cocky under Herbartian approval. And as super-concepts, the attitudes of secularism and sympathy for the common man joined to support moral self-determination and reconstruction. This gave new vigor to a re-definition of democracy in connection with the New Deal ideas of welfare, but eventually led men like Rugg and Brameld to lend support to journalistic tendencies that faced away from inquiry and toward indoctrination. Articles published as "philosophic research" often lacked scholarship and became impassioned essays.

The humane and liberal attitudes of the depression provided the nutrients on which talk about Experimentalism ripened. A different concept, however, governed the *manner* of expression. By insisting on the inseparability of means and ends, John Dewey sought to weld talk about goals to be achieved (ends) to concrete means for their accomplishment (means). But in such an immediate and practical activity as teaching, an unimpeachable connection between ends and means depended on some empirical proof of what instructional techniques accomplish. The link between idea and practice depended on information. Trial-and-error experimentation during the 1930's had not added appreciably to the reservoir of proven techniques or even increased the supply of information about what worked, where, with whom. Yet, in the expression of aims, Experimentalist talk reached as far as the imagination could stretch without worrying too much about the reliability of techniques for accomplishing the ends-almost-in-view or the availability of skills by which practitioners would make the general method work. Not only did aims outreach proven technique and available skills, but they sometimes reached beyond, first, the possibility of proof, and second, the likelihood that necessary talents and skills would ever be in extensive supply.

Either the aims would have to be restated to fit in with proven

---

* It was in unifying the general method of teaching under concepts from just such areas of inquiry that Rugg found the sources for his Foundations. In actuality, this seems to have been a set of premature generalizations from other areas of inquiry thrown as an intellectual blanket over general method in the name of a general discipline of education.

methods, or the statement of methods could not be made in operational terms. Unwilling to be constrained to proven or even provable techniques, yet committed to the ends as stated, talk about Experimentalism retained only a verbal link with practice. Talk about methods became as purely rhetorical as talk about aims, and the link remained unstrained, since the two kinds of verbalizations were indistinguishable. This can be dramatically illustrated by the accompanying chart, which shows the dual usage of basic concepts in Experimental talk. The same words serve interchangeably as process terms for explaining internal operations, such as thinking, or as product terms for designating the results of processes, such as when consensus is achieved.

PROCESS-PRODUCT INTERCHANGEABILITY		
	Individual	Instructional	Institutional
intra	Need satisfaction	Self-initiated learning. Problem-solving	Democracy
inter	Cooperation	Cooperative planning	Social adjustment
super	Consensus	Scientific valuation	Peaceful revolution

This interchangeability of process and product terms accelerated the tendency to speak of aims and achievement as internal happenings taking place within the individual, the group, or society. Unintentionally, no doubt, a sense of mystery gave process explanation a literary flavor. Philosophy of education, historically the matrix from which statements of aims emerged, became saturated with introspective talk. Further, talk about methods of teaching began, increasingly, to resound with philosophic statements about human nature and the nature of experience, both immediate and ultimate. Once talk about practice lost connection with operational procedures, talk about education struggled less to build theory capable of being validated and more toward pulling a general discipline from the magic hat of rhetoric. Although that rhetoric used the vocabulary of philosophy and of psychology, it was neither of these but, instead, simply professional shop talk: practice-centered abstractions out of scholarly context. As such verbalizing took over in teacher-training courses, it became even more sensible to say, "That sounds good, but I don't know how to make it work." And this, after all, is the sum of what teachers meant when they offered the misstatement, "It's O.K. in theory, but it doesn't work in practice." In fact, many complex ideas in the educational field have no practical bearing but continue to be graced with the name "theory."

The responsible use of knowledge from psychology and sociology for the improvement of practice became almost impossible when the ends lost touch with the means. Talk about both became more a matter of style than of substance. The interchangeability of process and product talk obscured this gap by making the ends and means seem one and the same. As a consequence, as "faith" in a general discipline grew, practice operated increasingly on expedience, even though practitioners believed that they had the benefit of guidance from the behavioral sciences and philosophy.

The Condition of Practice. Wearing no girdle, public schooling had to take the shape of whatever was poured into it. Blinded by rhetoric and left to the devices of expedience and trial-and-error experimentation, practice struggled to implement requests for elbow room. The absence of a lowest common denominator of achievement meant, inevitably, that some practices would be ugly and that the rhetoric of their defense would become grotesque in the extreme.

The faults of "progressive" practice do not rest so much with a particular philosophy or theory but rather with the difficulties inherent in a system of public instruction. The search for elbow room and for something that everyone could do posed most formidable, practical problems for the teacher. The mistakes, and the successes too, were the failures and triumphs of necessary trial-and-error experimentation. The presence of more errors than triumphs should not be surprising.

Child study and object-teaching generated the elbow room which "progressive" practices employed, but no program of reform can be immunized against those techniques and thoughts which its opposition has planted so deep that they cannot be exorcised. Elements of Herbartianism had to be included in the experimentalist general method. Further—and this is the point—just as heredity blends indissolubly with the effects of environment in the adult, so experimentalist education emerged as much the product of its revolt against formalism as of its inheritance from elbow room and the search for novelty. The neighborhood in which it grew encouraged extremes. The dichotomies that grew up around the general methods sought defense and justification in the practice-centered attempts at a general discipline such as the foundations concept. Too often journalistic excesses emerged.

Advocates of elbow room in the classroom found in the stages of scientific method a step-by-step method of instruction which could replace the Herbartian five steps of formal instruction as a general method that teachers could implement. The new method would require an increase in physical activity, and it would encourage the asking of questions. But it could not be limited to handling the sciences or even academic content if it were to become a truly general method of instruction for all the students then in school. As the model for all problem-solving, however, it could be comprehensive without being linked to any particular content. Thus, as the generalized scientific method grew into a prescribed technique for solving moral problems as well as informational ones, so did it seem to be a general method for teaching everything. By making this general method the major instrument in the development of behavior during daily instruction, experimentalism purported to explain the relationship between social ends and pedagogic means without losing contact with the demands of practice. That philosophers did not like the logic of the connection mattered less than the fact that teachers did. Such an appeal by foundations courses in teachers' colleges to the new personnel, rather than to an objective criterion of cognitive sense, proved to be an intellectual dead end camouflaged as a short cut to a general discipline of education. It produced considerable speculation about how to improve human behavior.

6. CURRENT ACADEMIC EMPHASIS

Our nation's greatest economic boom followed so closely after this century's worst depression that attitudes and practices had little opportunity for graceful revision. Total war completely filled the brief space between the beginning of recovery and the flush of surplus. The demands of war production changed many industrial habits quite rapidly; but when the nation awoke from the nightmare of war in 1945, people were not prepared to find the noontime of prosperity already striking. Just as newly discharged GI's found only ill-fitting civilian clothes in their closets, so did education have only prewar talk and practices, once the military-preparedness programs were scrapped. The kind of instruction used "to give something to anyone when jobs were scarce for everyone" did not fit prosperity, with its increased college attendance. More important, the rhetoric of discontent which encouraged peaceful social revolution through the schools no longer sounded like honest and healthy criticism, as the possibility of communist-inspired revolution and conquest suggested conspiracy.

And again, rocks thrown at the distribution of wealth seemed harmless enough when the economy could go no other way than up. As what seemed to be an economic zenith approached, such criticism of output could only disrupt the precarious balance needed to keep production and consumption at the summit. In the absence of positive proof of the superiority of techniques arrived at by trial and error during the depression, the change in outlook accompanying inflation and the cold war made the practices and rhetoric of experimentalist education seem, at best, naïve and obsolete and, more likely, unsound and subversive. During the depression, the problems of ordinary living were the most immediate and pressing and were therefore considered the most important. The ordinary problems of the great bulk of people seemed subject to common-sense solutions. Education promised to help all citizens to reason better about such matters. Further, the development of behavioral science promised to provide as much precise information about ordinary human and social matters as physics had supplied about ordinary objects and events. During the depression, science and welfare had converged on the common man as sufferer, and education approached him as a potential savior.

By contrast, however, after World War II, rocket supremacy and turning the atom into horsepower depended on the exceptional man who could understand and apply mathematics and physics. Nuclear defense and the exploration of space could be best facilitated by the talented few. Ordinary people once more became common and just a little obsolete, albeit necessary.

To implement the moral commitment that everyone is of equal worth as a human being, instruction during the 1930's offered something for everyone. In its extreme form, this descended to anything for anyone. As the standard of living climbed, however, questions of human worth and dignity receded before problems of military preservation and expansion of production and population. The postwar tensions forced the admission that equal worth as a person could not be translated directly into equal importance for cold-war survival. Since inclusion in the public schools of almost everyone in the appropriate age groups had already been accomplished, it became time to worry about achievement. And, indeed, as the accompanying chart of problems and conflicting attitudes suggests, there was much to worry about.

DIFFICULTIES ASSOCIATED WITH PROGRESSIVE EDUCATION		
(Some problems which led to a decline of confidence in Experimentalism)		
Individual	Instructional	Institutional
intra Failure to control student behavior was too often defended as the need for freedom and expressive activity.	Activities and projects drew attention from practice in composition and training in reading, spelling, and arithmetic skills.	1. Multiplication of committees 2. Committee opinion not used even when given. 3. Groups manipulated by administrators and teachers
inter 1. Group work in committees and on projects aggravated discipline problems. 2. Concern for social adjustment became an excuse for ignoring quality of accomplishment and organization of control.	1. Lack of over-all organization led to repetition of activities and of content. 2. Many courses were invaded by trivial content.	1. Services to the community multiplied beyond possibility of efficient control. 2. Excessive noninstructional teacher responsibilities, such as milk money and athletic supervision at evening games
super 1. Delinquency increase was blamed on lack of firmness in control. 2. Increase in sexual experimentation among adolescents was blamed on social adjustment programs. 3. Moral confusion was blamed on doubting of established values encouraged by educators.	1. Some students were encouraged to write compositions questioning some things done in the U.S., praising some things done by the Soviets, and expressing the need for world government. 2. Interest in the humanities and scholarship was replaced by interest in engineering and more immediately useful pursuits.	1. Fear that the U.S. might give up some sovereignty to U.N. 2. Feeling that patriotism and fighting power of soldiers declined in the Korean War. 3. Concern over loss of initiative in such proposals as socialized medicine—fear of the welfare state. Conflicting concepts of security

Broadly speaking, the difficulties confronting American education after 1950 converged from three angles:

1. *Natural change.* The switch from depression to prosperity, from isolation to internationalism, from what had seemed secure peace to cold war had been so gross as to produce a new national posture without a commensurate change in outlook.
2. *Institutional expansion.* Nowhere, ever, had so many youngsters been included in a schooling program. The great diversity of abilities included in a classroom made it necessary to expand the available choices open to youngsters so far as to make it almost impossible to achieve efficient organization and effective instruction.
3. *Strategic miscalculations.*
   3.1 Quality Control. In quality of instruction and effectiveness of discipline, educators had assumed that methods would soon be found which would accommodate unlimited diversity and still maintain high levels of achievement. (They were not found.)
   3.2 Idealization before Inventory. Having emphasized education as a profession, teacher-training institutions conveyed the idea of the teacher as a master-craftsman-turned-artist without bothering to take inventory of the techniques available for achieving minimums of control and accomplishment. Talk about the ideal covered up ignorance as to the mechanics of instruction.

Under pressure of such problems, it made good sense to seek something safe, and safety had two practical meanings: one pedagogic and the other national. Pedagogic safety rested with method and content which would be credited, in some sense, as tried and not found wanting. This policy dictated that the ends would be controlled by the means previously found useful in such incontestably important matters as basic skills and behavior control. In addition, national safety demanded talent in the professions, engineering, science, and military planning—all areas with intellectual-skill and academic-content prerequisites and populated by those who had made the most of sequential organization of content offered within well-regulated study routines.*

In moments of panic, this twin concern for safety became "to each student according to Soviet successes; from each according to Cape Canaveral failures." In more sober form, however, this foraging for safety

---

* Good study habits can be taught, but there is no guarantee that good study habits, so necessary to achieving entrance into a profession, will make one a successful practitioner or will lead to that other "habit" of mind, creativity— that is, looking at the familiar from a new angle so as to alter the perspective.

(sometimes characterized as a return to sanity) produced the Rockefeller Report, *The Pursuit of Excellence,* and the Conant reports on the high school and the junior high school.

If *The American High School Today* can be taken as representative, the following outline of its specific recommendations shows the current academic emphasis as far as it seems to have developed by 1960.

1. General education for everyone (9th and 10th grades)
   1.11   4 years of English (50% devoted to composition)
   1.12   3-4 years of social studies   (5 periods per
   1.13   1 year of mathematics   week throughout
   1.14   1 year of science   the academic year)
2. For the academically talented (repeating elements prescribed for general education)
   2.1   4 years of mathematics
   2.2   4 years of one foreign language
   2.3   3 years of science
   2.4   4 years of English
   2.5   3 years of social studies
3. For marketable skills (with vocational programs tied to employment and opportunities)
   3.1   Office skills for girls   (½ day in 11th and
   3.2   Home economics for girls   12th grades)
   3.3   Vocational agriculture, trade, and industrial program for boys.
4. Guidance (one full-time person to every 250-300 pupils)
   4.1   Individualized program: no classification of students according to tracks, such as college preparatory, vocational, commercial
   4.2   Ability grouping: grouped by ability, subject by subject, according to ability to perform in that subject
   4.3   Elective program: "Through consultation, an attempt should be made each year to work out an elective program for the student which corresponds to the student's interest and ability as determined by tests of scholastic aptitude, the recorded achievement as measured by grades in courses, and by teacher's estimates." [22]

The Conant report courted three virtues: balance, scope, and quality. Balance required that the teacher take into account the terminal student as well as the college-bound. He could ignore no one: the retarded, the slow, the average, the talented, or the gifted. Scope required the some-

---

[22] Conant, 1959: 14.

thing-for-everyone that a school's general program would provide: options of home economics, vocational training, and cooperative work projects. Quality could be found in those academically safe areas such as mathematics, composition, science, and foreign languages. Here, the content has been sufficiently standardized so as to suggest a sequence in which mastery must precede promotion and to insure the possibility of nationally standardized tests of achievement.

The appearance of balance dissolves, however, in a comparison of the amount of attention given to different areas of instruction. The retarded and the slow student are to be accounted for by specially trained teachers and ability grouping. Further, with ability grouping and a sliding standard of achievement, Conant would adjust the same general program to the slow and the average student. Guidance, cooperative work programs, and electives take care of the terminal student. Having mentioned these categories, Conant* gives fully 80 per cent of his attention to the talented and the gifted college-bound student. It is the student with special academic talents, not the depression's "common-man," that interests him.

The only program given a specific and detailed structure is the one which continues as the present-day vestige of Herbartianism. From the general program through the mathematics, science, foreign languages, English, and social studies of the last two years, the academic core provides the backbone on which all other programs must be draped—the norm from which all else is a departure. For all the talk about individualized courses of study, scope becomes a matter of fitting the student to the academic curriculum rather than fitting a curriculum to his capacities. The "interest" and "ability" employed in guidance are *"determined* by tests of scholastic aptitude, the recorded achievement as measured by grades in courses, and by teachers' estimates." Such a determination of *interest* takes the word back to an earlier Herbartian meaning. Mention, not attention, created the illusion of scope.

Progress in pedagogy is so slow that no one knew any better in 1960 than they did in 1930 how to have something for everyone and still maintain quality of instruction and achievement. The Conant report, and the academic emphasis in general, insist on quality. How to get it in a thoroughgoing way for everyone has not been solved, except in some journalistic oversimplifications that receive so much popular attention. The Current Academic Emphasis is not yet a general method in the sense that the five mentioned earlier have been. Yet its characteristics seem to be as outlined in the accompanying chart.

---

* It remained for Conant to revitalize the kind of inquiry that Rice initiated in 1895 and to show the truth of Thorndike's statement that the investigation of what goes on in schools is at least as complex as the geological surveying of a continent.

CONCEPTS BASIC TO CURRENT ACADEMIC EMPHASIS		
Individual	Instructional	Institutional
intra — The key virtues are initiative and integrity, especially as concerns intellectual matters, and they must be insisted upon. Eventually natural curiosity should triumph.	Knowledge of experts and the talents of gifted teachers will be made available to most youngsters through such devices as educational TV, tape, and teaching machines.	High achievement for the majority of youngsters in such subjects as mathematics, sciences, and foreign languages sets the tone on which the rest of the school should be organized. Yet it must be run, like an efficient business, by a board of directors.
inter — Students must have the courage to resist conforming to group pressures. Love for knowledge will supplant need for acceptance in a club or gang.	The content will be so well organized throughout the curriculum and from year to year that performance in skills will be high for most youngsters, they will learn foreign languages well, and will be prepared for professional training earlier.	The school is a basic training program for the professions, the arts, and science. National and even human survival—military, economic, and cultural— depend on the quality of that training. Basically, public school is preparatory for college, the professions, and technical institutes.
super — This should produce 1. Dedication to science and to scholarship in general. 2. Breadth of understanding. 3. Discipline which leads to excellence. The child is seen as a natural resource essential to national survival.*	The dedication to scholarship and high achievement best illustrated in science foundation scholarship projects will become widespread, yielding scholars, scientists, professionals, and military leaders.	Enlightened nationalism

The academic emphasis recognized clearly that diversity of student ability, accommodated through the complete abandonment of standards, invites the apathy and mediocrity of performance that make any claim to equal opportunity a farce. The whole emphasis on academic subjects hangs on the fact that high standards of scholarship can be built into lectures. With the quality of instruction thus prefabricated by scholars and with the required level of accomplishment set by experts on a national basis, local deficiencies in instruction and, to some extent, in student incentive could be minimized. Insistence on this approach to quality depends, in part, on a conviction that previous programs underestimated the academic abilities

---

* In the hands of super-patriots, who profess a return to individual initiative, the school could be turned into an instrument for molding the child into whatever the state needs (for survival, to be sure).

of youngsters and failed to tax them anywhere near capacity and, also, on the conviction that *broadcasting* is the better part of communication. Neither Conant nor other advocates of the academic emphasis have faced the possibility that the instruction might not be understood and remembered by the great majority of secondary-school students. They say nothing about what per cent of the present student body will be educationally expendable in the name of academic broadcast quality and test achieve- ment of this sort. With virtually everyone in school, the issue of who shall be educated has been supplanted by concern for the kind and level of in- struction currently employed. This is a direct, practical concern. And since those programming instructions are only guessing about the outcomes to be achieved by this book, that TV broadcast, or another lesson on a teach- ing machine, they must be prepared to have their trials result in more error than success. It will be interesting to see whether the automation of in- struction evolves into a general method applicable in most phases of the current academic emphasis. In the past, confidence in a general method applicable across many subject-matter fields has given impetus to the mistaken belief that "how" something is taught can be separated from "what" is to be taught. This, in turn, strengthens the view that a teacher who knows the method can get along with less than a thorough subject- matter mastery—a convenient professional fiction.

Yet a growing tendency to talk about producing a generation of technician-teachers who work under a master teacher could give added force to the older normal school outlook that it is more important to know how to teach than to be thoroughly acquainted with the subject-matter content to be taught. Teacher-technicians could become mere audio-visual aid experts. If you have ever stood in a cinema projection booth, you know that the last thing the operator wants to do is to look at the movie. For- tunately for the movie audience, they can't see him; but once in a while, he forgets to switch projectors in time, and the weighted hand of his pro- fessional detachment becomes apparent. As a technician, the audience's reaction means nothing to him. His critical faculties remain unexercised, even uncultivated. Already the zeal with which school administrators have taken to building conferences around the new technology suggests that they have the same fascination with it that hi-fi fans sometimes have with rec- ords of boat whistles and train noises.

In sum, practices in the schools have grown up around certain single views of generalizable method: monitorial drill and memorization; object- teaching's handling of things and play activities; Herbartianism's five steps and the (Culture Epoch) arranged curriculum; child study's vague directive concerning creative expression and self-discipline; experimentalist problem- solving and the scientific method; and the current academic-emphasis re- liance on the new teaching technology. These, it seems, have been linked in a common-sense way with differing models of child nature, as is exhibited by the accompanying chart.

The Tradition	Method	View of Child	Controlling Theme
Monitorial Method	Drill and Memorization	Trainable beast	Obedience
Object-Teaching	Handling Things	Flower to be cultivated	Discovery
Herbartianism	Five Steps	Social Embryo to be molded	Will power
Child Study	Self-Expression	Potential Artist	Sensitivity
Experimentalism	Problem-Solving by Scientific Method	Responsible Rebel	Involvement
Current Academic Emphasis	New Technology	Greatest Natural Resource	Mastery

The method seemed a description of how to teach, and the common-sense view of child nature served as the model for understanding child behavior. Given such a controlling theme as I have suggested for each tradition, efforts to build a discipline of education could reach out to discuss such philosophic issues as free will versus determinism or any other subject. As in the construction of an essay, these efforts at building a literary discipline of education knew no natural limits. The method seemed general, and so did the discipline. Change the controlling theme, and the essay will dip into some other field of inquiry for its substance. Change the model of child nature, and the whole ground shifts. Change the general method, and you have a different universe of ideas to work in. Even within each of the six traditions specified here, no single set of values can be posited as necessary for *this* general method or *that* view of child nature.

From this analysis the magnitude of Weisberg's recommendation that the values implicit in each special tradition must be ferreted out from its local context becomes apparent. If these be literary, poetic, constructs, they do not yield to careful analysis in that the poetry of what is implied but not stated cannot be sifted by the finest mesh of logic. The criticism of literary concepts is itself an art in which the standards of excellence and/or scholarship remain unexpressed and possibly unexamined. It is to be expected that efforts at building a general discipline of education on a foundation of literary concepts should exhibit the same disorder that has prevailed in areas having the same inheritance.

As teacher training and as independent research, the development of the intellectual content about education has passed through four stages. The first stage began with the monitorial method at the beginning of the nineteenth century and finished with the twin development of Herbartianism and child study at the end of that century. Stage two, confidence in an empirical science of education, covered the first quarter of the twentieth century. Stage three, in which two different kinds of research were mixed, overlapped the stages before and after it with no clear dates of beginning or end. The fourth stage, the attempt at subjective unity, began in 1929 and continues through the present.

These stages of development do not chart the evolution of a discipline of education so much as they show the failure of such an evolution to take place. They chronicle the major turns in the issue of whether to develop explicit areas based on descriptive information or to substitute emotionally charged, practice-centered thought as the means for creating personal belief.*

Nineteenth-Century Approaches to Teacher Training

Innovation in the way of training teachers in the United States developed during the nineteenth century. Monitorial method, object-teaching, Herbartianism, and child study each faced different sides of that changing

14

---

* Thus filling talk about education with journalistic statements that often inhibit teacher training and virtually prohibit broad standards of scholarship.

Literary Patterns
in General
Disciplines of Education

practical problem, and each sought to solve it in different ways. The way these teacher-training programs talked about education set the precedents for the discussion of education as an intellectual discipline in the century that followed.

Monitorial method trained boys to perform the teaching function with the same techniques it employed in classroom instruction. Talk about the practical task of teacher training was one with talk about instruction. With monitorial method frankly based on rote memorization, extensive drill, and unswerving obedience, *talk* about education quite easily *described* the techniques and content of monitor training in *common-sense* terms designed to *improve practice*. Chart One presents a synopsis of the nature of monitorial method, one of four major approaches to teacher training which set precedents for ways of talking about education in the nineteenth century. These precedents severely influenced how education would be conceived as an intellectual discipline at the beginning of the twentieth century.

Monitorial method had to make progress against widespread illiteracy with a minimal kind of instruction, and hence had to maximize routine in order to provide strong control. Technical skill in conducting drill and recitation and forceful techniques for commanding obedience were ade-

CHART 1

Monitorial Method—Practice-Centered Talk, 1820 *

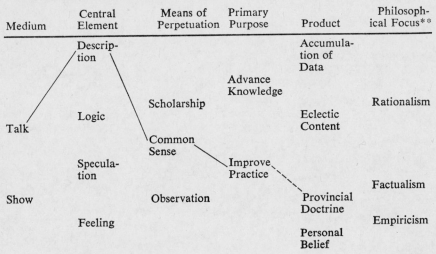

Medium	Central Element	Means of Perpetuation	Primary Purpose	Product	Philosophical Focus**
	Description			Accumulation of Data	
			Advance Knowledge		
		Scholarship			Rationalism
Talk	Logic			Eclectic Content	
		Common Sense			
	Speculation		Improve Practice		Factualism
Show		Observation		Provincial Doctrine	
	Feeling				Empiricism
				Personal Belief	

---

* Solid line—well-developed tendencies.
  Dotted line—latent tendencies partially developed.

** Absence of connecting line indicates that development stopped short of next category.

quate to the straightforward assignment of achieving almost letter-perfect repetition. The concept of instruction was narrow and simple; the standards of achievement were explicit and, taking into account the necessity for obedience, did not tax common sense. In all respects, straightforward explanations of practical skills and techniques sufficed; practice-centered talk was adequate even in its simplest, nontechnical form, common sense.

Much of monitorial method was so straightforward in its explanations that the talk could be called nontheoretical. Object method, as originally discussed by Froebel and Pestalozzi, continued to engage in talk on the common-sense, descriptive level; but the speculation which both men introduced concerning the nature of mind and the symbolic significance of objects opened the way for much more imaginative kinds of talk about things of a less immediately practical nature. Chart Two traces out the more complicated pattern of *talk* and *show* generated by that mid-nineteenth-century teacher-training program which offered the first simple glimpse into the possibility that education might develop as an intellectual discipline and thereby enhance its effectiveness in changing the conduct of practice.

CHART **2**

Object Method—Feeling-Centered Thought, 1860 *

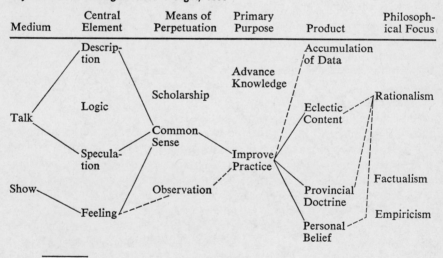

* Solid line—well-developed tendencies.
  Dotted line—latent tendencies partially developed.

Viewing the instructional task and the teacher's role in more complicated terms than monitorial method had done, training in the object method had to go beyond common-sense talk devoted to the explanation of practice. The demonstration and practice-teaching parts of the program supplemented practice-centered talk of method with the explicit showing of technical skills. On one level, talk and show fit together in a common-sense approach to providing information about a less narrow, more complex kind of instruction than monitorial method had been concerned with. Practice-centered show and talk accomplished that much through explicit expression.

But object-method teacher training went beyond the demonstration and explanation of technical skills. Practice-centered talk and show did not deal with the connection between the method of instruction and the concept of how the mind operated. The speculation of rational psychology had to be brought in to do this. Froebel's talk about the spiritual and symbolic significance of objects gradually added a kind of amateur speculation to object-method theory. Explanations of "reality" often went beyond common sense. Thus, on a second level, practice-centered show and talk were surrounded by speculation-centered talk—a kind of metalanguage considered more professional theory than scholarship.

Yet even these two levels did not complete the structure of object-method teacher training. Somehow, the model of the teacher as a sympathetic adult responding sensitively to the behavior and the needs of children had to be achieved. Since this could not be built up explicitly from the sum total of technical skills and understandings developed, the best to be hoped for was that the needed sympathy and sensitivity would accrue as impressions from exposure to the totality of practice-centered talk, show, and speculation. Talk of the spiritual and symbolic meaning implicit in objects and activities could only hope to arouse appropriate feelings in the practitioner. The sensitivity and the sympathy which the teacher was supposed to feel had to be evoked in like manner—not defined or described. To a degree, such attitudes could be exhibited, but the combination of talk and show mustered to create this feeling were summoned up as resources to take over where straightforward, narrow, explicit, descriptive, practice-centered language stopped. Such feeling-centered show and talk constituted the top level from which the logical meaning of the speculation and the technical meaning of the practice-centered thought derived their value. The humane interpretation of the teacher's role and the extension of the instructional task to include a way of looking at life had begun to absorb practice-centered talk. Information was necessary but no longer sufficient for the development of the desired attitude.

The issue became whether to give primary attention to improving ways of talking, as the Herbartians did, or to attend to influencing attitudes as directly as possible, along the lines of child study. This was the first fork in the road toward developing an objective discipline or something subjective to serve in its absence.

CHART **3**

Herbartianism—Logic-Centered Theory, 1890 *

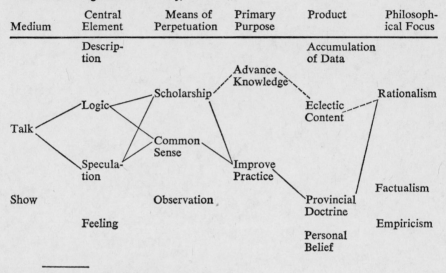

Medium	Central Element	Means of Perpetuation	Primary Purpose	Product	Philosoph- ical Focus

Description

Accumulation of Data

Advance Knowledge

Scholarship

Logic

Rationalism

Eclectic Content

Talk

Common Sense

Specula- tion

Improve Practice

Show   Observation   Provincial Doctrine

Factualism

Feeling   Empiricism

Personal Belief

---

* Solid line—well-developed tendencies.
  Dotted line—latent tendencies partially developed.

The Herbartians updated the monitorial concept of instruction as focused on drill in necessary skills and the recitation of important works. Alongside their finely polished concept of instruction, the Herbartians stood a limited concept of the teacher's role. Although the Herbartian model of the teacher did not call for the extraction of obedience through a rigid chain of command, the teacher-to-student relationship was decidedly cool and formal, demanding little of such intangibles as sympathy and sensitivity as expressed in Pestalozzian terms. The view of the teacher and of instruction had been cut back to where technical skills which could be shown and practice-centered talk of only a slightly technical nature offered minimal training. With such a floor under practical training, the rationale built around such mechanical routines and explicit directions as the five steps of instruction could be expanded indefinitely.

In this spirit the Herbartians set out to make the first full use of the intellectual machinery imported with the object method. They pursued speculation back to metaphysics and sought to establish the moral aim of all social organization and human effort. Detailed speculation on the rational psychology of apperception and the rational anthropology of the culture-epoch theory produced pieces of an elaborate intellectual jigsaw puzzle. Some parts locked with the tight-fitting logic of scholarly reasoning. Other parts touched one another in the smooth fit of common-sense thought. Still others were held in place by interlocking analogies. With all parts in place, the puzzle spelled out the same message that practice-centered talk conveyed, namely, that instructors should use the five-step general method.

Conversational reasoning, with its common-sense agreement, and the documented logic of scholarship mingled on equal terms in Herbartian talk about the educational entailments of speculation on "life." Overcompensating for limited descriptive information about mankind, Herbartian verbalization gave the illusion of great learning, confirming a general method of instruction bound to lead to the successful conduct of practice. Taken in by their own illusion, the Herbartians declared such talk a rational science.

Being the first to make full use of the available intellectual tools for talking about education in the context of ideas about all of life, the Herbartians assumed that these tools had been used with maximum effect and efficiency. Prone to consider their mixture of scholarly and common-sense logic systematic because it fit together into a pattern of their own design, the Herbartians encouraged the belief that such teacher-training talk could be cultivated into a general discipline of education productive of both knowledge-for-its-own-sake and useful generalizations comparable to those derived from the application of established science.

The Herbartians had faith in the eventual utility of the pursuit of information and reasoning having no apparent, immediate value—they had the research attitude necessary for building a discipline. In addition to having the research attitude, advocates of child study expected educators to spend more time looking at children and less time worrying over logical theories. They had an empirical attitude. In directing attention to the feelings and the information to be gathered from the observation of children, the early stage of child study was the only one of the four nineteenth-century training programs to envision the full extent of the job involved in cultivating education as a specific *literal* discipline.

Object-method instruction and the sympathetic teacher underwent a face-lifting by child-study advocates. During the pursuit of a general method of instruction, the handling of objects grew to include such activities as self-initiated investigation and imaginative invention. Not free from its rationalistic inheritance, however, child study pursued the internal responses and feeling states which accompanied object-method interest in learning through sensory contact. Tapping these internal feeling states so that they would come out as creative expression became a primary consideration in teacher training. To inspire, recognize, and channel such internal sources of written, spoken, or acted expression, the teacher had to be more than sympathetic to the needs of children.

Such a teacher had to have internalized an understanding of how the child works on the inside as well as outwardly. That grasp of how chil-

CHART **4**

Child-Study—Observation-Centered Reasoning, 1895 *

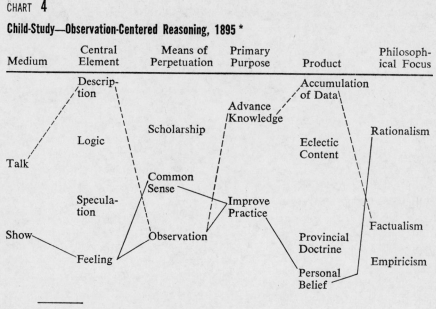

Medium	Central Element	Means of Perpetuation	Primary Purpose	Product	Philosophical Focus

Description

Talk

Logic

Scholarship

Advance Knowledge

Accumulation of Data

Eclectic Content

Rationalism

Common Sense

Speculation

Improve Practice

Show

Observation

Feeling

Provincial Doctrine

Personal Belief

Factualism

Empiricism

---

* Solid line—well-developed tendencies.
Dotted line—latent tendencies partially developed.

dren behave inside had to be felt, not explained. To achieve that feeling, detailed observation of children was added to the practice teaching and skill demonstration developed in conjunction with object-method training.

Demonstration lessons, practice teaching, and observation made full use of the machinery of look and show. Child-study advocates had confidence that their training program was adequate to their enlarged definition of the instructional task and the teaching function. To develop this internal dimension of practice and practitioner, child study cultivated direct exposure to the activities of children and supplemented the exposure with talk. Observation of practice became the most important part of teacher training because of its effect on attitudes. The right attitude, moreover, was considered a prerequisite to understanding anything else about teaching. The sum total of talk and technical skills could not insure such attitudes, but without it talk and skills lacked over-all integration.

The classroom had become a stage on which feelings about life were to be expressed. As director of that daily drama, the teacher had to coach his students like a Stanislavski-trained expert. Empathy, not logic, provided the key. The talk which supplemented the direct exposure of observation owed less allegiance to Herbartian scholarship and logic than to the sympathy and tolerance upon which object method insisted.

Child-study training produced numerous accounts of child behavior written in a common-sense descriptive style by amateur observers who thought the sum total of reports would lead to a general discipline of education. To the Herbartian belief that talk about education could be organized into a science, advocates of child study added their conviction that reports by amateur observers could be added up to yield a literal account of child behavior. Confidence in the ability of the untrained but dedicated amateur to grasp a fruitful line of inquiry overlooked by experts seems to have been at the bottom of the early-twentieth-century belief that a science of education was imminent. This same naïve confidence in the amateur scientist prompted later students of teacher training to accept the reports of measurement and survey researchers as facts instead of as experiments in description. The accounts of child behavior reported by student observers were, however, early experiments at refining a language of description.

As the task of training teachers took on new dimensions, both talk and show had been expanded from narrowly practical tools for explaning technical skills into broad instruments for conveying the feelings implicit in a way of looking at life. In child study the task of creating attitudes and feelings had been so completely taken over by the direct exposure to the activities of children that new attention could be given to limiting the language used in making the reports. Instead of having to use talk as a primary instrument for creating broad impressions and attitudes of sympathetic acceptance, the student of child study could restrict it to the job of careful description. The sum total of careful descriptions gathered or read by any one student did not have to add up to a change in attitude. The change was achieved in the act of observing. Recorded observations were a bonus, and they could be treated in the same detached way in which the Herbartians had approached their attempts at systematic reasoning— as research for a discipline. The child-study efforts at building a general discipline did not follow up this attitude but degenerated into human-interest stories and autobiographic accounts. When, because of limitations inherent in common-sense explanations, concern is for panoramic explanations rather than detailed inspection, practice-centered thinking leads toward journalism, not scholarship.

Cultivating the Research Attitude

Through teacher training, Herbartianism and child study cultivated the research attitude, although each put practice-centered considerations first. Under the encouragement of men like Royce, James, Dewey, and Munsterberg, clinical research in laboratory schools promised to improve on-the-job descriptive reporting similar to the kind that child study had experimented with. The linking science of education sponsored by James and Dewey encouraged the scholarly investigation of established science and the careful processing of personal experience by middleman theorists who voluntarily limited their speculation. Critical talk about practice had a good beginning. A high point of hope came in 1912, however, when Paul Monroe, Thorndike, Henmon, Ruediger, and Parker distinguished between the immediately useful rationalism convenient for teacher training and the careful observation, objective description, and limited generalizations essential to an empirical discipline of education.

Under the Herbartians, practice-centered talk seemed to be tightening into more precise, technical explanations of a five-step general method. There was concentration on the development of the skills that could be demonstrated in a straightforward manner—another aspect of general method. Such a move could have left rationalistic theories, with their broad speculation about all of life and their detailed deductions for practice, in the hands of scholars such as James and Dewey. Reports of child-study observations might have been refined into records of laboratory-school clinical research. It seemed that the research attitude born in the company of speculation about life and of feeling-centered observation would act first as a built-in governor against excesses of unscholarly talk and sentiment in teacher training, and second, as a boost to the liberation of scholarly and scientific inquiry from the demands for immediate utility.

Instead, however, of bursting forth as a newborn force aiding in the development of education as an independent intellectual discipline, the research attitude conceived within the overlapping frameworks of Herbartian and child-study teacher training became circumscribed by practice-centered demands for common-sense explanations. Thus, strength was given to the belief that the most important inquiry was that which could be turned to immediate use. The next development was an impatience with the long-range view that Thorndike summed up when he likened the complexity of descriptive research in education to the geographic charting of a continent.

By using scholarship to back up speculation about all of life, to buttress drooping logic, or to find talk to fit preferred feelings, practice-centered research obscured the tasks of developing a language of careful description, a body of objectively described data, and a set of theories to be tested. Practice-centered research siphoned off energy that could have gone into experimenting with descriptive ways of talking. It flooded the literature with the speculative and feeling-centered vocabulary of teacher training, and it dragged the scent of rationalism along the trail of empirical research.

The attempt to extract maximum immediate utility from scholarship and observation reduced the attention paid to the objective investigation of present conditions. Yet it fostered the belief that the practice-centered research attitude and the disinterested research attitude needed for the development of education as an independent intellectual discipline were mutually supportive, if not synonymous. As a result, experiment in ways of describing practice had to proceed by trial and error through the survey and measurement movements.

Accounts of the activities of children, of their deepest personal feelings, and of their needs ran through the clinical reports like those that Dewey solicited from the practitioners of progressive methods. The development of philosophies of life with implications for the conduct of instruction filled talk about education with controversy over seemingly contradictory accounts of experience drawn from unrelated points of view. The measurement and survey movements produced bundles of information which could neither be piled up nor laid end to end. Workers exploring each little niche of practice and each chink in speculative reasoning could not foresee that the sum total of their efforts would be random and repetitious rather than organized and cumulative. The improvement of the language of objective description and the extensive development of information gathered from a standardized point of view had not been accepted as problems in need of direct attention. It had been assumed that these problems had already been solved. Under that assumption, confidence in an empirical science of education took the form outlined in Chart Five.

CHART **5**

Confidence in an Empirical Science, 1912 *

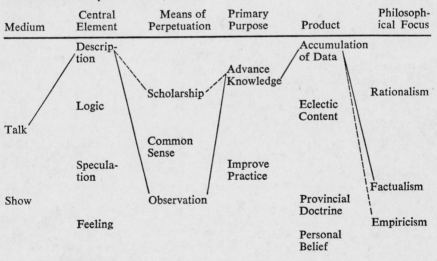

| Medium | Central Element | Means of Perpetuation | Primary Purpose | Product | Philosophical Focus |

* Solid line—well-developed tendencies.
  Dotted line—latent tendencies partially developed.

Mixing Observation-Centered and Practice-Centered Research

By 1912 many leaders of educational thought had argued well for the liberation of research from the task of supplying immediately useful material, but more powerful trends forced teacher training to bind investigation to the production of intellectual content which would reach for a broad subjective euphoria rather than narrowly descriptive information. Three such trends which kept much investigation practice-centered but highly speculative were: (1) the rapid expansion of public schooling as an institution for social services in addition to instruction, (2) the further development of object-method and child-study concepts of instruction through experimentalism, and (3) the increasing popularity of the idea that, in addition to technical skill, the teacher must be guided by a philosophy of life. In providing an understanding of public schooling as a social institution, teacher training had to account for a vast enterprise still unexplored as to its structure, its function, and its effect. Concepts of instruction which spoke of cultivating the expression of feelings and of satisfying deeply felt needs looked for light to illumine the unknown regions of consciousness and the depths below. And an educational philosophy of life had to make all this intelligible, somewhat consistent, interrelated, and applicable to explanations of method and of technical skills. In order to develop some useful "feel" for the child, instruction, the school, the community, and society within an account of the nature of experience, those building the content of teacher training had to rely heavily on the imagination and the authority of established scholars. Practice-centered research developed the habit of using older philosophies imaginatively but without the precision and careful criticism that makes "research" scholarly. Practice-centered talk thrived on secondary scholarship which cared more for what could be done with an idea than for its precise meaning in the context of its original appearance. Interest in the imaginative use of an established idea sometimes ignored the genealogy of its development to the point of accepting second-hand interpretations of the thought, for example, of such philosophers as Plato, Aristotle, Aquinas, and Dewey.

Secondary scholarship in the area of philosophic speculation set a precedent for the subsequent assimilation of information, vocabulary, and generalizations from the sciences of human behavior into talk about education. Information was often selected to support speculation. Vocabulary was often adopted without the restrictions of meaning which gave it precision on home grounds. Generalizations were stripped of restrictive qualifications and used to support philosophic speculation about the nature of human nature. Such journalistic sleights-of-mind too often passed as "research."

This eclectic assimilation of philosophic and scientific thought left deep rents in the patchwork of secondary scholarship. Speculation about the nature of experience had to be stretched to touch on the technical skills known to be useful in the classroom. To create a feeling for the institution of public schooling, for general methods of instruction, and for the guidance which a philosophy of life could give to practice—to create an attitude which would cover up the absence of objective information—teacher training had to encourage extravagant talk. Practice-centered "research" that fabricated speculative content for training teachers overran rather than supplemented the observation-centered research of the measurement and survey movements.

Further, while the measurement and survey researchers experimented by trial and error with ways of making the language of objective description more precise, the secondary scholarship of practice-centered research facilitated extravagant talk about education by oversimplifying scientific and philosophic thought. Although practice-centered talk often included measurement and survey findings readily, it accepted those findings at face value as facts at the very time when the experiment in ways of describing were in need of careful criticism and evaluation.

Teacher training took whatever it could grasp and used it as a springboard from which to speculate. Otherwise expressed, uncritical acceptance plus invention enabled it to make a proposed general method seem derived from sound scholarship and quite capable of improving practice. Measurement and survey research attempted to give an account of everything in sight, in the belief that each account was one of a finite number of descriptions needed for an empirical discipline of education. Differently stated, uncriticized reporting and undirected selection of observation marked the frenetic activity that seemed to be part of a descriptive task comparable to the geographic surveying of a continent. Separately, practice-centered and observation-centered research each produced considerable material. Added together as secondary scholarship and factualism, the sum total of "educational research" suggested an emerging discipline of education, especially in the peak years of the early 1920's.

The bulk of educational research produced, however, could only be organized by categories, mechanically; and such a method did not suffice to turn a miscellany into a discipline. Libraries used alphabetical organization to put everything into some category. Individuals in teacher training cultivated particular philosophies of life and incorporated whatever findings could be accommodated from that provincial point of view.

The redundancy and inconsistency in content among courses with the same name annoyed Henmon and Ruediger in 1912 and confounded Pangburn in 1932. Even in 1912, teacher-training programs were organized by categories into courses in educational psychology, principles of education, administration, and method; and concurrently individual courses exhibited the provincial point of view to which the instructor subscribed. Suzzalo used a change in organization to conceal the perpetuation of a provincial point of view when he suggested having educational philosophy changed to educational sociology without a change of content. By addition and by splitting of content categories, the teacher-training program managed to make room for the expanded volume of practice-centered and observation-centered content. But the provincial viewpoints developed through practice-centered research gradually became power blocks, such as Instrumentalism, or Perennialism; and they injected the same quasi-philosophic questions into each categorical division of content, such as curriculum, administration, or principles of education.

As advocates of particular provincial viewpoints teamed with those who favored a particular approach to the description of human behavior, the same information, vocabulary, and generalizations taken from observation-centered research began to appear in all the divisions taught from that one point of view. And as provincial points of view differed within a division, so did the content. The only order in teacher training came through the individual instructor or the instructional teams committed to a provincial point of view, and that order was so limited as to encourage repetition and duplication.

Committed to the restoration of unity in professional training, the advocates of the foundations of education viewpoint sought to build a composite intellectual discipline which each of the various specialties, such as administration, curriculum, and guidance, could have in common. Such a composite discipline was to be built by informed yet imaginative middleman conceptualists operating between established science and the professional practitioner. In accepting Dewey's idea of the middleman conceptualist, the advocates of the foundations of education concept also accepted his view that the only place for educational science was in the mind of the practitioner. Thus, the foundations programs bypassed the construction of an objective discipline focused on knowledge about education and sought after the practice-centered result of conviction in the mind of the practitioner. Chart Six maps out the route by which the foundations program sought to encourage subjective acceptance of a point of view by offering a literary discipline of education.

Although educational course work had taken up permanent residence in colleges and universities by 1920, no literal discipline yet existed to supply objective information about instruction on which all disputing viewpoints would rely. For the structure of course work, teacher training relied on the powers of organization possessed by conceptualists. Lacking a descriptive language which compelled consensus on what constituted objective observation, attempts at empirical research were unsuccessful in building a body of content on which all parties to provincial disputes might appeal.

Teacher training had neither a straight line of scholarly thought

CHART **6**

An Attempt at Subjective Unity—Foundations of Education, 1950 *

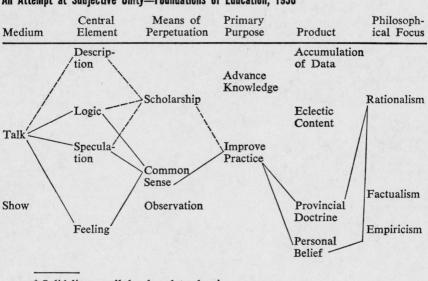

Medium	Central Element	Means of Perpetuation	Primary Purpose	Product	Philosophical Focus

* Solid line—well-developed tendencies.
Dotted line—latent tendencies partially developed.

from which to trace speculation nor a clear line of clinical research from laboratory schools with which to justify certain methods or to attest to the efficiency of certain practical skills. Meanwhile measurement and survey research lacked the power to generalize with authority. Middleman theorists were the only bulwark against the intellectual anarchy of unsupported personal opinion when, in 1929, Dewey began the move to relegate observation-centered reasoning to the established sciences and to install personal belief as a compensation for the deficiency in scholarly discipline. Spread-eagled, with one side tied to scholarly findings and the other tied to practice, the middleman conceptualist shouted that his general method would work in the classroom, and that, if he could just hold on to both sides, he would soon come up with a general discipline of education—its intellectual-emotional foundations.

Dewey's book *The Sources of a Science of Education* proposed that observation-centered research be left to the empirical sciences. With established science as the source of factual information and limited generalization, the middleman theorists would all have a common set of findings from which to begin. Although the faculty at Teachers College, Columbia, were willing to relegate observation-centered research to established science, they preferred to search out in conversation the foundations of American society as the basic platform from which middleman theorists would talk up an educational philosophy of American life—at best, a literary task.

In the 1930's the polemics of political science, social philosophy, and behavioral science replaced information from the more established science as the requisite background for practice-centered speculation. In the 1940's, Rugg added the expressions of "the men of force" acting as creative artists in the sciences of feeling-body response, the arts, ethics, and aesthetics. In the 1950's, the Illinois authors of *Theoretical Foundations of Education* added the poetic and ritualistic celebration of general ideals, and Brameld suggested that anthropology and the world's great religions be included. In searching for an over-all general discipline that would integrate all kinds of understandings from such diverse regions as empirical science, art, and religion, they could neither satisfy the scholarly demands from any one field nor keep from oversimplifying quite complex ideas and offering them up as sophisticated common sense. Complex ideas, stripped of the qualifications that kept them sound, stretched beyond elastic limits to be used as suggestions for practice, and set alongside other ideas equally deprived of their credentials, gave such middleman theorists as Rugg the feeling of making a new synthesis of knowledge.

These advocates of the foundations of education sought to combine the various complex modes of expression found in established science, the sciences of feeling and body response, political science, social philosophy, literature, the fine and applied arts, and religion into a subjective, practice-centered educational philosophy of life. It would be a general discipline of education supporting a general method of practice.

The Evolution of Extravagant Talk about Education

Before the Civil War, monitorial training explained particular technical skills of instruction and control in practical, descriptive terms leading toward the development of nontheoretical talk about method. Concerned with implementing drill and extracting obedience, monitorial method remained common-sense in character throughout.

During the Reconstruction Period, object-method teacher training continued the expansion of descriptive, practical content, supplemented by extensive demonstration. In addition, however, object-method training incorporated a popular variety of speculative talk that was designed to further practice-centered aims. Froebel's talk about symbolic and spiritual significance of his "gifts" fit well with popular religious beliefs. And further, speculation and talk about methods were encased in the conviction that an attitude of empathy and a feeling of sympathy for childhood were necessary before technical skill in instruction could be made effective. Introspective talk and spiritual speculation had been grafted onto objective description.

In the last decade of the nineteenth century, Herbartianism took the emphasis off technical skills and instructional methods which could be directly talked about or shown. Skills and attitudes were secondary to rationalistic understandings. But, as James pointed out in his attack on the pedagogical idea of apperception, the scholarship of one generation had led to the educational commonplaces of another. Herbartian logic and speculation mixed descriptive and non-descriptive ways of talking as indiscriminately as they mixed scholarly inquiry and cracker-barrel curiosity. Practical in intent, they had to bend scholarship to support a preconceived general method. Scholarship, stretched beyond its elastic limit, ceases to be scholarship.

During the same period, child study sought to distinguish between the reports of amateur observers and the practice-centered feelings evoked by watching children. Desired attitudes and usable skills were to result primarily from observation, demonstration, and practice-centered description of method. Speculative theory would supplement such implicit understandings.

Confidence in an empirical science of education grew strong around 1912, when it seemed that amateur observers were being replaced by experts. For the next decade, the belief that a language for objectively describing educational conditions was available and being used profitably by experts remained strong. The innumerable research studies which make up the measurement and survey movements between 1910 and 1925 were not looked on as experiments in various ways of describing. They appeared, instead, to be the content of a science of education. Meanwhile, during the 15 years in which observation-centered research experimented with ways of describing educational phenomena, teacher training continued to mix explanations of method, subjective talk of internal feeling states, and conversational philosophies of life with clinical reports from laboratory-school practitioners and an elaborate display of speculation. Throughout, the teacher-training ideas of the nineteenth century were recast in the terminology of twentieth-century behavioral science.

During the depression and the post-World War II years, the foundations-of-education viewpoint made that amalgam of practice-centered talk even more extravagant by making skill, information, and logic subordinate to the emotional attitude, and feeling tied to beliefs held by practitioners. Thus, with the exception of the early child-study experiment in modes of description, the influence of teacher training has been to turn talk about education away from anything that could be called disinterested scholarship and toward a practice-centered doctrine of personal belief frequently conveyed in terms unscholarly enough to be called journalistic.

The evolution of talk about education has not followed the path taken in the organization of content and the demonstration of skill cultivated in legal, in engineering, and in medical training. Instead of a rigor-

ous discipline of detailed scholarship and precise demonstration focused on
the objective explanation of a narrow segment of practical affairs, talk
about education has summoned the secondary and tertiary scholarship of
amateurs to the task of assembling the shaky scaffolding of what was
thought to be a general discipline of education at once scholarly sound and
immediately useful. Throughout, the dominant trend in classroom practice
has been one of trial-and-error experimentation conducted under the belief that a general method of instruction was being perfected. Expressing
the viewpoints deeply embedded in the American way of living, such general disciplines of education and such general methods of instruction
changed as rapidly and as radically as the patterns of living and of popular thought changed. For example, the attitudes of the 1930 depression
differed as much from the attitudes of post-Warld War II prosperity as
socially conscious permissiveness differs from current concepts of corporal
and intellectual discipline. In the United States the evolution of talk about
education has been a reflection of the evolution of popular, rather than
academic, thought concerning human nature and human society. Lacking
a discipline, teacher training has depended on prophets and their disciples.
It seems that too often prophets and disciples, who are not mystics, come
closer to being journalists than to being scholars. From this it seems apt
to quote Whitehead's statement that: "pure speculation undisciplined by
the scholarship of exact logic, is on the whole more useless than pure
scholarship, unrelieved by speculation." [1]

---

[1] Whitehead, 1959: 111.

W hat is involved in a scientific structure? A novel? A tragedy? A well-designed machine? What is involved in conceiving them? In realizing the conception? Such researches would not be immediately fruitful, for they are a far cry from early efforts at comprehending intellectual effort and from current inquiries into emotional circumstances and conditions. The necessary premises and frames of reference are yet to be constructed. Such research would also, undoubtelly, give rise to its own congeries of partial truths. But only in this way can we eventually hope to give a full set of dimensions to doctrines in psychology.

Finally, since it takes two to make a corruption, there is a contribution to be made by the working teacher and administrator in our schools. They can bring common sense to bear on bright and shiny doctrines of behavior, the common sense that warns us that, about things as complex as the human person and human society, short and simple generalities must be either empty, false, or incomplete.[1]

In their efforts to understand instruction simply yet comprehensively, teachers have been quite ready to believe that one or another general method would work wonders in the classroom. In their eagerness to have a comprehensive theory which would both provide a basis for training teachers and enable education departments to take a respected position in the university community, educators have been too willing to believe that a general discipline was at hand. It may be that the

[1] Schwab, 1958: 95.

15

Improving Education
As a Subject
of Study

beginning of enlightenment rests with the admission that no general method is likely and that no general discipline other than a literary one is possible. The next question, then, asks, "What is possible?" What approach will lead to a better understanding of practice and to the improvement of education as a subject of study?

General methods of teaching, like general methods of science, grow from certain stages of understanding of the process involved. Careful examination of how scientists work and careful examination of the statements made in science have led philosophers of science to question Huxley's presentation of the method of science. Dewey, in turn, amplified Peirce's formulation and added details that had not been stated by Huxley. In general methods of teaching, the gross simplicity of monitorial or Montessori methodology seems shocking until it is realized that the schools had, as their basic problem, merely to overcome illiteracy. Experimentalism, on the other hand, sought to encompass a complexity concerning the individual, instruction, and the institution of public schooling that Lancaster could not have imagined. Each new and detailed description of the process of teaching shows up inadequacies in previously accepted general methods. Hence, attention must be given to careful description of the classroom situation.

General disciplines of education, like societies for the unification of all knowledge, frequently grow from practice-centered concerns similar to those put forth by Philip H. Phenix in *Education and the Common Good:*

> In treating so wide a range of problems as appear in this study, adequate documentation and scholarly support of the statements made would require erudition that the author cannot claim. Specialists in every one of the fields considered can doubtless find many faults with what is said— faults that could have been avoided had each field been treated by an expert. The present overview is nevertheless offered, with all its short- comings, as an illustration of the kind of integration that every person must attempt in his own way. Everybody must come to terms in some fashion with the whole sweep of human concerns. Every citizen, every parent, every teacher and administrator must make decisions about what shall be taught in homes, schools, churches, industry, and community. Everyone must * somehow put together his convictions about such matters as knowledge, the mass media, art, manners, work, play, nature, health,

---

* This imperative gains strength from Russell's statement: "It is only when you come to expressing your thought in words that you approach logical precision. Both in introspection and external perception, we try to express what we know in *words*. . . . The purpose of words is to give the same pub- licity to thought as is claimed for physical objects." (*An Outline of Philosophy,* p. 11.) But these first formulations of Everyone come closer to being jour- nalistic than to being scholarly. Whatever practical value they may have, they do not belong to the subject matter of a discipline of education.

sex, class, race, economics, politics, international relations, and religion into a pattern for the formation of character through the curriculum. [2]

Rugg envisioned the Teachers College, Columbia University, staff of the 1930's and 1940's as building a general discipline of educational foundations similar in spirit to the synthesis which Phenix attempts. Useful as such a synthesis might be for teacher preparation, its confessed faults make it inadmissible as scholarship that could contribute to establishing education as an independent, specialized subject of study that is not primarily practice-centered and literary. Analogy is provocative but cannot be definitive; hence, one's poetry cannot do the job assigned to science.

General methods fail as practical recommendations when confronted by more complex conditions than they were designed to account for. General disciplines fail when the "theories" encounter facts and arguments that they were not designed to include. Yet both general methods and general disciplines continue in business long after their practical uselessness and their intellectual unsoundness have been pointed out. General methods and general disciplines hold their shape like sucked-out eggshells: kept rigid by the tension of fictional hypotheses supporting poetic analogies. In 1898 William James crushed the shell of Herbartian "apperception," but the Herbartians continued in teacher training, almost untouched, until 1920 or later.

In 1949, with the publication of *The Concept of Mind,* Gilbert Ryle brought quite formidable charges against ways of talking about how thinking is done. Herbartians and Experimentalists frequently employed such ways of talking about thinking as Ryle derides in the following terms:

> As if, for example, John Doe could and should sometimes be described as having woken up and started to do some judging, conceiving, subsuming or abstracting; as spending more than three seconds in entertaining a proposition, or in moving from some premises to a conclusion, or as sitting on a fence, alternately whistling and deducing, or as having had an intuition or something a moment before he coughed. [3]

It was in just such a sense that Kilpatrick took the idea of purpose as "the typical unit of the worthy life in a democratic society" and converted it into "the typical unit of school procedure." From a unit of procedure to being a unit of behavior, Kilpatrick had only to change the grammatical form as follows:

Product	*Infinitive*	*Process*
Purpose	To purpose	Purposing

[2] Phenix, 1961: 85.
[3] Ryle, 1949: 94.2.

With "purposing" as a typical unit of human behavior, Kilpatrick and Monroe and others went on to build what they thought were causal hypotheses which explained how humans worked. About just such hypotheses Ryle says:

> The imputed episodes seemed to be impenetrably "internal" because they were genuinely unwitnessable. But they were genuinely unwitnessable because they were mythical. They were *causal* hypotheses substituted for functional descriptions of the elements of published theories. [4] [*]

One need not accept Ryle uncritically to recognize that he has thrown doubt on the utility of intellectual chameleons that can suddenly become explanations of processes by changing their suffix. A judgment can be recorded by the court clerk, but the process by which it was reached is not explained by the term *judging*. Ryle casts these doubts on a whole list of process terms: *judging, reasoning, conceiving, confessing, reflecting, concluding, proposing, considering*. Confusion mounts if we seek to explain further by joining terms: *considering judging, proposing abstracting*.

Yet something of a similar sort happened with the process terms set forth in connection with experimentalism:

problem-solving process	critical judgment
cooperative planning	attitude formation
decision-making	scientific reasoning
creative thinking	scientific valuing
personality-building	consensus-forming

In such talk, present participles were put forth as process terms and then used to explain human behavior, social interaction, and the "dynamics" of classroom learning. These were the ingredients of a practice-centered general discipline, it seemed. Further, they fit well with the poetic analogies of the child as beast, as flower, as artist, or as rebel. Thus, it seems that the basic intellectual ingredients of general methods and of general disciplines of education have been apt analogies and fictional hypotheses. Although this deduction has not escaped the attention of scholars, they have not seen fit, or not been able, to do much about it.

As history, genius, interpretation, and opportunity combine in different proportions to mold the institutions of any age, so do rationalism, poetic analogy, and sloganeering go into general methods and general

---

[4] Ryle, 1949: 94.3.
[*] One need not accept Ryle as having the last word concerning the defensible use of process terms to admit that his cautions about their possible misuse must be carefully considered in connection with such basic ideas as Dewey put forth concerning the process of valuing in *Theory of Valuation*. Professor Rossi-Landi, of Milan, has stated that much of what Ryle has said defies straightforward application in other languages such as French and Italian. Yet users of English must consider his challenge.

disciplines. The history of the Darwinian hypothesis and the genius of Herbart mingled in the interpretation with which Charles and Frank McMurry launched American Herbartianism. Without the opportunity which the rapid expansion of American secondary schooling provided, however, this concept of instruction might have remained inconsequential. With a general method to support, it became possible to build a general discipline from rationalistic concepts and provocative analogies.

As a practical movement becomes powerful, some of its leading concepts get translated into slogans. And such slogans often point to problems which have defied analysis. The solace found in the phrase "Families that pray together stay together" suggests both the danger and the fear of divorce. The slogan "Peace through world brotherhood" has much the same quality as the educational dictum "An active child is a learning child." Both face the problem summarily so as to provide a working model for all situations. Such general models, however, do not consider that brothers kill brothers or that busy folk may be the most ignorant. Having mistaken the part for the whole, slogans such as "teaching the whole child" or poetic analogies that liken children to beasts cannot help but lead to only partial answers.

Yet teacher training often employs more slogans, analogies, and summary general methods than thorough investigation, be it careful observation or scholarly analysis. At times a problem appears to be so urgent that the need for immediate summary solution leads to the wholesale adoption of slogans in defiance of step-by-step analysis. The detailed examination of complex problems takes so long and is itself so involved that the man faced with an immediate practical decision often becomes exasperated. This situation—when aggravated by lack of training, lack of patience, and the dissatisfying nature of extensive qualification—makes him easily susceptible to the temptation of adopting or accepting a slogan which promises, though falsely, to solve the whole problem. It may even tempt a whole body of professionals to put forth a general discipline as a scholarly one.

Such pre-analytic summary solutions offer the practitioner hope with which to face the immediate future and often, to boot, suggest that deeper examination may not be necessary. When the answer is at hand, why ask the same question again? When, however, the same pre-analytic conclusions parade as the product of deep and careful investigation, they do positive harm to the development of a discipline in the same way that inferior materials and unskilled workmanship detract from the quality of a house.

HOW TO BEGIN

A discipline is a protected area, a kind of intellectual game preserve where all who hunt must follow the same rules. At bottom stands the attitude that the area set aside is worth protecting, and on the surface exist the rules which the hunters make and enforce. Different preserves harbor different game, and the hunt proceeds by locally defined rules. Beyond this, little can be said of all disciplines; but it suggests that initially the development of a discipline such as physics demanded the same distinctive kind of activity it took to discern a body of "art" among the world's abundant supply of paintings. Whether in "taste" or in cognitive meaning, the initial step involves a judgment that separates the acceptable from the unacceptable.

Further, an emphasis on utility has led to what amounts to an obsessive search for "practical implications." Psychology and sociology have been combed for clues translatable into directives for the conduct of instruction, principles for the organization of the curriculum, guides to improved administration, and techniques for counseling. In turn, for the most part, educational philosophy more nearly resembles political debate about diplomacy than philosophic scholarship. Thus, no matter how skillful and academic the argument, the final justification of the credo will be its implications for practice. Where practical implications are not forthcoming, the attitude is "apology before abandonment."

Implications for practice are the *raison d'être* for much of educational philosophy, educational psychology, educational sociology, and just about all of educational administration, supervision, curriculum, and methodology. Designed not as areas of separable knowledge, but as special provinces of practitioner training, with rare exceptions they continue as such. Indeed, in the materials catalogued in libraries under "Education," the search for practical implications so far outweighs pursuit of new information that it makes some sense to say that education as a subject of study does not yet exist.

A QUESTION OF QUALITY

The poor performances frequently exhibited by, and accepted from, both students and faculty in teacher-preparation and advanced-degree programs stand as a severe embarrassment to the American academic world. Teacher-training texts, professional articles, dissertations, and published "research" all supply overwhelming evidence that a bureau for the suppression of unintelligent expression might be both benevolent and beneficent. With but rare exceptions, the bulk of what is written about education fails in substance, form, and vocabulary. It fails as scholarship, as interpretation, as communication, and as guidance for instruction. In *substance,* what begins as if it were an inquiry into human behavior too often ends as a pronouncement on human nature. In *form,* the attention given to speculation usually outweighs the effort given to observation or to logical analysis. In *vocabulary,* technical terms imported from other fields soon lose the precision which gave them distinctive meaning and become nothing more than pretentious synonyms for common words.* Since less censorship can be imposed on what a professor says than on what he writes, course work in departments of education generally achieves an even lower quality than what they and their graduate students commit to paper. Thus we are confronted, in education, with an illiterate literary discipline.

"Talk" about education needs some yardstick with which to measure out sense, so that it can be dissociated from nonsense. This study has explored the historical traditions of American instruction to see if some basic ground for distinguishing sense from nonsense in talk about education could be found. It did not assume that such criteria had been established by any particular writer or philosophical school. Nor did it assume that the great bulk of what has been written about education must make sense. It did assume that the search for criteria must begin somewhere, and the established historical traditions like Monitorial Method and Object Teaching seemed likely grounds for prospecting.

If the libraries could be purged of all materials about education which employed poetic analogy as substantive knowledge and fictional hypotheses as causal explanations, the bare shelves would mock advanced-degree programs. Teacher training would be cut back so far by a forthright admission of ignorance that courses in methods, curriculum, administration, and supervision might have to be dropped altogether. Ridding talk about education of its misapplied poetic analogies and fictional hypotheses is not likely to be a popular activity among those charged with the responsibility for training teachers and for developing a discipline —that is, faculties of education. If it is to be done, *it will have to be forced* from the outside. Like racial integration, it will never be done voluntarily. Too many jobs, too many texts, too many programs of instruction, and too much power are at stake.

It would be well for a university to set up a special committee to look into what their colleagues in departments of education are saying in their courses and having their students read.† Someone has to arbitrate over what makes sense and what does not make sense in talk about education. And there is every reason to suspect that those least equipped, least trained, and especially least disposed to police talk about education are those who engage in it most freely. Practice-centered thinking, whether directed toward defending a general method or building a general discipline, is not, strictly speaking, disinterested. It is time to admit, about

---

* See George Orwell, "Politics and the English Language," in *A Collection of Essays,* Doubleday Anchor Books (A 29). New York: Doubleday & Company, Inc., 1954.

† Not that other departments could not likewise benefit from such scrutiny.

education, what H. L. Mencken said long ago about faculties of economics, political economy, and theology:

> In brief, human reason is a weak and paltry thing so long as it is not wholly free reason. The fact lies in its very nature, and is revealed by its entire history. A man may be perfectly honest in a contention and he may be astute and persuasive in maintaining it, but the moment the slightest compulsion to maintain it is laid upon him, the moment the slightest external reward goes with his partisanship or the slightest penalty with its abandonment, then there appears a defect in his ratiocination that is more deep-seated than any error in fact and more destructive than any conscious and deliberate bias. He may seek the truth and the truth only, and bring up his highest talents and diligence to the business, but always there is a specter behind his chair, a warning in his ear. Always it is safer and more hygienic for him to think one way than to think another way, and in that bold fact there is excuse enough to hold his whole chain of syllogisms in suspicion. He may be earnest, he may be honest, but he is not free, and if he is not free he is not anything. [5]

Yet jobs, texts, programs of instruction, and even power in departments of education are not the most debilitating aspects of the practice-centered thinking that seeks to defend one general method over another or one general discipline over another. Worse, by far, is the demand that ideas be made immediately practical, and this demand will continue so long as research in education must be carried on in departments primarily committed to training practitioners.

Those who would develop a theory of education must heed the comment that Mencken directed at proposals for governmental reform: "The thing they propose is intrinsically, or at all events most probably, beyond accomplishment."[*] The search for a universal and workable general method and attempts at constructing a plenary and valid general discipline have led middleman theorists to try to fuse rules of thumb about instruction to broad philosophic, almost religious, social and world views. The intellectual flux has frequently been educational idealism, educational realism, educational pragmatism, or educational scholasticism. But super-scholarship, like super-patriotism, too often lacks the virtues it espouses. Practice-centered concerns and journalistic salesmanship have sometimes made a comic figure of educational scholarship. Middleman theorists, inexpert as scholars, have naïvely striven for some impossible synthesis that would be at once faithful to scholarship, useful to the practitioner, intelligible to the populace and thus comprehensive as a discipline, workable as a general method, and defensible as a social institution.

---

[5] Mencken, 1958: 67.
[*] See frontispiece.

By contrast, modest inquiry into the art of teaching might yet seek to explain "balance" in terms of such coordinates of instruction as deportment, organization of content, and permitted activity. The description of behavioral components of elbow room and constraint might not be beyond immediate accomplishment. With scholarship directed toward the examination of elements of instruction, it might be possible to arrive at an outline for the study of teaching as responsible as the one set forth for the study of literature by Wellek and Warren in *Theory of Literature.**
Some sense of what the beginnings of such an outline might be like can be gained from looking at the effort to describe the components of aims of instruction edited by Benjamin Bloom: *Taxonomy of Educational Objectives: Part I: Cognitive Domain.*†

---

* Wellek and Warren, *Theory of Literature,* Harvest Books (H.B. 22). New York: Harcourt, Brace and Company, 1956.
† Benjamin Bloom, *Taxonomy of Educational Objectives: Part I: Cognitive Domain.* New York: (now David McKay Co., Inc.) 1956.

If the attempts to develop education as a literal discipline involved looking at teaching practices intently and in detail, it might be possible for some jury to identify a body of good practices. It might be possible, with the help of a motion picture camera, to establish a body of practices in the art of teaching as comparable in worth to education as a discipline as the fairly stable body of "approved" paintings is to art. Just as harmony, balance, and complexity are concepts which guide art critics, so might certain elements of instruction guide the judges of teaching practices. Deportment of youngsters, the organization of content, and classroom activity could be subdivided, respectively, in terms of such common-sense divergent tendencies as constraint versus elbow room, sequence versus spontaneity, and didactic versus ostensive. Allowing for a neutral area where many ordinary practices are as much one as the other, the elements and their components could be arranged along a continuum as shown in the accompanying chart.

Accounts of the behavior which earned medals for soldiers in World War II would, no doubt, encompass an astonishing range of activities. Fact would have to be sifted from fiction, impressions glorified after the fact from eyewitness accounts, hero worship from envy, and much more. Yet, in the broad, a general concept of "exceptional" or "heroic" behavior might be extracted from such a body of material. And, informally, such a conception has been distilled in the history and even in the fiction of each war. In much the same manner, there is a general conception of "delinquent" and "well-adjusted" child behavior. Gov-

16

Judging
Practices

Elements of Instruction	Three-Part Continuum			Terminology
	DIVERGENT TENDENCIES IN INSTRUCTION			
Deportment	Constraint	Neutral Area	Elbow Room	Deportment Continuum or Constraint-Elbow-Room Continuum
Organiza-tion	Sequential	Neutral Area	Spontaneous	Organization Con-tinuum or Sequential-Spon-taneous Continuum
Activity	Didactic	Neutral Area	Ostensive	Activity Continuum or Didactic-Ostensive Continuum

ernments are branded "tyrannical" or "benevolent," parties "liberal" or "conservative," in roughly the same way. Central tendencies, fuzzy to be sure, are thus discerned much in the manner which Huxley suggested for sociology in 1854.

In the same general manner, central tendencies toward deportment, organization, and learning activity might be identified. In fair measure, broad concepts already useful in daily communication could serve without giving a false sense of exactness or precision where none exists, without leading to polar extremes. Underlying such comon-sense conceptions as cowardice, heroism, delinquency, or, in this instance, constraint and elbow room, sequential and spontaneous, and didacticism and ostension, rests the bedrock assumption that each, at some future time, could be more precisely defined in terms of observable behavior. Meanwhile, someone judging the art of instructing might set up guidelines of this sort:

Constraint

1. Functional:
   1.1 Not having two students speak at once.
   1.2 Inquiry into the cause of absence or tardiness.
   1.3 Discouraging the reading of comic books, chewing of gum, or eating candy in class.
   1.4 Having youngsters occupy the same seats every day until a change in activities necessitates a shift.
   1.5 Insistence that clothes be clean and dress be appropriate to the occasion.

2. Regulative:
   2.1 Insistence that a hand be raised and recognized before speaking.
   2.2 A rule that absences must be excused by the parent in writing.
   2.3 Forbidding the reading of comic books, chewing of gum, or eating of candy in class.
   2.4 Using an alphabetical or boy-girl seating arrangement as a general rule.
   2.5 No shorts or blue jeans allowed in normal class sessions.
3. Rigid:
   3.1 Extension of the hand-raising rule to all activities such as fixing a window or going to the boy's room.
   3.2 Specifying the excuses which will be acceptable and those conditions which will not qualify as excused absences.
   3.3 Forbidding that comic books, gum, or candy be brought to class.
   3.4 Insisting on the same seating arrangement for all class work and activities and extending it to control seating outside of class in assembly, for instance.
   3.5 Specification that white shirts, sport coats, and neckties will be worn by boys.
4. Punitive:
   4.1 Extra assignments for unauthorized talk even when motivated purely by enthusiasm to respond.
   4.2 Excluding from class anyone who fails to bring an excuse for absence.
   4.3 Searching students for contraband.
   4.4 Designating a "dunce seat" or seating youngsters according to performance (highest grade gets the front seat in the first row, and so forth).
   4.5 Forcing a boy who forgot his tie to wear a crepe-paper one.
   4.6 Forbidding certain kinds of haircuts under threat of expulsion.

Elbow Room

1. Functional (same as for "Constraint")

2. Self-contained:

   2.1 Allowing students to raise questions without putting up their hands or receiving formal recognition.
   2.2 Accepting students' explanations of absences.

2.3 Having students specify whether, to what extent, and when comic books, gum, and candy will be allowed.

2.4 Letting students sit-at-will on the first day of class.

2.5 Saying nothing about dress until a problem arises.

3. Unfettered:

3.1 Allowing students to interrupt one another and argue in class as they might outside (when they keep to the subject and avoid violence).

3.2 Accepting any explanation of absence so long as one is offered.

3.3 Letting each individual regulate his use of comic books, gum, and candy voluntarily.

3.4 Permitting students to adjust their seating arrangements as the activity indicates.

3.5 Allowing students to wear blue jeans if they care to.

4. Anarchistic:

4.1 No control over talk.

4.2 Absences need not be excused.

4.3 Allowing students to import anything into classroom.

4.4 Letting students wander the classroom at will.

4.5 Any dress within moral-legal bounds.

No one phase of any stage assures the discovery of a central tendency. Taken together, however, examples of the kind given above point definitely toward certain attitudes and serve as signs that legitimate distinctions of degree can be made, giving meaning to the following coarse division of the deportment continuum:

Constraint			Neutral sector		Elbow Room		
punitive	rigid	regula-tive	func-tional	func-tional	self-contained	unfet-tered	anarch-istic

STAGES OF THE ORGANIZATION CONTINUUM

Instruction, like murder, can be premeditated or governed mainly by impulse. Premeditation—careful planning—unfolds as a sequence of organized steps. Although action taken on impulse may have a design about it—a certain organization—such spontaneous organization emerges from contextual conditions more than from any abstract plan. Again, examples should clarify the attitudes and their stages.

Sequence

1. Contextual:

1.1 Building history lessons around local battlegrounds and monuments.

    1.2 Arranging English and spelling lessons on the basis of errors in composition.

    1.3 Working up projects for science foundation scholarships by using war surplus electronic equipment.

    1.4 Incorporating museum exhibits in the study of American Indians.

2. Established:

    2.1 Units on subjects worked up in lesson plans which go unchanged from year to year.

    2.2 Standard lectures based on past precedent in the subject.

    2.3 Standardized divisions of a subject, as in physics—mechanics, thermodynamics, electricity.

    2.4 Unalterable college-preparatory curriculum in mathematics—algebra I, plane geometry, algebra II, trigonometry, and solid geometry.

3. Expert:

    3.1 Revised programs of modern mathematics or physics worked up by Nobel prize winners.

    3.2 Textbooks or teaching machines programmed by subject-matter experts.

    3.3 TV lectures given nationwide by outstanding scholars.

4. Crystallized:

    4.1 Texts in fast-changing field used even though out of date.

    4.2 Teaching designed merely to satisfy board of regents' requirements; to prepare for college boards.

    4.3 Practice on standardized achievement and intelligence tests in order to insure higher scores.

    4.4 Unchanged tests given year to year to students who have samples to study.

    4.5 Unchanged projects which students anticipate.

Spontaneity

1. Contextual (same as under "Sequence")

2. Cooperative: (instead of the usual sequence of a subject as understood by the teacher, some approach is planned in the class in conference with the students)

    2.1 The writing and production of a play as an approach to both composition and appreciation.

    2.2 Identification of significant problems by students and teacher and arrangement of activities to solve them.

        2.21 Building science experimentation apparatus in shop rather than the usual pump-lamp project.

        2.22 Surveying community opinion about school consolidation as part of social studies.

3. Immediate: (spur-of-the-moment organizations)
    3.1 Relying mainly on student questions.
    3.2 Having youngsters bring in whatever they want and then talking about these things.
    3.3 Relying on current news happenings for substance of class.
    3.4 Depending on student interest as basis for deciding what to teach without evaluating its worth.

4. Chaotic: (breakdowns due to absence of organization)
    4.1 Repetition, continuity gaps, and omissions resulting from reliance on student interests.
    4.2 Digression in tangents brought in as distractions by students.
    4.3 Much time spent on trivial matters merely because students are interested, such as hot-rods, rock and roll, and so forth.

Sequence provides efficiency and to some extent assures significance. Experts will spend time organizing trivia only by mistake. Like earning money, sequence can become an end in itself apart from its utility. Under such circumstances, pedantry is difficult to distinguish from scholarship. From the other side, however, spontaneity captures the verve and zest of a situation the way a good performer capitalizes on the mood of his audience. Teaching worthy of being called a refined art can breathe the life of student enthusiasm into otherwise inert information. Somewhere on the following continuum a point of aim must be selected:

Sequence			Neutral Sector		Spontaneity		
crystal-lized	expert	estab-lished	contex-tual	contex-tual	cooper-ative	imme-diate	chaotic

STAGES OF THE ACTIVITY CONTINUUM

Didacticism emphasizes "telling" over "showing" and violates the Pestalozzian dictum, "Never tell a child what he can discover for himself." Ostension is "showing" in such a way that the child "sees" directly through some one or a variety of senses—Alberty's oblique approach. Didactic activity would emphasize the verbal definition of a circle as the locus of all points in a plane equidistant from a single point in that plane. In contrast, ostensive instruction would emphasize what could be learned from looking at and drawing circles, along with handling circular things. Good instruction in geometry would include both, but one could be emphasized over the other. In the absence of information as to results, balance is a matter of taste. Yet a student may pitch a baseball quite well for ten years and not learn the first thing about trajectory or the aerodynamics of a curve-ball. In an English class, the same student could learn to define beauty as "the harmony of opposites in dynamic balance" and never see a painting or listen to a symphony. As instructional activities, didacticism and ostension have the following stages:

Didacticism

1. Deliberative—the intellectual discussions between teacher and student or among students (directly related to the subject at hand).
   1.1 Lectures and assigned readings integrated with questions and a recitation session.
   1.2 Seminars devoted to more intense discussion than recitation allows (often associated with library research).

2. Impersonal—fixed concepts formally presented.
   2.1 Formal lectures with only five minutes for questioning.
   2.2 Lectures unchanged from year to year.
   2.3 Readings assigned but not discussed.
   2.4 Drill and memorization.

3. Broadcast—one-way presentations.
   3.1 Full lectures with no questions whatever.
   3.2 Centrally programmed teaching machines with unchangeable programs.
   3.3 Courses given over television, film, tape, record, radio, or through correspondence.

4. Dogmatic—intentionally biased presentations.
   4.1 Propagandistic lectures, broadcasts, films, and so forth, such as medical or military-minded groups present on the evils of Communism or socialized medicine, and the like.
   4.2 Lectures stipulating or promulgating a "correct" set of attitudes or tastes in such equivocal matters as art, morality, religion, and politics.

Ostension

1. Deliberative—the same kind of intellectual discussion as above, except that it is stimulated by a project or some other activity.
   1.1 Discussion of civil rights stimulated by a re-enactment of "sit-ins": role-playing.
   1.2 Written papers stimulated by field-trip activities.

2. Allied—contacts initiated because they seem related to the learning outcomes sought but from which no deliberation is is expected.
2.1 Modeling clothes of the Civil War period.
2.2 Building a model airplane as part of a unit on transportation.
2.3 Making soap as the Colonists made it.

3. Terminal—activities and contacts with things for appreciation alone and without any effort being made to relate them to other areas of learning.
3.1 Mechanically sewing a dress together just to make a dress, because it is required.
3.2 Building a lamp by following directions but learning next to nothing about electricity or woodworking.
3.3 Walking through the steps of a dance.
3.4 Learning the mechanics of starting, steering, and stopping a car without reference to the motor, laws, or physics.

4. Trivial—terminal activities lacking significance.
4.1 Fixing a hot-rod in shop.
4.2 Building models because it keeps the student quiet.

Which kind of didacticism or ostension achieves what kinds of results with which students may be determined empirically some day. In the meantime, however, those who train teachers must take a position on the following continuum with only the precedent of historical traditions to guide them:

Didacticism			Neutral Sector			Ostension	
dogmatic	broad-cast	imper-sonal	deliber-ative	deliber-ative	allied	ter-minal	trivial

CLASSIFICATION IN INSTRUCTIONAL SPACE

The stages of each tendency toward constraint or elbow room, sequence or spontaneity, and didacticism or ostension would have to be defined fully in terms of directly observable behavior before the literal description of actual practice could proceed on the same level with, say, mapping a continent. Yet even as they stand, these categories provide a rough framework for suggesting how a judge of the art of teaching might go about discussing what he was looking for in practice. This could be his rating sheet:

		SHEET FOR RATING PRACTICE		
Stages	General Areas	Deportment Continuum	Organization Continuum	Activity Continuum
four	Negative Extreme	Anarchistic Elbow Room	Chaotic Spontaneity	Trivial Ostension
three		Unfettered Elbow Room	Immediate Spontaneity	Terminal Ostension
two		Self-contained Elbow Room	Cooperative Spontaneity	Allied Ostension
one	Common Border ➤ Concept	Functional Elbow Room	Contextual Spontaneity	Deliberative Ostension
	Neutral Area			
one	Common Border ➤ Concept	Functional Constraint	Contextual Sequence	Deliberative Didacticism
two		Regulative Constraint	Established Sequence	Impersonal Didacticism
three		Rigid Constraint	Expert Sequence	Broadcast Didacticism
four	Negative Extreme	Punitive Constraint	Crystallized Sequence	Dogmatic Didacticism

With some similar rating sheet in hand, judges of the art of teaching might be able to come to sufficient agreement about the standards of good practice to be able to sketch in the details of three dimensions of instructional space:

THREE DIMENSIONS OF INSTRUCTIONAL SPACE

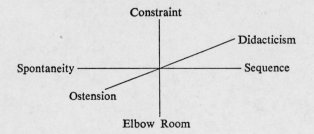

Further, a rating sheet of observable characteristics would make the following account of the cyclical swing of major conceptions of practice more meaningful than such polarization as progressive versus traditional education:

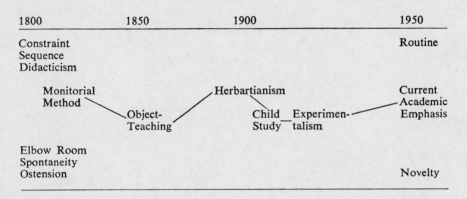

The appraisal of actual classroom practices can be at least as careful an undertaking as the judging of the artistic merit of a painting or a poem. Art critics care much about their judgments and they defend them constantly. The better ones seem to find something to say about the painting as such. Instead of defending their judgment of actual teaching practices, educators have argued the merits of major conceptions of practice. These conceptions have been seen as general methods, and efforts have been made to broaden them into general disciplines of education. But both the general methods and the general discipline seem to be diamond-like abstractions which only reflect images of practice while fascinating the "theorist" with the glitter of deeper philosophic fires beneath the surface.

A short time, only, am I here,
And come, devoted and sincere,
To greet and know the man of fame,
Whom men to me with reverence name.
                    Faust, First Part, Scene IV.

As a boy I watched Hooverville grow atop four square miles of the city dump across the highway from Newark Airport. Human derelicts defeated by the depression, even whole families, mined the slagg heaps of refuse for materials with which to build corrugated roofs, tin-can walls, and tarpaper window shades, until thousands of huts dotted the low, blackish hills. Each day they sifted the new droppings for food, furnishings, things to trade, and rubber tires to be burned for heat. There were patches of gardens, even flowers, and a maze of paths woven throughout the dump. Was it a society, a city, a collection of towns, or just a lump of humanity cast off from society—one with the refuse on which it stood? Whatever it was, it disappeared within six months after Pearl Harbor Day. It lasted for a decade, and when the conditions which had made it necessary no longer existed, it vanished.

Much of what is gathered together as educational theory or lumped into a larger package as the discipline of education seems no more solidly established than Hooverville. It subsists on the verbal refuse of ignorance as a necessary accommodation to conditions we cannot control and would rather ignore, only to be bulldozed away as soon as possible with no assurance that anything more serviceable will be built to replace it. Mean-

17

The
Courage
to Judge

while, there being no equivalent of Pearl Harbor Day in sight for education as a subject of study, the task of assessing its parts and examining how they function remains. Even if much of educational philosophy or methods of instruction are destined to dissolve when behavioral science provides more reliable information from which to generalize about teaching, learning, and the organization of the curriculum, the task of judging the worth of each item of present doctrine cannot be put off. It seems a job for a jury of scholars. The problems ahead of them are formidable—possibly insurmountable—yet the attempt must be made. At the first level, a jury comparable to the one selected by Paul Monroe about 1908 could be convened. Working from their implicit understanding of what constitutes the best of what has been said in the special areas of their expertness, each could designate those materials which constitute the most reliable items of scholarship. Hopefully, they would be able to offer some synthesis within each specialty, stating reservations which would caution against misuse and overgeneralization. To some extent this is being done in some of the reports put out by the Russell Sage Foundation. Even so, this jury would have to examine the question of how to divide education as a subject of study into categories which represent a tentative classification of the field into special areas of inquiry, after the manner exhibited for goals in *Taxonomy of Educational Objectives* under the editorship of Benjamin Bloom. Lacking a common language, common standards of scholarship, agreement on the nature of theory in education, and consensus on what constitutes literal and literary statements, such a jury would face the same problems of communication that the General Systems Theory group took up under the editorship of Von Bertalanffy and Anatol Rappaport after gathering together at Palo Alto in the Foundation for Research in Behavioral Science (where I had the pleasure of being a janitor).

By drawing together an encyclopedia of basic scholarship in education as a subject of study and by offering a tentative synthesis of the meaning of those documents for a potential discipline of education, such a jury could set forth a minimum core of materials from which those who wish to talk about the practice (or art) of teaching might profitably draw, thereby offering an alternative to excessive reliance on the personal experience of practitioners in teachers' colleges and the collective rules of thumb sprinkled, and often at odds, throughout the profession.

The difficulties involved in collecting such a body of material to be presented as the best scholarship in each category of investigation within education as a subject of study cannot be overestimated. Yet some jury must be struck and set to the task, setting its own guidelines much in the same way which international biological conferences were begun in the wake of the revolution in botanical investigation and classification set off by Linnaeus' taxonomy, if the present anarchy in education and in behavioral science is to be overcome. It may be agreed that any such designation of content for education as a discipline will be confining, restrictive, arbitrary, within the range of outlooks included by the jury. But, without such a designation, there can no more be a discipline of education or a designation of what constitutes adequate educational theory or satisfactory scholarship than there could be meaning to the term *art* without critics. Questions of quality involve judgments to be made by judges; and, until the judgments are made explicit, not much can be said about the basis upon which subsequent judgments might be made. Unless all talk about education is to be called "theory," and unless all that is said about human behavior and human nature is to be a part of "the discipline of education," the questions of quality of content must be entrusted, initially, to some judge or jury. Any group puts its wisdom to the test when it selects its judges, since it is from their decisions that laws will be written. Even Hooverville had its judges, I suspect.

If the materials chosen as the nucleus of a scholarly discipline of education are to survive longer than Hooverville did, they must be selected with a view to the faults which plague practice-centered talk and journalism. The guideline has been stated by Bertrand Russell:

> What passes for knowledge in ordinary life suffers from three defects: it is cocksure, vague, and self-contradictory. The first step toward philosophy consists in becoming aware of these defects, not in order to rest content with a lazy scepticism, but in order to substitute an amended kind of knowledge which shall be tentative, precise, and self-consistent. [1]

---

[1] Russell, B., 1960: 92.

A MEMORANDUM BY PROFESSOR JOHN DEWEY TO
PRESIDENT WILLIAM RAINEY HARPER OF THE
UNIVERSITY OF CHICAGO ENTITLED "PLAN
FOR ORGANIZATION OF WORK IN A
FULLY EQUIPPED DEPARTMENT
OF PEDAGOGY"
January 6, 1897*

The various lines of work which are naturally included within the scope of a University Department of Pedagogy may be reduced to a few main heads. We have:

1. What may be termed for convenience, Educational Physics and Physiology, dealing with the whole plant of educational work and the adaptation of that to the physical being and welfare of the pupils.

2. Educational Sociology which concerns itself with the organization and administration of the educational system, both in relation to other social conditions and institutions and in its own external mechanism and workings.

3. Educational Psychology which deals with all matters appertaining to the adaptation of the school resources and the subject matter of the curriculum to the child. Its problem is how, out of the plant and school system described above, to get the maximum of result from the standpoint of the individual pupils.

4. We have the subject matter of general pedagogy occupying itself with the theorical considerations regarding the nature, ends and aims of educational work and the intellectual organization of curriculum and methods corresponding thereto.

---

* Unpublished. The memorandum is preserved in the Archives of the University of Chicago.

Appendix

5. Educational History dealing both with the systems which have actually obtained at various times and in various countries, and also with the development of the theory of education as such.

I   Educational Physics and Physiology.

1. School buildings and grounds; city and country; heating, lighting, ventilation, and plumbing; laboratories; school furnishings, desks, blackboards, etc.; school decoration and aesthetics; all this to be inclusive from the Kindergarten to the University. Besides giving courses, the person in charge of this work would be responsible for the collection of plans, drawings, photographs, etc., from all available sources. Summaries should be given in original investigation along these lines, the construction of proper plans, etc. The work should look ultimately to co-operation with school boards in furnishing information upon these points, copies of plans, etc.

2. School Hygiene. The adaptation of the matters mentioned above to the health of children, including the investigation of the normal and abnormal conditions of the sense of the muscular system in relation to the physical conditions of school work. The nervous and other diseases of children so far as they act and react upon the work of education, should be included, as also the theory of physical exercise and culture in relation to health. The person in charge of such a course ought to be, if not a physician, one who has had a thorough training in physiology and is in close contact with physicians. The seminar work would involve an examination of the actual school buildings from the standpoint of all their sanitary arrangements. On the practical side there would be such cooperation as occasion might suggest with the City Board of Health and with physicians and others interested. Through the museum and library there should also be formed here a sort of bureau of information to which those engaged in actual school administration might apply.

II   Educational Sociology.

1. Systems of education in their relation to political, economic, religious and intellectual conditions of society, involving such things as a comparative study of the various European systems in their special adaptation to their surroundings and a study of the various types of the systems found in this country, in their adaptation to their local environments. It would also involve a study of industrial, technical and professional education from the same standpoint.

2. Internal School Organization and Management. This would include a study of the business side; the raising and expenditure of money for school purposes and the proper divisions of labor involved there. It would take up the functions of school boards: the Superintendent, Supervisors, Principals, etc., and their relations to each other. The question of the methods of preparing teachers for their work and so on, would come under survey also. In fact all the problems which have to deal with the actual administration of

the school system. The advanced work would consist in an actual examination of systems of Chicago and other cities near enough to be personally investigated with a view of discovering both the methods actually pursued, the defects and the suggesting of remedies.

III   Educational Psychology.

1. Child study, both on the side of its methods and the undertaking of actual work, should receive attention.

2. Course or courses should be given in Psychology as applied to instruction. The question of methods in relation to the learning process of the mind.

IV   General Pedagogy.   This is the head which receives most attention, and in some cases, exclusive attention, in the existing status of Pedagogy in colleges. It deals with the philosophy of education as such and the question of educational aims and means. Beside this general work it should include a more special and detailed study of the school curriculum; of the studies actually pursued in the schools, of their respective values and relations to each other; also a study of the various sub-divisions of the educational system, elementary, secondary, and higher, from the standpoint of their curriculum and their methods.

V   Education History.

1. The history of educational systems as actually organized, for example, the Chinese, Greek, Roman, Medieval; the history of the development of the modern common school system; the history of the development of the curriculum. This is the historical counterpart of what is treated theoretically in III.

2. The history of the theoretical discussion of educational matters. The study of educational classics from Plato down. The study of the epochs of educational reform and the writings which influenced them; the relation of educational thought to philosophical, ethical and religious thought; a consideration of educational theories in their relation to the general culture and intellectual atmosphere of the times.

The above takes up the work of the department from the standpoint of its logical sub-division. From another point of view it may be said that at least four courses should be given as undergraduate courses. These four are general in character and to be taken by those interested in education, apart from specialization along any particular line.

1. The history of educational doctrine.

2. Educational psychology on its theoretical side.

3. Child study.

4. A synoptic view of school organization; the resources of the school; their administration; the chief contemporary problems in educational administration.

In the above nothing has been said about work in the actual training of teachers as it is assumed that for the most part, at least at the outset, the whole stress must be thrown upon the culture side rather than upon the professional. There are two phases, however, of training work whose comparatively speedy inauguration is worthy of consideration.

I. When the Manual Training School is definitely annexed to the University, and its location changed so as to be sufficiently in close contact with University work, it would be highly desirable to have it include a special course for training teachers in the direction of manual training. The introduction of this line of work in the public schools is hindered now more by the lack of properly trained teachers than by any other one thing, as public opinion in general is now decidedly in favor of it. The New York Training School for teachers is the only college of rank now making a specialty of this matter.

II. We have already begun to have applications for teachers who are trained in the methods in use in our University Primary School. As soon as means are sufficient to give us a good supervising principal (a thing very much needed in itself) we should aim at securing a person who should be able to take oversight of and give direction and criticism to a number of assistants who should, at the same time, be taking theoretical work in the University. Such a move would be economical in more ways than one as it would enable us to derive a revenue from our assistants instead of having to pay anything for their services.   R. S.

John Dewey

1. Alberty, H. B., *A Study of the Project Method in Education*. Columbus: The Ohio State University Press, 1927.

1.1	p. 7	1.6	p. 27
1.2	p. 18	1.7	p. 63
1.3	p. 20	1.8	p. 54
1.4	p. 25	1.9	p. 65
1.5	p. 73	1.10	pp. 81-82

2. Anderson, Archibald W., *et al., The Theoretical Foundations of Education*. Urbana: Bureau of Research and Service, The College of Education, University of Illinois, 1951.

2.1	p. iv	2.5	p. 4
2.2	p. v	2.6	p. 9
2.3	p. 2	2.7	p. 84
2.4	p. 3	2.8	pp. 91-92

3. Axtelle, George, "Philosophy in American Education," *Harvard Educational Review*. Vol. 26, No. 2 (Spring, 1956), p. 185.

4. Bain, Alexander, *Education as a Science*. 1897 edition. New York: D. Appleton and Co., 1879.

4.1	p. 9	4.2	pp. 12-13

5. Baldwin, Bird T., "The Present Status of Education as a Science: The Principles of Education," *The School Review Monographs: No. II*. Chicago: University of Chicago Press, 1912, p. 128.

Bibliography

6. Barnard, F[rederick] A[ugust] P[orter], "Education as a Science," May 1, 1882, reprinted in *The Rise of a University*. Wm. F. Russell, editor. New York: Columbia University, 1937.

    6.1   p. 299   6.2   p. 307

7. Black, Max, "A Note on 'Philosophy of Education,'" *Harvard Educational Review*. Vol. 26, No. 2 (Spring, 1956), p. 154.

8. Brameld, Theodore, *Cultural Foundations of Education*. New York: Harper & Row, 1951.

    8.1   p. 265   8.2   p. 273

9. Brown, J. Stanley, "What Is Meant by a 'Science of Education'?" in Manfred J. Holmes, editor, *The Fourth Yearbook of the National Society for the Scientific Study of Education*. Part. II. Chicago: University of Chicago Press, 1905, p. 72.

10. Buckingham, B. R., "Our First Twenty-Five Years," *National Education Association of the United States, Proceedings*. Vol. 79. Washington, D. C.: National Education Association, 1941, p. 347.

11. Burnham, William H., "Child Study as the Basis of Pedagogy," *Proceedings of the International Congress of Education of the World's Columbian Exposition. Chicago, 1893*. New York: National Education Association, 1894, p. 720.

12. Cameron, Edward H., "Experimental Pedagogy," in Paul Monroe (editor), *A Cyclopedia of Education*. New York: The Macmillan Co., 1911. 2:551-552.

13. Chapman, James Crosby, and George Sylvester Counts, *Principles of Education*. New York: Houghton Mifflin Company, 1924, pp. xi-xii.

14. Conant, James B., *The American High School Today*. New York: McGraw-Hill Book Company, Inc., 1959, p. 45.

15. Cowley, W[illiam] H[arold], "The Need for Conceptually Oriented Research in Education," *California Journal of Educational Research*. Vol. 7, No. 2 (March, 1956), p. 64.

16. Cowley, W[illiam] H[arold], "Two Kinds of Research," *California Journal of Educational Research*. Vol. 5, No. 1 (January, 1954), p. 12.

17. Crombie, A. C., *Augustine to Galileo*. Toronto: William Heinemann Ltd., 1957, pp. 291-292. Reprinted by permission of William Heinemann Ltd. and Harvard University Press.

18. Cubberley, Elwood Patterson, *An Introduction to the Study of Education and to Teaching*. New York: Houghton Mifflin Company, 1925, p. 151.

19. Dearborn, Ned Harland, *The Oswego Movement in American Education*. New York: Teachers College, Columbia University, 1925.

    19.1   pp. 69-71   19.2   pp. 73-74

20. De Garmo, Charles, "The Herbartian System of Pedagogics," *Educational Review,* Vol. 1 (January, 1891), p. 35.

21. De Garmo, Charles, "Co-ordination of the Normal School and University in Training of Teachers," *National Education Association: Journal of Proceedings and Addresses, Session of the Year 1892.* New York: National Education Association, 1892, pp. 411-413.

22. Dewey, John, "Interpretation of the Culture Epoch Theory," *The Second Yearbook of the National Herbart Society for the Scientific Study of Teaching.* Bloomington: The Pantagraph Printing and Stationery Co., 1896, p. 91.

23. Dewey, John, "Plan for a Fully Equipped Department of Pedagogy." 1897. Unpublished. See Appendix.

24. Dewey, John, "Psychology and Social Practice," *Contributions to Education.* No. II. Chicago: University of Chicago Press, 1901.

    24.1 p. 17   24.2 pp. 33-34

25. Dewey, John, *The Educational Situation.* Chicago: The University of Chicago Press, 1902, pp. 96-98.

26. Dewey, John, "Experiment in Education," in Paul Monroe (editor), *A Cyclopedia of Education.* Vol. 2. New York: The Macmillan Co., 1911, pp. 550-551.

27. Dewey, John, "Progressive Education and a Science of Education," *Progressive Education.* Vol. 5, No. 3 (July-September, 1928).

    27.1 p. 197   27.4 p. 200
    27.2 pp. 197-198   27.5 p. 204
    27.3 p. 199

28. Dewey, John, *The Sources of a Science of Education.* New York: Liveright Publishing Corporation, 1929.

    28.1 p. 7   28.6 p. 32
    28.2 pp. 9-10   28.7 pp. 35-36
    28.3 p. 13   28.8 p. 40
    28.4 p. 23   28.9 p. 50
    28.5 pp. 26-27

29. Dewey, John, *The Thirty-Third Yearbook of the National Society for the Study of Education, Part II, The Activity Movement.* Guy Whipple (ed.). Bloomington: Public School Publishing Co., 1934, pp. 85-86.

30. De Witt, Norman J., "The Humanist Should Look to the Law," *The Journal of General Education.* Vol. 4, No. 2 (January, 1950), p. 142.

31. Faculty of the State Normal University, Normal, Illinois, "The Relation Between Theory and Practice in the Training of Teachers," *The Second Yearbook of the National Society for the Scientific Study of Education.* Part II. Charles A. McMurry, editor. Chicago: University of Chicago Press, 1903, p. 9.

32. Feibleman, James K., "Some Problems in the Philosophy of Educa-
    tion," *Harvard Educational Review*. Vol. 26, No. 2 (Spring,
    1956), p. 151.

33. Findlay, Joseph John, "The Scope of the Science of Education,"
    Educational Review. Vol. XIV. New York: Henry Holt and
    Co., 1897, p. 247.

34. Frankena, William, "Toward a Philosophy of Education," *Harvard
    Educational Review*. Vol. 26, No. 2 (Spring, 1956), pp. 94-95.

35. Gill, John, *Systems of Education*. Boston: D. C. Heath & Co., 1887.

    35.1 p. 162   35.3 pp. 175-178
    35.2 p. 166   35.4 p. 202

36. Gordy, John Pancoast, *Rise and Growth of the Normal School Idea
    in the United States*. Washington: Government Printing Of-
    fice, 1891.

    36.1 p. 23   36.7 p. 84
    36.2 p. 24   36.8 p. 86
    36.3 p. 25   36.9 pp. 108-109
    36.4 p. 44   36.10 p. 120
    36.5 p. 64   36.11 p. 124
    36.6 p. 74

37. Greene, S. S., "Object Teaching," *National Teacher's Association
    Proceedings and Lectures of the Fifth Annual Meeting*. Hart-
    ford: Office of the American Journal of Education, 1865, pp.
    267-268.

38. Hall, G. Stanley, "Child Study as a Basis for Psychology and Psy-
    chological Teaching," *Proceedings of the International Congress
    of Education of the World's Columbian Exposition. Chicago,
    1893*. New York: National Education Association, 1894, pp.
    717-718.

39. Halleck, Reuben Post, "What Is Meant by a 'Science of Education'?"
    in Manfred J. Holmes (editor), *The Fourth Yearbook of the
    National Society for the Scientific Study of Education*. Part II.
    Chicago: University of Chicago Press, 1905, p. 73.

40. Hansen, Allen Oscar, *Liberalism and American Education*. New
    York: The Macmillan Co., 1926, p. 45.

41. Harris, William T., "Discussion: The Pupil as a Social Factor,"
    *Journal of Proceedings and Addresses of the National Educa-
    tion Association*. Chicago: University of Chicago Press, 1896,
    p. 196.

42. Haskell, Ellen M. (editor), *Child Observations*. Boston: D. C.
    Heath & Co., 1896.

    42.1 p. viii   42.3 p. 241
    42.2 p. 1   42.4 p. xxxiii

43. Henmon, V. A. C., "The Present Status of Education as a Science:
    The Problem of Educational Psychology," *The School Review*

Monographs: No. II. Chicago: University of Chicago Press, 1912.

43.1	p. 75	43.5	p. 79
43.2	p. 76	43.6	p. 80
43.3	pp. 76-77	43.7	p. 81
43.4	p. 78		

44. Highet, Gilbert, *The Art of Teaching*. New York: Alfred A. Knopf, Inc., 1950, pp. 37-38.

45. Holmes, Manfred J., "Report of the Secretary," *The Fourth Yearbook of the National Society for the Scientific Study of Education, Part II.* Chicago: University of Chicago Press, 1905, pp. 72-77.

46. Huxley, Thomas Henry, "On the Educational Value of Natural History Sciences," delivered July 22, 1854, in *Lay Sermons, Essays and Reviews*. New York: D. Appleton & Co., 1915.

46.1	p. 83	46.2	p. 88

47. James, William, *Talks to Teachers on Psychology*. New York: Henry Holt & Co., 1901.

47.1	pp. 7-8	47.3	pp. 155-157
47.2	pp. 8-9		

48. Jefferson, Thomas, "Letter to James Madison, December 20, 1787," *The Writings of Thomas Jefferson*. Paul L. Ford, editor. New York: G. P. Putnam's Sons, 1894. 4: 474.

49. Jefferson, Thomas, "Letter to Col. Charles Yancey, January 6, 1816," *The Writings of Thomas Jefferson*. Paul L. Ford, editor. New York: G. P. Putnam's Sons, 1899. 10:497.

50. Judd, Charles Hubbard, *Introduction to the Scientific Study of Education*. New York: Ginn and Company, 1918, pp. 305-306.

51. Kandel, I[saac] L[eon], "University Study of Education," *Twenty-Five Years of American Education*. New York: The Macmillan Co., 1924.

51.1	pp. 29-30	51.3	pp. 39-41
51.2	p. 30	51.4	p. 46

52. Keller, Robert J., and Mary Corcoran, "Educational Psychology," *Annual Review of Psychology*. Vol. 8. Palo Alto, California: Annual Reviews, Inc., 1957. 8:176-177.

53. Kilpatrick, William H., "The Project Method," *Teachers College Record*, XIX (September, 1918), 4.

53.1	p. 322	53.3	pp. 334-335
53.2	p. 323	53.4	pp. 332-333

54. Kilpatrick, William Heard, "Tendencies in Educational Philosophy," *Twenty-Five Years of American Education*. New York: The Macmillan Co., 1924.

54.1	pp. 83-84	54.2	p. 86

55. Kilpatrick, William Heard, *Selfhood and Civilization*. New York: Bureau of Publications, Teachers College, Columbia University, 1941, p. 114.

56. Kirkpatrick, Edwin A., "Child Study," *A Cyclopedia of Education*. Paul Monroe, editor. New York: The Macmillan Co., 1911. 1:616.

57. Lawrence, Irene J., "A History of Educational Sociology in the United States." Unpublished doctoral dissertation, Stanford University, September, 1951.

    57.1   pp. 133-134   57.2   p. 145

58. Leary, Daniel B., "Development of Educational Psychology," *Twenty-Five Years of American Education*. New York: The Macmillan Co., 1924, p. 103.

59. Lin Yutang, editor, *The Wisdom of Confucius*. New York: Modern Library, 1938, p. 225.

60. Luckey, G[eorge] W[ashington] A[ndrew], "Child-Study in its Effects upon the Teacher," *The Child-Study Monthly*. Vol. 1, No. 8 (February, 1896).

    60.1   p. 238   60.2   pp. 238-244

61. MacVannel, John Angus, *The Educational Theories of Herbart and Froebel*. New York: Teachers College, Columbia University, 1906.

    61.1   p. 70   61.2   p. 88

62. McMurry, Charles A., "Plan and Purpose of the National Herbart Society," *The Second Yearbook of the Herbart Society. Proceedings*. Bloomington: The Pantagraph Printing and Stationery Co., 1896, p. 170.

63. McMurry, Charles A. (editor), "Proposed Plan of Work for the NSSSE," *The First Yearbook for the National Society for the Scientific Study of Education*. Chicago: University of Chicago Press, 1902, p. 62.

64. McMurry, Frank, "Value of Herbartian Pedagogy for Normal Schools," *National Education Association: Journal of Proceedings and Addresses, Session of the Year 1892*. New York: National Education Association, 1893.

    64.1   pp. 424-425   64.5   p. 428
    64.2   p. 425   64.6   pp. 428-429
    64.3   pp. 425-426   64.7   p. 430
    64.4   pp. 426-427   64.8   pp. 431-432

65. McMurry, Frank, "Concentration," *The First Yearbook of the Herbart Society for the Scientific Study of Teaching. Proceedings*, 1894.

    65.1   p. 28   65.2   p. 33

66. McMurry, F[rank] M[orton], "What Is Meant by a Science of Education?" in Manfred J. Holmes (editor), *The Fourth Yearbook*

of the National Society for the Scientific Study of Education.
Part II. Bloomington: Pantagraph Printing and Stationery Company, 1905, p. 74.

67. Mencken, H. L., "The Dismal Science," *Prejudices: A Selection* (edited by James T. Farrell) in *Vintage Book,* vol. 58. New York: Random House, 1958, pp. 150-151.

68. Mencken, H. L., "The Cult of Hope," *Prejudices: A Selection,* in *Vintage Book,* vol. 58. New York: Random House, 1958, pp. 84-85.

69. Monroe, Paul, "Cooperative Research in Education," *The School Review Monographs: No. 1, Research within the Field of Education, Its Organization and Encouragement.* Chicago: University of Chicago Press, 1911.
    69.1   p. 27   69.2   pp. 27-29

70. Monroe, Walter S., "Projects and the Project Method," *University of Illinois Bulletin,* XXIII (March 29, 1926): 30. Educational Research Circular, No. 43.
    70.1   p. 3   70.3   p. 16
    70.2   p. 6   70.4   p. 20

71. Monroe, Walter S. (editor), "Preface," *Encyclopedia of Educational Research.* New York: The Macmillan Co., 1941.
    71.1   p. vii   71.3   p. ix
    71.2   p. viii

72. Monroe, Will S., *History of the Pestalozzian Movement in the United States.* Syracuse: C. W. Bardeen, 1907, p 77.

73. Munsterberg, Hugo, "Psychology and Education," *Educational Review,* Vol. 16 (September, 1898), pp. 130-132.

74. Nagel, Ernest, "Principles of the Theory of Probability," *International Encyclopedia of Unified Science.* O. Neurath, R. Carnap, and C. Morris, editors. Chicago: University of Chicago Press, 1955, pp. 345-346.

75. National Herbart Society, "Proceedings of the Meeting for Reorganization of the National Herbart Society," *The First Yearbook of the National Society for the Scientific Study of Education.* Charles A. McMurry, editor. Chicago: University of Chicago Press, 1902, p. 70.

76. Pangburn, Jessie M., *The Evolution of the American Teachers College.* New York: Bureau of Publications, Teachers College, Columbia University, 1932.
    76.1   p. 7   76.2   p. 79

77. Parker, S. Chester, "The Present Status of Education as a Science: Educational Methods," *The School Review Monographs: No. II.* Chicago: University of Chicago Press, 1912.
    77.1   p. 135   77.4   p. 138
    77.2   pp. 136-137   77.5   p. 139
    77.3   p. 137   77.6   p. 150

78. Paulsen, Freidrich, "The Evolution of the Educational Ideal—II," *The Forum,* Vol. XXIII (March-August, 1897), pp. 675-676.

79. Payne, W[illiam] H[arold], *The Education of Teachers.* Richmond: B. F. Johnson Publishing Co., 1901, p. 145.

80. Peirce, Charles S., "The Fixation of Belief," *Popular Science Monthly,* 1877. Reprinted in *Chance, Love, and Logic.* Morris R. Cohen, editor. London: Kegan Paul, Trench, Trubner & Co. Ltd., 1923, p. 14.

81. Peirce, Charles S., "Pragmatism in Retrospect: A Last Formulation," *The Philosophy of Peirce.* Justus Buchler, editor. New York: Harcourt, Brace & Co., 1950.

   81.1 p. 271   81.2 p. 272

82. Peirce, Charles S., "How to Make Our Ideas Clear," *Popular Science Monthly,* 1878. Reprinted in *Chance, Love, and Logic.* Morris R. Cohen, editor. London: Kegan Paul, Trench, Trubner & Co. Ltd., 1923.

   82.1 pp. 44-45   82.2 p. 45

83. Pestalozzi, Johann Heinrich, *How Gertrude Teaches Her Children.* Authorized translation by Lucy E. Holland and Francis C. Turner. Syracuse: C. W. Bardeen, 1898, p. 315.

84. Peterson, Francis Edwin, *Philosophies of Education Current in the Preparation of Teachers in the United States.* New York: Teachers College, Columbia University, 1933.

   84.1 p. 31   84.2 pp. 31-34

85. Phenix, Philip H., *Education and the Common Good.* New York: Harper & Row, Publishers, Incorporated, 1961, p. 16.

86. Reigart, John Franklin, *The Lancasterian System of Instruction in the Schools of New York City.* New York: Teachers College, Columbia University, 1916.

   86.1 p. 90   86.4 p. 97
   86.2 p. 93   86.5 p. 99
   86.3 p. 94   86.6 p. 100

87. Rice, J. M., "The Futility of the Spelling Grind," *The Forum.* Vol. XXIII (March-August, 1897).

   87.1 p. 163   87.2 p. 164

88. Royce, Josiah, "Is There a Science of Education?" *Educational Review.* Vol. 1 (January, 1891), pp. 17-24.

89. Ruediger, William C., "The Present Status of Education as a Science: The Principles of Education," *The School Review Monographs: No. II.* Chicago: University of Chicago Press, 1912.

   89.1 p. 89   89.5 pp. 102-103
   89.2 p. 90   89.6 p. 115
   89.3 p. 91   89.7 pp. 116-117
   89.4 p. 95   89.8 pp. 117-118

90. Rugg, Harold, *Foundations of American Education*. New York: Harcourt, Brace & World, Inc., 1947.

90.1	pp. xvi-xvii	90.6	p. 207
90.2	pp. xix-xx	90.7	pp. 578-579
90.3	pp. xxi-xxii	90.8	p. 802
90.4	p. 23	90.9	pp. 802-803
90.5	pp. 23-24		

91. Rugg, Harold, "Is There a Widespread Interest in the Theory of Education?" *Educational Theory*. Vol. 1, No. 1 (May, 1951), pp. 33-34.

92. Russell, Bertrand, *An Outline of Philosophy*. New York: Meridian Books, Inc. (M 97), 1960, pp. 1-2.

93. Russell, E. H., "Observation and Experiment Essential in Pedagogical Inquiry," *Journal of Proceedings and Addresses of the National Education Association*. Topeka: Kansas Publishing House, 1889.

93.1	p. 279	93.3	pp. 283-284
93.2	p. 283	93.4	p. 284

94. Ryle, Gilbert, *The Concept of Mind*. New York: Barnes and Noble, Inc., 1949.

94.1	pp. 310-311	94.3	p. 318
94.2	p. 292		

95. Schwab, Joseph J., "On the Corruption of Education by Psychology," *The School Review* (Summer, 1958). Chicago, Illinois: The University of Chicago Press, p. 84.

96. Sears, Jesse B., "The Development of Tests and Measurements," *Twenty-Five Years of American Education*. I. L. Kandel, editor. New York: The Macmillan Co., 1924.

96.1	p. 127	96.4	p. 136
96.2	p. 130	96.5	p. 138
96.3	p. 134		

97. Sinclair, Samuel Bower, *The Possibility of a Science of Education*. Chicago: University of Chicago Press, 1903, pp. 22-23.

98. Smith, Walter Robinson, *An Introduction to Educational Psychology*. New York: Houghton Mifflin Company, 1917, p. 35.

99. Smith, Walter Robinson, *Principles of Educational Sociology*. New York: Houghton Mifflin Company, 1928, p. 43.

100. Snedden, David S., "What Is Meant by a Scientific Study of Education?" in Manfred J. Holmes (editor), "Report of the Secretary," *The Fourth Yearbook of the National Society for the Scientific Study of Education. Part II*. Chicago: University of Chicago Press, 1905. p. 76.

101. Snedden, David, "Some Basic Assumptions," *Second Yearbook of the National Society for the Study of Educational Sociology*. New York: Teachers College, 1929, p. 8.

102. Thorndike, Edward L., "Quantitative Investigation in Education: With Special Reference to Cooperation with This Association," *The School Review Monographs: No. I. Research within the Field of Education, Its Organization and Encouragement.* Chicago: University of Chicago Press, 1911.
　　　102.1　pp. 34-35　　　　102.2　p. 35　　　102.3　p. 42

103. Ulich, Robert, *A Sequence of Educational Influences.* Cambridge: Harvard University Press, 1935, p. 6.

104. Van Liew, C. C., "The Educational Theory of the Culture Epochs," *The First Yearbook of the Herbart Society for the Scientific Study of Teaching,* 1894, p. 105.

105. Waddle [Wadell], Charles W[ilkin], *An Introduction to Child Psychology.* New York: Houghton Mifflin Co., 1918.
　　　105.1　p. v　　　　　　　　　　105.3　pp. 18-19
　　　105.2　p. 17　　　　　　　　　　105.4　p. 20

106. Waller, Willard, *The Sociology of Teaching.* New York: John Wiley & Sons, Inc., 1932, p. vi © 1932 by John Wiley & Sons, Inc. Reprinted with permission.

107. Weisberg, Harold, "Tradition and the Traditionalist," *Philosophy and Education.* Israel Scheffler (ed.). Boston: Allyn and Bacon, Inc., 1958, p. 234.

108. Wesley, Edgar B., *N.E.A.: The First Hundred Years.* New York: Harper & Row, Publishers, Incorporated, 1957.
　　　108.1　p. 185　　　　　　　　　　　　　　　108.2　p. 187

109. Whipple, Guy M., "The Contributions of This Society to the Scientific Movement in Education with Special Reference to the Trends in Problems and Methods of Injuiry," *The Thirty-Seventh Yearbook of the National Society for the Study of Education. Part II. The Scientific Movement in Education.* Bloomington: Public School Publishing Company, 1938.
　　　109.1　p. 259　　　　109.3　p. 262　　　　109.4　p. 264
　　　109.2　p. 261　　　　　　　　　　　　　　　109.5　p. 270

110. Whipple, Guy M., "The Inner Workings of the NSSE," *School and Society.* Vol. 54, No. 1393 (September 6, 1941), p. 164.

111. Whitehead, Alfred North, *Adventures of Ideas.* New York: © 1933, The Macmillan Company; copyright renewed, 1961 by Evelyn Whitehead, pp. 112-113. Reprinted with the permission of The Macmillan Company.

112. Whitehead, Alfred North, *Science and the Modern World.* New York: © 1925, The Macmillan Company; copyright renewed, 1953 by Evelyn Whitehead, pp. 48-49. Reprinted with the permission of The Macmillan Company.

113. White, Jessie, *The Educational Ideas of Froebel.* London: University Tutorial Press Ltd., 1905

114. Wiggins and Smith, *Froebel's Gift: The Republic of Childhood.* New York: Houghton Mifflin Co., The Riverside Press, 1896. Frontispiece.

Index

Date Due